Ukrainian Minstrels

"David took pity on the blind and gave them a mountain of gold so that they could mine it and thus support themselves. But Solomon said that this was not wise because, if blind people had money, then sighted people would attack them and take the gold away. So David gave the blind his lyre and said that they should go out into the world and sing and people would give them money and this would be money that no one could take away."

Folklores and Folk Cultures of Eastern Europe

SERIES EDITOR:
Linda J. Ivanits
Department of Slavic Languages
Pennsylvania State University

Ukrainian Minstrels
And the Blind Shall Sing
Natalie Kononenko

Ukrainian Minstrels

And the Blind Shall Sing

SKETE OF
SAINT MAXIMOS THE CONFESSOR
P.O. Box 356
Palmyra, VA 22963-0356

Natalie Kononenko

M.E. Sharpe
Armonk, New York
London, England

Library of Congress Cataloging-in-Publication Data

Kononenko, Natalie O.
Ukrainian minstrels : and the blind shall sing / by
Natalie Kononenko.
p. cm. — (Folklores and folk cultures of Eastern Europe)
Includes bibliographical references (p.   ) and index.
ISBN 0-7656-0144-3 (C : alk. paper)
ISBN 0-7656-0145-1 (pbk : alk. paper)
1. Kobzari—History. 2. Minstrels—Ukraine—History.
3. Ukraine—Social life and customs. I. Title. II. Series.
ML399.K65   1997
782.42162′91791—DC21   97-28498
CIP
MN
Printed in the United States of America

EB (c) 10 9 8 7 6 5 4 3 2 1
EB (p) 10 9 8 7 6 5 4 3 2 1

To Peter and Paul, successors of the Apostles

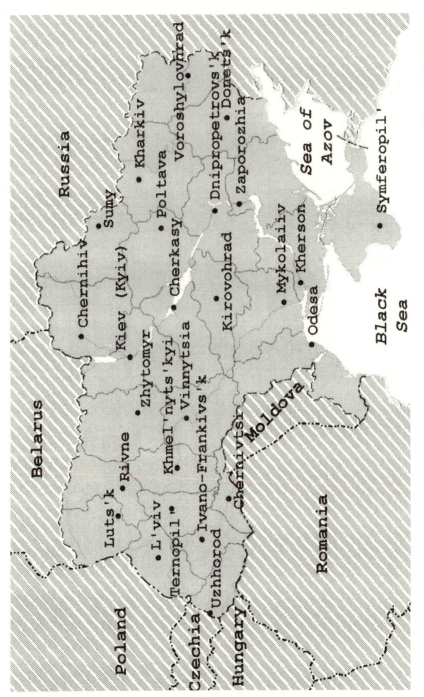

Map by Peter Holloway

Contents

Songs

Foreword

The present volume is the first in M.E. Sharpe's series on the "Folklores and Folk Cultures of Eastern Europe." The series aims to offer the English-speaking public a wide range of primary texts and scholarly works on major subjects in Eastern European folklore and folk culture. Natalie Kononenko's *Ukrainian Minstrels: And the Blind Shall Sing* is a model study with which to launch this series; it illuminates a fascinating, and for a Western public, little known tradition of oral poetry. The focus is on the performers, the *kobzari* and *lirnyky* of the Ukrainian countryside, but the study also includes new translations of the basic songs of their repertory. Kononenko's book should be the standard work on Ukrainian minstrels for years to come.

Kononenko shows that Ukrainian minstrelsy is unique in several ways. Most notable is the fact that blindness was obligatory. In the nearby Russian, Turkish, and South Slavic traditions, singers are sighted (legends of great blind performers of the past notwithstanding). Another difference is the elaborate guild system, which controlled the admittance of new minstrels, handled financial matters, and, at times, punished errant performers. Kononenko includes detailed chapters on the evolution of this system, its links with beggars' guilds, and its connections with the Orthodox Church. The extensiveness of the repertory of the Ukrainian singers may come as a surprise to some readers. Kononenko has lengthy discussions on the various types of songs the minstrels performed and the probable influence of religious songs and laments on the epic.

Trained at Harvard under Albert Lord, one of the pioneers in the study of oral narrative in this century, Kononenko is familiar with other folk traditions, especially the Turkish one, in which she has conducted extensive fieldwork. Her present study has been in the making over ten years, during which she made numerous trips to Ukraine, worked extensively in archives, and consulted with living singers. *Ukrainian Minstrels: And the Blind Shall Sing* should go a long way in fostering appreciation for the richness of Ukrainian folk culture.

Linda Ivanits, Series Editor

Preface

*T*his work began as a study of texts. When I left for Ukraine in 1987, my intention was to compile a complete edition of Ukrainian epic poetry, the *dumy*. Though Kateryna Hrushevska's collection of 1927 and 1931 contained all known variants of every epic song and was the most complete collection ever published, there were several reasons to update it.[1] Other variants had been collected after Hrushevska, and some of these were published by Borys Kyrdan in his *Ukrainian Folk Epics* (*Ukrainskie narodnye dumy*), but there were no doubt other texts to be found in archives.[2] Perhaps there was even the possibility of collecting new texts, especially of the *dumy*, such as "Duma about Lenin" (*Duma pro Lenina*), composed during the Soviet period, and granted, of somewhat dubious authenticity.[3] Above all, it was necessary to make Hrushevska's already published texts available, since her collection was suppressed by Soviet authorities and most copies destroyed. If the Ukrainian epic were going to be a subject of serious scholarly inquiry, then Hrushevska's collection had to be republished, preferably in the updated form that I had in mind.

But this study is not primarily about texts. It is an investigation of their performers, a special type of minstrel, the blind mendicant. For a long time, I had trouble accepting that blindness was obligatory to minstrelsy in Ukraine. I assumed that blindness in the Ukrainian tradition functioned the same way that it did in other traditions with which I was familiar: more as a symbol of past excellence than as a real trait of actual performers. Working in Yugoslavia, Albert Lord found legends of blind performers who were reputed to be especially talented, but he did not find the performers themselves.[4] I had run into something similar during my field work in Turkey: legends about great blind performers of the past, a few rather mediocre living blind minstrels, but no dominance of the tradition by the blind. Ashik Veysel was the only actual performer of special merit who was blind. Yet even he seemed of lesser stature than the legendary singers of the past, for he was not so much a teller of tales as a composer of short, lyric verses, which seemed a degeneration of the former tradition in which the lyric songs were imbedded in long, epic narratives. The fact that Ukrainian minstrels were all blind was striking by contrast. Did this mean that blindness somehow facilitates art, as popular belief so often claims? Was there something about specifically Ukrainian beliefs that irrevocably linked blindness to art?

Obligatory blindness of minstrels turned out to be just one of the many intriguing characteristics of the Ukrainian tradition. Ukrainian minstrels were members of professional guilds. These guilds were complex and elaborate structures that provided for the training of new members and for their support throughout their careers. Guild membership also differentiated Ukrainian minstrelsy from all traditions with which I was familiar. In Turkey, I had encountered masters and apprentices working in a one-on-one relationship. I had read about similar situations in Yugoslavia and Russia. The master-apprentice relationship turned out to be very important in Ukraine also. What made the Ukrainian situation unique was that the master- apprentice pair was part of a whole minstrel network, a network that did not exist in other Slavic areas. In fact, at least in some instances, the master and the apprentice were not a pair, but just one part of a complex training system. I found evidence of whole schools of minstrelsy where older apprentices helped train younger ones and where the school worked like a miniature version of the minstrel guild.

The phenomenon of the guild linked Ukrainian minstrelsy to a string of other professions and institutions. Minstrel guilds were patterned on trade guilds, and minstrelsy was seen as a profession. The governance of the guilds was remarkably democratic and egalitarian, and resembled the political structure of Cossack administrative units. Minstrel guilds, like trade guilds and Cossack regiments, were linked to Orthodoxy, and helped support churches or monasteries. Interestingly, the guild type that minstrelsy most resembled was the guild of beggars. Beggars and minstrels seemed to overlap, sharing some repertory items, such as a begging song (*zhebranka*), and terminology for guild members.[5]

Ukrainian minstrels performed a variety of songs and other materials, and the more data about minstrelsy comes to light, the more complex and varied the minstrel repertory is seen to be.[6] Yet, only one category of minstrel song, the epic, has been extensively studied, and this category has acquired a political importance so great that working on it becomes almost impossible whenever the atmosphere is politically charged. The epic is seen as legitimizing Ukrainian culture: the fact that Ukraine has its own independent epic tradition, one that is clearly distinct from the Russian epic, is viewed as proof that Ukraine is a legitimate, separate culture, which implies that it should be a legitimate, separate state. Because of the nationalist meaning assigned to the epic, the *dumy* have been glorified, and many writers have sought nationalist content in them, or at least, expressions of striving toward independence. By emphasizing *dumy* over other genres shared with other Slavic peoples, particularly the Russians, scholars with nationalist inclinations have been responsible for the lack of attention that the rest of the minstrelsy repertory has received. By the same token, powers trying to suppress Ukrainian nationalism have consistently targeted *dumy* and everything and everyone associated with them. Such was the motivation for the attacks on Hrushevska and the confiscation and destruction of her collection and for the greatest tragedy of all—Stalin's massacre of Ukrainian minstrels in 1939.

Working on a collection of epic texts proved too politically sensitive. While the Soviets were still in power, their goal was to prevent the publication of national epics, no matter by whom. Like all manifestations of nationalism, real or presumed, a collection of Ukrainian *dumy* was to be thwarted for fear that it might be the straw that would break the back of Communism in Ukraine. Now that Ukraine is independent, quite the opposite is true, and everyone seems to be competing to get an epic collection to press. Unfortunately, the competition has not yet produced an actual compendium of *dumy*.

Politics has dissuaded me from pursuing a collection of Ukrainian epic poetry and from overplaying the nationalistic dimension of minstrelsy. My only political statement is that Ukrainian minstrelsy is worthy of study in its own right, regardless of nationalist or other implications. Perhaps more than anything else, I want to establish the legitimacy of the study of Ukrainian minstrelsy for its own sake. I want to get away from a nationalist interpretation of Ukrainian minstrels and the Ukrainian epic. I want to show that a romantic portrayal of minstrels is unnecessary to make them interesting. Minstrels were an underclass, and they can be studied as such. They do not need to be turned into something else to make them legitimate artists.

Unfortunately, the tremendous prestige assigned to the epic has not brought prestige to the singers of *dumy*. For a long time, scholars felt that the performers whom they encountered were not the true owners of the genre. *Dumy* were supposedly created by people from a high social stratum. They descended to the blind mendicants who sang them in the nineteenth and twentieth centuries only later, when the institutions in which the epic had arisen began to disintegrate. Usually, the creators of *dumy* were thought to be Cossacks. One prevalent interpretation was that they were rank-and-file Cossacks, men who, when they could no longer fight, took up singing about their past deeds and the deeds of their comrades. The other was that they were special military bards, kept by Cossack regiments for entertainment and moral support. In either case, they were not like contemporary minstrels. Because minstrels were seen as an imperfect conduit for someone else's art, not artists in their own right, very little information about them was collected. What was recorded either was not published, or was published as articles in journals, rather than as part of a book. The exceptions to this came only in this century with the work of Mikhail Speranskii, Borys Kyrdan, and Fedir Lavrov.[7] Thus my major sources have been archives and old journals including *Kievan Antiquities* (Kievskaia starina), *Ethnograhic Survey*

(Etnograficheskoe obozrenie), and *Living Antiquities* (Zhivaia starina). I am grateful for the many people who have helped me work with these rather difficult to obtain sources. In this country, Angelika Powell of the University of Virginia Library's Slavic Division helped me borrow or otherwise secure sources that were not in the library's collection. I am also most grateful for the patience of the microform staff at the University of Virginia and the help of the tremendously knowledgeable librarians in the Slavic Division of the University of Illinois Library. In Ukraine, I worked in the library of the National Academy of Sciences at the University of Kiev and in the archives of the Academy of Sciences Folklore and Literature Institutes. I am especially indebted to Valentyna Borysenko and the staff of the Folklore Institute for their guidance. Ivan Honchar, a sculptor and enthusiastic collector of folk memorabilia, granted me access to his collection and permission to copy his many old photographs of minstrels. The actual copying was done by Volodymyr Fedko, a professional photographer. Credit for all but one of the photographs published here belongs to them.

Besides thanking the library and research personnel, I would like to thank those who provided financial support. IREX, the International Research and Exchanges Board, paid for my travel in 1987 and then again in 1994. The University of Virginia has provided research leave and the Center for Russian Studies at the University contributed some money toward my travel to Ukraine in 1993.

Moral support and intellectual guidance were vital. Andrij Hornjatkevych provided both. He and Frank Sysyn encouraged me to undertake the project when political obstacles seemed insurmountable. Hornjatkevych helped further by guiding me through the intricacies of the secret language of minstrels, deciphering difficult folk texts, and reading my manuscript and offering suggestions. Norman Ingham, Valentina Izmirlieva, and others helped me with religious texts and concepts. James Bailey, Ronelle Alexander, and Boris Putilov offered insight into minstrels and epics in other Slavic cultures. Colleagues here and at other institutions read various versions of my manuscript and offered suggestions and corrections. Any errors that remain are my responsibility and not theirs. My students Jann Lacoss, Anne Ingram, Bruce McClelland, and LeAnn Judd helped me put my bibliography and my notes in order. Linda Ivanits, my editor, provided guidance, encouragement, and above all, wisdom. Patricia Kolb, executive editor at M.E. Sharpe, gave me the courage to start the publishing process. My family here and in Ukraine were sources of the love and support that make a major undertaking possible. Pavlo and Nadiia Suprun became my adoptive family, helping me understand the meaning of blindness and minstrelsy.

Note on Transliteration

*T*ransliteration presented special difficulties in this work. Some of the sources were written in Ukrainian, and others in Russian; some prior to the orthographic reforms, and others after. In addition, many scholars, when quoting their informants, tried to capture dialect features and invented their own, unique transcription systems. Some writers invented their own orthographies for nationalistic reasons, trying to distinguish Ukrainian from Russian.

To maintain consistency, the decision was to render names used in the text in standard literary Ukrainian, transcribed according to the Library of Congress system, with all diacritical marks, such as apostrophes for soft signs, omitted. Diacritical marks were omitted for ease of reading, because in Ukrainian, several may appear in close proximity, as in Ryl's'kyi. Names of authors who were known by the Russian version of their names (Borzhkovskii) or authors who were primarily Russian scholars (Speranskii) are given in Russian. Words and terms of folk origin, or widely used by minstrels, are rendered as closely to the original as possible, with variants where these existed (*odklianshchyna, odklynshchyny*). Since this is a book about the folk, it seemed inappropriate to impose standards from written literature on an oral tradition.

In the notes and bibliography, all material is given in a form as close to the original as practical. Thus, all works that appeared in Ukrainian are cited in standard, contemporary, literary Ukrainian, transcribed according to the modified Library of Congress system, with appropriate diacritical marks. All works that appeared in Russian are cited in standard, contemporary, literary Russian, transcribed in the same way. I have modernized spellings (*istoricheskogo* instead of *istoricheskago*). At the same time, I have tried to maintain author intent and have not standardized to modern

Russian when an author was writing in Russian but trying to create a Ukrainian flavor (*Ukrain's'ki zapisi*).

If an author wrote in both Ukrainian and Russian, the Ukrainian version of his or her name is given first, followed by the Russian version in parentheses. Even if an author wrote in Russian only, the Ukrainian version of his or her name is given if the Ukrainian version is cited in the text or if the person was widely known by his or her Ukrainian name.

Ukrainian
Minstrels

Part 1

Ukrainian Minstrelsy

"After Christ, came the Apostles. When all of the Apostles died, God sent the blind. And God said that the blind should sing, that they should spread God's word and teach the people truth and goodness."

Chapter 1

The Singers

*T*he heart and soul of Ukraine is its countryside: the black, fertile soil; the fields of golden wheat dotted with the red of poppy flowers and the blue of cornflowers; the white adobe houses with thatched roofs; the sparkling blue streams. In the late nineteenth and early twentieth centuries, this countryside was peopled with the usual peasants, craftsmen and peddlers, but also with others who were unique—blind, mendicant minstrels. There were two types of minstrels: *kobzari*, who played the strummed string instrument called the *kobza*, which later developed into the distinctive, asymmetrical *bandura*; and *lirnyky*, who used a crank-driven hurdy-gurdy called the *lira*. *Kobzari* and *lirnyky* were professional performers who lived mostly from their art, though they did occasionally take on such crafts as plaiting ropes, which did not require sight. Because they did not farm as did the rest of the population, and relied on the charitable impulses of their audiences for their living, they were associated with beggars. But Ukrainian minstrels were much more. They were the repositories of tradition and culture. They were the disseminators of the word of God and the major source of folk historical and religious information. Ukrainian singers were disabled people who used minstrelsy as a social welfare institution, and yet many among them were true artists, great performers. This book is their story. It presents an account of traditional minstrelsy as it was reportedly practiced in the nineteenth and early twentieth centuries, the period for which we have the most data. This will be supplemented by the sparser information from earlier periods and my personal experiences with contemporary *kobzari*.

The years from approximately 1850 to 1930 represent the zenith of traditional minstrelsy, or at least, of available information about this phenomenon. During this time, scholarly interest in minstrelsy was high: We have a relative abundance of data, documenting a continuous, if not a totally stable, tradition. *Kobzari* and *lirnyky* probably existed well before the nineteenth century. Songs like those in the repertories of these minstrels were recorded well before then.[1] By the time performers were studied, the various institutions associated with them, such as professional brotherhoods, were so well

bandura   *lira*

developed and so complex that they must have been in existence for centuries. Some of the historical material in the repertories of *kobzari* and *lirnyky* dates back to as early as the fifteenth century and the battles against the Turks and the Tatars. If songs containing this material were composed shortly after the battles took place, then the profession that sang them must have originated at a date closer to AD 1400.[2]

At the start of the twentieth century, when the musicologist Filaret Kolessa began his wax cylinder recordings of minstrels, he observed evidence of deterioration and change. Certain of the men he recorded had learned their texts from books rather than from other minstrels and were trying to develop a more ornate style to please the educated public that had replaced villagers as their most important customers.[3] Questions of how the tradition would have proceeded to develop, and indeed, whether it would have continued or ceased to exist are now moot. Stalinist intervention ended traditional minstrelsy. From what we know, Stalin liquidated the majority of Ukrainian minstrels by summoning them to a conference in Kharkiv in 1939 and having them shot.[4] Thus, most minstrels disappeared, if not shot at the conference in Kharkiv, then exterminated individually or repressed into inactivity. But a few survived, and when interest in minstrelsy revived with the Khrushchev Thaw, they were available as subjects of study and as performers of a new, Sovietized folklore, who sang properly adapted traditional texts and composed songs on acceptable contemporary topics, such as the "Duma about Lenin."[5]

Pavlo Suprun

With the birth of the newly independent Ukrainian state and the drive to uncover and encourage all the aspects of culture perceived as truly Ukrainian, minstrelsy is experiencing a renaissance. Efforts are underway to revive the handcrafting of traditional instruments, and there have been several attempts to establish schools of minstrelsy. While most of the efforts to rejuvenate minstrelsy are done by sighted people and for political reasons, there is at least one *kobzar* working today who became a minstrel for reasons similar to the ones that prompted the minstrels of the nineteenth and

early twentieth centuries to take up their craft. He is not completely apoliti-
cal, though he does not sing for political reasons. Like traditional minstrels
and unlike almost all of his contemporaries, he is blind. Pavlo Stepanovych
Suprun lives on the outskirts of Kiev and has been singing since the early
1970s. I met Suprun in 1987. This was a difficult time because Ukraine was
still a part of the Soviet Union and people feared that *perestroika* (*pere-
budova* in Ukrainian) would not last and that any show of enthusiasm for
reform would soon bring reprisals. Ukraine's loyalty to Russia and to the
Soviet Union was always suspect, and *perestroika* seemed a way of flushing
out all those of dubious loyalty: Ukrainian nationalists, bourgeois sympathizers, any and all subversives. The political atmosphere was tense, and the
weather was awful. It was a chilly and wet October evening, and Suprun was
performing in a dingy classroom at the University of Kiev. His audience was
Lydiia Dunaevska's folklore class, plus assorted people interested in folklore
and minstrelsy, like me and my escort, a second-rate Ukrainian poet living in
Moscow, evidently a KGB agent assigned to watch me.

Lydiia Dunaevska introduced Pavlo Suprun and he began his concert. He
sang the obligatory "Duma about Lenin," an epic song dedicated to Lenin.
Then he went on to traditional material: epics and historical songs. He sang
about the pain of captives languishing in Turkish captivity, not allowed even a
glimpse of daylight for "three and thirty" years. He sang about Baida, suspended by his rib from a meathook and still defiant toward the Sultan. He sang
about Morozenko's mother, her premonition that her son was in mortal danger
and her horror at the discovery that her premonition was right. He sang songs
of the Second World War, how Kateryna supported her lover with her last crust
of bread while he fought for the Ukrainian cause and how she then killed him
in hand-to-hand combat when he decided to defect. I was transfixed. I forgot
the miserable weather, and the room no longer seemed dingy. Best of all, I
forgot my poet and all the unpleasantness of dealing with an ultra-suspicious
Soviet state. It was not just Suprun's baritone, powerful though it is. It was not
just his ability to play his *bandura*, though he is a master. I now understand that
it was Suprun's deep feeling for the content of his songs. After about a week, I
called Pavlo Suprun, and he invited me to visit, in spite of the risks of inviting a
foreigner to one's home. Thus began a friendship that lasts to this day.

Pavlo Suprun is a man of medium stature, with a stocky, Ukrainian build
and long "Cossack" whiskers. When he performs, he plays up the Cossack
image by wearing embroidered Ukrainian shirts. At other times, except for
his blindness, he looks no different from any other citizen of Kiev. He lives
with his blind wife, Nadiia Mykolaiivna, in a small apartment on the south
side of the city. While the Soviet Union still existed and social programs for
the disabled were functional, this region of Kiev was especially geared

toward the blind. A number of blind people lived in the Supruns' apartment complex, and a factory built to employ the blind stood across the street.

Suprun was born in 1937, in a village outside the city of Konotop, where his sister still lives. When he was six years old, one of his playmates picked up a land mine left over from the Second World War. The mine was still active, and it exploded, killing several of the boys and leaving the others seriously injured. Suprun received a head wound and was left totally blind.[6] Even now, he has a deformed skull and fragments of shrapnel imbedded in his head and his body. Suprun refuses to talk about this incident, but Nadiia gave me an extensive account of what happened to her when she was involved in a similar accident. From this, we can get a good idea of what Suprun's experiences might have been like.[7]

Nadiia comes from a village near Kiev. According to her, toys were very hard to come by after the Second World War, and a soldier stationed in her village showed her and some other children how to dismantle land mines. There were two balls inside each mine, and these were particularly prized playthings. Nadiia had dismantled many mines and grown quite confident of her ability to do so, when she ran across one mine that looked somewhat different from the rest. She proceeded to take it apart as the soldier had taught her, and it exploded, injuring her arms and face. With time, the skin on her arms and face grew back, but she never regained her sight.

Worse than the physical injury was the psychological trauma that came with blindness. Nadiia was afraid that this meant the end to her dreams of schooling. She was terribly frustrated, trying to move about the village as she had in the past, trying to play with the other children. Things were both familiar and strange at the same time. She knew certain paths, like the one down to the swimming hole at the river, and yet she had trouble running down these paths with her playmates. Perhaps the most horrible thing of all was being treated like an object rather than a person, having people behave as if she were not there. A neighbor came over and started telling Nadiia's mother, right in front of the blind child, that it would have been better if the girl had been killed outright. Nadiia started screaming. "She is a horrible, horrible woman," she told her mother. "Make her leave." This tendency to treat blind people as objects, to see them as "other," is very important to this book. Many traits of traditional minstrels can best be understood if we keep in mind that something in the human psyche wants to label a disabled person as outside the human sphere, perhaps even belonging to another world. Suprun told of a similar instance, where someone treated him as if he were not present, or at least, not sentient. He was performing one evening in a restaurant, and a woman, pleased by his singing, came up to the restaurant owner and asked him to convey her sentiments to Suprun. "Tell him that we really liked his performance," she is supposed to have said. Suprun, who was standing right next to the restaurant owner at the time, was furious. As he told me afterward, "What is this? I may be blind, but I am not deaf. And as far as I know, I am still of sound mind. What does she mean 'tell him that we really liked his performance'?"[8]

In spite of physical and psychological injury, Pavlo and Nadiia managed. Nadiia did go to school. In fact, she pressured her mother into enrolling her in a school for the blind almost immediately. This meant entering at mid-year and required special dispensation and extra effort on Nadiia's part to catch up with the other pupils. At the school, Nadiia learned how to read Braille, she learned mathematics, and she got some job training, so that she could work at the factory for the blind.[9] Since the school staff believed that blind people were especially inclined toward music, she received music training. It was at the school for the blind that Nadiia met Pavlo, whose experiences appear to have been similar to hers. But Suprun was judged musically gifted and was therefore sent for outside schooling at the Kiev Conservatory, where he learned how to play the *bandura* and received instruction in voice.[10]

Pavlo and Nadiia married, were assigned an apartment, and went to work at the factory across the street. The factory was their primary source of income. Suprun sang, but singing was a hobby, an avocation, not something he did for pay. The performance that October evening at Kiev University was typical. Suprun would go to schools and various civic organizations, and although he earned nothing by singing, performing meant a great deal to him. When the audience was limited to schoolchildren and various civic groups, he expressed a desire to learn all of the songs that were in any way related to people or events covered in history books. He felt it was his duty to contribute to the children's education, to make the stuff in books more moving, more meaningful.[11] He told me with pride how emotionally the children had reacted to his singing, how teachers told him about his successes with otherwise unresponsive pupils.[12] Having this effect obviously was very important to him.

The collapse of the Soviet state changed everything. New opportunities beckoned, and Suprun entered a cooperative of artists and entertainers, a post-Soviet substitute for an agent, and later made his own arrangements with the owner of a restaurant located in Podil, the former merchant section of Kiev and now the section with the most rapid urban renewal.[13] Recently he has taken an additional job in a modest cafe in the same sector.[14] Suprun enjoys performing in the restaurant and the cafe, and the money, especially from tips, is very good. Yet, singing in various dining establishments does not satisfy him as an artist, because the patrons want to hear cheerful songs as they eat, and what Suprun finds most meaningful are traditional songs, like the ones that first caught my ear, and his own new compositions in the traditional mode, songs on topics like the disaster at Chernobyl.[15] To have an opportunity to perform his traditional, melancholy material, Suprun continues to sing for schools and civic groups, where he appears without compensation.

Suprun sees these appearances as a public service, and he feels that people need to hear the traditional songs as much as he needs to sing them. He extends the belief that a *kobzar* is a public servant to contemporary material, and feels that he is obliged not only to compose songs on current events but also to provide a news service to his neighbors. Thus, he and Nadiia listen to as many newscasts as possible, including the voice portion of television news, and then present what they have heard at a backyard forum.[16] The Supruns feel that minstrels, and particularly blind minstrels, have a moral imperative for their songs and for the information that they provide others and that this imperative takes precedence over other considerations. Thus, they were willing to listen to Voice of America when it was still dangerous to do so, and they invited foreigners into their home when having foreign contacts was suspect.[17] The Supruns see themselves as intermediaries between the world of the sighted and the world of the blind, and perhaps between Ukraine and the outside world. They are also intermediaries between the past and the future of Ukrainian minstrelsy.

To my knowledge, Suprun is the only blind minstrel in Ukraine today; all other contemporary *kobzari* are sighted. A number of blind people sing in public places for money but are not minstrels, because they play no musical instrument and they sing to beg; they do not try to reproduce traditional minstrel songs and they do not strive for musical excellence.[18] Yet, in the past, blindness was obligatory. Many of the features I see in Suprun were once institutionalized. Just as Suprun cannot settle for being an entertainer only, just as he feels he needs to sing serious songs with a higher purpose, so traditional minstrel songs were not meant solely for entertainment, and traditional minstrels were mediators on the grandest scale possible: between man and God. Minstrels sang lighthearted songs like those that Suprun sings in the restaurant, but these were nothing next to the core of their repertory: melancholy epics, religious songs and historical songs; songs that provided a spiritual experience for the living; songs that served as prayers for the dead. The emphasis on spirituality was institutionalized, in the sense that there was some pressure on minstrels to sing serious songs only. Any singing that was done for alms was supposed to be morally uplifting; entertainment was not its goal.

Like the Supruns, traditional minstrels lived lives similar to those of their neighbors. They owned homes and small plots of land in their native villages. They raised families. Like the Supruns, they were simultaneously people apart. They traveled great distances, while most peasants were sedentary. They belonged to professional guilds, while most peasants had no professional status. Not all had the Supruns' dedication. Being blind and being a minstrel did not guarantee achieving strength of character. Minstrelsy was a way of overcoming disability; it was available to all blind people, though not all chose to use it or succeeded in using it. Those who did succeed often proved strong and compassionate, willing to help all who suffered, sighted and blind alike. Many, though not all, loved their songs with a passion similar to Suprun's. Like Suprun, they felt a real obligation to sing. Many also performed other duties designed to provide spiritual and religious fulfillment, which can be compared to the Supruns' efforts to provide an objective and complete news service.

Traditional Minstrels

As used here, the term traditional minstrel applies to minstrels active in the period roughly from 1850 to 1930. It applies to *kobzari*, like Pavlo Suprun, and also to *lirnyky*, the musicians who play a hurdy-gurdy rather than a lute. *Lirnyky* are few in modern day Ukraine because when scholars began writing extensively about minstrelsy, the *lira* came to be considered a less prestigious instrument than the *bandura*, and, of course, the latter became the instrument of choice. In the heyday of traditional minstrelsy, however, *lirnyky* were numerous, and in many regions, far outnumbered *kobzari*.[19] We do not know when *lirnyky* came into being or at what time they came to be considered the same type of performer as the *kobzari*. Although minstrels probably existed from the fifteenth or sixteenth century, the first documentary evidence of them comes from the eighteenth, refers to *kobzari* only, and consists of the court records of minstrels being held for trial. One such document refers to a sighted *bandura* player, strongly suggesting that *kobzari* were not always blind.[20] *Lirnyky*, on the other hand, were probably always disabled. Because at least some *kobzari* were sighted and even more because of the striking dissimilarity of their instruments, we can assume that *kobzari* and *lirnyky* were once two distinct categories of musician. How *kobzari* and *lirnyky* came together is one of the subjects of this book. But from the middle of the nineteenth century to the Soviet period, *kobzari* and *lirnyky* were one category of minstrel. They knew each other, belonged to the same guilds, and even learned songs from each other.

To be a *kobzar* or a *lirnyk*, a person had to be blind. Some were born blind, and some suffered head injuries, like Suprun. More typically, a child would develop an illness, such as smallpox or scrofula, that would lead to blindness. At about the age of ten or twelve, a blind child could be apprenticed to a master minstrel, which meant moving into the teacher's home and living there for a period of three to six years. During apprenticeship, the child received musical training, learned songs and how to play an instrument. The child learned a secret language (*lebiiska mova*) that minstrels used to communicate among themselves, and was also taught how to live the special life of the blind mendicant, including how to cope with blindness, how to travel, and how to behave so that people would be willing to give alms. The apprentice paid for training in cash, or more often, by begging, turning over the proceeds to the master. Upon completion of training, the apprentice went through an elaborate initiation rite that granted entry into the profession and permission to perform and beg for oneself. In some areas, initiation also conferred the right to take on apprentices of one's own, though more typically, a minstrel had to work approximately ten years and complete a second rite before he was granted the status of master and given permission to teach.

Gender issues are important to minstrelsy. Apparently, training was available to both boys and girls, yet our information about mature performers is almost exclusively about men. In published sources, there are a few texts and oblique references to women singers: a wife of a *kobzar* or a *lirnyk* who also sang, a woman someone had heard perform, usually someone other than the collector writing the article.[21] The general impression that minstrelsy was a man's profession is probably due more to scholarly bias than to fact. Because the epic has been considered the most prestigious of all of the genres sung by minstrels, there has been a tendency to ignore the rest of the minstrel repertory, to focus on the military subject-matter of the epic, and to associate minstrelsy with war, male activities, an exclusively male sphere. Women *kobzari* and *lirnyky* did not fit scholars' ideas of what minstrels should be, and few collectors recorded from them. Porfyrii Martynovych, most of whose work exists in manuscript only, is an exception.[22] In the description of traditional minstrelsy that follows, most of the discussion will be about male minstrels, but wherever possible, every effort will be made to complete the picture by drawing on the Martynovych manuscripts and talking about women. A very different picture of Ukrainian minstrelsy emerges when we realize that women could be professional performers along with men. The existence of women singers shows that minstrelsy served the entire population and provided a means of artistic expression to all, not just men, that it offered a potential livelihood for the disabled of both sexes.

Once initiated, a *kobzar* or *lirnyk* would return home to his family and then begin to travel and beg, hiring a boy or a girl to serve as guide (*povodyr*). Children who accepted this job were orphans or crippled in some way; they too needed an alternative livelihood because they could not participate in the normal farming economy of the Ukrainian countryside. The guide would live with the minstrel, receiving food, clothing, and a small wage. When a guide had earned enough money to live independently, he or she parted with the minstrel, and usually became a craftsman or a trader, most often making musical instruments, presumably having learned about these from the master. The minstrel then would hire another guide.

A minstrel tended to avoid begging in his own village and to have a circuit of villages other than his own that he would visit on a regular basis. Arriving in one of these villages, he would stop at a home and sing outside its windows, beginning with the begging song (*zhebranka, proshba,* or *zapros*). This announced his presence and allowed the inhabitants to decide whether they could afford to give him alms. If they could give nothing, they would so inform the minstrel, and he would proceed to the next dwelling. If they could give only a small amount, they would come out to the street and offer a coin or a cup of flour before sending the minstrel on. People who could give more would invite the minstrel into the courtyard or into their home. Here the minstrel sang for as long as he was welcome. He would sing religious songs (*psalmy*) and historical material (*dumy* and historical songs—*istorychni pisni*). Sometimes he would be asked to sing a few happy songs for the children. In payment for this extended performance, he might receive a piece of cloth or some baked goods, some sausage, a larger amount of flour, or several coins. If the residents were particularly interested in minstrels and wanted to chat with their guest, they might invite him to stay for a meal. After the minstrel had concluded his performance or his meal, he would sing a song of thanks and farewell (*blahodarinne*) and proceed to the next household. When night fell, the minstrel would sleep in the home of the local *kobzar* or *lirnyk* or at the church. The next day he would sing at other homes in the same village or travel on down the road to the next one.

The best time to go begging was when people had the most money and the road conditions were still good: between harvest and the winter snows. But this optimal time was of short duration so minstrels travelled whenever weather permitted. If a minstrel arrived at a village in summertime, then all of the men would be out working in the fields and the people at home would be women and children. This means that a substantial part of a minstrel's repertory had to appeal to a female and juvenile audience.

Performances at homes seem to have allowed the minstrel the greatest opportunity to display his artistry and range of songs. Religious songs were basic to minstrelsy, and a man might start with these, singing about Varvara the Great Martyr, who endured horrible torture because she refused to marry a pagan king, or about Oleksii, Man of God, who went off into the desert for the sake of his faith and returned thirty years later, so transformed by his experience that he was not recognized by his own family. Very popular was the song called "Lazar" (Lazarus) or "The Two Lazars," the story of a rich brother who mistreats his sibling and is punished by God in the afterlife (based on Luke 16:19–31). A minstrel might sing "The Orphan Girl," a song resembling a fairy tale, only with a sad ending, which tells of an girl mistreated by her stepmother, or he might sing about the Last Judgement or the premonitions of the Virgin Mary. This was a safe and lucrative repertory. Behaving in a seemly manner was extremely important to minstrelsy. Suspicions of impropriety always dogged the profession, and when in doubt, it was best to stick to pious material. Reminding people of their mortality with mentions of death and the Last Judgement, and giving the audience positive examples of charity and piety and negative examples of punishment for stinginess, this material predisposed the listeners to generosity.

People who invited a minstrel into their homes might be pious folk wanting to hear religious material; but more likely, they were familiar with the minstrel's art, perhaps even aficionados of it, and they would want to hear the full range of what a singer could do. In a home, a minstrel might be asked to sing historical songs and *dumy* in addition to religious songs. *Dumy*, or epics, are songs about war. There are *dumy* about the conflict with the Turks and the Tatars, and about Khmelnytskyi and the uprising against the Polish-Lithuanian Commonwealth. Among them are many songs about the deaths of heroes in battle. A whole cycle of epics tells about Cossacks in Turkish captivity, languishing in prison and suffering beatings and privation. A very interesting group of epics, called the *dumy* about everyday life, tells about widows, sisters, and wives, and has little to do with battle except in the sense that the women suffer because their men go off to war. This group of songs was likely aimed at the many women who would be in a home, listening to an invited minstrel.

Historical songs, another category likely to be performed in a home, are related to epic songs in content but distinguished from them in form. They are more melodramatic than epics and tell of such historical figures as Baida, Semen Palii, and Ivan Sirko, recounting their often gruesome deaths and the sufferings of their surviving family members.[23] There are also many historical songs about generic figures—a Cossack, for example, identified only as such, who as he lies dying on the field of battle instructs his horse to go home and inform his mother. There are songs about a mother meeting her daughter among the new captives just brought into the sultan's harem; about a brother and sister, separated at birth, who meet and marry, and only much later discover that they are siblings. Historical songs were apparently quite popular and probably good money makers. Religious songs directly equated damnation with lack of charity; historical songs presented a tragic view of life and made people mindful of death. They also articulated problematic family relations typical of rural Ukraine and provided descriptions of battle and high adventure. They were the popular drama of their day.

Toward the end of a performance, a minstrel might be asked to play something with a lighter touch, a satirical song perhaps, or something to entertain the children. Many minstrels were apparently reluctant to do this, sensing, evidently, that a happy listening public, one not quite so worried about the fires of hell and redeeming one's soul through charity, paid less well. Once a singer had received his payment or gift, a bit of frivolity was quite acceptable—perhaps the song about the two brothers Khoma and Iarema, who always got things confused and did everything backward, or the song about Hrytsko, who was incurably lazy and succeeded only through a series of lucky coincidences. Religious songs, historical songs and epics, and satirical songs are the genres about which we have the greatest amount of information, but minstrels could do much more. They probably knew lyric songs and could tell prose stories.[24] If his hosts were willing, a minstrel could entertain them for hours.

Besides travelling to other villages and singing at various homes, minstrels liked to go to fairs and to religious festivals. Here there would be large crowds, and a performer could earn a relatively large amount of money in a single place. Both fairs and religious festivals would predispose audiences to generosity; fairs because they would put people in a spending mood, and religious festivals because they would encourage alms giving for the sake of salvation. At fairs (*iarmorok*), minstrels would stand or sit in one place, singing songs to attract attention—either the same begging song used to start a performance at a home or a special one suitable for fairs.[25] Afterward, the minstrel would sing whatever the audience requested. Anyone requesting a song was expected to pay for it by placing a coin in the begging bag (*torba*) that the minstrel would set by his side. At fairs, payment was usually made in coins rather than in goods, because coins were readily available.

Religious festivals (*vidpusty*) were somewhat analogous to fairs. These were events held at cathedrals or monasteries on religious holidays. Pilgrims would gather to pray for forgiveness of sins or for relief from an ailment, and merchants would come to sell refreshments and candles or religious artifacts. Minstrels sat or stood among the merchants and sold spiritual, rather than concrete, wares, songs that were supposed to provide moral uplift and bring people closer to God. Categories of songs that clearly fit this definition were few, and there was considerable ambiguity about other song types, making minstrels wary of honoring all song requests. No one questioned whether begging songs and religious verses were appropriate to religious occasions; but historical songs and epics would be considered appropriately serious material by some members of the audience and censured by others. Similarly, songs like "Justice and Injustice" could either be interpreted as pious glorifications of the meek, which presented suffering as the path to salvation, or they could be seen as songs of social protest, which by siding with those who were the victims of injustice, encouraged rebellion.[26] With such material, minstrels were torn between the desires to please the audience and earn money and the fear of angering their listeners, possibly prompting them to call the authorities; and police punishment could be quite severe, including incarceration, beatings, and having one's musical instrument smashed.

As events where a large number of minstrels gathered in one place, fairs and religious festivals served as occasions for professional meetings of minstrel brotherhoods or guilds. Here, apprentices would be presented to the brotherhood as candidates for initiation, and the actual initiation ceremony would be held. The meetings might serve as occasions for trying errant members accused of theft, of cheating on their brothers, or of performing without having passed the initiation test. Other guild business conducted at the various meetings might include electing officers, collecting dues, and distributing cash awards to members in need, such as those whose homes had burned down.

When not travelling, minstrels lived lives similar to those of their neighbors. Almost all married and raised families. It would usually take several years from the time a man passed his initiation and started working on his own for him to earn enough money to take a wife; but as soon as they could afford to marry, minstrels did. Having a wife and a family was the village norm, and this norm extended to blind people. Besides, there were a great many advantages to being married. While most minstrel wives were not prime marriage material and many were widows or had a physical defect, they nonetheless could contribute to the work that needed to be done on the farmstead. Most would eventually have children, and children, if sighted, could contribute a great deal more, especially as they grew older and stronger.

A married minstrel and his family would live at first with the minstrel's parents. Eventually they would inherit their family lands and take care of these by hiring farmhands with the proceeds from the farm, from begging trips, and from work such as plaiting ropes. As the children grew older and became able to take care of the family farm, the need to hire outside workers decreased, and the minstrel's family functioned almost identically to the families of the neighbors. A minstrel's children did not follow in their father's profession unless they too were blind. A son or a daughter might serve as a guide while still young and unable to do heavy farm labor. This would eliminate the need to hire someone, and save the minstrel and his family money. As the children grew, they did farm work only, often discouraging their father from begging if the farm could sustain the family without his contribution. Because of the awkwardness of begging and the shame of asking for alms, even in payment for singing or praying for deceased relatives, children tried to keep the father at home as soon as this was economically feasible.

While at home, a minstrel might be hired to perform at a wedding, which was not considered begging. Here a minstrel did not have to initiate the interaction between himself and his audience by singing first and then hoping that the performance would move someone to charity. Rather, the family of the groom, the side that normally paid for a wedding in rural Ukraine, would approach the minstrel and contract with him for a specified fee. This was a straight exchange of a service for a predetermined amount of money, and none of the minstrel's family members sought to deter him from making such an arrangement. At weddings, minstrels played dance tunes and sang joyful, satirical songs, like the ones performed in private homes to entertain children. The dance tunes were quite different. There was, of course, no sound amplification in rural Ukraine, and when the dancing started, the room became too noisy for even the most powerful singing voice. For this reason, dance tunes (*kozachok*) were instrumental pieces, perhaps with a line of verse or two sung or shouted every so often. A successful minstrel might have a repertory of many *kozachky* to meet audience demand.[27]

A traditional minstrel was probably ambivalent about his profession. He was happy that he did not have to rely on begging, that he could do some kind of work to earn his daily bread. At the same time, his line of work was something he had not fully chosen; it had been forced upon him. It was both an honorable and a demeaning form of work. Perhaps these mixed feelings can be seen in the way minstrels treated their musical instruments. Kharkiv notes that some minstrels did not care for their *bandury* or their *liry* and would readily sell these to scholars or collectors. When not performing, they would neglect them, even to the point of letting the wood warp.[28] At the same time, other minstrels loved their instruments so much that when forced to sell them out of economic necessity, they would lament and shed tears.[29] As we shall see, duality characterized many aspects of minstrelsy.

Chapter 2

The Traditional Repertory: An Overview

*P*avlo Suprun sings quite a variety of songs, and the number of separate pieces that he knows is impressive indeed. His personal favorites are traditional epics and historical songs and his own compositions, modern epics which he creates by composing music to the words of poems that he especially likes. However, his repertory is not restricted to these. He sings lyric songs, folk songs known by virtually all Ukrainians. His audiences like to hear familiar pieces with which they can sing along, led by Suprun's magnificent voice. He sings satirical and drinking songs if necessary, as in the restaurant where he works. Though he prefers to speak Ukrainian only, he sings Russian romances because there are many Russian speakers in Kiev, especially among the restaurant clients.

Traditional minstrels, at least the better ones among them, like Pavlo Suprun, had huge and varied repertories. Scholars credit minstrels with knowing three categories of song: religious, historical, and satirical. In all probability, they also knew folk songs, prose legends, folktales, and many other genres that did not attract attention because they were performed only in the privacy of homes rather than in the more public settings of the street, the fair, and the religious festival. Possibly scholars did not associate genres not restricted to professional performers with minstrels; possibly they even collected these from minstrels, but published the folk songs and tales separately from minstrel material and without attribution, meaning they did not name the teller or singer who had provided the text. Even the begging song, the traditional opening of a performance in a home or at a fair or festival, has not been extensively recorded or analyzed, because it was not exclusive to minstrels but was shared with regular beggars, men and women who sang nothing more than this request for alms.

The Begging Song, or *Zhebranka*

Often addressed specifically to a woman, the begging song is a plea for generosity that can extend for as many as one hundred fifty lines. The line length is variable, usually ranging from eight to sixteen syllables, though some lines can be as short as three.[1] There is no discernable rhyme scheme. Collectors like Borzhkovskii have tried to arrange parts of the begging songs they published into four-line stanzas, but either couplet rhyme or rhyme between alternating lines is more common.[2] When rhyme occurs, it is not necessarily maintained throughout a song. One of the dominant poetic features of the begging song is repetition, often of the initial word or phrase of a line. Internal rhyme occurs occasionally. A great deal of variation was permitted in the begging song. While any one minstrel probably sang a fairly similar begging song from one performance to the next, the differences between the begging song of one minstrel and that of another could be quite substantial in both form and content.[3]

Despite the differences between begging songs, certain themes appear regularly. Begging songs speak of the transitory nature of life and earthly possessions; what is really important is the afterlife, for which one should prepare by practicing charity. A common image used to show how fleeting life can be is that of the poppy, which fades quickly and is swallowed by the soil; and the soil, meaning the measures of earth in which one is buried, the songs tell us, is man's only permanent possession.[4] The message is clear: The listener, standing to gain nothing by clinging to earthly treasures, should secure a place in heaven by giving alms to the mendicant. Often the begging song emphasizes that the singer is not asking for much: just a small coin, just a scrap of cloth, anything the listener can spare.[5]

Most begging songs have a section where the performer apologizes for seeking alms, emphasizing that he has no choice, and describing the plight of a blind person by listing what he cannot see: the dawn of day, the coming of night, the seasons, the beauty of nature. The minstrel says that his eyes are sealed, as if covered by the leaves of an oak tree, and complains that he depends on someone else's eyes to see where he is going, on someone else's work to provide his livelihood. Sometimes the singer adds that blindness is so awful, it would be better to be dead, to never have been born, to have rotted in the mother's womb. The singer states that if he had any other choice, if he could work, he would much rather ask the listener for employment than for charity.[6] This section, too, is often followed by statements to the effect that the supplicant is asking only for a small donation.

A very interesting and unexpected theme found in several begging songs is the theme of cloth. The singer makes a particular plea for cloth to wipe his sightless eyes or to cover his nakedness, comparing the desired act of covering the mendicant to what God does when he covers the earth with grass, the tree with leaves, the sky with clouds, the fish with scales, the bird with feathers, and so forth.[7] Even more interesting is the use of a short narrative about Mary, Mother of God, who is sometimes replaced by Saint Paraskovia, the patron saint of cloth and of activities such as spinning and weaving. In this story, Mary, or Paraskovia, divides her mantle into three parts, keeping one for herself, giving one to the church, and giving another one to the poor to cover their nakedness. By doing so, she earns her place in heaven. The listener is then urged to be like Mary, or Paraskovia, and to give the singer a piece of fabric.[8]

Cloth is emphasized also in other ways. The *lirnyk* Varion Honchar told the collector Volodymyr Kharkiv that a special effort, perhaps an especially elaborate and poignant song, was needed to get a piece of cloth.[9] The *lirnyk* Mykolai Doroshenko gave Martynovych two different songs of thanks, one for an ordinary donation and a special one for the gift of a piece of fabric.[10] The emphasis on fabric has a practical and a symbolic basis. If the audience was primarily female, then the gifts that this listening public could supply would be first and foremost food and fabric. Much food was perishable, but a piece of cloth lasted a long time and could be sold later at a bazaar for cash. Fabric also had a magical quality. Specially embroidered long strips of cloth called *rushnyky* were used, and with the end of the Soviet era, are now again used, to protect people and places. They are draped around doors and windows to shield the inhabitants of a house from anyone or anything entering the building's openings. They are tied around the waist of a bride and placed on newborns and the dead to guard them as they journey from one stage of life to the next.[11] They are hung over icons, and may have had a sacred meaning similar to that of the icon. The prestige that embroidery enjoys among Ukrainians even now attests to the special position that fabric and fabric-related activities hold in Ukrainian culture. Magical properties assigned to cloth probably have a pre-Christian basis, but this did not stop them from being included in the belief system associated with minstrelsy.

Whether asking for a piece of cloth or for a coin, whether asking the listener to give alms for the sake of the listener's salvation or because the performer had no other way of supporting himself, the singer always promised to pray for his benefactor. He promised to pray for his health and prosperity on earth and he promised to pray for his peaceful rest in the afterlife. The minstrel also offered to pray for the dead relatives of his audience, especially those who had died young and suddenly, accident victims, and people killed in battle.[12] The promise to pray for the listener and his or her deceased relatives was carried out either at the close of the begging song, if that was the only item performed, or separately, at the end of the entire session.[13] The begging song thus sought to secure concrete and symbolic benefits for the minstrel—the alms and the gift of cloth—and in return, it promised the listener symbolic, spiritual services in the form of prayers.

Religious Songs, or *Psalmy*

Religious songs, which also provided spiritual services for the audience, formed the central portion of the minstrel's repertory. Usually called *psalmy*, these are not really psalms as such, but songs on Biblical and other religious topics. Their form is more rigid than that of the begging song. Line length is constant throughout the song, though occasional lines with a missing or an extra syllable are possible. The most common number of syllables in a line is eight; but songs with six-syllable lines exist, as do songs with longer lines of twelve, fourteen, and even sixteen syllables. The lines are most often grouped in four-line stanzas, with an underlying couplet structure, so that the usual rhyme is aa, bb, cc, and so forth. Often a single line is repeated, to form a couplet of sorts. As P. Demutskyi, who published one of the few collections devoted to religious songs, points out, this genre resembles a cross between church chant and folk songs. Interestingly, religious songs for which the instrument is tuned in a major key are more like church singing, and the ones where the instrument is tuned in a minor key are more like folk songs.[14]

The content of religious songs is varied. There are a number of songs about the passion of Christ and the Last Judgement. Biblical topics include the story of Adam and Eve, which curiously says nothing about the expulsion of the pair from Eden, but in keeping with the importance of cloth, emphasizes their perception of their nakedness after eating the forbidden apple. An interesting version of the Great Flood, published by Demutskyi, has people climbing trees as the waters rise, repenting for their sins, and bidding each other farewell. In this version there is some confusion between the dove sent out by Noah to find dry land and a raven, which seems to have survived the flood without the aid of the ark.[15] Other songs tell about Judas' betrayal of Christ, about John the Baptist, Mary Magdalene, Saint George the Dragon Slayer, and various other religious figures.

The most often repeated message in this material is that life is short, that one never knows when death will come, and that one had better repent and start preparing for the afterlife immediately. This is quite literally the topic of "About the Hour of Death" (*Ob smertnomu chasu*) and of the song variously called "Archangel Gabriel" and, after its first line, "If only I knew."[16] In the song about the hour of death, the first-person narrator has a conversation with Death itself. He complains that Death had promised him a life of a hundred years, leading him to think that he could drink and celebrate and still have plenty of time to atone for his sins. Death has broken its promise, he implies, and here it is forcing him to rot in the ground much too soon. The narrator then asks Death for an extra hour of life to say good-bye to his family. Death grants his wish but seems to break its word again leaving enough time for the whole family to gather, but not enough time for the farewells. Still, the narrator of the song manages to ask the angels to save his soul while consigning his body to the earth.

Good deeds and avoidance of sin are as necessary as repentance, religious songs say, and the catalogues of good and sinful deeds they provide offer an interesting perspective on the worldview of the Ukrainian peasant. In the song about the passion of Christ, the Virgin Mary comes to view her son's suffering and asks Him for instruction. He tells her to take her keys and to open the gates of Heaven and Hell. She is to release all righteous people and to condemn all who have committed unforgivable sins: those who have sung songs on Fridays, failed to wash on Saturdays, eaten early on Sundays, disobeyed and angered their parents, argued with elder siblings, and failed to keep the fast.[17] The listener is then urged to avoid all of these sins so as to be saved from damnation. All of the Last Judgement songs tell how the righteous will rejoice on the last day and how the sinners will mourn. These songs, again, urge proper behavior before it is too late.[18] In the song called "Guardian Angel," the angel of the title awakens the human soul and urges it to do what is right. The soul, however, proves lazy. It fails to attend church, it fails to light candles, and it fails to care for widows and orphans or to host pilgrims. As a result, the soul is condemned to Hell and the Guardian Angel refuses to intercede on its behalf.[19] Some versions of the Lazar song present arrogance as a sin. The rich brother not only fails to care for his poor and sickly sibling, he also assumes that he can buy off death with his riches or hold death at bay with his armed forces. When death comes, of course, neither physical nor financial might proves effective, and the arrogant rich man bemoans his failure to secure himself a place in Heaven.[20]

A more hopeful picture appears in the various songs addressed to women and to Saint Nicholas (*Mykolai* in Ukrainian). Mary, Mary Magdalene, and Paraskovia prove more compassionate than the Guardian Angel. They pray and seek to intercede on behalf of all sinners, to lead people from their errant ways in this life, and to save them from the torments of Hell in the next.[21] Nicholas is presented as even more powerful and helpful than the women. He is pictured not only as the savior of souls but also as the savior of bodies, rescuing people from prison and from fire, guarding their health, protecting those on the field of battle and those in need, such as widows and orphans. All one needs do to secure the help of Saint Nicholas, the songs tell us, is to humble oneself and ask.[22] The songs about Saint Nicholas were apparently quite popular, indicating that religious songs do not paint a totally bleak picture. They offer hope and help in this life, as well as promises of salvation after death. Religious songs, then, contain both the tough approach of threats of damnation for those who need to be frightened, and the comforting approach of the Saint Nicholas songs for those who need reassurance.

As with much folk material, genre boundaries are hard to draw, and it is difficult to determine what is and what is not a religious song. Many collectors, including Demutskyi and Valerian Borzhkovskii, include a very popular item called "The Orphan Girl" in the religious song category even though it has no overtly religious subject-matter and resembles a religious song only in the ending, where the orphan dies and her soul ascends to Heaven, while the soul of the wicked stepmother who had tormented her is banished to Hell.[23] A narrative in which the Virgin Mary intercedes in a battle is normally considered a historical song, in spite of the presence of a holy figure.[24] "Oleksii, Man of God," already mentioned as a religious song, is grouped with historical songs by Amvrosii Metlinskyi.[25]

Historical Songs and Epics: *Istorychni Pisni* and *Dumy*

Historical songs are very close to religious songs in form. Like religious songs, they have a stable line length based on an eight- to sixteen-syllable line. The most common line lengths are eight and sixteen syllables. Depending on the collector or publisher, the sixteen-syllable verses are printed either as sixteen-syllable lines with couplet rhyme or eight-syllable lines with alternating rhyme. Some songs have true eight-syllable lines rather than eight-syllable lines that are part of larger, sixteen-syllable units, and in these, we find rhyme at the end of each eight syllable line and couplets built of eight-syllable units. Not all sixteen-syllable structures break up into units of eight plus eight, and sometimes ten-syllable lines alternate with lines of six syllables. Other divisions are also possible, though less frequently used.

In terms of subject matter, historical songs, like religious songs, tell of events that both the singer and the audience believed really happened. These events include the supernatural and the miraculous. As Saint Varvara survives being boiled in pitch, walking on broken glass, and being entombed for thirty years, so Baida survives being suspended by his left rib from a meat hook for three days before he dies. Likewise, Cossack heroes like Perebiinis and Nechai battle hundreds of enemy soldiers before being killed or captured.[26] As human beings talk with Death, with angels, and with deceased and buried relatives in religious songs, so in historical songs animals speak with human voices. Horses inform the family back home that their riders are dead, and cuckoos sing laments over fallen Cossacks.[27] There are remarkable coincidences. Two or even three sisters, or a mother and a daughter, may find themselves in captivity in the same Turkish harem.[28] The differences between historical and religious songs are differences of scale: the historical songs tell of events that are important on a personal or a national level, while religious songs function on a cosmic scale. There are also differences of time and place: historical songs occur in Ukraine in a past that is recent enough to bear strong resemblance to the current situation, and religious songs occur a very long time ago, and often, in faraway lands.

Historical songs cover a wide range of topics, and thus are difficult to characterize from the point of view of content. Some are about famous people, such as Mazepa.[29] Many are about people who are nameless: an unnamed Cossack, a brother and a sister, a mother and a daughter. Many historical songs have a lyrical dimension and describe or address nature. Most tell of the death or suffering of their protagonists. In many regards, historical songs represent a continuation of religious songs, the latter treating events in the distant past and the former treating more recent occurrences. It is easy to see why for minstrels and much of their audience historical songs and religious songs were of one type: serious, morally uplifting material.

Dumy, or epic songs, also were considered serious. In content, they are similar to historical songs, and they are often published alongside the latter, as in the collections of D. Revutskyi, V. Antonovych and M. Drahomanov, Metlynskyi, and others. *Dumy* deal with fewer topics than do historical songs: there are approximately thirty stories that indisputably belong to this genre. The usual division of their subject matter is into three categories: songs about the Turko-Tatar period, songs about the rebellion led by Bohdan Khmelnytskyi, and songs about everyday life. Sometimes the first category is further subdivided into songs about the field of battle and songs about captivity. Like historical songs, some epics tell about real historical figures, and others describe events in the life of an unnamed Cossack, brother, or widow.

While the subject matter of *dumy* is quite similar to that of historical songs, their form is radically different. Both religious and historical songs are sung; epics, however, are chanted. Their performance style is often called recitative, and the effect resembles church chant more than singing. Epics do not have a melody, as songs do, and most performers sing them differently every time because the words, rather than the music, drive the performance. Like the begging songs, epics have a line length that is extremely uneven, varying from three to sixteen syllables. Rhyme is also irregular. The usual rhyme unit is called a tirade, a group of rhyming lines with no set dimensions resembling, the *laisse* of French epic poetry. The tirade can be several lines long, or it can have a rhyme that repeats for five, six, or sometimes as many as twenty lines. Couplet rhyme also occurs, though rarely, and is most often found in epics that describe later historical periods, such as the ones about Khmelnytskyi and his men. R. Jakobson demonstrated that the Ukrainian epic shares features with the other Slavic epic traditions.[30] It is, however, in form at least, quite different from the other historical material performed by Ukrainian minstrels.

Though in form distinct from religious and historical songs, *dumy* were of the same category in the eyes of their performers. Minstrels used the word *rozkaz*, a generic term for narrative, usually applied to prose, for all serious material, prose narratives, epics, historical songs, and religious songs.[31] They even blended what scholars consider distinct genres: Borzhkovskii recorded a lengthy piece that he called simply "a minstrel's song," which has the formal features of religious song and resembles a religious song in content at the beginning but then proceeds to describe deaths on the battlefield using imagery commonly found in the epic.[32]

Satirical Songs and Songs on the Periphery of the Minstrel Canon

The begging song formed the shell, and religious, historical, and epic songs the core of a typical performance. This constituted the basic minstrel canon. But there were other songs, related in form and content to those already described, which some minstrels chose to include in their repertory and other singers did not. For example, some minstrels readily performed "Justice and Injustice," while others feared that this song would offend certain audiences. "Justice and Injustice," which defies genre assignation, is published either in twelve-syllable lines with couplet rhyme or in six-syllable lines with alternating rhyme. Thus the line length is somewhat shorter than the eight syllables basic to the songs discussed so far, but with the variation permitted especially in epics and begging songs, not drastically different. The content of "Justice and Injustice" is similar to that of a religious song, except that the action takes place in the present. The song emphasizes that things are not as they should be: justice is vilified and neglected, while injustice is celebrated and praised. Injustice, personified in the same way that death is in religious songs, sits at table with the rich and receives their bribes, while justice is trampled underfoot.[33]

The other song category that, like "Justice and Injustice," is built on a six- (sometimes seven-) syllable line with couplet or alternating rhyme was always outside the serious sphere. It could be sung at weddings, where the minstrel was paid for reasons other than charity and it could be sung "for the children," as long as the performance was in a home and thus relatively private, and a proper number of serious pieces had already been sung. This is the category called satirical songs. The formal features of satirical songs are similar to other song types except that line length is always short to produce a more jovial, staccato tempo.

The content of satirical songs differs markedly from that of other songs. Some resemble folktales and tell of a simpleton who means well but always uses the wrong polite expression. He sees a corpse being carried out of the church for burial and wishes the members of the funeral party many more. After he gets beaten up, he turns to his mother, who tells him that he should wish the deceased eternal memory and everyone else long life. Kosmina, the simpleton, then runs across a wedding party and says what his mother had just taught him. After he gets beaten again, his mother advises him to wish the wedding party success in finding brides for all their sons. Kosmina then sees a man preparing to take a pig to market and wishes the man success in marrying the pig to his son.[34] The song continues in a similar vein for as many as one hundred lines, depending on the abilities of the performer. An analogous song about two brothers, Foma or Khoma and Iarema, tells of their misfortunes in business. Like Kosmina, the two brothers fail at endeavor after endeavor. The song about Khoma and Iarema is a wonderful example of the repetition with variation that characterizes much of minstrel material, and it is tempting to view this as a training song used to teach oral composition and minstrel aes-thetics, especially since some minstrels claim that satirical songs were the ones taught first.[35] Throughout the song, Khoma performs one action and Iarema performs the same action slightly differently. For example, Khoma gets dressed and Iarema dons his clothes; Khoma tries his hand at selling and Iarema tries to run a business; Khoma tries selling pots and Iarema tries selling bowls; people will not buy from Khoma and they will not do business with Iarema, and so forth. The two words used for the similar actions or objects either rhyme or alliterate, and the minstrel must produce near synonyms with repetitive prosodic features line after line. This is exactly the same sort of thing we see in epic where the hero is wounded by bullets, cut by a saber, and injured by a spear. Thus, even satirical songs, as different as they are from the minstrel material already described, share some of its structural and prosodic features.

Some satirical songs are misogynistic. An old man who can no longer see well mistakes an old woman for a beauty and falls in love. When he gets her outside into daylight and takes a good look at her, he realizes his mistake. He tries to drown her in the stream, and the song makes fun of the fact that the woman will not drown and that the old man must push her under with his cane again and again. In a song called "Noblewoman" (*Dvorianka*), the wife tells her husband to sell the various farm animals and to buy her fine clothes, rare cosmetics, and costly food and drink so that she, along with her husband, can entertain guests as befits her noble birth. The husband does as he is told, but the next day, he makes his wife do the work of all of the missing farm animals. After the man makes his wife pull a cart with him sitting in it all the way to the forest to chop wood, and all the way back loaded with logs and with him sitting on top, the woman has a change of heart. She promises to be a good wife, to love, cherish, and honor her husband. All that she asks in return is that he sell her fine clothes and cosmetics and buy back the farm animals.[36] Although the misogynistic satirical songs may seem at odds with the rest of minstrel material, they are not. The serious minstrel songs provide a positive picture of women and attribute a great deal of power to them, especially to mothers and old women. A mother's curse can cause a man to be defeated in battle, and a mother's anger can bring crop failure and ruin.[37] Conversely, a mother's prayers can save one even from the bottom of the sea. In "The Orphan Girl," we see that a mother's love is so desirable, her child will seek her even when she is dead and buried. In the song "Justice and Injustice," the only good thing left in the world is a mother's love. The satirical songs provided a corrective balance to this perceived overprivileging of women. Thus, satirical songs were not at odds with the rest of a minstrel's repertory, even though, at least in the data available, they were always sung outside a serious performance.[38]

One widely recorded song, "Misfortune" (*Bida*), seems to bridge the serious and the humorous. The beginning of this song resembles "Justice and Injustice" and religious material: it laments the human condition, saying that misfortune follows man from the cradle to the grave, wherever he goes, whatever he does. The remainder of the song is slapstick and resembles "Khoma and Iarema" or "Kosmina, the Simpleton." In this part, which can be quite long, as many as one hundred lines, a personified Misfortune walks the earth, walking in and out of various homes and establishments, and either tricking people, or more often, getting tricked and beaten up herself.[39]

The song types described here are usually associated with minstrelsy, though they are probably just a fraction of what the best minstrels knew.

They are the song types proper to professional singing: the begging situations in the home and at fairs and religious festivals, and the contractual situation that prevailed at weddings. Knowing this material required excellent memory, a quality minstrels themselves prized, and superior oral composition skills.[40] It is striking that people who came from a necessarily limited pool of potential performers, namely all blind people, achieved a level of artistry and knowledge as great as the one possessed by Pavlo Suprun and traditional *kobzari* and *lirnyky*.

Chapter 3

Common Stereotypes of Minstrels

*P*eople react to Pavlo Suprun and his wife in opposites and extremes. Some treat them as less than human and speak past them as if they were not there. Others consider them especially privileged and rely on them for objective information, be it on historical topics or the day's news. Similarly, traditional minstrels were treated in opposite and extreme ways. Some considered them the successors of the Apostles, and thus, trustworthy spiritual guides. Others suspected them of drunkenness and thievery. Negative stereotypes are the most destructive, though positive ones laid their own burdens upon minstrels and minstrelsy. The reasons for negative perceptions had a great deal to do with the performance situation in which a minstrel found himself, one which had many of the traits of begging. Except when he played at weddings, a minstrel was not a hired performer. He was a supplicant, and paying for his songs was up to the listener, an amorphous arrangement that was hard on the minstrel. The fact that it no longer exists attests to its problematic nature. Traditional minstrelsy was a recognized profession which gave the blind a way to earn a living, and thus, a degree of dignity; it was work, much better than simple begging. Yet, paying for a song was not making a purchase; it was akin to giving alms. Thus, the stigma of begging attached itself to minstrelsy.

Suspicions of Drunkenness and Depravity

Jozef Dzierzkowski gives the most negative picture of minstrels, lumping them together with professional beggars.[1] His description depicts what allegedly occurred every year at the monastery of St. Vasilian in Hoshov, Dolinskyi region:

> Among them were the dirty and the naked, the broken and the lame, with faces marked by the worst calamities that can destroy human nature. There

were men among them and women, the old and the young. There were the
crippled and the grossly deformed. There were those who had the most
hideous wounds which they displayed without shame, as if they were the
finest trophies. There were dwarfs with huge animals, so huge that they
seemed to have been stolen from giants. And there were broad-shouldered
giants with staffs that seemed suited only for the activities of a highwayman
and heads so small that it was hard to believe so many evil passions could fit
inside. When the king of the mendicants, Vasyl, treated all those present to
vodka, the scene changed beyond recognition. Inspired, the beggars came to
life and began to move—and there were no more blind or lame among them.
There were no more hunchbacks or those stooped to the ground. They were
all dancing in their various ways, jumping as if they wanted to cast aside
their myriad disabilities as quickly as possible. And they threw away their
staffs. The dwarfs grew to full height. The deformed hands and fingers disappeared. The raw wounds were gone, as if washed away. And their voices
changed. They were no longer plaintive, but became strong and natural; they
were all speaking as loudly as they could, calling to one another, each in his
own manner. The whole scene moved in a way never before seen and a
happy hum rose above it, full of a strange mix of swear words, religious
songs, and laughter. It was a scene capable of destroying one's physical and
moral sensibilities.[2]

Dzierzkowski's description is sensationalistic; yet it reflects a widely
held belief that the cadres of the disabled, to which blind minstrels belonged, were deformed not only physically but also morally, and that their
suffering did not lead to righteousness but to depravity. The professional
meetings of minstrels and other beggars were secret, and it is not that hard
to understand why outsiders might have pictured these as freak shows rather
than serious business gatherings. Furthermore, beggars and minstrels were
widely suspected of feigning piety and meekness to cover their real natures.
They were routinely reputed to be alcoholics and suspected of stealing to
support their habits.

Speaking specifically about minstrels, Dzierzkowski says that they reveal their true nature in the tavern when they get drunk.

> Only then can one truly see the extent of their cunning. Only then is one fully
> convinced that their piety is but a mask and that their prayers and religious
> songs mean nothing to them and are just a way to earn money. There they
> boast to each other about how well they feign disability to rouse the emotions
> of passers-by, what clever tricks they use to get the public to give them alms.
> There the incorrigible drunkard is revealed for what he is and the full extent
> of his depravity becomes clear. A devilish malice appears on the faces of
> these men, and all sorts of foul passions. These are criminals who hide
> behind the cloak of Lazarus and who deceive merciful people to such an
> extent that the public then denies alms to sufferers who are truly needy.[3]

Again, Dzierzkowski's views are extreme, but his words express attitudes that were held widely in a milder form. Why these attitudes toward minstrels existed is a complex question. Part of the answer may be an almost universally held belief that the poor are somehow less moral than the rich. In the English language, "nobleman" and "gentleman" mean someone in a high social position as well as someone of good character, though with time, the first term has come to refer more to position and the second, to character. Part of the reason minstrels were accused of a love for alcohol may have been an equally popular association between art and narcotics. Writers, poets, jazz musicians, rock stars, and so forth are frequently assumed to have a special affinity for alcohol and drugs. Similarly, at the end of the nineteenth century and the beginning of the twentieth, Ukrainian peasants, nobles, and law-enforcement officers all assumed that artists, the *kobzari* and *lirnyky*, had a tendency to drink. There was even a belief that the greater the artistry, the more massive the alcohol consumption—a belief that was sometimes shared by the artists themselves. Fedir Hrytsenko-Kholodnyi had a reputation among his fellow minstrels for a prodigious musical talent and an equally immense capacity for alcohol. Profirii Martynovych noted that Hrytsenko would not play without first getting a drink, and that he would drink enormous amounts, costing his hosts much money.[4] Vasyl Horlenko reported hearing about Vircheskii Anton, a man reputed to have a fiery nature, an ability to drink vast amounts, and an enormous musical repertoire.[5] Whether these beliefs have a basis in fact is another matter. Horlenko never found Anton, and he complained that no one else had recorded him either. As for theft, in one of the Bilozerskyi manuscripts there is an isolated and unattributed statement that *didy*, a term that could refer both to minstrels and to other organized beggars, steal, and that there are incantations to prevent them from doing so.[6]

Ukrainian minstrels were artists and they were poor. Thus they were doubly suspect. Even the most sympathetic of patrons, the scholars who worked with minstrels and tried to get government assistance for them, seem to have had some doubts about minstrel sobriety and honesty. They often excused *kobzari* and *lirnyky*, and argued that in fact, they were not drunkards. Almost invariably, they felt they had to differentiate minstrels from beggars. Nikolai Sumtsov, Oleksandr Malynka, Konstantin Bich-Lubenskyi, and Hnat Khotkevych all published virtually identical statements to the effect that minstrels are people who want to work and cannot, whereas beggars are people who can work and do not want to.[7] Lesia Ukrainka, in a letter to Filaret Kolessa about her experiences recording songs from the *kobzar* Hnat Honcharenko, wrote at length about how noble the minstrel was in bearing and behavior, how unlike a beggar. She described his artistic hands, his fine manners, and his refusal to accept a handout, and noted that even when someone did Honcharenko a favor, he insisted on playing and singing as payment for the kindness.[8] It almost seems as if she praises too much. One senses that before she actually met Honcharenko, she was anticipating some of the traits that appear in Dzierzkowski's descriptions. Klement Kvitka's guide to collecting information about *kobzari* and *lirnyky* is very telling: its first two series of questions are aimed at ascertaining the relationship of minstrels to beggars and establishing the moral qualities of the former.[9] Thus, even in the twentieth century, folklorists still had their doubts about both these matters.

Police Persecution

Suspicions that minstrels drank and stole existed at all levels of society. Various city officials and petty bureaucrats were prone to such suspicions, and evidence of severe police persecution exists in a number of sources. Hrushevska contends that one reason police harassed minstrels was to suppress the nationalistic feelings that *kobzari* and *lirnyky* supposedly instilled.[10] Soviet scholars wrote that minstrels were Communist sympathizers, often engaged in subversive activities such as carrying secret messages, and were persecuted for these activities. They further argued that police harassment which occurred prior to the twentieth century must have been in reaction to similar class-struggle acts on the part of minstrels.[11] There is probably some truth to these arguments, but a full picture requires a psychological explanation as well as a political one; at least some attacks on the part of the police and other authorities probably stemmed from an image of *kobzari* and *lirnyky* akin to the one presented by Dzierzkowski.

Even Ehor Movchan, the composer of "Duma about Lenin," beloved of Soviet authorities, suffered at the hands of the police. According to Pavlo Suprun, several policemen in Kiev once arrested Movchan for loitering, drove him far outside the city in the middle of a snowstorm, and left him to get back on his own. Movchan, one of the last traditional *kobzari*, was blind, and making it back into town through a storm was an almost impossible task. But the city police chief panicked when he learned what had happened to this emblem of the Soviet people and sent a search party to help find the old man, who returned safely. Perhaps to help him through the many times when he suffered police harassment and arrest without cause, Movchan had a special walking stick made for himself. It was a bit thicker than an ordinary blind man's staff and hollow, with a screw cap, and it held exactly one liter of vodka. Movchan was supposedly found in his jail cell more than once, drunk from some inexplicable source.[12]

The *lirnyk* Vasyl Lypnyk told a particularly sad story to Mykola Bilo-zerskii. It seems that Khvedor Lysyi of Chernobyl, a man with a beautiful voice and a large repertory, was given permission to travel and to beg by a priest. The police arrested the minstrel during his journey and chided the priest for his complicity because "such a man will only go and drink what-ever he collects by begging." Lysyi was given a three-month sentence and died in jail.[13] Terentii Parkhomenko avoided big cities for fear of arrest. He started performing in places like Kiev and Kharkiv only when he had be-come so well known that he felt confident he could find an intellectual to protect him wherever he went.[14] In a report to the Twelfth Archeological Congress, a priest noted that a *lirnyk* whom he had interviewed displayed constant nervousness, always seeming to listen to what was going on out-side. When asked why he was behaving as he did, the man confessed that he feared being arrested or beaten.[15] Apparently the minstrel did not feel safe even in the home of a priest. Kuchuhura-Kucherenko told Martyn-ovych that several women once asked him to sing the *duma* about a brother and a sister and he complied. While he was singing, he suddenly felt some-one strike his *kobza*. It turned out to be the constable, who then accused him of forming an illegal assembly, arrested him for four days, and broke his instrument.[16] By the beginning of the twentieth century, persecution was so prevalent that the instructions a minstrel gave his apprentices routinely included warnings about the police. Petro Dryhavka's teacher, for example, told him to honor his master, the minstrel brotherhood, and his biological family. He told him to pray whenever he set out to go begging, and when he entered a new village, to avoid the police.[17]

A statement that Mykhailo Kravchenko made to Opanas Slastion is telling. Slastion was trying to arrange for the singer to travel to St. Peters-burg, "in the footsteps of Ostap Veresai," and he asked Kravchenko what he would do, should he, like Veresai, a famous minstrel from the past, get to see the tsar. Kravchenko answered that he would ask nothing for him-self but he would request that minstrels be allowed to travel and work freely. The same Kravchenko had had trouble getting a talented boy to become his apprentice because the boy's father feared that being a minstrel would expose his son to police harassment. Slastion also remarks that the *kobzar* Opanas Bar complained that various civil authorities would tear the strings of his *bandura* and threaten to break the instrument itself without reason. Protest was useless and elicited beatings from the police. Once Bar turned and addressed an officer, "Your excellency, where am I supposed to get a crust of bread? No one will bring it to my house, you know. Am I supposed to lie down and die?" The answer, according to Bar, was, "Lie down and die, you cur. Just don't go around with your *bandura* anymore. It is not permitted."[18]

Minstrels themselves fell under the influence of the stereotyping; they suspected each other of sticky fingers and a love for the bottle. Veresai accused some of his masters of drunkenness, and Zlatarskyi reported how one minstrel tricked another by getting him drunk, almost as if he knew that the man would drink however much was offered.[19] Porfyrii Martynovych, who managed to gather details about minstrels' training which eluded other collectors, notes admonitions against alcohol that suggest drinking might be a particular temptation.[20] When Martynovych asked an informant about the gifts which a youth was supposed to distribute as part of the initiation rite, the man answered that a hat or a pair of boots were suitable gifts for a master. He noted that he himself had given his master, Nazarenko, a hat, but heard that the latter pawned it for alcohol almost right away.[21]

Alcohol served as a currency of sorts among minstrels. Vodka paid for entry into a guild and for readmission if one committed a misdeed that caused him to be ejected. A drink was also a way to buy information from a fellow minstrel, such as the text of a new song. Kharkiv stated that minstrels were "not impartial to drink" and when one minstrel wanted to learn a new song from another, he paid for it with a shot of vodka.[22]

One of the most touching stories of drinking and theft among minstrels comes from Martynovych's informant, Dryhavka. It seems that Dryhavka's master taught him the rudiments of begging and sent him out on his very first money-earning trip with the master's son as guide. When the two returned, the master's wife accused her own son of stealing. The boy denied concealing any of the money he and Dryhavka had collected, but the mother searched him and found over four rubles. According to Dryhavka, on another occasion, the master and his wife tried to avoid sharing vodka with their fellow minstrels. Both of these events must have affected the new minstrel deeply. They were not part of his formal training and they are told in a language quite different from that used to describe apprenticeship proper. Yet Dryhavka told them to Martynovych as if they were integral to his apprenticeship, and they must have been important to him as coming-of-age experiences, tales of his discovery of human flaws.[23] If even the master's own children could steal and a respected minstrel might try to trick his fellows, then all sorts of things were possible. It should not be a surprise, then, that Kuchuhura-Kucherenko's teacher advised him to keep a low profile in the company of other minstrels, just in case.[24]

Minstrels as Descendants of the Apostles

Minstrels may have been suspected of misdeeds, but they were also revered. As numerous as descriptions of their supposed depravity are statements which give *kobzari* and *lirnyky* an almost saintly quality. Positive descriptions abound in scholarship on minstrels. Panteleimon Kulish described villagers turning to a *kobzar* to learn the words to prayers and psalms and the methods of reciting these correctly. He also commented on the efforts of *kobzari* to teach others by example, with their church attendance and pious behavior.[25] Vasyl Horlenko called minstrels "the people of God" and described their participation in various religious events. Valerian Borzhkovskii discussed minstrel participation in religious celebrations and contrasted the spiritual importance that their singing held for ordinary folk with the lack of such meaning for the elite attending the event. An elderly peasant told Borzhkovskii that mendicants were capable only of good, that their words led to salvation, and that in the eyes of God, the *lirnyk* performing at the time of the interview was the most worthy human being. In interviews with *lirnyky* at home, Borzhkovskii found that piety and righteousness were qualities important to both the minstrels and their families. Andrii Dovhaliuk, for example, though young, had already established a good reputation, and the *lirnyk* Nikon, an older man, was renowned for his piety and was a community leader.[26]

What we have, then, are descriptions of minstrels that tend to extremes. The positive ones picture *kobzari* and *lirnyky* as saintly and even make them direct spiritual descendants of Jesus Christ by way of the Apostles.[27] The negative descriptions go so far as to link minstrels with the devil. This is not as surprising as it may at first seem. In the nineteenth-century Ukrainian countryside, minstrels were a marginal group, and such groups tend to be characterized in extremes and opposites. What made minstrels liminal was that they were professionals, that is, they were not farmers, unlike the vast majority of the population. It is precisely that which is unusual, which is at the edge, or limen, of society, which people tend to see as either all black or all white but never in shades of gray.

While images of minstrels tend toward black or white simplifications, even in scholarly literature, the truth is much more complicated, as close scrutiny of minstrel biographies reveals. Perhaps what is most remarkable in these biographies is how noble many minstrels appear even when their character flaws are acknowledged. Ivan Kravchenko-Kriukovskyi is a good example. He remained unembittered despite extreme adversity, and harbored no desire for revenge. The nobleman's son he was supposed to serve as companion physically abused him, eventually making him blind, yet his autobiographical account of this event is told in a dispassionate tone and conveys no hatred for the man who so terribly affected his life.[28] And, indeed, Kravchenko-Kriukovskyi was highly regarded by his peers. He was a leader among minstrels: their elder, a master teacher and the head of his guild. Slastion's description of Kravchenko-Kriukovskyi as a grand, tall man with long, flowing hair and an even grander, more imposing personality captures his stature well.[29] True, Kravchenko-Kriukovskyi tended to drink, especially when he was trying to stimulate his artistic powers for Martynovych and to recall the *dumy* that he had not sung for thirty years, yet this drinking did not detract from the impression he made on the collector. Slastion, serving as Martynovych's young assistant when the latter interviewed Kravchenko-Kriukovskyi and recorded his autobiography and some of his songs, was so affected that, although a painter by training and profession, he took up folklore and became a major contributor to folklore scholarship.

While not saintly, many minstrels were men of great personal and moral stature. It was, evidently, the power of Andrii Shut's personality that prompted Hryhoryi Basylevych to make him the subject of the very first *kobzar* biography.[30] Mykhailo Kravchenko, of course, refused to ask for anything for himself should he be granted an audience with the tsar. Kravchenko, incidentally, had plenty of reasons for requesting personal favors because, in addition to supporting his own wife and children, he supported his sickly brother and the brother's family. Fellow minstrels commented on Kravchenko's altruism. Kushneryk reported that Kravchenko gave him a *bandura* for free and Symonenko said that Kravchenko was equally generous with his knowledge, teaching him *dumy* without requesting compensation.[31]

Metafolklore and Scholarly Stereotypes of Minstrels

Kobzari and *lirnyky* have had image problems even among scholars. Because traditional minstrelsy was associated with begging, Ukrainian scholars have had trouble dealing with it objectively. Traditional minstrelsy developed two images in Ukrainian scholarship as well as in Ukrainian popular belief. The scholarly images were different from the popular ones, but they discouraged the study of real *kobzari* and *lirnyky*. One image of the minstrel was that of a social outcast, romanticized into the quintessential artist. Because most people, especially the elite who wrote about *kobzari* and *lirnyky*, would see a minstrel only on his begging trips or at fairs and religious festivals, they imagined him to be a loner with no family, no home, and no ties to the village community. This is the image presented in

Taras Shevchenko's poem "Perebendia," where the *kobzar* is pictured as an artist alone and apart, misunderstood by his audience. The image of quintessential artist was a positive one and brought attention to real performers, but it also encouraged collectors to distort the facts to fit the image, or to ignore the many performers who were less than consummate artists. Scholarly perception of minstrelsy shaped popular views—making people believe, for example, that this was an exclusively male profession. Some scholarly approaches to minstrelsy have affected the tradition itself.

Hrytsenko-Kholodnyi: A Real-Life Perebendia

Some imagined the minstrel as a man who sang for art's sake and was oblivious to money and his bodily needs. The most famous such treatment is Taras Shevchenko's poem "Perebendia." Shevchenko, a poet who is identified with Ukraine and whose name graces its streets, parks, and universities, called a collection of his poems *Kobzar*, thus equating his own poetry with the minstrel's art; and it is in this book that we find the image of the minstrel Perebendia. Perebendia has no home and sleeps by the roadside. He entertains the villagers, and they are thrilled by his singing; yet, the songs that Perebendia performs for others are not the ones that he finds truly meaningful, and to be able to sing these, he withdraws to a barrow in the steppe, where he sings to nature and to God Himself.[32]

Perebendia is alone in the middle of a steppe as blue as the sea, his mustache and his special Cossack forelock (*chupryna*) blown by the wind, and he is singing to the clouds, as lonely as the sun in the Heavens—this is a wonderful and romantic image which gives us the impression that money was not a concern for minstrels.[33] Unfortunately, this image does not correspond to reality. Among the minstrels whose biographies are available, there is only one who lived like Perebendia. His name was Fedir Hrytsenko-Kholodnyi, and he was a loner and a man apart. Kholodnyi, meaning "the cold one," was a nickname bestowed on this man because of his strange habits. He literally owned nothing. He slept outdoors, although various people, including the nobility, would try to take him in, feed and clothe him and exchange his boots with their iron, wear-proof soles for ordinary, comfortable shoes made of leather. But the minstrel could take this life only for a day or two, and soon he would be back out on the street in his old boots, sleeping in the cold.[34] One gentleman made a point of telling Martynovych that Kholodnyi had no home of his own. The fact that he bothered to point this out suggests that a homeless *kobzar* was exceptional.[35]

Shevchenko's Perebendia is an artist of exceptional skill, able to move his audiences with sad songs and to excite them with joyful ones.

Hrytsenko-Kholodnyi seems to have been as great a performer as his fictional counterpart. His musical talent was prodigious, and both scholars and fellow minstrels were in awe of him. His talent rendered Martynovych, an experienced collector who had listened to many performers, speechless: "Kholodnyi was a remarkable minstrel. Sometimes, when he would play the *bandura*, his notes would flow together and his playing would sound like a violin, so that you could not hear the strumming. And when he played the *kobza*, it sounded like his *kobza* was uttering words. His playing took my breath away the first time I heard him. And when he asked me how I liked his playing, I was silent for a long time because I had lost my ability to speak, because I was so full of wonder, and could not, at first, say a word."[36] Kravchenko-Kriukovskyi, himself an outstanding *kobzar*, reports that when Hrytsenko-Kholodnyi would start to play and sing, people would be so moved, money would just pour into his collection plate: "When he sits down, when he starts to strum and to give free rein to his melancholy, then he himself cries and everyone cries along with him; and as for the money—it is like dried peas being poured onto a plate—trr, trr, trr . . . "[37] Fellow minstrels Bar and Doroshenko claimed that Hrytsenko was so good, he could play dance melodies on a *bandura* with his bare feet.[38]

Yet Hrytsenko-Kholodnyi, like Perebendia, seems to have disdained the audience that was so taken with him, and would perform only when he absolutely had to. He did not withdraw to the steppe to practice his true art, however. Slastion reports that he would literally drink the shirt off his back, and only then would he go and play. And he would play only until he had earned enough money to barely sustain himself.[39] Kholodnyi was asocial, but in a less attractive way than Perebendia. A Polish gentleman, Pan Tvardovskii, notes that Kholodnyi was willing to use Tvardovskii's resources without a hint of embarrassment, and when he stayed at his house, he cost his host a *karbovanets* a day in drink alone, quite a large sum in 1885. In spite of the cost, Tvardovskii and others were willing to indulge Kholodnyi, just to hear him play and sing.[40]

Thus, minstrels like Perebendia really existed, and the romantic image of the *kobzar* has some small basis in fact. This is a colorful image, and it is not difficult to see why Shevchenko, though he was the son of a serf and familiar with village life, chose to use it for his poem. As much as Perebendia and Hrytsenko-Kholodnyi may capture the imagination, they were not the norm.

Ostap Veresai, the "Last" Minstrel

If one extreme was to see *kobzari* as quintessential artists, the other extreme was to see them not as artists at all but as imperfect remnants of a former, glorious artistic tradition. Some scholars, uncomfortable with the fact that minstrels were mendicants, assumed that this situation came into being only recently, after the tradition had begun to collapse, and that the original *kobzari* had nothing to do with beggars. There was one contemporary minstrel who was a good artist and yet had trouble getting along with his peers and functioning within minstrel institutions. Scholars seized upon him as concrete evidence of the imminent collapse of minstrelsy and made him famous around the world. Ostap Veresai was atypical in many respects, yet he became the darling of scholars and exerted tremendous influence on both scholarly and popular approaches to minstrelsy. He and his songs became the standard against which minstrels and minstrelsy were judged.

In the years 1852 to 1856, the artist Lev Zhemchuzhnikov lived and worked in the Poltava region, painting landscapes and portraits. He met and befriended Ostap Veresai, drew him, recorded one of his *dumy* and several of his songs, and wrote down his biography. While Zhemchuzhnikov drew and painted other performers, both *kobzari* and *lirnyky*, and did a fair amount of collecting, it was Ostap Veresai who made the strongest impression on Zhemchuzhnikov, and who through Zhemchuzhnikov would make an impact on the future study of Ukrainian folk performers and color the world's perception of what it means to be a *kobzar*.[41] Veresai appeared before the special meeting of the South-West division of the Imperial Geographical Society, held in Kiev, September 28, 1873, and thus became the first Ukrainian folk artist to be brought before an educated and urban audience. Veresai subsequently became the topic of several significant studies and collections: Chubynskyi wrote down and published the texts of his songs, Lysenko produced a study of minstrel music based on his recordings of Veresai, and Rusov wrote an essay on minstrel life based on Veresai's biography.[42] Since it was Veresai whom the French scholar Rambaud observed when he attended the Kiev Geographical Society meeting mentioned above, it was his image that the West initially received of Ukrainian minstrelsy.[43] Veresai was also the performer taken to St. Petersburg, the Russian capital, to showcase Ukrainian folklore for the Russian nobility and intelligentsia.

The attention paid to Veresai is both curious and unfortunate, because he was not a typical *kobzar*. He never completed any of his several apprenticeships and was never initiated into a minstrel guild. He had only one pupil of his own and that one left him for another master. His existence on the periphery of the profession gave the erroneous impression that Ukrainian minstrelsy was rapidly disintegrating and that he was one of the last, if not the very last, of its representatives.

Veresai affected not only the perception of minstrelsy, but also the evaluation of *dumy* and other folklore texts. He was not the best or most talented of *kobzari*. As he himself admitted, in his circle of acquaintances there were people who were technically better performers, had better voices, and were artistically more gifted, able to recite a fuller, more aesthetically pleasing text. Yet, because of the attention Veresai received, his versions became virtually canonical, so that subsequent performers, especially in the most recent period when learning is done from books rather than through apprenticeship, have tried to memorize his texts.[44]

Veresai's personality does not seem to have been particularly pleasant. We have fuller biographical data on him than on any other performer living in the nineteenth century. From these data, which include many statements directly from Veresai, he emerges as pushy, insensitive to people close to him, and self-centered. One does not wonder that he was unable to complete any of his apprenticeships, in spite of excuses such as illness, the drunkenness of the master, the master's exploitative tendencies, or Veresai's sense of possessing a superior talent. Nor does one wonder that Veresai's own apprentice left him. It does not seem strange that he had a much harder time marrying than most *kobzari*, and that when he became a widower, it took him seven years to coax the widow that he was in love with to the altar. Nor is it hard to believe that when he was allegedly mistreated by his son-in-law, the court ruled in the younger man's favor. This event in Veresai's life supposedly gave his rendition of the song, "Justice and Injustice," which begins with the line, "There is no justice in this world," particular poignancy. Veresai's attitude prompted his biographers to present him as a martyr, suffering unjustly because of his poverty and blindness. However, the more one reads about Veresai's life, the more one suspects that he deserved some of the ill treatment that came his way.

At the same time, there must have been something enormously attractive about Ostap Veresai. None of the other performers whom Zhemchuzhnikov encountered had the appeal for him of Veresai. Newspaper articles attest that the scholars at the Geographical Society meeting in Kiev and the nobility and intelligentsia in Petersburg were quite taken with him.[45] True, they knew no other *kobzari*; and perhaps Veresai's personality appealed more to the urbane and the elite than to his fellow villagers. And perhaps some of the appeal was precisely that Veresai was unable to function within the minstrel tradition, and reinforced notions about its imminent collapse. Veresai still continues to color many people's perception of the Ukrainian *kobzar*, even though this image is not an accurate representation of the Ukrainian folk tradition. The real tradition was complex, and it still flourishes. It may not have functioned for Veresai, but it did for the vast majority of minstrels. The various institutions of the system, like apprenticeship, had evolved to accommodate a variety of abilities and needs. The very fact that minstrelsy tolerated performers as atypical as Veresai and Hrytsenko-Kholodnyi is proof of its vitality and its efficacy as a social welfare institution.

Stereotypes Derived from Ukrainian Nationalism

One persistent image of the minstrel was derived more from the nature of the epics he sang than from anything to do with real performers. Scholars were especially interested in *dumy* because the existence of the epic on Ukrainian soil was a matter of great national pride. It legitimized Ukrainian culture. Ukraine has enjoyed very limited political independence, its eastern section being under Russian rule and its western part under Polish. Russians in particular were reluctant to see Ukraine as a separate entity, calling it "Little Russia," regarding its language as a dialect of Russian. Under these circumstances, Ukrainians felt a special need to establish the distinctiveness and validity of their culture; and since, rightly or wrongly, epic was considered great literature, a genre from which other genres evolved, the possession of an indigenous epic tradition distinct from the Russian one met that need. As heroic literature, epic is associated with warriors rather than mendicants. This, plus the striving to glorify Ukraine, led scholars who wrote about Ukrainian epic to downplay the role of the seemingly lowly beggar-minstrels and to spend time hypothesizing about a different type of epic performer, one associated with Ukraine's warriors, the Cossacks. It also discouraged them from trying to describe and understand mendicants, because to them, mendicants represented a devolution of the hypothetical warrior-*kobzar*.[46] This group, too, was happy to see Veresai as proof of the demise of the tradition.

While a special type of warrior *kobzar* is likely to have existed, to see mendicants as a devolution is to fail to do justice to a complex institution that had its own integrity and value. Traditional minstrelsy had meaning and purpose in the village setting, and traditional minstrels were much more than inferior remnants of warrior-bards. If anything, mendicant minstrels were part of an older tradition that absorbed warrior-bards when the Cossacks who supported them lost power and status. By focusing precisely on mendicants, this book will try to compensate somewhat for the overemphasis on singers employed by the Cossacks and try to give a truer picture of art in rural Ukraine.

Ukrainian scholars have not studied *kobzari* and *lirnyky* extensively, because they had a hard time being objective. In the West, where scholars did not have the burden of exalting Ukraine, Ukrainian minstrelsy has received virtually no attention except in the émigré community perhaps due to the general ignorance of the existence of Ukraine as a separate entity. Émigré scholarship has been limited to a dictionary of the secret language of the *kobzari* and *lirnyky*, a few collections of song texts, and a guide to playing the *bandura*.[47] The stigma that discouraged objective analysis, the link between minstrelsy and begging, is precisely what makes studying Ukrainian traditional minstrelsy so important. Analyzing a tradition in which blindness is obligatory yields an unusual perspective on the nature of art and beliefs about the artist.

Conclusion

Records of minstrels trying to live up to the pious standards expected of them, such as those provided by Borzhkovskii and Kulish, are probably the most accurate description of the majority of minstrels, namely that they were people trying to measure up to an ideal. Some, like Parkhomenko, Bratytsia, and Veresai, were entrepreneurs and hustlers. A few, like Nykolenko, found their singing and playing to be absolutely necessary for spiritual well-being, while others played and sang to earn money and viewed their music as nothing more than a livelihood. *Lirnyk* Masliukov asserted frankly that as soon as he had earned enough money on any given day, he would quit and rest; on being informed about a school where the blind were taught a trade, he expressed an earnest desire to be sent to such a school and to be relieved of the burden of being a *lirnyk*.[48] We also have evidence of the exact opposite. Some minstrels regarded art as a moral obligation and a service to the community, and did not stop singing after earning enough money. Rather, they sat and told stories "to teach people about the past."[49] In a word, the profession accommodated all sorts, as it would have had to if it was a potential means for taking care of all blind persons. To quote the *lirnyk* Nikon, "There are those who will sing a song through as quickly as they can, just to get their alms. And there are those who wouldn't think of doing that, because it is a sin." Even Nikon, who was of the latter category, sometimes slipped from grace "May God forgive me," he said, "but sometimes when a song is very long and I am very tired, I will start it at one house and finish it at the next." As Borzhkovskii noted, among the *lirnyky* there are those who are real men (*liudi*) and those who are something less (*liudishki*).[50]

Experiences with contemporary *kobzari* confirm that there is no one type which dominates among minstrels. If the question in the nineteenth and early twentieth centuries was the piety of minstrels, the question in recent times has been minstrel patriotism: were minstrels willing to fight for Ukraine, or were they going to toe the Soviet line? The reaction to this dilemma was as varied as the reaction to formerly obligatory piety. Among the *kobzari* working during the late Soviet period, some were noble and sang for the glory of Ukraine. They were willing to risk censure, and performed songs that were considered nationalistic, and therefore, taboo. Some of the men were mercenary and sang for a nice apartment. To please the Soviet authorities that might get them financial rewards, they would sing *dumy* about Lenin and songs about the glories of the Soviet system without hesitation. Pavlo Suprun provided some interesting information on the subject of the "Duma about Lenin." Ehor Movchan, the composer of this song, experienced a severe swelling of his extremities in his old age. The swelling in his fingers eventually became so severe that it prevented him from playing his musical instrument and providing himself some solace with music. Movchan, who was living in an old age home when Suprun visited, attributed the swelling to God's punishment for having composed the Lenin *duma*.[51]

As brave as Suprun was, he did not fight the Soviet system, and for a long time, the "Duma about Lenin" was a regular part of his public repertory. A nationalistic friend interpreted Suprun's decision to omit the obligatory "Duma about Lenin" from a concert as a significant political statement. Yet Suprun still sang Russian songs, particularly Russian romances, unlike many who try to advance the Ukrainian cause by refusing to have anything to do with Russian culture. As much as Suprun was altruistic and acted for the good of art and the good of Ukraine, he was quite willing to try and improve his economic position. Thus, he came to the United States on a concert tour not just because he wanted to spread Ukrainian culture but also to make money. In much the same way, minstrels at the turn of the century were probably driven by a noble desire to promote religious faith, as well as by more mundane economic motives. They were careful not to offend the powers that be and were responsive to audience likes and dislikes.

The negative extreme of the image ascribed to minstrels cannot be totally dismissed. There was some fairly innocent duplicity among *kobzari* and *lirnyky*, and collectors complain that some minstrels were quite willing to make up whatever the scholar wanted to hear, especially if the pay was good.[52] Borzhkovskii found a man who was not blind or even physically disabled, yet wanted to be a *lirnyk*. His name was Oleksandr Dimnych, and he feigned blindness so that the public would accept him and pay him for his music. Yet, he did this out of love for minstrelsy, and he was willing to serve as a guide for almost no pay, and later, to accept the financial burdens of a blind wife and a blind guide just so that he could play and sing.[53]

There was some alcoholism and stealing among minstrels. Hrytsenko-Kholodnyi drank a great deal; Kravchenko-Kriukovskyi used alcohol to try to stimulate memory. Yet, if minstrels, as the popular misconception claimed, spent all their earnings on alcohol, they could not have supported their families and farmsteads. But support them they did. Furthermore, some men provided more than mere subsistence. Musii Shuga, for example, saved enough money to lend to others, which he did without charging interest, earning himself great community admiration and gratitude.[54] As for theft, most of the stealing that minstrels report is peripheral to the profession: guides or apprentices not turning over to the minstrel all that is his due. Dovhaliuk's father claimed that the sighted guides would cheat a *lirnyk* but certainly minstrels would never cheat each other.[55] One apprentice admitted short-changing his masters; but most minstrels, if they mention stealing at all, accuse someone else—always someone other than a fellow performer.[56]

On occasion, criminals who found the disguise of a blind or crippled mendicant convenient used minstrelsy as a cover for illicit activities. In his article on hospices, the church-supported quarters which housed minstrels and other mendicants, P. Efimenko says that the institution went into decline because "questionable elements" used the hospices as hiding places.[57] At the time when the Polish-Lithuanian Commonwealth ruled much of Ukraine, people trying to escape from Polish authorities and people trying to resist them supposedly hid among minstrels, probably disguised as mendicants.[58] Soviet scholarship offers a variation on this idea in claiming that minstrels themselves used their profession as a cover for non-professional, revolutionary efforts. According to Fedir Lavrov, minstrels carried secret information orally from one revolutionary cell to another. They were even able to smuggle books and papers by hiding them in their musical instruments and in the linings of their boots and their clothing.[59] We will never know whether minstrels actually supported the Soviet Revolution or whether this was an element required by Soviet ideology, and as such, added to all biographies. Nonetheless, its persistence indicates that using minstrelsy as a cover for illegal activity was not a new idea.

In sum, traditional *kobzari* and *lirnyky* were ordinary men with some strivings toward piety and righteousness and with a big economic stake in minstrelsy because it was their primary source of income. These men were professionals rather than farmers. As such, they were on the fringes of Ukrainian society, and thus were pictured in extreme terms, either as saintly or as corrupt. Negative images, stimulated by the association between minstrels and beggars, and possibly also by the fact that some truly immoral men, such as criminals, used minstrelsy as a cover for their illegal activities, were particularly burdensome to the profession. But positive images brought their own set of problems. Scholars writing about minstrels wanted to see them in a positive light, as quintessential artists, as defenders of Ukrainian nationhood, often using them to debate issues irrelevant to the profession. When the disparity between living minstrels and scholarly ideas became too evident, scholars often claimed that contemporary singers were but the inferior remnants of a glorious minstrel past.

Chapter 4

Blindness

*T*o understand *kobzari* and *lirnyky* and how they functioned as artists, we must examine the surroundings of the blind children who became minstrels, especially the financial pressures to which they were subjected. Life in the Ukrainian countryside in the nineteenth century meant agricultural work. Everyone participated in farming: men and women, young and old. Work plus gender defined the space of the house and farmstead. Certain jobs were considered men's work and others were appropriate to women; the house and the farmstead were accordingly divided into men's and women's work areas. The stove and its immediate surroundings belonged to the women; there they did the cooking and various chores such as spinning, weaving, knitting, and mending. Men worked near the door, making and repairing farm tools, shoes, nets, and harnesses. Outside, women tended the garden, while men did most of the work in the fields. The very young and the very old did not have specific work areas, but they did have jobs, mostly chores that required less strength, such as sorting seeds. Yet, should the need arise, gender and age distinctions were ignored, and at times like harvest, everyone helped do whatever was most urgently needed.

A number of studies dealing with change in Ukraine and Russia in the nineteenth century underscore the importance of work. They show that the qualities sought in a bride were industriousness and physical strength and that the ability of the young woman to work was essential when the family supported itself by farming alone. As the soil was depleted, family income had to come from a combination of agricultural and industrial sources. Men left the farm to work in factories; women stayed behind in the village, where their strength and willingness to do hard labor were crucial to survival, since they now assumed their husbands' agricultural duties in addition to their other tasks. Young men who were going off to the city to look for manufacturing jobs were often required to marry before leaving so as to provide the family with a replacement farm worker in the person of their wives.[1]

When a contribution to labor was not forthcoming on the part of a family member, great bitterness resulted. The most common motive for division of a rural household was resentment over providing support for non-working household members. Even though divisions produced smaller units which were often far less viable economically than a large household, peasants seemed to prefer them to supporting those who ate but contributed nothing (*darmoiidy*). Splits would occur if one subfamily felt it was working to compensate for too many non-workers from another subfamily, usually meaning the children of other couples or disabled siblings.[2]

Living in a Ukrainian village in the nineteenth century also meant living in conditions where disease was common and medical care was virtually unavailable. Most accounts of the health of the rural population, and especially its children, read like horror stories. Infant mortality around 1900 was close to thirty percent. About forty percent of children died before they reached the age of two. The rural population had no understanding of infection, what caused it, or how to prevent it. People continued to give the deceased a farewell kiss, even when the cause of death was not old age but infectious disease. At times of epidemics, groups of the faithful would visit the homes of all of the afflicted, thus exposing themselves and their families to infection. Babies were given pacifiers made of bread wrapped in cloth and chewed by an adult and were thus put in contact with adult bacteria.[3] Peasants would not drink stagnant water, but believed that all running water was pure. Diseases spread by drinking water, such as scrofula, were epidemic, while stagnant water was simply ignored and left to breed mosquitoes which carried malaria.[4] Vaccination was unheard of, and the population suffered from smallpox, measles, diphtheria, and scarlet fever. Trachoma and scrofula were everywhere.[5] As a consequence, of the children who survived early childhood, an unusually high percentage ended up blind. In its early twentieth-century study of hygiene among the peasantry, the Pirogov Commission complains, "In no country in Europe is there such an enormous number of blind people as among us in Russia, where two out of every thousand are blind."[6]

Blindness was common and not life threatening, but being blind was very difficult, especially in a society which demanded that everyone participate in agricultural work. Again quoting a Pirogov Commission pamphlet: "All know how dear is sight and what sadness there is without it. . . . The blind person is helpless and defenseless as a child . . . lives as a burden to himself and to his near ones. For him there is no happiness in life, eternal night surrounds him."[7]

Yet there were certain things that a blind person could do, such as make ropes and harnesses.[8] But this, apparently, was not enough. Ukraine was much richer than Russia; nonetheless, there were many families for whom the burden of a blind member was just too much. In minstrel biographies, there are terrible stories like that of Andrii Nykyforovych Ermylov. According to the data collected by Volodymyr Kharkiv, Ermylov's father kept telling him how useless he was because he was blind, and allowed him to wear only the clothes discarded by other family members.[9] There were, of course, kind fathers, as well. The father of the well-known *kobzar* Terentii Makarovych Parkhomenko wanted to keep his son home and take care of him himself. He was a carpenter as well as a farmer, and felt he could absorb the expense. But the boy himself did not want to encumber his parents.[10]

As a version of the begging song collected by Porfyrii Martynovych puts it:

> Give me alms; have pity, oh righteous people,
> Oh father, (have pity) on me, on one caught in darkness,
> That I cannot see and cannot go and ask you for work,
> That I have to ask you, oh father and mother, for alms.
> Look upon me in my dark darkness!
> If I could but see this world,
> Then I would not stand in your path and in your way.
> I would go and ask you for work.
> But because of my darkened eyes,
> I must go and ask you for alms.[11]

In other words, a man would support himself by farming if he could. When blindness prevented him from doing so, he turned to singing and begging.

Kharkiv gives an excellent summary of a blind person's situation in another manuscript. Citing the well-known proverb "He who does not work, does not eat," Kharkiv goes on to expand on the problems of the blind family member. If he is not resented by his parents, then he is surreptitiously attacked by his in-laws, to the point that they sometimes take the proverb literally and withhold food. The blind person feels indebted for his support, and feelings of indebtedness are encouraged by in-laws and neighbors who threaten that there might be no support once the parents of the blind person pass away.[12]

The solution to the economic burden of blindness and other disability was reached in the distant past: the blind, the sick, and the crippled were permitted to beg, and thus they became wards of the community at large.[13] Giving them alms was considered an act pleasing to God, and certain legends affirmed that beggars are necessary for the spiritual and physical health of a community. A beggar at the Lavra monastery in Kiev, for example, tells how the rich people in a certain land decided to get rid of their beggars by selling them to a foreign king. The wealthy began to drink and to celebrate their freedom from the obligation to support the destitute. Soon they forgot God, and a great famine came. When the foolish rich men realized the cause of their problems, they tried to buy the beggars back; but the foreign king refused, and the land without beggars was doomed.[14]

But blindness was a special disability. The blind could, of course, be beggars, but they alone were permitted to be something more. They could become minstrels.

Becoming a Minstrel: The Causes of Blindness

We know that all nineteenth-century minstrels were blind. We do not always know how they became blind. Where information was recorded, it tells that the usual sequence of events was illness followed by loss of sight. In most cases, the disease that led to blindness was smallpox or scrofula contracted before the age of ten. The *lirnyky* Nykifor Dudka and Oleksii Pobihailo, for example, contracted scrofula at age six, and Mykhailo Pohrebnoi, at age seven. The *kobzar* Terentii Parkhomenko went blind from the same illness at the age of eleven.[15] Oleksii Terentevych Masliukov, according to Oleksandr Malynka, had had a tendency toward scrofula since birth, and finally went blind at age sixteen. As Masliukov describes it, the actual onset of total blindness was very rapid. He picked up a cup and began to drink, and by the time he finished, he could no longer see the cup.[16] Prokop Dub went blind from smallpox at age four, Antin Ivanytskyi at age five, Vasyl Moroz at eight, and Andrii Kornienko and Evdokim Mokroviz lost their sight from the same illness at age ten.[17]

The *lirnyk* Ivankho attributes his blindness to a cold he contracted at the age of sixteen months. Petro Tkachenko gives the same reason for his blindness, the difference being that the cold which deprived him of his sight occurred when he was older, some eight or nine years of age. T. Pashchenko, the man who collected information from Tkachenko, explains that the boy came from a very poor family and was probably predisposed to illness. Chills and hypothermia were believed to be the cause of a variety of physical problems. A chill made Pavlo Kulyk blind and killed his friends. When he was twenty-three, Kulyk and a group of youths fell through the ice on a river. All of the young men became ill as a result, and all but Kulyk perished. Kulyk, it seems, was lucky to have escaped with just the loss of sight.[18]

Kobzar Petro Harasko reports that he went blind during a cholera epidemic, although he does not connect his vision problems to the cholera.[19] Ananii Homyniuk suspects that he went blind because he was unnecessarily moved during an attack of epilepsy (*chornaia bolist*, an affliction he also calls the "falling sickness"—*paduchaia bolist*).[20] One of the more recent performers, Ehor Movchan, born in 1898, went blind from measles at the age of ten months.[21] Measles, supposedly contracted by drinking raw eggs, made Hrytsenko blind at age thirteen.[22]

Some of the men who became minstrels were born blind. This was true of Demian Symonenko, Andrii Dovhaliuk, also known as Zoria, Iahor Okhremenko, and Iakiv Zlatarskyi.[23] Fedir Kushneryk reports that the circumstance of his birth predisposed him to blindness: his mother was working in the field when he was born. She apparently laid him aside, finished her work, then wrapped him in her skirt to carry him home. Kushneryk believes her coarse skirt skinned his newborn shoulders and predisposed him to disease, like the one which took his sight when he was six.[24]

Ostap Veresai claims that his blindness was the result of "the evil eye" (*oslip z prystritu*). He says that, when he was still little, a journeyman carpenter came to his house, asked ridiculous questions about his mother, then cast an evil spell by hammering several times on the side of the house as he left. Veresai developed a headache, then his eyes became sore, and finally he lost the ability to see. Veresai says that he knew the carpenter must have cast a spell because the man had "bad, mean eyes."[25] A less colorful explanation is probably closer to the truth. While Veresai's mother was sighted, his father was blind. Veresai himself was quite sickly, and probably had a predisposition toward infirmity, especially the sorts of illnesses which left children blind in nineteenth-century Ukraine. Thus, Veresai's blindness, like that of most minstrels, was probably due to disease.

There are heartbreaking accounts of parents trying to cure their sick sons, but usually only when the children were beyond help. Harasko's father tried and tried to cure him. Only when he had used up all of his money did he resign himself to having a blind son.[26] There were some successful attempts, or at least partially successful. According to the *lirnyk* Andrii Dovhaliuk, his father knew from the moment that he was born that he would be blind, so he gathered money for his son's treatment. Not long after, some Russians (*moskali*) stopped by Ianov, Andrii's village, and gave Andrii's father the name of a doctor. As the family was about to set off to consult this doctor, a Jewish moneylender talked them out of it, convincing them that the venture was useless. Nevertheless, the parents kept hoping, and hearing of miracles at the local church, started taking Andrii there. The priest gave them holy water to put on the boy's eyes, and according to Andrii, this did help. The holy water treatment was supposedly so efficacious that by the time that he was interviewed, Andrii could distinguish night and day and even make out the moon.[27] Fedir Kushneryk's encounter with the village priest was less fortunate. There was no hospital or other medical facility in his village, and when he started to go blind at age six, the priest offered his family "drops." As Kushneryk tells it, by the time he got home following this drop "therapy," he was totally blind.[28] Vlasko underwent what we would consider more conventional medical treatment. His bout with scrofula produced cataracts. These were removed, but for reasons not specified in the interview, from one eye only. This meant that Vlasko could see and was able to work as a guide for the *kobzar* Kulyk. After working for two years, Vlasko decided to become a minstrel himself, and switched from being Kulyk's guide to being his apprentice. The fact that he was still blind in one eye qualified him as disabled.[29]

The most unusual account of going blind and entering the special world of the disabled comes from Ivan Kravchenko-Kriukovskyi's interesting and moving autobiography. As the minstrel told Porfyrii Martynovych, he was born into a serf family named Kravchenko and lived on the estate of the Kriukovskyis. Within three weeks of Ivan's birth, a son was born to the landowners. When the boys reached age three, Ivan was taken into the household of the noble family to act as a companion for their son. It was apparently at this time that the nobles' family name was added to his own. Under normal circumstances, living with the landed gentry would have ensured better food and medical care and possibly also travel and education. Unfortunately, the landowner's son (*panych*) whom Kravchenko was to serve as companion turned out to be a sadist.

When the rich boy and Ivan were sent to a boarding school in Hadiach, the landowner's son tortured him every chance he had. He would pinch him and pull his hair and beat him. He would make him walk on all fours and would ride on his back, beating him again. Ivan's eyes started to hurt and then to water terribly. When Ivan's bed became wet from his tears, the landowner's son teased him and accused him of having urinated in bed.

After a year and a half of boarding school, Ivan went home. His parents made various attempts to cure him. First they went to the local *znakhari*, or folk medicine practitioners. One Jewish woman offered to cure him, and worked on him for three months, but to no avail. Neighbors told the Kravchenkos about a doctor in Poltava, and the family took the boy there. The doctor kept the boy for a month and then sent him home with instructions that he be kept indoors, in the dark, for another month, to complete his cure. The parents did as they were told and even kept Ivan indoors longer than instructed, but this, too, did not help. Finally someone told them about a doctor in Kiev, and the family traveled to consult with him. This doctor examined Ivan and informed the parents that the boy's pupils had been eaten away and that there was no cure for his blindness.

Although Ivan was blind and no longer officially serving as companion, this did not stop the landowner's son. The boy would chase Ivan around the yard and in and out of various farm buildings, hoping to cause an accident. One day, the landowner's son steered Ivan toward a well, which was uncovered for repairs, and Ivan fell down the shaft. Ivan was seriously injured and recovery was difficult and slow.[30] After Ivan recovered from his fall, the nobleman let him go. The elder Kriukovskyi showed no sympathy for his plight and no remorse for any of the injuries that his son had inflicted. He did not even give his former servant any land, which, it seems, Kravchenko expected. He simply said, "You are blind now. Go—you will be supported by the people."[31]

It may be that other minstrels went blind from injury; one report of blindness caused by trauma is available in manuscript form. The *lirnyk* Mykolai Khvedorovych Doroshenko, a serf on a nobleman's estate, had a terrible accident when he was eight. He was sent to fetch his master's horses from the stable and as he was leading them across the barnyard, one of them reared and kicked him in the bridge of the nose. A servant was dispatched to the city to summon the doctor and bring medicine. The doctor, who arrived the next day, could not save the child's sight. After that, supposedly because his family was so poor, everyone gave up and did nothing further for the boy, even though for seven years Doroshenko suffered debilitating headaches and was unable to tolerate even the least bit of sunlight. Once the headaches passed, he was able to function and eventually went on to become a successful minstrel.[32]

One report attributes blindness to psychological trauma and consequent physical self-abuse. The *lirnyk* Ivan Kherlamovych Morozhka was poor, as a youth, and had to hire himself out as a laborer. But he was industrious, and by age twenty-two, he had earned enough to buy a small plot of land, pay a bride-price, and marry. He and his wife had a baby. Everything seemed fine until Morozhka lost both wife and child to an unspecified illness. At that point, Ivan threw himself into his farming, and apparently, overworked himself to the point that, by age twenty-six, he was blind. He traveled to a famous specialist in Kharkiv. When the doctor informed him that he had "dark water" (*temna voda*) on his eyes and that there was no cure. In spite of his affliction, Ivan managed to marry again and have yet another family, becoming, of course, a professional performer as well as a farmer.[33]

Blindness Automatically Leads to Minstrelsy: Questions of Talent

Not all blind children became minstrels. Those who did were apprenticed to a master performer and worked and studied with him an average of three to six years. How it was decided whether or not a particular child would be apprenticed is poorly documented. In a few cases, the decision was based on the boy's musical abilities. Money was sometimes a factor, because minstrels earned more than people who begged without singing. Toward the end of the nineteenth century, monetary incentive was counterbalanced by fear of police persecution. Master *kobzar* Mykhailo Kravchenko (no relation to Ivan Kravchenko-Kriukovskyi) told Opanas Slastion that he found a blind boy whom he considered gifted and whom he wanted to have as an apprentice. The boy's father, however, refused because he feared this would make his son the target of police harassment. He felt that it was better for the boy to make a lesser living as a plain beggar than be subject to beatings and arrest.[34] Police persecution aside, minstrelsy was the routine choice for a blind child, and it seems that, more often than not, blindness was the sole criterion on which this choice was based. Morozhko, for example, explained his taking up the *lira* by saying simply that it was the appropriate way to "feed the blind."[35]

Most biographies present apprenticeship as the logical consequence of blindness. Ivan Kravchenko-Kriukovskyi's story of the beatings is immediately followed by the statement that he was apprenticed to a man whose name was Ivan Kravchenko, the same as his own. *Kobzar* Petro Harasko says simply that when his father gave up all hope of curing him, he apprenticed him to Prokop Dub in Mokievka.[36] Iakiv Zlatarskyi also states quite matter-of-factly that because he was blind, he was apprenticed to a *lirnyk*. Zlatarskyi must have been very young when this happened, because the first time he mentions his age, it is eight, and by then he was already traveling with his second master.[37] The *lirnyk* Vasyl Moroz says that after he went blind at age eight, the landowner on whose estate he lived took him into his own house and gave him menial tasks. A guest at the nobleman's house suggested that the boy be apprenticed to a minstrel, apparently simply on the basis of his blindness. According to Moroz, he thanks the gentleman to this day for giving him the opportunity to earn his bread with honest work.[38] A nobleman was instrumental in getting Hrytsenko apprenticed also. The boy's father did not want to send his son to a master minstrel but the gentleman convinced him to do so, arguing that minstrelsy was the only way Hrytsenko could manage to survive once his father and the landowner passed away.[39]

Sometimes money prompted men to seek the training that apprenticeship provided. This was most often true if the choice was being made by the blind person himself, especially if he was an adult rather than a child, or if the decision involved retraining and additional instruction. The first time Nykifor Dudka became an apprentice, it was simply because he was blind. When he was thirteen, his father sent him to the *lirnyk* Vasylii Antonovych

Harbuzov. Following his apprenticeship, Dudka traveled and sang a capella, but after two years he decided that his income would be better if he had instrumental accompaniment. He acquired a *lira*, and apparently, the appropriate training.[40] *Kobzar* Demian Symonenko tells a similar story. He studied with Hrytsko Dubyna, who taught him how to sing, but who did not play a musical instrument. After working for a while, Symonenko decided he could make more money if he played a *bandura* and apprenticed himself to Andrii Hoilenko of Syniavka. He says that he did not like Hoilenko's singing style but that learning an instrument was important enough for him to willingly complete the apprenticeship.[41] The *lirnyk* Ananii Homyniuk says that he begged until the age of twenty-two, when he noticed that *lirnyky* made more money than ordinary beggars. Within a year, he apprenticed himself to Petro Kremynskii and began to study the *lira* and appropriate songs.[42]

The line delineating ordinary beggars from minstrels was sometimes fuzzy. In certain regions, training which did not teach a boy a musical instrument was not considered training in minstrelsy. It was, however, considered apprenticeship, and the ordinary beggar who offered such training was called a master (*panotets*), just like a minstrel master. According to the materials collected by Kharkiv, learning first from a beggar master and then deciding to seek training from a minstrel master was common enough to be institutionalized to an extent. Minstrels told him that the usual length of apprenticeship was three years and included training in how to manage blindness, as well as musical instruction. If someone had already studied with a beggar master, he could shorten the period of apprenticeship to two and perhaps even one year, because only musical, and perhaps only instrumental, training was then necessary.[43]

Financial concerns of a different sort made Oleksii Masliukov a *lirnyk*. Here again we find something like an automatic assumption that a blind person who cannot be otherwise supported should be apprenticed to a minstrel. After Masliukov went blind, his father kept him at home as long as he could. When the father could no longer support his son, he sent him to Mykola Slidiuk in Hlukhiv.[44]

Terentii Parkhomenko was motivated largely by money and quite successful at increasing his earnings by responding to audience likes and dislikes. Parkhomenko studied with Hodienko, learned to play the *bandura* and three epics, some religious songs, satirical songs, and lyric songs. He tried out the *lira*, presumably to see if it would improve his income, but abandoned it.[45] Probably due to his experiences at the Twelfth Archeological Congress held in Kharkiv in 1902 and his acquaintance with Hnat Khotkevych, a writer, musicologist, and folklorist, Parkhomenko identified the educated public and the scholarly community as his best customers. He decided to learn *dumy*, especially *dumy* of interest to intellectuals, such as the ones about Bohdan Khmelnytsky, even though these had long disappeared from the folk oral tradition.[46] And learn epic Parkhomenko did, apparently from books. By the time that Speranskii worked with him in 1906, he knew nine *dumy* and was working on a historical song related to *dumy*, namely the one about Morozenko. Parkhomenko's efforts did indeed bring financial rewards: his income jumped from an average of two hundred rubles a year to an average of six hundred.[47]

Musical talent plays a role in a few biographies. After he went blind, Fedir Kushneryk would nonetheless follow the other children to school so that he could listen to what they were reading. One day, he picked up some wood and fashioned himself a makeshift fiddle. When his father heard him playing, he recognized his talent and bought him a real fiddle, first one for fifty kopecks and then one that was more expensive. Kushneryk's knowledge of the *bandura* came later, when he was given the instrument by Mykhailo Kravchenko.[48]

Veresai was driven by a great love of music and probably possessed great musical talent.[49] Veresai's father, who was blind, played the fiddle, and thus the boy was exposed to music from birth. In addition, Veresai's father frequently hosted passing *kobzari*. When one of these men would begin to play, Veresai would become so agitated that he wanted to "either crawl inside the man's shirt or take him inside my own." It was one of these passing *kobzari* who recognized how attracted the boy was to minstrelsy and suggested to his father that he be apprenticed.[50] Veresai had a great deal of trouble being an apprentice. He kept falling ill and having numerous conflicts with his masters. Nonetheless, his love of music, and particularly *kobzar* music, was so intense that he simply could not stay away, and it was only after his third master announced that he had no more to learn that Veresai gave up trying to receive the customary training.[51]

Collectors comment on the talent or the skill of performers more frequently than the minstrels themselves. Opanas Slastion, Hnat Khotkevych, and Filaret Kolessa all evaluate the voices of the various minstrels they recorded. Khotkevych even tried to improve the voices of his charges when preparing them for their appearance at the Twelfth Archeological Congress.[52] Describing the *lirnyky* of Galicia, Studynskyi reports that the ones who completed the well-known schools were indeed particularly adept at playing the *lira* and could get an extraordinarily clear tone out of this rather awkward instrument.[53]

Here and there, minstrels mention the pleasure of music. Oleksii Masliukov told Malynka that, while the *lira* did nothing to improve his income, it did make his life a little more bearable. Begging was bad, especially so if he was alone, without his guide. The *lira* then acted as a companion, easing some of the misery. Iahor Okhremenko said something quite similar: he liked having a *lira* because it gave him pleasure.[54] After his days as a professional performer had ended, Pavlo Bratytsia still loved his *bandura*. He had had the same instrument for thirty years and was so attached to it that he refused to part with it, even though he could have earned some badly needed money by doing so.[55] Ehor Movchan said that he loved his *kobza* as if it were a living thing.[56] Arkhyp Nykonenko said that he could not go for more than a week without playing, and confessed to performing just for himself, sometimes even at night.[57] One curious account ascribes a love of all things beautiful to a minstrel, implying that this somehow encouraged him to be an artist. According to Mykhailo Polotai, the *kobzar* Petro Tkachenko, nicknamed Halushka, was a very poetic person and insisted on living in the prettiest part of Syniavka, even though he could see nothing of the town.[58]

Discussions of love of music or of artistic talent are not common, however. While there is some indication that minstrels had musical ability or were attracted to music, this simply was not a concern in choosing minstrelsy as a profession. Veresai expressed a love for music, and others noted his talent, yet neither of these was foremost in Veresai's mind when he decided to become a *kobzar*. In his own words:

> And I thought to myself, "Oh my God, what if I live a long time? Oh my God! My father may be blind, but at least he knows how to play a fiddle. He'll go and play at someone's wedding and then those people will come and plow his fields for him. But what about me—how am I going to live in this world? And what if God gives me a long life and I outlive my father and my mother? What will I do in this world then?" I would lie down to sleep, and I—I can't sleep! As soon as I start to think, I start to cry, and my mother says to me, "Why are you crying, you fool?"[59]

This was the point when Veresai went out on his own to seek yet another master.

It should be noted that questions which we would find important, questions of talent and artistic inclination, are raised in those biographies where outside influence is greatest. Thus, they appear in the most modern material: the biographies of Kushneryk and Movchan, and in that of Veresai, who though he lived in the nineteenth century, received a great deal of scholarly attention. Only Arkhyp Nykonenko seems to talk about love of music without the prompting of a collector. Choosing a profession on the basis of aptitude was just not something done in traditional Ukraine. In fact, since virtually everyone did agricultural work, professions were essentially nonexistent. If a boy was blind, agricultural work was impossible, so he could be either a minstrel or a beggar. Begging was shameful, but minstrelsy was "honest work." This is precisely what the *lirnyk* Moroz claimed when he expressed his gratitude to the man who had suggested he be apprenticed to a minstrel.[60] Only police persecution of minstrels made some people see begging as preferable. It is true that, of the blind, only a small percentage actually became minstrels and the reason many did not was most likely talent: they lacked the musical and poetic ability required. Yet, it is also true that the blind and their parents chose minstrelsy automatically, without taking talent into account.

There is some evidence that apprenticeship was once universal, that all blind children, girls as well as boys, were sent to master minstrels. Klement Kvitka, a musicologist who did some important ethnographic work, including writing a field guide for interviewing minstrels, interviewed Ivan Humeniuk, son of the *lirnyk* Sydor Humeniuk, who affirmed that almost all blind boys were sent to study with a minstrel and that blind girls were also sent, but they were only taught songs, not how to play an instrument.[61] While there is little mention of women performers in print, the Martynovych manuscripts contain evidence that women received training and had extensive, if gender-specific, repertories.[62] Perhaps at some point in the past, all blind children were automatically apprenticed, and those who lacked the talent or the perseverance dropped out before training was complete. Even if training was not universal, it clearly extended beyond those who actually entered the ranks of professional performers. Minstrel biographies and descriptions of training create the misleading impression that apprenticeship automatically led to professional status. Had there been more studies of beggars and more data on training, we would probably see that others were trained but did not complete their course of study. The repertory of ordinary beggars overlapped with the beginning stages of minstrel training, and as Kolisnyk told Kharkiv, beggar repertory could be fairly extensive.[63] If we had more knowledge of this repertory, we might see even greater coincidence with the material performed by minstrels.[64]

If talent or musical aptitude played a role in this whole complex, it took the form of a belief that blindness fostered musical expression. Some sort of musical activity was expected of all of the blind, almost as if their physical condition produced musical ability. Most accounts of beggars, such as Valerian Borzhkovskii's description of a religious festival (see pages 201–203), refer to their chanting or singing.[65] These same accounts usually add that singing is particularly appropriate to the blind. When V. Danyliv interviewed beggars at the Lavra in Kiev, he was told that most ask for charity with a begging chant several lines long. The informant added that when requesting alms, women are more likely than men to perform longer pieces and to sing instead of chanting because their voices are more pleasant, and the blind are more likely to sing than the sighted.[66]

Some of the necessary associations between blindness and song persist today. The instructors of the school for the blind which Pavlo and Nadiia Suprun attended automatically assumed that all of their charges had a particular predisposition to music, and encouraged all of them to sing. The Supruns themselves shared this view and felt that blindness fostered better memory and thus made the blind better performers.[67] Nadiia gave another reason why blindness is associated with singing, reminiscent of the ideas in Shevchenko's "Perebendia"—namely that those who suffer have a particular need for song because singing relieves pain. The afflicted, and the blind foremost among them, are more strongly drawn to music because it helps alleviate their suffering. Nadiia's blindness, like her husband's, is the result of head wounds sustained in childhood. Because of this trauma and possibly also because blindness as profound as Nadiia's destroys the ability to distinguish between day and night and throws off a person's biological clock, Nadiia has severe insomnia. For her, deep depression follows prolonged periods of sleeplessness. The solution, Nadiia said, is singing. Asked if she sang happy songs to cheer herself up, Nadiia answered that the song can be a cheerful one, but much more often it is melancholy. What the sad song does is relieve Nadiia's depression by expressing it. She gets rid of her problem by "singing it out."[68] Collectors working with minstrels in the nineteenth and early twentieth centuries never asked their subjects why the blind should sing. Because they were part of the same tradition as the minstrels they studied, they may have simply assumed a link between music and loss of sight. While data were not collected, it is nonetheless not that farfetched to suppose that some of the reasoning given by Nadiia Suprun was operative in the traditional setting, especially since suffering was an idea central to minstrel songs.

The Financial Aspects of Minstrelsy: Paying for Training

Having chosen minstrelsy as a profession, a boy became an apprentice to a master minstrel. The usual age at apprenticeship was between fifteen and twenty-five. The length of apprenticeship was supposed to be three years in eastern Ukraine and six years in western Ukraine or Galicia, but a great deal of variation is evident. There was even variation within the broad east-west division. Mikhail Speranskii, a scholar who wrote extensively about Ukrainian and Russian epics and epic performers, says that the usual length of apprenticeship in the Kharkiv region, in the north, was four years, while in the Kherson region, in the south, it was six.[69] Some of the numbers may be based more on belief than on fact. Three especially seems to be a magic number, and when asked about the length of apprenticeship, most minstrels from the eastern part of Ukraine gave it as three years or three years and three months, even if their own apprenticeship period was different from this ideal. There was some correlation between the age of the young man when he became an apprentice and the length of time he was expected to train. (Actual apprenticeship terms, with the age of the minstrel at the time of apprenticeship, are given in the Appendix page 300).

Volodymyr Hnatiuk, who worked in Galicia and described the *lirnyky* in Buchachchyna, gives one of the most logical explanations of how the length of apprenticeship was determined. His information, collected from the *lirnyk* Iakiv Zlatarskyi through a trusted third party, is as follows: A disabled person anywhere from nine to thirty years of age can become an apprentice. Twelve is considered the best age; twenty-five is still an age when a man can learn, but beyond thirty is considered too old. The length of apprenticeship depends on the circumstances. It can be three, four, five, but no more than six years. Apprenticeship will be shorter or longer depending on whether the boy is talented or slow, mature or immature. When a young boy becomes an apprentice, he is not taught right away; rather, he is used as a servant (this means that he is sent out begging and required to turn over all the alms gathered to his master). Someone over twenty is apprenticed for only one year because he is already mature and does not need to develop. A young boy who can be sent out to work pays nothing because he provides a service. An older lad who is apprenticed for just one year pays twenty to thirty *zloty* (a Polish coin, roughly equivalent to a ruble). If he has the money, he pays for his own training; if he does not, then his parents or guardians pay for him.[70] No matter what the age of the apprentice, the master can keep him on for a longer period of time if he feels this is necessary. Masters extend the apprenticeship, Zlatarskyi makes clear, not so much because an apprentice has failed to learn all that he needs to know, but because the master has lost money on him. If the young man has been ill, for example, and thus unable to go begging as much as was normally expected, the master may require that he make up for lost time and revenue.[71]

What is available for other regions is less detailed, but confirms the information provided by Hnatiuk. Volodymyr Kharkiv, working in northeastern Ukraine, says that a young person, fifteen years old or younger, trains for three years. If the person is older, the period of apprenticeship may be shortened to two years or even less. The master and the novice agree upon a certain period before the boy enters apprenticeship. The agreement is strictly kept, and should the novice be unable to put in the necessary time, he must compensate the master by either making up for the lost service or paying a fee. Varion Honchar, for example, was seriously ill for three months during the period of his contract. He had to serve his master for that exact length of time beyond his original apprenticeship to make up for the begging income which the master had lost. A person who trains for at least three years does not pay the master a fee, but does turn over to him all of the proceeds of his begging. During training, he lives with the master, who is responsible for feeding him and providing a guide when he goes out begging. Clothing is supposed to be provided by the boy's parents. A youth who cannot live with the master for three years is considered unprofitable: the master cannot make enough money from the boy's begging to compensate for his training and upkeep. Such an apprentice must pay a fee. In Kharkiv's experience, this fee was twenty-five *karbovantsi* (about the same number of dollars) a year.[72]

Setting Up a Household as an Economic Unit

A few years after completing his apprenticeship, presumably after he had earned enough money for the bride-price, a young man married.[73] Since the family life of minstrels was of little interest to collectors, they did not record much information beyond the mere fact of marriage. Scholars like Horlenko and Malynka, for example, mention the marital status of their subjects in passing. Although data are not abundant, we know that marriage among minstrels was nearly universal, just like among the rest of the rural population. Martynovych collected a guide to living called "the wisdom of minstrels," from Ivan Kuchuhura-Kucherenko. This is a set of sayings in the special language of minstrels (*lebiiska mova*), which among other things, gives instructions on how to find an appropriate wife, and wishes that God grant a successful marriage.[74] Kvitka asked the younger Humeniuk if minstrels were expected to marry, and the latter answered, yes, indeed.[75]

Masliukov and Okhremenko are the only minstrels specifically listed as being single. Even so, they were young at the time that they were interviewed and could be expected to marry eventually.[76] It may be that even Hrytsenko-Kholodnyi was married, strange though he was. In the Martynovych manuscripts there is a folder labelled as being collected from Khvedir Hrytsenko. Inside, material from Hrytsenko seems to be mixed with material from Iaremenko and Doroshenko. Women and wives are mentioned several times, and it is not always clear whose wife is being cited. However, one statement in which the informant claims to have learned a certain song from his wife is quite clearly attributed to Hrytsenko.77 We have an explicit statement in the literature on minstrels for forty-one men, a sizable number, considering how little information on the personal life of performers is normally given. (See page 301 for a full list of married minstrels.)

Since work was so central to survival in a Ukrainian village and since a blind man could not work, how a man with poor economic prospects got a woman to marry him becomes an interesting question. Presumably women who married minstrels were themselves not prime marriage material: widows, spinsters, women with a physical deformity. In the few cases where we do know something about the wives, this is the case. Bratytsia's wife was blind, as were the wives of Iaremenko, Dimnych, and Khrystenko.[78] According to Humeniuk, a blind minstrel marrying a blind woman was rare.[79] Much more common was something like Zlatarskyi's situation. His wife was blind in one eye, so that, according to Hnatiuk, the couple would be teased with phrases such as "two people—one eye."[80] Kyrylo Kuzmyn-skyi's wife was sickly.[81] Semen Vlasko's wife was a widow, as was Pavlo Kulyk's; and Oleksandr Dimnych's wife was a spinster.[82] Koven's wife was supposedly quite good-looking and even knew a trade, but married a *lirnyk* anyway because she was a spinster. When asked whether she was ashamed of her decision, she answered, "And what am I supposed to do if no one else wants to take me as wife?"[83] The first woman Ostap Veresai courted was a spinster. There was apparently so great a difference in their ages that the woman's mistress discouraged the match for fear of a bad marriage. The woman finally agreed to marry Veresai, then backed out the day of the wedding. She later came back to Veresai, promising to go through with the wedding this time, but Veresai refused because the woman was rumored to be epileptic. Veresai then courted two other women before he was finally able to marry. Veresai's second wife was a widow, and even so, it took him seven years to convince her to marry him. This woman's reluctance is documented in the minutes of the Geographical Society meeting in Kiev where Veresai was first presented to the scholarly world. "It was his *bandura* that was the matchmaker," she said. "He would come to court me, and I would chase him away. He would start to play his *bandura*, and I would call him back."[84] Horlenko reported that Ivan Kravchenko-Kriukovskyi's wife was a woman with a tendency to drink. In the obituary for the *kobzar*, he described how he arrived at Kravchenko-Kriukovskyi's home to find it empty except for the soldier stationed there. Upon inquiring, he learned that the *kobzar* had died, that his children were off working in various distant parts, and that his widow was in the bar, drinking. The tone of Horlenko's article implies that the woman was of questionable character and unworthy of being married to the great *kobzar*.[85] Another Horlenko account pictures the wife of Pavlo Bratytsia in fairly negative terms. At the time of the interview, Bratytsia was staying mostly at home. His support

came from his fellow villagers, especially one wealthy peasant named Ver-
bilo, from the local nobleman, and from the begging done by his wife, who
was also blind. His wife jealously guarded his repertory and sent away all
minstrels who came to him to learn a few extra songs and thus fill out their
knowledge. Horlenko implies that the woman was accelerating the demise
of Ukrainian minstrelsy by restricting dissemination of information.[86]

A more positive picture of a minstrel's wife appears in Malynka's article
on Semen Vlasko. Vlasko's wife was apparently also a widow, for she is
listed as having a son from a previous marriage. Although as a widow she
was not the most desirable of brides, she seems to have been a good companion to her husband and someone who shared his art. According to the
article, she accompanied her husband when he went to Kiev to earn money.
She also sang, and she wanted to learn the *bandura* and become the first
female *kobzar*. Indeed, it appears that she had some knowledge of the
instrument, for Malynka says that she played only in private homes and was
too embarrassed to play in public.[87] A handful of other women are listed as
their husbands' travelling companions. Parkhomenko told Petrov about the
lirnyk Khydor Matiukhin and his blind wife. She not only traveled with her
husband but also sang for pay. Even more interesting, she was supposed to
have had a blind female pupil.[88] Kharkiv notes that Makar Khrystenko
would sometimes travel with his wife, and that the two would sing together.[89] Iaremenko's wife and possibly also Hrytsenko's wife sang and
taught their husbands some so-called "women's psalms."[90] Polotai says that
Kuzminskyi's wife, although she did not sing, knew her husband's entire
repertory and would remind him of songs as needed.[91]

An interesting and unusual account of a marriage appears in Borzhkovskii's "Lirnyki." The author worked extensively with Oleksandr Dimnych, nicknamed Plazun. This man was orphaned as a child and went to live
with his uncle, who hired him out as a guide to minstrels. This was a typical
fate for sighted boys who could not otherwise be supported. What was
unusual was that unlike most boys, who stopped working as guides as soon
as they earned enough money to become independent, Dimnych continued
to be a guide, often working for next to nothing. He had developed such a
taste for the wandering life of a *lirnyk* that he did not want to quit, even
though the police tried to restrict him to one village. Dimnych then started
making fiddles, which was an acceptable occupation for a former guide, in
fact just the sort of craft that guides were expected to learn while serving
with a minstrel. The problem was that Dimnych also started going around
and performing as a *lirnyk*, using the knowledge he had gathered while
working as a guide. This was not acceptable either to the other *lirnyky* or to
the general public. Although fellow *lirnyky* felt obliged to Dimnych because

he had worked essentially for free, they still felt that he needed to go through the formal training of an apprenticeship. The general public was less kind, and would do anything from refusing to listen to a sighted man to pouring ashes into his begging bag, thus ruining whatever food was in there. Sensing that the problem was Dimnych's sightedness, his friends arranged a marriage to a blind woman who was a spinster. They thus created the unit of one blind and one sighted spouse that was typical for minstrels, only in reverse, with the minstrel being sighted and his spouse blind. While this did not solve Dimnych's public acceptance problem, the marriage, according to Borzhkovskii, was a happy one. The wife accompanied Dimnych to nearby villages. She took care of the money he earned, and she earned a bit of money herself by babysitting.[92]

Although minstrels were poor peasants, they were not destitute. Most had a house and garden; many had some livestock and even some arable land. Oleksandr Dimnych and his wife had only a small apartment, not much more than a room, but they paid very little for it. Two rubles a year went to pay a woman to do the wash, and they had to buy wood for heat in winter. The *lirnyk* Andrii Dovhaliuk lived with his father and had one-half of the house and one-third of the garden. Borzhkovskii states that the minstrel had no fields yet, with the implication that his father would pass these on to him later, most likely when the children grew big enough to take care of the plowing and reaping. The house that Andrii Dovhaliuk and his father owned had caught fire, but the two men were able to contribute forty rubles each to repairs. The *lirnyk* Nikon had a large, two-part house and a large family: two sons and three daughters.[93] Efim Perepelytsia did quite well; he owned his own house and two *desiatiny* (tithes) of land (about five and a half acres). The land was farmed by others, and first among them the *lirnyk*'s thirteen-year-old son, a very mature and responsible boy.[94] Pavlo Kulyk did even better. He had two houses and five tithes, or about twelve acres. He hired laborers to farm his land, and rented his second house out to other minstrels for one ruble a month. Police pressure forced him to stop renting and to turn the second house into a barn, but this seems not to have been a serious financial loss, because the house had been rented for a minimal fee and functioned more to help fellow minstrels than to generate income for its owner.[95] Bratytsia, by contrast, lived poorly. He had a small house located on the land of nobleman, which meant that he had no land of his own, not even a garden.[96] It appears that Evdokim Mokroviz was married, with seven children, and that his wife took care of their small land holdings.[97] Vasyl Moroz, too, was married, and his family took care of the farm work.[98] Semen Vlasko had one tithe of land, and Antin Ivanytskyi owned his house.[99] Nykifor Dudka had a small plot of land, as did Prokop

Dub.[100] Ivan Kravchenko-Kriukovskyi owned his house and was unfortunate enough to have it burn down twice. In spite of the disasters, the *kobzar* managed to rebuild each time.[101] Mykhailo Kravchenko was also plagued by misfortune and still survived financially, holding onto his house and small plot of land. The younger Kravchenko supported not only his own wife and family, including three children from his first marriage, but also the family of his sickly married brother.[102] Parkhomenko's property, as recorded by Malynka in 1903, included a house, a half tithe of farm land, and a cow, which because he had no outbuildings, he kept in the house.[103] Kuzminskyi's property included a garden, several farm animals, and a large house that even had electricity.[104]

Iakiv Zlatarskyi told Hnatiuk that the *lirnyky* of Galicia did not do as well financially as the minstrels of Eastern Ukraine. Most owned only a house, and according to Zlatarskyi, usually this was so small that you "had to get in sideways." To the informant's knowledge, only Onufrii of Tovstii owned enough land to be able to live off of the landholdings alone. While Zlatarskyi complained about the poverty of the local minstrelsy, he also boasted that the *lirnyky* had built a church entirely with their own money. It was small and had a thatched roof, but it was a church nonetheless. Apparently it became the center of a village inhabited mostly by minstrels and their descendants.[105]

Perhaps the best proof that minstrels were part of regular peasant society is the fate of their children. The children of minstrels did not themselves become *kobzari* or *lirnyky* unless they were blind. Minstrel children were farmers, just like everyone else in the village. Sydor Humeniuk's son Ivan told Kvitka that the children of minstrels took care of the land which their father owned. If things were really bad, they hired themselves out as laborers or, perhaps, guides. As the children grew bigger and the household prospered, the children preferred relying on the agricultural income alone. They would stop their father's wandering and begging, and keep him home.[106]

Kharkiv presents an almost identical picture. He says that a minstrel's family did the farming. If the children were small and the family could not till the land, then they rented it out, usually for half of what the soil produced. Renters tended not to take good care of someone else's land, and the minstrel's family would take over the farming just as soon as they were able. Kharkiv too says that if the family prospered and did not need the money the minstrel contributed, the children preferred to keep their father home.[107]

When farming ceased being the sole occupation of Ukrainian peasants and more and more of them took up various trades, the children of minstrels became tradesmen and professionals, just like the children of other peasants. Hnat Honcharenko's son became a railway worker and lived in Sebastopol. The elder Honcharenko spent the winters with his son, and in the summer, returned to his native area, a village near Kharkiv.[108] Another minstrel from the Kharkiv area sent his son to a technical school, meaning that the boy was receiving post-secondary education.[109] One of Kuzmin-skyi's sons became a forester (*lysovyk*).[110] The middle son of Ivan Kravchenko-Kriukovskyi, when Horlenko interviewed him in 1882, was training to be a blacksmith.[111] Some minstrels were successful enough to advance the social position of their families. Thus, Shut, the first *kobzar* ever recorded, was able to educate his son.[112]

The Argument for Women Minstrels

The participation of women in the tradition is both intriguing and poorly documented. Scholars were interested in *kobzari* and *lirnyky* as bearers of heroic poetry. Women were not part of the heroic image and hence were ignored. Yet there must have been a way to take care of blind girls as well as blind boys. As noted in the section on work, the categories of men's work and women's work were central to the village worldview. There is at least some evidence, mostly in manuscript form, that women were trained and did perform for money. One of Martynovych's informants told him that there was special training for girls: *divchacha nauka*.[113] In a Martynovych manuscript dealing primarily with initiation rites, there is an aside that "women, too, blind women, if they are worthy, can be initiated."[114] Several informants mention a special women's repertory and state that strict gender distinctions applied to repertory, so that women were not permitted to sing men's songs, and men, women's. These same informants indicate that while the gender restrictions were disappearing, they still applied to women, so that a wife could teach her husband women's songs, but should a woman sing men's songs, "they will go and break her cups."[115]

Most intriguing are the several huge folders in the Martynovych collec-tion that seem to be collected from women. Although Martynovych's docu-mentation becomes erratic after 1880, when he either does not write down or writes down only sporadically where, when, and from whom he collected the songs and other material he presents, it is clear that women had huge repertories. An unspecified source praises one woman, Hanna Rudykha, and the extent of her knowledge:

> She was such a woman that she knew everything. All these tales and Christ-mas carols and other holiday songs and all sorts of songs, *kobzar* songs and *lirnyk* songs. She knew all of the Cossack and Zaporozhian songs, all the haidamak songs, the Cossack-haidamak songs. Hanna Rudykh was the sort of woman that would be in the company of priests and of wealthy men. She was such as wise woman. Even though she was a woman, her intelligence resem-

bled that of a man. She was like a man and when she would tell something, her words would come out like those of a man. Oh, Baba Hanna Rudykha, praise and glory to her![116]

The folders include many items that women were not supposed to know, such as the *dumy* and the psalms that "get one's cups broken." Kharkiv also mentions a woman who knew Cossack songs, which could be either historical songs or epics, but would not sing them in public.[117] Thus, women knew a great deal, even if they were not allowed to perform it publicly or for money. Unfortunately, from the Martynovych manuscripts it is unclear whether his women informants were sighted or blind. In one of the Kharkiv manuscripts there is a brief notation about a blind woman who knew many, many historical songs and possibly epics (*kozatski istorii*) but who would sing only psalms in public, presumably because she feared reprisal.[118] Thus, there is reason to suppose that female performers were not sighted.

Published sources give even less information than manuscripts, yet even here there is evidence of female participation in minstrelsy. Of course, the wives of some minstrels traveled and sang with their husbands. Andrii Shut, the first great *kobzar* to be recorded, said he learned "from a blind woman."[119] When Kolessa collected material for his book on *duma* music, one of his informants was a woman, Iavdokha Iukhymivna Pylypenko.[120] Lack of documentation of women minstrels does not mean that they did not exist; it means, rather, that scholars and collectors were less interested in women performers and perhaps less comfortable with them. It is also possible that male fellow minstrels restricted women, likely for financial reasons. If they ensured that women sang nothing but women's songs in public by threatening to go and "break their cups," then they may have denied them access to collectors, especially when these were seen as a source of prestige and better pay.

Conclusion

In conclusion, a minstrel was an ordinary peasant who could not continue living as a peasant because he was blind. When such a person reached his teens, he was apprenticed to a master minstrel for approximately three years. Upon completion of the apprenticeship, the young man worked for several years and then married. Most minstrels had families, owned their homes, and had small plots of land, which were usually managed by their wives, and eventually, their children as well. The children of minstrels returned to the ranks of ordinary peasants; they were not obliged to be minstrels unless they, too, were blind. Blindness was considered a great curse, and minstrelsy was not a desirable profession, but it was still honest work and thus preferable to begging. Ivashchenko's article on Pavlo Bratytsia and Propik Dub beautifully expresses the idea that minstrelsy is the substitute for normal work or farming. When asked about what they did, the two minstrels supposedly pointed to their instruments and said in unison: "This is our scythe and our plow. This is our livelihood. This is how we live and pay taxes."[121] The fact that they described their work as minstrels using agricultural imagery confirms that the minstrels themselves recognized farming as the basic form of work for which minstrelsy was substituted when disability demanded.

Minstrelsy was thus a solution to disability. It existed to provide for the blind, not to foster art. There were great artists among the *kobzari* and *lirnyky*. Andrii Shut, Ivan Kravchenko-Kriukovskyi, Fedir Hrytsenko-Kholodnyi, and Ostap Veresai are just a few of the men acknowledged to be gifted musicians and poets. Yet no man became a minstrel because of his musical and poetic abilities; a man became a minstrel because he was blind. Musical talent led people to play and sing for pleasure, but a professional *kobzar* or *lirnyk* was always a disabled person who became a professional out of necessity and not by choice.

Because music was a way to support those who could not do normal work, a far greater range of musical ability was tolerated and financially rewarded than has been widely documented. We have only passing references, like Borzhkovskii's description of a religious festival, to indicate that all who sang or chanted must have been paid regardless of talent, or they could not have survived. Collectors naturally sought the most talented of *kobzari,* and especially the ones who knew the prestigious *dumy,* but there were also many men of lesser talent who belonged to the ranks of minstrels and earned enough to support themselves and their families. Unfortunately, the only records of them are, again, passing references and calls from scholars to document minstrels who had escaped attention.[122] Because the disabled were expected to substitute musical performance for farming, some sort of musical instruction must have been almost universal for the blind and possibly for all who could not work.

Chapter 5

Minstrel Institutions: The Brotherhoods or Guilds

M instrels were both members of their villages and people apart. While all of their neighbors were farmers and their own children would probably become farmers, the minstrels themselves were professionals, and as such, they belonged to organizations which were called either guilds (*tsekhy*) or brotherhoods (*bratstva*). These complex organizations effectively served the needs of their members into the early part of this century. For most minstrels, the guild was an integral part of professional life.

To understand minstrels, learning about their guilds is as important as learning about their villages. Unfortunately, gathering information about these organizations is considerably more difficult than finding data on rural life. All scholars who have written about minstrel guilds complain about lack of information.[1] The guilds were secret and even when traditional minstrelsy was breaking down at the beginning of this century, getting *kobzari* or *lirnyky* to talk about their professional organizations was difficult at best. There were many reasons why minstrels were so reticent to talk, and one was surely that the guilds served to mediate some of the tension between art and making money. The guilds acted for the good of the profession: they served to protect the interests of their members. To protect member minstrels, the guilds had to attend to practical, financial matters and they also had to defend the profession's image. Image problems often stemmed precisely from concern with money. Thus, guilds took care of practical matters, and at the same time, hid them from public view, leaving visible pious and charitable acts, such as the donation of money or a candle to the church with which a guild was affiliated. Anything that would upset this delicate balance, such as revealing the secret, practical aspects of the guild to outsiders, was scrupulously avoided. As Opanas Slastion noted, every time he asked Mykhailo Kravchenko about guilds, the minstrel would deftly steer the conversation in a different direction.[2]

But some information does exist. The most thorough published study is Mikhail Speranskii's *South-Russian Song and Its Contemporary Performers (on the subject of T. M. Parkhomenko)*. Other published materials and manuscripts, especially those collected by Porfiryi Martynovych, serve to supplement Speranskii. The published sources, however, are somewhat problematic, since most scholars were forced to rely on minstrels who were alienated from their guilds or on people peripheral to the profession. Terentii Parkhomenko, Speranskii's primary informant, was especially interested in money and in pleasing intellectuals. Valerian Borzhkovskii got much of his information from a sighted, would-be *lirnyk* rather than from a guild member. Kyryl Studynskyi began with someone even more peripheral: a guide. Fortunately, Martynovych, perhaps because he did not publish his data and reveal guild secrets, had access to the minstrels themselves. His data show that the published studies, despite their problematic sources, are accurate.

Speranskii, using published and manuscript materials and data collected from Parkhomenko, isolated eight traits of minstrel guilds:

(1) Minstrel guilds are territorial. Each guild claims professional hegemony over a certain geographical area, a certain set of villages, towns, and cities where its members, and only its members, can function. A guild protects its territorial rights from the members of other guilds and from unaffiliated persons.

(2) Each guild has a headquarters. This is a church or a monastery. The guild has a formal affiliation with the religious establishment and supports either an icon, a candle, an icon-lamp or some combination of these within the church.

(3) Minstrel guilds are democratically governed. All guild officials are elected by the entire guild membership, and the final say in any matter belongs to the membership as a whole. This also applies to the administration of justice: the guild has the right to try, convict, and punish errant members. It also applies to the disposition of guild funds and the acceptance of new members.

(4) Each guild has its own treasury. The money in the treasury comes from the dues paid by the members.

(5) Guilds grant the right to teach minstrelsy to certain of their members, and control the teachers by submitting them to examination.

(6) Minstrel guilds have an initiation ritual with strong religious overtones. This is the sole means of entry into a guild.

(7) Entry into a guild requires professional competence: the ability to play a *lira* or a *bandura*, knowledge of a certain minimum number of songs, and familiarity with minstrel secret language, the *lebiiska mova*.

(8) The personal and family life of guild members is their own business and outside of guild jurisdiction.[3]

Jurisdiction over Territory

Isolated statements indicate that territory was both controlled and subdivided. There was a sense that resources were limited and a given area could provide only so much charity. Those already drawing support from the area evidently wanted to control the access of others and to use the territory as efficiently as possible, perhaps dividing it among themselves. At some point in the past, this probably was what guilds did. Speranskii reports that in the Kozeletsk region, if a man served an apprenticeship in the district (*uezd*) in which he resided, he was permitted to beg in that district only and he belonged to only one guild. A man who served an apprenticeship in another district could work in the district of his own residence, his master's district, plus a third district nearest to the residence of his master. He would have membership in three guilds.[4] Talking about the Mena guild, to which he belonged, Parkhomenko said that each minstrel, upon successfully passing initiation, was assigned specific villages, towns, and cities where he could work. In other words, his guild subdivided its territory among its members.[5] There were provisions for switching guilds. According to Ivan Humeniuk, should a man permanently settle in an area belonging to a guild other than his own, he could become a member of the new guild by passing its initiation rite. It is possible that he could be allowed to play and sing in the new territory without being submitted to an initiation; but in such a case, he was not allowed to take apprentices.[6]

While the system of territorial jurisdiction was once clearly articulated, by the end of the nineteenth century it was breaking down. All of the statements above are unique. They complement each other nicely and form a cohesive structure, but they are not corroborated elsewhere. Furthermore, while minstrels stated that territorial restrictions existed, they did not seem to follow them. We do not know which villages, cities, and towns were assigned to Parkhomenko, for example; but his choice of places to travel was governed more by financial considerations and attempts to avoid the police than by the directives of his guild. There is even doubt whether guild territories corresponded to administrative districts which Speranskii's description of Kozeletsk would imply. In all probability, they did not and minstrel divisions followed their own, rather than official, lines.[7] Certainly, from what we know of the circuits actually travelled by minstrels, they do not fall within a single administrative district.[8]

The reasons for the breakdown of territorial hegemony are many. One is the Ukrainian ethos which champions sharing of resources: those who were better off were expected to share with the less fortunate, whether it was harvesting a crop for a neighbor short on manpower, giving food to fellow villagers in need, or sharing access to territory. This ethical principle caused tension when there was an overall shortage and no one had much of anything.[9] The desire to limit the sharing of meager resources was behind guild attempts to limit access to their territories, but at the same time, sharing was the cornerstone of minstrelsy. *Kobzari* and *lirnyky* were regarded as disabled people who could do nothing except sing and so should be paid for their music. Minstrels called on able-bodied people to share their food, their clothing, and their money with poor, blind minstrels, who could not get these things for themselves.[10] Many of the religious songs, "Lazarus" being a good example, say that the rich who do not share, like Lazarus' wealthy brother, will be damned to eternal torment in Hell. As Ianko from the village of Iuzefivka, Sharhorod region, told Borzhkovskii:

> There are lots of poor people among us. He who is stronger supports him who is weaker. One will go and buy flour, and then give you a piece of bread. That's how we live. God will give to one and take away from another. If you give something to one person, he will pass on part of it to another. That's how we make it.[11]

Ivan Kuchuhura-Kucherenko's master advised him to keep a low profile in the company of other minstrels. He added that if possible, his pupil should avoid staying in the same quarters with other minstrels, because "if you sleep with them, you will have to share. The bread and the money which you gathered begging, they will make you share it."[12]

Practical motives were as important as ethical ones. When collectors asked about the circuits they travelled, minstrels said they decided where to go on the basis of two considerations: where they would make the most money and where they would most successfully avoid the police. Guild territorial boundaries were not mentioned. Valerian Borzhkovskii and Klement Kvitka both report that fairs and religious festivals were favorites because they were good places to make money. Vasyl Horlenko's obituary for Ivan Kravchenko-Kriukovskyi states that, in his youth, he travelled all over Ukraine, visiting not just villages, but cities, especially city fairs.[13]

Iakiv Zlatarskyi traveled far and wide, crossing over into Russia by mistake while still a boy, and later travelling a wide circuit of Galician villages, including villages along the Russian border.[14]

There is one more factor that worked against territorial restriction. It would appear that in the past, there was a federation of guilds to which all of the smaller, regional guilds belonged. The territory of this federation was huge, encompassing both Galicia and Eastern Ukraine, and possibly the adjacent parts of Belarus and Russia. An elderly Cossack from Kholodna Hora named Khoma Semenenko reported that a huge meeting which included both minstrels and regular beggars and attracted hundreds of participants was held each spring in the Brovariv forest between Kiev and Pereiaslav. According to Semenenko, the "super-guild" had a system of offices patterned on the military (*otomany, sotskie, desiatskie*), and vacancies were filled at this time. Trials of those accused of a misdeed took place at the huge annual meeting, and finances were allotted for the coming year, including the granting of dowries, especially to those who, upon marriage, would cease being beggars.[15] This description, although published third-hand, has so much in common with other accounts of minstrel meetings that it seems credible. Furthermore, other evidence of a super-guild exists. In his analysis of the secret language used by minstrels, Kyryl Studynskyi shows that the *lebiiska mova* of the Galician minstrels from whom he gathered his data has a great deal in common with that used by the minstrels of Eastern Ukraine. Zlatarskyi, Hnatiuk's informant, compared the finances of minstrels in Eastern Ukraine to those of Galician minstrels, and showed familiarity with minstrel life in a geographical area far removed from his own. Both Studynskyi's and Hnatiuk's data indicate extensive professional contact over a large territory, just the sort of thing that would happen under a guild federation encompassing all Ukrainian areas. Volodymyr Kharkiv reports that the men he interviewed knew *kobzari* and *lirnyky* from all over Ukraine.[16] If there was such a super-guild, it is understandable that with time, it might displace smaller, district-size divisions, especially if there were other factors working against such divisions.

While there is little evidence that minstrels tried to stay within the territory of their own guild and to protect this territory from members of other guilds, there is abundant evidence that they guarded their profession from intrusion by outsiders: they protected professional territory rather than geographical territory. It is possible that the minstrels' emphasis on this form of protection was mistranslated into an emphasis on geography in Spernaskii's study. Efforts to protect professional territory are widely attested and often took physical form, namely, someone who had not gone through the training and initiation process that normally led to guild membership was literally attacked and beaten. Borzhkovskii affirmed that guild members would beat someone posing as a *lirnyk* and destroy his instrument.[17] Describing practices in the Kozeletsk district, Speranskii tells us that should *kobzari* and *lirnyky* find out that a man is performing without having achieved membership in a guild,

> they will savagely beat the "pretender" with sticks, with their staffs, with their fists. They will break his musical instrument. They will forbid him from ever again travelling through the villages with "a *lira* and a song," and they will allow him to beg only "in the name of Christ." This means that he has to beg without playing or singing.[18]

By trying to access guild privileges without paying guild dues, a man doomed himself to the less lucrative and more painful status of an ordinary beggar.

Zlatarskyi, probably aware of the practices in Eastern Ukraine, told Hnatiuk that *lirnyky* in Galicia did not punish an errant youth physically. However, they did have a whole system of fines which could be levied on a young man who had learned to perform without serving a master or who had been indentured to a master but had not fulfilled his obligations to him properly. In extreme cases, a master could notify the other members of a guild about an insubordinate apprentice, and when they caught such a man performing, they would interrogate him and take away his instrument or even break it.[19] Kuchuhura-Kucherenko told Martynovych that if fellow minstrels caught you teaching minstrel "science" (*nauka*) to someone who should not be privy to this knowledge, such as a sighted person, "you would lose your livelihood."[20] It is little wonder that most scholars had trouble collecting data on minstrel brotherhoods, and quite remarkable that Martynovych succeeded in spite of these stringent sanctions.

Oleksandr Dimnych, the sighted ex-guide interviewed by Borzhkovskii, had a great deal of trouble because, being sighted, he was technically ineligible for apprenticeship and subsequent guild membership. Yet it is clear that *lirnyky* objected to Dimnych's not having served an apprenticeship as much as to his not being blind. They said that he needed to "submit himself" (*pokorytysia*) to a master and that his "wisdom needed to mature." Fortunately for Dimnych, his past services as a guide made minstrels more lenient toward him than they would have been to another sighted person, and at the time of the interview, he was finally serving an apprenticeship with Andrii Dovhaliuk. Prior to apprenticeship, Dimnych had suffered a great deal for his desire to be a *lirnyk*. He himself confessed that he once made the mistake of teaching a blind boy the begging song and taking him along to the religious fair in Brailiv. By doing so, Dimnych broke a number of guild rules, including teaching without permission. He was caught by a group of guild-affiliated minstrels and would have been beaten had he not broken free and run, an escape probably made easier by the fact that he was a sighted man fleeing blind pursuers. He returned and made peace with the *lirnyky* after they had calmed down, but at the moment of their anger, he needed to flee, he felt, or risk brutal physical punishment.[21]

In sum, intrusion onto guild space, space not in the sense of geographical area, but in the sense of professional terrain, prompted minstrels to defend their turf with fervor. The importance of the profession as a boundary is underscored by Borzhkovskii's statement that once a person had been initiated and properly instated as a minstrel, "no one has the right to take away his *lira* or break it."[22]

The Secret Language: *Lebiiska Mova*

Speranskii calls the secret language of the guilds, the *lebiiska mova,* one of the marks of minstrel professional competence. Other scholars, such as Studynskyi and Horbach, have examined this language as a secret code and a means of protection.[23] Some, like Borzhkovskii and Martynovych, give samples and dictionaries of minstrel language without speculating on functions.

The secret language is a mix of encoded Ukrainian words and borrowings from modern Greek, Romanian (the language of Ukrainian gypsies), Hungarian, Turkish, Hebrew, Russian, and even a few western European languages, such as Swedish. The encoded Ukrainian words are derived by the addition of prefixes (*bi-mene* for *mene*, 'me') and suffixes (*chuzhivnyi* for *chuzhyi*, 'strange'). In some cases, a root is used with a derivational suffix that does not normally go with it *(batii* for *batko*, 'father'). Some words are formed by metathesis and some are metaphors, such as *khodulia* for leg, foot (Uk. *noha*). It comes from the verb *khodyty,* meaning 'to walk,' and thus, *khodulia* is a thing which walks, a foot or a leg.[24]

Scholars looking at the secret language have always been intrigued by its origins and its similarity to the languages of other liminal groups, namely beggars (*zhebraky*), peddlers *(ofeny;* Russian, *korobeiniki*), hatters (*shapovaly*), and bandits or thieves (*zlodii*). All of these groups have less-than-savory reputations. Hatters and peddlers were thieves of sorts: they were itinerant merchants who travelled from village to village, selling their wares, and were notorious for cheating their customers, short-changing them or selling them shoddy goods, and then disappearing. Both had permanent residences in cities but were perceived as inaccessible once they had left the village. Peasants felt that the secret languages of the peddlers and the hatters and the thieves were a way to obscure their conniving until they could get out of town. Needless to say, the existence of the minstrels' secret language and its similarity to that of thieves and suspect merchants did not reflect well on *kobzari* and *lirnyky*. It implied that minstrels, too, were up to no good, trying to cheat the public and to cover their deceitful ways with code. Nor did it help that minstrels themselves claimed that their language originated at the time when Ukraine was governed by the Polish-Lithuanian Commonwealth, and served as a cover-up of illegal activities, such as plotting attacks against the Polish nobility.[25]

The suspicion surrounding minstrels' secret language is an example of the ease with which negative imagery attaches itself to a group which differs from the majority population. As Oleksa Horbach argues, there are two possible reasons for a secret language: to hide what one is saying from others and to test a stranger, to make sure the stranger belongs to one's professional group by seeing whether he possesses the appropriate secret knowledge. In the case of Ukrainian minstrels, Horbach favors the latter explanation and there is much support for this choice.[26] The *lebiiska mova* was something that minstrels used among themselves when no one else was listening. If a stranger approached, minstrels would switch to ordinary speech. Thus, what they were hiding was the language itself, not what was being said.[27] According to Borzhkovskii, they hid the language so well that even some peasants did not know it existed.[28] Minstrels hid their secret language not only from fellow villagers but also from collectors. They were extremely reluctant to have it documented. Borzhkovskii got most of his information from Dimnych, the sighted ex-guide who was not a guild member.[29] Hnatiuk collected from Zlatarskyi through "a third party who had the *lirnyk*'s trust."[30] Studynskyi reported a great deal of trouble collecting the language, including having to promise his sources that he would not reveal their names to other minstrels. The material for his first article on secret language was not collected from a minstrel, but from a guide.[31] Curiously, Studynskyi claimed that when he addressed *lirnyky* using their language, they tended to warm up to him and take him for one of their own.[32] Martynovych was the only one who seems to have collected *lebiiska mova* directly from minstrels, and one of his informants actually said something close to what Horbach theorized. Kuchuhura-Kucherenko stated:

> And why do we need this language? To know who is who. To know who a man is—is he good or is he bad? Is he a policeman? Can you play and sing in front of him or not?[33]

Later in the same document, he said,

> If you learn it, they will talk to you, and if you don't, they won't acknowledge you.[34]

Even the similarities between the secret language of minstrels and the secret languages of peddlers, hatters, and thieves, if viewed from a different perspective, can be seen as proof that it was used to test strangers rather than to conceal shady acts. All of these groups were subject to suspicion and needed to shield themselves from strangers who might believe the negative image and act upon it, be it valid or not. All of them needed to know if a person seeking entry was friend or foe. According to Studynskyi, the thieves, who were the most likely to be attacked, had the most elaborate system. In addition to a secret language, they had certain words which changed daily and acted essentially as passwords. Someone who did not know both the language as a system and the individual passwords was an outsider and immediately barred.[35]

The supposition that the secret language was a way of ascertaining guild membership and thus a means of protection is confirmed by the existence of other methods for testing strangers. Speranskii tells us that when minstrels met an unfamiliar *kobzar* or *lirnyk*, they inquired about his teacher. All of the teachers in a given area were known, and if the stranger was not able to give a satisfactory account of his apprenticeship, he was considered an outsider and could be attacked.[36] Perhaps the most interesting test is the minstrel greeting formula, which is analogous to the passwords used by thieves. It did not change on a daily basis like the passwords; but like passwords, it was an additional element drawn from the secret language, but also isolated and assigned special status, which all minstrels were expected to know and to produce correctly.

Guild Governance and Guild Finances

Of the things within the jurisdiction of the guild, the most open to public view was the guild's affiliation with a church. Minstrels were an integral part of the church. Whether minstrels were allowed to sing and solicit alms on church grounds and during church services is open to debate, but there is much to indicate that they were. The *lirnyk* Evtakhvii Dovhopalyi, in describing his repertory, listed a special begging song that was to be used outside a church and another, different song which served as a request for alms when people were leaving after a church service.[37] Minstrels were welcome as worshippers, parishioners who contributed valuable goods and services: they had their guild icon and icon lamp or candle. During their annual business meeting, they allotted money for the maintenance of the icon and for the purchase of wax for the candle or oil for the lamp. According to Pavlo Efimenko, some of the finest artifacts in the churches were the ones provided by the poor. Zlatarskyi boasted that *lirnyky* built an entire church with their own monies. Efimenko also wrote that the indigent, minstrels included, who lived on church property were responsible for keeping the church and the grounds clean. In addition to their regular contributions to their churches, some guilds would assess candle wax or lamp oil as a fine for misdeeds.[38]

Minstrels provided monies for their churches and they used them as the sites for their annual guild meetings. In all probability, the churches with which guilds chose to affiliate and which acted as the locations for their meetings were the bigger ones located in religious complexes, usually consisting of a cathedral, a monastery, a hospice, and a school. As major institutions, religious complexes served as sites for the festivals that would attract large numbers of minstrels and thus were convenient places to hold annual guild meetings.[39] During the meetings, the guild took care of its business: governance, finance, and the granting of membership and teaching privileges.

The Mena guild described by Parkhomenko elected officers, collected dues, and allotted monies to its church. It also tried members accused of crimes and assigned penalties to those found guilty. The assembled brotherhood tested new members and admitted those who passed their initiation, assigning them territories where they could work.[40] According to Speranskii, the meetings of other guilds were essentially the same. In the Kozeletsk region, one of the most important offices was that of the treasurer. This office was divided between two people, the person who kept the trunk with the guild's money and the person who kept the key. They were elected at guild meetings and held their positions for an unspecified length of time. Apparently, minstrels feared that their brothers might be tempted by the guild monies, and purposefully selected trunk and key keepers who lived far apart.[41] The report from Minsk is that the most important office was that of guild head (*tsekh-meister*). This is a term that appears in the descriptions of a variety of guilds, including beggars' guilds and religious brotherhoods. Like the treasurer, the *tsekh-meister* was elected at the annual meeting for an unspecified period of time.

Some information about the trials of errant brethren held at guild meetings also comes from the Minsk region. We are told that in the past, penalties for guild members found guilty of crimes could include corporal punishment. The guild determined what the punishment should be, and if the decision was to subject the guilty brother to a whipping or a beating, the guild members themselves administered the sentence. By the time this information was collected at the beginning of the twentieth century, the Minsk guild had ceased to inflict corporal punishment, but was still assessing fines. The monies collected were used for things like the purchase of candle wax. The most severe sentence was the "cutting of the begging bag" (*obrizuvannia torby*), which signaled expulsion from the guild and retraction of the right to beg. This was virtually a death sentence. In most cases, people who were caught performing without permission were still permitted to beg, although they were barred from ever playing and singing. The "cutting of the begging bag" meant that even begging was prohibited; and as begging was the last available option, removing it was eliminating all possibility of survival.[42]

An interesting version of a fine for misdeeds appears in a Martynovych manuscript. It seems that the guild could force an errant member to renew his vows by going through the equivalent of a second initiation. Martynovych had apparently asked his informant, Mykolai Doroshenko, to give the Poltava version of an initiation. During the course of his testimony, Doroshenko seems to confuse information about an apprentice requesting an initiation to permit him to terminate training and the guild requesting a reinitiation. Doroshenko thus gives a list of accusations of misdeeds, the material appropriate to the reintegration of a guild member who had fallen from grace.[43] The possibility of the guild forcing an extra initiation on someone is logical. The ritual required the initiate to make a considerable cash outlay and was thus analogous to fines that went to brotherhood coffers or brotherhood supported projects, like the candles in their church. The initiation also emphasized proper behavior more than musical knowledge and would indeed be a good way to reintegrate a brother whose behavior had alienated him from the group. The terms for the initiation rite, *odklianshchina* and *vyzvilok,* have more to do with gaining permission and paying things off than their English equivalent, and it would make sense that these rites could be used for both entry and reentry into the guild.

In addition to the big annual meeting, guilds held smaller meetings when necessary. These were called by the guild head (*tsekh-meister*) and took place in conjunction with events where large numbers of minstrels gathered, such as fairs. Trials could be held at these meetings, and novices could undergo initiation. If a guild member suffered a calamity, such as a house fire, his fellows could apportion a sum to help him rebuild. If a member died, the guild could vote to give financial aid to his widow. This was especially common if the children were too small to help support the family.[44] After the business of the guild was concluded, the members enjoyed themselves. They played and sang for each other the songs that they performed for the public, and guild meetings provided good opportunities for minstrels to learn new material. Sometimes minstrels enjoyed secret musical entertainment. The Martynovych manuscripts contain a magical song called "Zhachka" (see Part 2, "Secret Songs" pp. 273–81), which was supposed to keep the Devil at bay.[45] Other sources claim that minstrels, once out of earshot of the public, sang parodies of sacred religious verses.[46] There are, however, no texts of these, and rumors of minstrels making fun of the material that they were supposed to revere may have been but one more manifestation of the suspicions of impropriety that those outside a closed organization held about those within. Guild meetings that included initiations sometimes ended in a special form of revelry. A young man who successfully completed the rite was allowed to perform a special mendicant dance (*lebiiska skakomka*), a dance that other young *lirnyky*, and sometimes older men, would join.[47]

Accounts of guild meetings give us some clues to guild structure. We know that there was a single person in charge, the guild head, or *tsekh-meister*. Konstantyn Bich-Lubenskyi attributes a good deal of power to the guild head, saying that he could make many decisions by himself, without calling an assembly of brethren. The control over his decision-making was his term of office. It was unspecified, as stated in other sources, but if too many of the decisions made by the guild head without consultation displeased the brothers, he was removed.[48] The procedure for disciplining or even removing the head of the guild appears in an unpublished manuscript. According to the material collected from Vasyl Hovtan, if the head of a guild has done something wrong, such as drinking, or falsely accusing a guild member, or disciplining him unjustly, then the others gather at a church or a fair without the guild head. They discuss the matter, then summon the guild head before them. They either reprimand their guild head or say, "You are not capable of serving the brotherhood." At this point, they can either elect a new leader or, if the old leader expresses remorse and asks to stay, they can leave him in his position.[49]

Another important guild office was that of treasurer, an office which was often shared by two people, the key-keeper (*kliushnyk*) and the money-keeper, or counter (*shchotchyk*). They were supposed to keep each other honest, and would unite and open the trunk with the guild's monies only at the time of the annual meeting when dues and fines would be added to the coffers and offerings to the church and funds for brothers in need removed. As time passed and the guild system, and probably also the guild treasury, declined, the two treasurer positions were reinterpreted in interesting ways. In Poltava, for example, there was still a sense that both the *kliushnyk* and *shchotchyk* were important people, but what they were supposed to do was forgotten, the *shchotchyk* becoming literally "one who counts," except that he no longer counted money. Rather, during the initiation rite, the *shchotchyk* was supposed to count prayers and make sure that each was said twelve times. Apparently, he did just that, saying "one" after the first recitation of a prayer, "two" after the second, and so on. The key-keeper in this system became the person in charge of handing out food and drink during the initiation ceremony.[50]

The Minsk guild had the curious additional office of a scribe, a person whose duties included registering the names all those admitted into the guild in a ledger.[51] Whether this was a sighted person is an interesting question. We are told that sighted persons were excluded from all guild activities, and yet it is difficult to image a blind person keeping a ledger.

Among the rank and file, there were two levels of membership, "the older and the lesser brothers" (*bratiia starsha i mensha*), as appears in some of the formulas for addressing the guild.[52] By the turn of the century, the two-tier system was breaking down. Where it still existed, there are indications that it affected dues and that there were two rate levels. In some areas, the rate for elder members was zero, and dues were paid by the younger members only.[53] There are even indications that only the younger guild members were subject to punishments, while their elders were exempt. The democracy that Speranskii attributes to guilds might not have been as extensive as he claims, and it is likely that the various guild decisions were made by elders only. This seems especially true of initiation tests and trials. Borzhkovskii tells us:

> Young *lirnyky* behave with great respect toward their elders and have to obey them in everything. If a young *lirnyk* does something wrong, then his elders, when they gather at a religious festival or a fair, question witnesses about the event. They then decide how to deal with the accused. Because of these trials, a young *lirnyk*, as A. Zoria's (Dovhaliuk's) father told me, "is more afraid of an elder *lirnyk* than of a policeman or a magistrate."[54]

The status of elder not only brought respect and power; it conferred the right to teach, and thus brought financial rewards. Entry into the group of elders was shrouded in even greater secrecy than entry into the guild, but we do have some information about it. It appears that after about ten years of being simply a *kobzar* or *lirnyk*, a man was eligible to undergo a rite similar in format to the initiation which first admitted him to the guild. According to Drahomanov, the two rites, although similar in structure, have different names: the first rite of initiation is called *odklynshchyny* (meaning, roughly, the paying off of debts), while the rite that grants permission to teach is called the *vyzvilka* (the granting of permission). Successful completion of the second rite meant that the candidate was allowed to take apprentices and received the special title of master (*maister* or *pan-maister*).[55] Martynovych's informant, the *lirnyk* Mykolai Khvedorovych Doroshenko, confirms this information.[56]

Apprenticeship from the Guild's Point of View

Being a teacher, or a *pan-maister*, was an honor. Apprentices retained a tie to their masters throughout their lives and continued to offer them gifts and thanks on holidays.[57] Being a *pan-maister* was a very responsible position and it carried financial rewards. Students improved the economic position of their teacher by paying a fee for instruction and by begging and turning their earnings over to the master. Thus the master could sit at home and have someone else do the begging for him. Ostap Veresai, who complained about nearly everything, complained about this aspect of apprenticeship. According to his account, his various masters would soon recognize Veresai's superior talent and send him out to sing and beg while they sat in their warm, dry houses. Because he was the most talented, they would send him out more than any of the other apprentices. Only when he would fall ill from the physical strain and exposure would his masters take pity and not force him to work. Sometimes they would just get rid of Veresai when he could no longer be exploited and send him home to his parents.[58] Veresai's accounts are melodramatic and most masters did not exploit pupils.[59] Nevertheless, having apprentices was a bonus.

Pupils, of course, knew their masters and many teachers remembered their students. Using this information plus the fact that outstanding masters had a reputation over a large territory, Speranskii attempted a genealogy of the tradition, tracing pupil-teacher relationships, in some cases over several generations.[60] This work allows us to determine that in the nineteenth and early twentieth centuries, most masters had from one to several pupils at any one time. At some point in the past, however, there were probably whole schools of minstrelsy. The fullest account of such a school comes from the *lirnyk* Vasylii Moroz. According to Moroz, his master Mefodii Kolesnichenko, of the Podile region, ran a school with thirty students. The school was located on the master's land in a large building separate from the cottage in which the master and his family lived. The school building housed pupils and instructors. There were two instructors for every five students and they took turns going out to sing and beg. While one teacher was out touring villages, earning money, the other one was back at the school, working with the students. Once a week the two instructors would switch. Also once a week, the master Mefodii's son would drive out and pick up all that had been earned by the teachers who had been out begging. This was mostly food, and it sustained the pupils, their instructors, and the master and his family. According to Moroz, pupils were apprenticed for six years, although the more obtuse ones (*bolvanuvaty*) could take longer and the more clever ones (*khytrenki*) could take less. The latter, the ones who completed their own training rapidly, formed Mefodii's staff of instructors. Anyone who had completed his studies could become an independent *lirnyk* with Mefodii's permission.[61]

This school may have been one of the last. According to Moroz, it fell apart after Mefodii's death, and there was nothing like it in existence at the time of the interview (1896); but there is every reason to believe that such schools were once common. Minstrels and peasants alike told Borzhkovskii that large schools housing approximately twenty pupils existed in the past. They even gave the location of a school near Kiev, told him the approximate date of its closing, and described its structure, a system much like the one used by Mefodii.[62] In Western Ukraine or Galicia, where Studynskyi did his work, schools were more numerous and more recently active. *Lirnyky* gave Studynskyi whole lists of the better-known schools. The biggest of these housed approximately fifty students and functioned like mini-guilds, with the pupils electing officers from amongst themselves to enforce discipline. Sighted persons could enter these schools if they chose. Whether they became professional *lirnyky* or received musical instruction for their own pleasure is not documented, but considering the restrictions on professional performers, it is safe to assume that sighted persons performed only privately. Studynskyi testifies that he heard the playing of people trained in the better-known schools and that their artistry was indeed marvelous. Thus, *lirnyk* schools could have been places where lovers of music with no professional aspirations sought instruction. Perhaps some of the sighted persons were orphans or other poor people who entered minstrelsy-related trades. At least some Galician schools taught the making of musical instruments, and sighted people could have selected this as a profession.[63] In any case, Studynskyi's account gives the impression that schools were a well-developed institution. If some form of musical instruction was available to all blind persons in the heyday of the tradition, then the existence of large schools is to be expected. At such schools a variety of people would receive musical training; a small portion of these would go on to become *kobzari* or *lirnyky*.

It is possible that schools were a specifically *lirnyk* phenomenon. All of the descriptions of schools come from *lirnyky*, and in Galicia, where Studynskyi worked, minstrels were exclusively *lira* players; there were no *kobzari*. Perhaps *lirnyky* were traditionally trained in large schools while *kobzari* studied in a one-on-one relationship with a master.

It is interesting to examine what established minstrels earned and the degree to which apprentices contributed to earnings. According to Studynskyi, schools had a relatively set fee structure, and men contracted to pay a certain amount when they entered. This amount varied according to the means of the pupil, from sixty *karbovantsi* to eight gold pieces (between sixty and eighty rubles, a *karbovanets* being roughly equivalent to one ruble). If a man wanted to shorten his apprenticeship, he had to pay an extra exit fee, which could be as much as twenty *karbovantsi*.[64] Where there were no schools, youths contracted with an individual master. Masters insisted that teaching be worth their effort, and if they did not make enough from the begging of the apprentice, they wanted payment in cash. We have records of what a number of specific individuals actually paid for apprenticeship. Ostap Veresai, Oleksii Masliukov, Petro Harasko, Andrii Kornienko, Dubrova, Demian Symonenko, Fedir Khrytsenko, Antin Ivanytskyi, Semen Vlasko, and Terentii Parkhomenko paid for their studies by turning over what they had earned begging. Borzhkovskii reports that this was the system used in the Podile region, and E. Krist says the same for the Kharkiv region. In both areas, the master and apprentice could also agree to the payment of a cash sum in lieu of begging services. Ivan Petryk paid a combination of a six-ruble fee and the proceeds of his begging. Ananii Homyniuk paid ten rubles. Nikifor Dudka and Evdokim Mokroviz each paid twenty rubles annually. Babenko paid twelve rubles a year to his master.[65]

In return, the master taught the pupil and, presumably, lost begging time while doing so; that is, while he was at home teaching his apprentices, he was not out performing and making money. The master provided minimal upkeep: food, shelter, and possibly also clothing and a free guide. In some regions, the master paid for the initiation rite. If the aspirant failed and had to retake an initiation test, the cost of the second initiation was then his responsibility.[66] In some regions, when a pupil completed initiation, the master gave him his first musical instrument. Babenko, for example, got a *lira*, which would have cost about four or five rubles. In the material examined by Drahomanov, the master gave his apprentice a *bandura*, an even more expensive instrument.[67] Even where the master did buy the *lira* and pay for the initiation, however, the cost to the master was much less than the apprentice's fee. Furthermore, if a master felt that he had lost money on an apprentice because the young man had been ill and unable to beg, he could keep him beyond the contracted period and send him out to make up for lost revenue.[68]

The fees apprentices paid were neither enormous nor insignificant. Minstrel earnings were approximately two hundred rubles or *karbovantsi* a year, supplemented by pay in kind: gifts of grain, other foodstuffs, and clothing. A ten- to twenty-ruble annual fee from an apprentice, especially if a master had several apprentices at once, was quite significant. The begging services of an apprentice were probably significant also. Mefodii's pupils earned so much in one week that a cart was needed to deliver it back to the school, and these earnings sustained thirty students, plus the staff and Mefodii and his family. If not exactly lucrative, having apprentices was at least profitable. It is, therefore, not surprising that minstrels tried to recruit apprentices. Mykhailo Kravchenko approached a particularly talented boy, only to have the boy's father refuse for fear of police persecution.[69] Kharkiv makes the general statement that minstrels could offer their services as teachers, and quotes what Tsarko said to Iakiv Bakhmut, "Come, I will teach you to earn your bread, to make a living."[70] Perhaps the most striking proof of the benefits of having an apprentice is Iakiv Zlatarskyi's autobiography. Zlatarskyi was apprenticed at a very early age to a man who, it turned out, did not have a teacher's credentials. As Zlatarskyi was travelling with this man, they ran into another minstrel, who literally stole the boy from his first teacher. He got the man drunk, walked out to Zlatarskyi, who had been left to wait outside, picked him up, and took him home. When Zlatarskyi's first master showed up to protest, the second pointed to his lack of credentials and let the boy choose. Zlatarskyi decided to stay with the man who stole him.[71] If an apprentice was worth stealing and then contesting, he must have been a valuable commodity.

Apprenticeship did not exist solely to make money for established minstrels, though minstrels like Veresai may have accused their masters of using it for that purpose.[72] In all aspects of minstrelsy, practical and lofty considerations existed side by side, and apprenticeship also served to insure the integrity of the profession. Masters tried to provide moral as well as musical and practical instruction. Something similar can be said about the initiation rite. This was a most serious and solemn occasion; yet, at least certain descriptions of the initiation show that it was a way for people already in the guild to collect an entry fee from those wishing to join them. The *vyzvilka* and *odklynshchyna* appear as money-making affairs most clearly in manuscripts. Perhaps openness about a desire to capitalize on the initiation was most apparent in Poltava, the region where Martynovych collected the fullest initiation descriptions, and perhaps minstrels hid the practical aspects of their rites from other collectors. In any case, Martynovych's informants state that the initiate must give gifts to his master and various other guild officials in addition to the apprenticeship fee. Mykolai Doroshenko gives the fullest list: a short coat (*chumarka*) for the master; a belt or a kerchief for the person who held the office of master's helper during the initiation rite; the same, only of lesser quality for the treasurer; and again, the same, only of lesser quality still, for the junior officer (*pidmolozhii*). Doroshenko even states that one is expected to spend about fifty kopecks on the master's helper, thirty to forty kopecks on the treasurer, and twenty-five kopecks on the smallest gifts.[73] Petro Dryhavka says that the aspirant must give gifts to all of the guild officers present at an initiation rite and that there should also be a gift for the master's wife because:

> She arose early in the morning,
> She cared for the apprentice and fed him;
> Thus she earned herself a gift and his thanks.[74]

According to Vasyl Hovtan, the appropriate gift for the master is a pair of pants or a shirt.[75] Another informant states that the gift for the master should be a hat, boots, pants, or a jacket; all the others in attendance receive the gift of food.[76] Gifts are not widely attested outside manuscript sources and may have been a relatively recent addition to the initiation ritual. This is what Fedir Hrytsenko told Martynovych in 1885. He considered gifts a bad idea because those receiving them did not always use them wisely. His own master, Nazarenko, supposedly took the hat that Hrytsenko gave him as an initiation gift and sold it for drink the first time he was in a city. A hat or boots, he claimed, was nonetheless the appropriate gift to give a master.[77]

In addition to the gifts for the master and other officers, the apprentice was obliged to treat the entire brotherhood to food and drink. In the verbal part of the Poltava rite, the apprentice asks for permission to join the guild, and the gathering of established minstrels responds that to do so, he must treat them to forty pails, or in some variants, a forty-liter barrel of vodka. The request is formulaic rather than real, and the amount is quickly negotiated down to a quarter of a pail of vodka. The vodka was seen as a payment, at least at some level, because the "fee" for the rite that permitted a man to enter the guild (*odklynshchyna*) was a quarter of a pail, while the rite that conferred teacher status and permitted accepting apprentices (*vyzvilka*) cost a half pail.[78] Presumably a man paid more for the more lucrative position. Initiation as payment is not as clear in other sources, but even in these there is mention of the apprentice having to save up some money to be able to pay for his initiation. Zlatarskyi gives the cost of initiation as part of the total cost of becoming a minstrel:

> For an initiation rite, the pupil needs two or two and a half gold pieces. If the initiation is being done very cheaply, then you need about one quarter of that. As for the *lira*, it depends on the circumstances. Sometimes the master will give the new *lirnyk* his own *lira*, sometimes he will have to buy it for himself. A good *lira* costs four or five gold pieces. A bad one costs two, maybe even one and a half. You commission a carpenter to make a *lira*, and so that he will know how to do it, you give him an "example" to follow.[79]

In the few remaining mentions of initiation, its connection to payment is less direct, but the informant almost invariably specifies for the collector the amount of money that going through the rite would require.[80]

Separation of the Personal and the Professional

To have a successful personal life, to function well within the family and the community, a minstrel had to separate his professional life from what he did at home. As Kharkiv reports, a *lirnyk* cannot beg among people who know him. He will never beg in his own village. If he lives in a larger town, he can beg in that town, but must avoid his neighbors. Hryhorii Kolisnyk told Kharkiv, "How can you go (and beg) among people you know?" Varion Honchar said,

> How can I beg at his house, when I paid him a visit yesterday, or he visited me? The farther away you go, the more boldly you can gather your livelihood.[81]

This articulates beautifully the tension between the normalcy of minstrel family life and the marginality of minstrelsy as a profession. Someone who worked as a minstrel could not be treated also as a normal person, and so those who saw a minstrel's family life could not deal with him as a professional. The ordinary life of a minstrel existed, but had to be separated from the professional. This is perhaps why minstrels abandoned their musical instruments as soon as they got home, something that scholars who wanted these men to be interested in minstrelsy for art's sake so often deride.[82]

Avoiding one's neighbors had a practical side of its own. A man could not work in his own village, but this does not mean that all minstrels were barred from performing there. What probably happened was that *kobzari* and *lirnyky* provided shelter in their homes for fellow minstrels. Printed sources contain virtually no discussion of where minstrels stayed when they went on their travels, but a bit of information is available in manuscript. While a hospice system functioned, minstrels probably stayed in these. In more recent times, minstrels stayed in hostels, which were available in big cities and where there might be a special section for wandering *kobzari* and *lirnyky*. A man staying in such a hostel would pay three to five kopecks, or give the owner some of the bread or flour he had collected.[83] Where there were no hostels or hospices—basically, everywhere outside the cities— minstrels stayed in homes, most often the homes of their fellow guild members. Martynovych does not give his source, but quotes a villager describing his neighbor's house as a place where *kobzari* routinely spent the night.[84] We noted earlier that Pavlo Kulyk rented to fellow minstrels.[85]

Kharkiv sums the situation up well by saying that the minstrel's neighbors knew him as an ordinary man and were often ignorant of the fact that he was a minstrel. Professional life was separate. As much as a minstrel was a professional musician, he was often ignorant of village songs. Sometimes he would know fellow minstrels living in other villages better than he would know his neighbors.[86] Perhaps the great virtue of the guild system was that it provided a home and a community for activities that were absolutely necessary to survival but that could find no home in the Ukrainian village. The nature of village life, with its emphasis on work, demanded that a blind person seek an alternate occupation. This same village made it difficult to be both its citizen and a professional. Minstrel guilds responded to this problem by offering a well-articulated structure for the professional part of life.

Chapter 6

Apprenticeship, Training, and Initiation

Minstrel guilds protected the boundaries of the profession and carefully controlled who crossed these boundaries and how. From their point of view, apprenticeship was the gateway to professional status, a gateway that needed to be jealously guarded. From the point of view of a blind child and his family, apprenticeship was the automatic reaction to disability. Sending a blind child to a master minstrel was what one did when it was impossible to care for him or her at home. Yet this reaction to blindness was very much in the interest of the minstrel guilds. It served their purpose to make sure that apprenticeship was seen as the only possible avenue for a blind person. Apprenticeship that drew in relatively large numbers of people was a good way of insuring an adequate talent pool, and until well into the twentieth century, apprenticeship was indeed universal. As Iakiv Zlatarskyi told Volodymyr Hnatiuk, there are no false *lirnyky*, meaning those who have not served an apprenticeship; there never were and there cannot be any. This is carefully monitored by the *lirnyky* themselves so that the others will not "spoil their piece of bread" for them.[1]

Apprenticeship was so critical that, when a man wanted to establish his credentials as a minstrel, proof of apprenticeship was more important than the ability to sing and play properly. Oleksandr Dimnych, Valerian Borzhkovskii's sighted, would-be *lirnyk*, could play and sing well enough. He had served as a guide to a number of minstrels, perhaps intentionally circumventing apprenticeship because he knew that his sightedness barred him from it. While working as a guide, he had learned both the words and the music of the standard minstrel repertory. By the time Borzhkovskii met him, his knowledge was comparable to that of many practicing, accredited professional performers and probably superior to that of some. But this was not acceptable to the true, guild-affiliated *lirnyky*. As they told

Borzhkovskii, they could overlook Dimnych's sightedness because, as an orphan, he was disabled in a sense. They were also favorably disposed toward him because he had served as a guide for virtually no pay. Apprenticeship was a must, regardless. If Dimnych wanted to be a *lirnyk*, he had to "submit" to a master, if not for the full term of a normal apprenticeship, then at least for a part of it. This is exactly what Dimnych eventually did; he became the pupil of Andrii Dovhaliuk, one of the other *lirnyky* interviewed by Borzhkovskii.[2]

Punishments were inflicted on men who acted like minstrels without going through the requisite apprenticeship and initiation. These included fines, beatings, confiscation of the musical instrument, and even prohibitions against receiving training in the future. Petro Dryhavka added that a man who performed without completing his apprenticeship risked having the strings of his musical instrument torn.[3] Always, the reason for punishing a man was his failure to secure the blessing of the minstrel brotherhood "to wander in all four directions"; it was not inability to sing or poor instrumental skills.[4] Ostap Veresai did not doubt his own musical ability. Nonetheless, he was worried when the last of his masters told him to leave because he had nothing more to learn.

> "What am I going to do, master?" he asked.
> "Take care of yourself as best as you know how," was the answer.
> "But what if the others attack me, saying that I have not completed the full term?" he pleaded.
> "No," the master said. "No one will attack you, and if they do, then send them to me; I'll take the responsibility. As for you, don't go be an apprentice again; just leave it as it is; use what God gave you."[5]

Although Veresai and some of his biographers claim that he avoided completing a full apprenticeship period and undergoing initiation because of his talent, it seems more likely that the reason was his quirky personality.[6] His statements given above indicate that his last master was getting rid of a troublesome pupil rather than bowing before superior talent. Certainly, as someone who had not been properly trained and initiated, Veresai did not have high status within the profession. Fellow *kobzari* called Veresai "Labza," a disrespectful nickname meaning something like "slob." Furthermore, they were amazed and annoyed at the attention Veresai received from the scholarly community. Opanas Slastion reported that at a meeting in Lokhvytsia, the assembled *kobzari* were incensed that Labza was the minstrel taken to St. Petersburg rather than someone whom they considered worthy and truly representative of the profession.[7] In St. Petersburg, Veresai sang before the tsar, who rewarded him with a gold cigarette case engraved with the royal insignia. Veresai always carried the cigarette case with him and used it as his "passport," a handy replacement for the credentials he would have received had he completed his apprenticeship.[8]

The Greeting Formula as Proof of Apprenticeship

Veresai had reason to worry when he was expelled by his master, because minstrels tested all fellow performers to make sure that they had completed training and passed their initiation rites. Sometimes they did so directly, questioning a man whom they did not know about his status and demanding the name of his teacher.[9] More often, the test took the form of long, formulaic greetings. These greetings are not termed "tests" and were viewed more as minstrel protocol, a formal obligatory act with perhaps some magical power. But the fact that these formulaic greetings were taught at the very end of the apprenticeship period insured that someone who could recite them had been through the full course of training. Furthermore, a minstrel was obliged to recite the greetings every time he met a fellow minstrel, thus demonstrating his knowledge of something that could only have come from apprenticeship.

In his account of a religious festival, Borzhkovskii gives a description of minstrel greetings and attests that minstrels consider it necessary to repeat these to each of their fellows. When minstrels meet, he says, they first wish each other a good day, using the secret language (*lebiiska mova*). Then, still speaking in secret language, they ask each other for permission to bow before the saints and honor the holidays. These requests to bow are followed by a long listing of saints and holidays, recitations which could go on for quite some time. Borzhkovskii adds that the minstrels themselves found this tedious, especially at a religious festival, where there would be many *lirnyky* and the formula would have to be repeated again and again.[10] The purpose of the formulaic greetings was not so much religious efficacy as the testing of those participating, making sure they had completed their apprenticeships. The fact that a *lirnyk* would recite the entire greeting every time he encountered one of his fellows, and would do so even at a religious festival, where the number of such recitations bordered on the extreme, confirms the importance assigned to it.

In Galicia, the greeting formula was quite different from the one described by Borzhkovskii, but equally complicated. It too was demanded of all minstrels and served a double function. The western version of a minstrel greeting was recorded by Volodymyr Hnatiuk, from the *lirnyk* Iakiv Zlatarskyi. According to Zlatarskyi, when two *lirnyky* meet, the younger man addresses the older one and says, "Praise be to God!" He then takes the older man by the hand and continues:

> May God grant you a good day. May you sleep well; may you rest well; may you live well and prosper in the morning and during the day. May fortune shine upon you along your paths, along your roads; may you find hospitality and kindness and respect and companionship, collegiality, just as our dear Lord did. What good things have happened to you in your travels? Are your wife and children well? Are all those in your household who have been baptized in good health: your sisters and your brothers, your father and your mother; are they still living; are they in good health? Are you yourself in good health? May God grant you good fortune at religious festivals and at fairs. God will grant you health and prosperity while Christ shows the path and the way!

Zlatarskyi adds that if the man being addressed is not married, the part about the wife and children is omitted. Once the greeting is completed, the elder man returns the good wishes by reciting the same formula. Like the material recorded by Borzhkovskii, this greeting expressed good wishes and also functioned as a test. It is no coincidence that the younger man had to display his knowledge first, since it would be more likely that he might not be a fully accredited *lirnyk*. It was he who needed to prove himself by producing the greeting, with no chance to imitate the example of his elder.

Zlatarskyi stresses that only *lirnyky* who have completed their apprenticeships are allowed to recite the full greeting. Men who are still apprenticed are supposed to say only "May God grant you good fortune" to fellow apprentices and fully accredited minstrels alike.[11] Thus, apprentices had their own verbal token, a short formula that was probably itself a means of establishing legitimacy, in this case showing that a man was an apprentice, with the right to travel and beg on his master's behalf. In western Ukraine, too, apprentices were not only prohibited from reciting the full formula but kept from knowing it until they had served virtually their entire term. The prohibition on the use of the full formula, plus the enforcement of the prohibition by teaching this material at the very end of training, confirms that it served not just to convey good wishes but also to test whether a man had completed his apprenticeship.

Porfyrii Martynovych's materials also show a distinction between the greeting used by a novice to address a full-fledged member of the profession and the greeting master minstrels used to address each other. Martynovych gives a bit of information not found elsewhere about the secret names for the days of the week. Intrigued by these names, which exist for every day except Sunday, he collected them from a number of minstrels. Martynovych learned that when two minstrels meet, they wish each other a good day using the appropriate secret name. Presumably, failure to use the proper word would indicate that someone was not a trained minstrel.[12]

It is instructive to contrast what Ukrainian tradition demanded of two minstrels meeting in their travels with what is considered requisite in other traditions. In Turkey, for example, when two minstrels meet, honor demands a verbal duel. Usually the younger or less established man challenges his elder with a poetic insult. The insult takes the form of a four-line stanza, with one of a certain possible set of meters, and an *aaba* rhyme scheme, sung to the accompaniment of the Turkish minstrel instrument, the *saz*. The man challenged must sing a return insult, couching it in a four-line stanza of the same meter, but now with a *bbcb* rhyme pattern, also to the accompaniment of a *saz*. The challenger must then reply with a stanza rhymed *ccdc*. The exchange continues until one man is unable to answer the other in the proper form. The Turkish minstrel contest, called *tashlama*, tests improvisational ability and verbal and musical mastery. A man establishes his credentials on the basis of his artistry. While he may be asked about his master in polite conversation, a Turkish minstrel does not need to provide proof of apprenticeship to be accepted as a performer. He will be accepted or rejected on his performance alone.[13] The contrast between the Turkish tradition and the Ukrainian one underscores the fact that issues other than the ability to sing and play were important to Ukrainian minstrels.

Pressure to Learn and to Complete Apprenticeship Quickly

While artistry may not have been the way to establish credentials as a minstrel in Ukraine, it was nonetheless important to both the audience and the performer. At a religious festival, for example, the better singers attracted larger audiences and thus earned more money. People tended to be more generous when the singing pleased them, as noted in the descriptions of Hrytsenko-Kholodnyi's virtuosity.[14] Also, when minstrels were hired for weddings and other occasions, the better performers would be the first hired and would command better pay.

To a certain degree, the public would support a minstrel regardless of ability, giving him alms for religious reasons rather than for his singing. Borzhkovskii says that at the religious festival in Brailiv, everyone who performed some sort of religious service, be it singing songs like the *lirnyky*, or reading the Scripture, or reciting it from memory, got something.[15] Oleksii Masliukov and Iahor Okhremenko both told Oleksandr Malynka that it did not seem to matter what they did or how well they did it: the public gave them alms, regardless. Both played the *lira* in addition to just singing and begging because the instrument made their life more bearable, not because it improved their income. Okhremenko, not an especially good artist, according to Malynka, was adamant that artistry did not matter.[16]

The tension between support for the sake of charity, regardless of artistic merit, and payment for artistic services is, of course, at the heart of the minstrel dilemma. Only people who needed charity were supposed to become minstrels, and yet minstrelsy meant precisely engaging in a money-making activity instead of relying on alms alone. Minstrelsy was an escape from the necessity of requesting alms on the basis of disability. It was a way to earn the kind of money and respect that beggars could not hope for. Minstrels could choose to emphasize either charity or artistry, and there was room in the profession for people like Masliukov and Okhremenko. Yet there were few who emphasized charity solely. Artistry was important to most minstrels. Ivan Kravchenko-Kriukovskyi lamented the adverse effect age had on his voice and his memory. He also resented the fact that making harnesses, especially plaiting ropes out of hemp, damaged his finger tips, ruining the sensitivity of his touch and the quality of his *bandura* playing.[17] Veresai complained about the loss of his voice with age:

> as the voice goes, so goes the song: when my voice isn't good—no! the words don't fall together. But when I am in proper voice, then, even if the words are sometimes not all that good, still the song is good regardless.[18]

Besides being able to sing and play well, it was important to know many songs, because these were a commodity of sorts, and a larger repertory meant better earning potential. Minstrels bought songs from each other. In certain areas there was a set, or at least customary, fee for a song request. According to Borzhkovskii, if someone in a *lirnyk*'s audience asked for a specific song, he paid three kopecks.[19] Needless to say, a minstrel who knew more songs and could meet more requests did better financially.

Perhaps the most interesting remarks are those where performers talk about the tricks they use to get more money. Bilokrypatskyi told Kharkiv that if he could manipulate the listeners' emotions, he would get more out of them. "I play in such a way as to make people cry," he said, "then they pay me with a towel."[20] Varion Honchar said something similar. If someone hears the right kind of music, a song with sorrow (*zhalib*), then:

> A person will listen to your songs and say, that's the way it is. If the song digs into his heart, then his heart will be predisposed toward you. But if you play something cheerful, something for the children . . . then he will simply say: "Look, kids, see how the man plays." And he will just sit down and rest

a bit. But the other way (with sorrow)—well, before you know it, they'll give you some bread, or some grain, or some bacon, or some flour.[21]

Ivha Khrystenko told Kharkiv:

If she (the mistress of the house) hears it through, hears the song about St. Michael, then tears come to her eyes; then she cries and she gives you everything that she has . . . and then I stop.[22]

It may be significant that all of the available quotes concerning manipulating audience emotion for better pay come from Kharkiv, which may indicate personal bias. Since Kharkiv worked in this century, they may also reflect the deterioration of the tradition. Generally, minstrels feared being accused of greed, and demanded from their fellows at least a show of piety and disinterest in money. Thus, admitting concern with audience payment, especially to an outsider such as a scholar, sounds suspect or symptomatic of decline. Kharkiv's bias and possible degeneration of the tradition aside, ability to manipulate emotion implies considerable artistic skill. All in all, it was to the minstrel's advantage to be as adept as possible, to have a large repertory, to sing and play well.

The place to learn how to sing and to play was apprenticeship. At the same time, apprenticeship was the gateway to the profession, the place where those who were already minstrels collected a toll from those who wanted to join their ranks. This created an inherent tension between master and apprentice. For the trainee, apprenticeship was his chance to learn as much as possible, while for the master and the brotherhood as a whole, apprenticeship was the place to collect dues, an initiation fee which a young man paid for the right to make money as a minstrel. Zlatarskyi's autobiography is a good example of the tension between master and apprentice, between apprenticeship as a way to teach the next generation of minstrels and apprenticeship as the place to make money from this future generation. It shows that established minstrels viewed him as a valuable commodity, valuable enough to steal him from each other:

I was born here in Zhyzhnomyr (a mispronunciation of Zhytomyr), blind. When I was still little, they sent me to a school (for *lirnyky*) to Iazlyvtsi, to Iasyk Iakymovych, who has since died. But I was with him for only two weeks. Then they gave me to some sort of vagabond in Lashkovytsi, called Hryts Tymniuk. I wandered with him all the way to Sadagura. There Hryts Tymniuk met Ivan Lukavytskyi from Stanyhora—and the two started to drink and sent me out to the street to beg. At that time I was eight years old. When they had gotten drunk, Lukavytskyi left Tymniuk in the inn and came outside. He came up to me and said, "Let's go, my son; your master said for you to come into the inn and get a drink of vodka." (They have both since died.) I got up, he grabbed me in his arms, threw me in a Jew's cart, got in himself, and rode with me to his house. Then he took me in his arms and carried me into the house; they gave me something to eat, and I was thinking that I didn't know what it is I was eating. After a while they told me to get up on the stove and go to sleep. In the evening, I'm asleep, and Tymniuk comes to the house with his wife and says, "Why did you trick me like that, brother?" The other one answers, "What did I do to you?" "Why did you steal my boy?"[23] "I did not steal him. I had every right to take him. You know that you don't have permission to keep a boy (because he was not a properly trained *lirnyk*)." Then they started to drink. They all got up early and that one got ready to leave Lukavytskyi, and said to me: "Get ready to go, son." And the other one said, "There is no need to get ready; stay here." And with that, they parted, and I stayed. There they dressed me in clean rags; there they washed and cleaned me, because when they put their hands down my back, they would pull up whole handfuls of lice. And there I stayed some two years. Then I understood that this was bad for me, because they beat me a lot and didn't teach me much—because he himself knew little—and Ivan Pokhovych from Sadagura took me in. He had me listed as his in the records; and I stayed with him two years also (and at home they had no idea where I was). There life was good for me, but then he died. Then Vasyl Hrytsko took me to Chornovitsi (a mispronunciation of Chernivtsi); he took me for a period of six years, but I stayed with him half a year. I didn't know where I was, in what country; I just knew the name of the city. And then a man came from Zalishchyky Velyki, a man named Filip Nykolik. He was studying himself, then, like me, but he had almost finished his training and I hadn't— and he said to me: run away from here, because you are in a foreign country. And I fled with him to Zalishchyky Velyki. When I arrived in Zalishchyky, I immediately reached an agreement with Ivan Khalus—he was from Tovstyi, from the Kitsman region. He was from Bukovyna by birth, living in Zalishchyky. I stayed with him three years and six weeks. Then I passed my test on Epiphany and went into the world. I went to Chornovitsi, Syrei, Sochavi, Humori, Dorni, Kimpoliunysi, Kachyky—and then I traveled along the Russian border—to Buviym in Okopa, Milnytsia, Kudryntsi, Skali, Borshchev, Husiatyni, to all of the villages that are in that area. Then I turned around and went home, thinking that they did not know how I am or any- thing. I came home (to Zhytomyr), I got married (I am completely blind and my wife is blind in one eye, and so everyone jokes: two people, one eye) and now I am settled down and I have started taking on apprentices, as it is supposed to be, and I have already had three pass their initiation tests.[24]

In the conflict between the interests of the pupil and the interests of the master, the institution of apprenticeship protected mostly the latter. As Zlatarskyi reported and Kharkiv confirmed, the master could lengthen the time of service if he felt that he had lost money on his charge.[25] Several sources state that a man must continue to honor and financially reward his master even after he has finished his apprenticeship and been initiated into the ranks of minstrels. The younger Humeniuk told Kvitka that a minstrel was supposed to bring his former master gifts at Christmas and at Easter, and Dovhaliuk told Borzhkovskii that the Easter gift was a special bread called a *kalach*, while the Christmas gift was a contribution to the meatless Christmas Eve supper.[26]

The apprentice did have some power over the master, however. According to the younger Humeniuk, a master minstrel had to accept all youngsters who wanted to become apprentices, no matter how talented or inept. During the initiation ceremony, the apprentice could speak against his master before the assembly of guild elders and could criticize him for failure to offer proper instruction.[27] Humeniuk's statement is unique, and comes from the son of a *lirnyk*, rather than from the minstrel himself. Other means existed to punish an errant master. An apprentice could not turn over all that he collected when he went begging. In the Kharkiv manuscripts, one apprentice actually boasts that he managed to hide some of the begging proceeds and keep them for himself.[28] This statement may be suspect, considering the unusual emphasis on money in the Kharkiv manuscripts. Most minstrels claim to have scrupulously fulfilled their financial obligations. Suspicions of cheating are usually directed at non-minstrels: the sighted guide, for example, who had the advantage of being able to see and of not being bound by minstrel codes of honor.

The surest protection a young man had against his master was his freedom of movement, and leaving was one resolution to the master-apprentice conflict. The younger Humeniuk contends that an apprentice could leave his master only if the latter died, but actual accounts of apprenticeship show that pupils switched teachers relatively freely.[29] Zlatarskyi, in the account given above, served six masters. Ostap Veresai served three.[30] Demian Symonenko, Mykhailo Kravchenko, and Terentii Parkhomenko had two.[31] Walking out on the master seems to have been a common recourse, when payment was in service. Zlatarskyi and Veresai, both of whom switched teachers more than the norm, paid only by turning over the proceeds of their begging to the master. Men who were paying cash or a combination of cash plus service, like the *lirnyk* Ivan Petryk, switched less.[32] Nonetheless, even with a cash investment, the apprentice seemed to have little to lose by leaving, since the master-apprentice relationship was more advantageous to the former. All pupils wanted to get out of the apprenticeship as soon as possible, even though knowledge acquired after apprenticeship came at a price. Ivan Kravchenko-Kriukovskyi had to pay twenty-five kopecks for each song he learned from Havrylo Vovk, and a whole ruble for "Samiilo Kishka," a long and complicate epic song that he particularly wanted to have in his repertory.[33] It would seem that a pupil would prefer to acquire such songs during the obligatory apprenticeship. But apprentices wanted their freedom as soon as they could get it, and Zlatarskyi says that if a man is paying for his training, it is his responsibility to complete the apprenticeship as quickly as possible.[34] He says nothing about an apprentice's responsibility to learn as much as possible during training. Even describing his own apprenticeship, he merely complains that certain of his masters beat him much and taught him little; he does not claim to have actively sought knowledge.

The Stages of Training

Minstrels and pupils alike viewed apprenticeship more as dues paid to men already in the profession than as the training ground of future minstrels. As a result, there is little information about what the master taught and what the pupil learned. Still, a great deal can be reconstructed by putting all of the oblique references to training together with the few available direct descriptions of apprenticeship. From these, we can abstract five stages of the training process:

(1) instruction in handling the practical aspects of life as a blind person
(2) the begging song and prayers—apparently prayers for the audience and their dead relatives, which are often given as part of the begging song performance
(3) the core of minstrelsy, the songs, usually meaning song texts, often without musical accompaniment
(4) music, meaning the playing of a musical instrument
(5) the secret language and minstrel customs, presumably items such as the greeting formula.

These steps are most clearly stated in Zlatarskyi's account of apprenticeship, though stage one is omitted. Oleksa Horbach's account, also describing the *lirnyky* of Western Ukraine, accords with Zlatarskyi's. His sources confirm that if a pupil is going to avoid paying cash and compensate the master with service only, then the minimum length of apprenticeship is three years. This is also the minimum amount of time needed for musical training. One year is required to learn prayers and the begging song. During the second year, the master teaches the pupil regular songs, meaning religious verses. During the third year, he teaches him how to play the *lira*, and toward the end, the special language of minstrels (*lebiiska mova*).[35] Borzhkovskii, speaking about *lirnyky* in Eastern Ukraine, also says that the begging song is learned first, before any other kind of song, but tells us nothing else about training.[36]

To look at the various stages in more detail, we need to combine the above data with those available in other sources. Zlatarskyi's information on practical training is the most elliptical part of his apprenticeship description. He merely states that an older apprentice, one in his twenties, "is already wise; he doesn't need it; he has already matured."[37] Studynskyi contends that the harsh life of the minstrel schools equips the novice for the demands of professional life; the suffering the boys experience in school teaches them the endurance they will need and develops the character and morals suitable to church affiliation.[38] Mikhail Speranskii confirms that a master teaches an apprentice how to properly request and offer thanks for alms, how to conduct himself, and how to maintain virtue, although he does not claim that he does so by making the boy suffer.[39]

Explicit indications that learning to live with disability was part of apprenticeship can be found in the Kharkiv and Martynovych manuscripts. According to Kharkiv, when Tsarko approached Bakhmut and offered to take him as an apprentice, he said, "I'll teach you how to beg for your bread, how to live." Varion Honchar told Kharkiv that a master teaches his pupil how to run his household, as well as the politeness and proper behavior he will need in his dealings with the public. When the pupil begins to travel with the master, the master shows him how and where to go and how to travel without a guide, should that become necessary. "When you are finished," Honchar told Kharkiv, "you know how and where to beg, how to enter a home and leave it properly, how to run your affairs."[40]

Martynovych collected interesting data on practical training, including several first-hand accounts from minstrels. The most detailed were recorded from Petro Dryhavka in 1913 and from Ivan Kuchuhura-Kucherenko in 1929.[41] While the manuscripts are difficult to follow, they nonetheless yield invaluable information. They prove that there was indeed a sense of discreet units or stages of instruction, which Dryhavka calls lessons (*nauky*) and Kuchuhura-Kucherenko calls books (*knyhi*). Another manuscript also notes that there are ten lessons of the *lirnyky*; unfortunately, it gives no description of these lessons.[42]

From the Martynovych manuscripts we learn that the first things taught are the basics of begging, the minimum a boy would need in order to be able to go about and ask for food. Dryhavka notes that this is the Lord's Prayer, followed by a song praising Christ, which is called "Christ, My Beloved" (*Isuse mii preliubeznyi*), and then a begging song.[43] Kuchuhura-Kucherenko notes only a begging song.[44] Both men give practical advice on how to properly enter the home of a potential alms-giver; how to address the host and his family, including the children; how to thank the family upon leaving, this time mentioning not only family members in the room but also their deceased relatives, who are "present in spirit."[45] There is advice against drinking; an admonition for a youth to keep to himself, even when staying overnight in the company of other minstrels; practical hints about avoiding the police, the clergy, and city officials.[46] Kuchuhura-Kucherenko talks about learning to "see" when one has no eyes:

> And my master said to me: "You will see,
> My dear boy,
> Even though we do not see with eyes,
> I tell you, you will see.
> We have to look, my friend,
> Not with eyes of the flesh, because we do not have those,
> But with spiritual ones, we have to feel;
> We have to sense;
> We have to feel with those eyes,
> Which sighted people do not see with,
> And most of them don't know about these,
> And a long, long time will come to pass,
> And maybe a whole age will pass,
> Before sighted people find out,
> And will be able to think the thoughts of the blind.
> And all of this is the same sort of ability to feel,
> Which they, too, possess."[47]

After practical matters, came instruction in the art of minstrelsy. The line between practical and artistic training is hard to draw, though both minstrels and scholars tried. Right at the boundary are prayers and the begging song. In the material collected by Martynovych, the prayers and the begging song are part of practical training, though they are obviously texts. They were probably placed here because they, along with information on how to live, were the minimum knowledge that a blind person would need to survive. In Zlatarskyi, the begging song is part of artistic training, probably because it was seen as an essential component of a multi-song minstrel performance.[48] But whether viewed as practical or artistic, it is clear that the begging song was the next step in training. No source mentions how the begging song was taught, and the only information we have is Zlatarskyi's comment that the process took about a year.[49] We can only surmise that this process was similar to that used for teaching other verses (see chapter 7).

After the begging song, the apprentice learned the other songs of the profession. This was the heart of the training process, the part that according to Zlatarskyi, took the longest. Learning songs was what an apprentice wanted most out of training and the songs were what truly made him a minstrel. Although the *kobzari* and *lirnyky* were named after their instruments, it was their songs rather than the *bandura* or *lira* that distinguished them from ordinary beggars. It is little wonder that Filaret Kolessa and others pointed out the dominance of words over music, particularly over instrumental accompaniment.[50] It is also not surprising that religious, historical, and epic song texts comprise the bulk of the apprenticeship material Martynovych collected from Dryhavka and Kuchuhura-Kucherenko.[51]

After songs, minstrels learned how to play a musical instrument. This, according to Zlatarskyi, can take as little as two months, sometimes even less if the pupil is particularly adept.[52] We know more about the teaching of *lira* play than about other aspects of apprenticeship. The *lira* is a hurdy-gurdy, a violin-shaped box with a crank-driven wheel at one end, three strings which run its length, and keys. The wheel is turned with the right hand and rubs the strings, producing a continuous drone. The melody is played with the left hand by lifting the keys which depress one of the strings. As the keys fall back into place, they make a clanging noise which gives the *lira* some additional percussion instrument qualities and makes it a good instrument to play at dances and weddings.[53] True virtuosity on the *lira* demands control over the wheel as well as the keys. Thus, according to Kharkiv, the master teaches the proper turning of the crank first. Then he combines the fingering of the keys with the turning technique. To teach the keys, the master either sits in back of the pupil and puts his left hand on the pupil's left hand, or he calls out to him which key to lift. A few masters, like the ones who taught Hrytsko Oblychenko, Babenko, and Kutsyi, tied their apprentices' fingers to their own to teach them the proper fingering. Kharkiv says that the various dance tunes, such as "Choboty," "Kamarinskyi," and "Melnyk," are taught first because they are the easiest to play. The ultimate goal was to learn religious songs, both the words and the music that goes with them.[54]

There is some information about how *kobzari* taught the *bandura*, but it is less abundant than information about the *lira*. Makar Khrystenko told Kharkiv that his master, Pavlo Hashchenko, taught him the layout of the *bandura* strings, then some easy dance melodies. Hashchenko was a good performer, and references to him appear in a number of sources, but he was apparently not a good teacher. Khrystenko was unhappy with what he learned because he could play with one finger only and had mastered only two or three religious songs. He improved both his instrumental skills and his repertory on his own, after he had completed his apprenticeship.[55]

Information about the last stage of training is as scant. We have dictionaries of the secret language of minstrels and discussions of its origin and function, but there is little commentary on the process of secret language learning. Dryhavka and Kuchuhura-Kucherenko gave Martynovych extensive samples of the secret language but did not tell him how they had acquired it.[56] The last stage of training also included formulaic greetings and other minstrel protocol, which Zlatarskyi calls the "peculiarities" (*kavalki*) of the *lirnyky*, and which was called customs (*zvychaii*) in Eastern Ukraine. Again, we know little about how these were taught.

Beggars and Minstrels: Shared Repertory

Apprentices may not have thought much of apprenticeship and may have wanted to get out of it as quickly as possible, but it was actually a very wise and flexible institution that accommodated the needs of the children being taught. It was in apprenticeship that the dilemma of talent was resolved. Apprenticeship was so structured that it could indeed take all blind children, regardless of talent, and offer them at least some instruction. Not all apprentices could complete all of the stages and emerge as minstrels, but each child could go through at least some of them. A child without the talent or the inclination for minstrelsy could leave after stage two, knowing how to handle life as a blind person and being able to perform the begging song and prayers. Such a child had basic survival training. A talented child could complete the full course of training and emerge as an artist.

There is evidence that at least in the past, many, if not all, disabled children entered apprenticeship. The items taught to minstrels first, the begging song and prayers, were known far beyond the sphere of minstrelsy. Virtually all beggars knew the begging song and could recite the prayer for the audience and their ancestors that normally went with it. V. Danyliv and V. Shchepotev recorded these from beggars at the Lavra monastery in Kiev and elsewhere. The quality varied from beggar to beggar. Some songs and prayers were quite long and elaborate, like those of minstrels; others were short and simple.[57] If a beggar's repertory was identical to the first thing taught to minstrels, it would be logical to hypothesize that at least at some point in the past, beggars and minstrels learned this material together.

It is possible that all disabled children studied together at the large schools described by Studynskyi. These catered to a varied clientele, even sighted amateurs. When they were numerous, they might well have taken in all children, training each to as high a level as he or she could go. From these schools some would emerge as beggars; others would go on to be minstrels. Universal training of the disabled would explain why children were apprenticed to minstrels simply because they were blind. Such disregard for talent could be possible if adjustments for musical and verbal ability were made in the schools, during the process of training. In all likelihood, when the system of common training broke down and the schools disappeared, beggars and minstrels began to train separately, but many links between them remained, one being the overlap in repertory.

In connection with the possibility of common training, it is interesting that Zlatarskyi distinguishes between schooled beggars (*vcheni didy*) who have an initiation rite (*terminatsiia*) and those beggars who are not trained (*ne vcheni*). He says that minstrels will interact with the former at events such as fairs and religious festivals, but not with the latter. Schooled beggars seem precisely a remnant of the beggars who trained together with minstrels, and this would explain the minstrels' willingness to treat them as their own.

Some of the minstrels in the Martynovych manuscripts seek to distinguish their begging songs from those of ordinary beggars. A number of Ukrainian words exist for the begging song: *prosba, zhebranka, klianchennia, zapros*. According to the *lirnyk* Ivan Peresada, these are not just different names for the same thing. Rather, the *zhebranka* is what a person sings if he knows nothing else; if he does not know any religious songs, then he sits and sings the *zhebranka*. The *zapros*, on the other hand, is what you sing as you go from house to house. It is part of the more complex performance characteristic of a minstrel.[58] Another, unnamed, source told Martynovych the exact opposite: the *zhebranka* is what a trained person sings, and it goes along with a full, presumably multi-song, performance; the *zapros* is what one sings if that is all that one knows.[59] Because the sources give contradictory statements and there is no difference in begging song content, regardless of the Ukrainian term applied, it is safe to conclude that the real distinction between minstrels and beggars was in extent of knowledge. Minstrels completed all the stages of training and had a correspondingly rich repertory, whereas beggars left after the early stages, knowing only the begging song. Minstrels naturally wanted to differentiate themselves from beggars, and with the many terms for begging songs, and probably in response to questioning by Martynovych, sought to draw a distinction using these terms.

The existence of stages of training permitted a great deal of flexibility. While most people, the ones who became ordinary beggars, emerged from apprenticeship either after an early stage, and the best studied group, minstrels, emerged after stage five, it was possible to leave at various intermediate stages. At least some people stopped at stage three. Demian Symonenko, Iahor Okhremenko, and Nykifor Dudka left apprenticeship knowing songs, but without the ability to play a musical instrument. They learned to play their *liry* or *bandury* after the completion of formal training. Leaving at this stage must not have been all that uncommon, because

Konstantyn Bich-Liubenskyi gives actual terms for singing only (*labiaty*) as a performance style versus being able to both sing and play (*psaliaty*).[60]

The existence of stages of training and the possibility of completing only some of these can help explain how blind female children were handled and how women acquired the extensive knowledge attested in the Martynovych manuscripts. Since women's work was as important as men's in the Ukrainian village, it seems logical that blind girls had an alternate occupation. They were likely apprenticed and trained together with boys, and like the boys, the majority learned only the practical aspects of living as a blind person and the begging song and prayers. Like boys, they became beggars, such as the one from whom V. Danyliv collected a particularly long and elaborate begging song text.[61] Those who went beyond the first stage and became something more than simple beggars could have learned songs, customs, and secret language. Women were prohibited from performing certain types of songs, and it seems that they were denied stage four, instruction in the playing of a musical instrument. But their knowledge was extensive enough to betoken the special training of apprenticeship.

Some indication exists that women were trained separatsely from men, and it is possible that this was a late development of the tradition. Petro Dryhavka's description of apprenticeship includes a section called training for girls (*divchacha nauka)*. It is not detailed, but it notes that girls went through an apprenticeship, albeit a shorter one than boys, and that they completed an initiation rite and became guild members.[62] Although Dryhavka mentions special girls' training, from his lack of a detailed description it seems evident that women were denied access to all the stages of apprenticeship. If the difference between beggars and minstrels was that the former had less knowledge due to lesser ability or desire, the difference between women and men minstrels was that the former knew less because they were not allowed as much training. This pattern is consistent with restrictions placed on women after apprenticeship. Although women knew a great deal, they were frequently not allowed to perform certain songs in situations where they could earn money. They were limited to a specific women's repertory of select religious songs (*zhinochi psalmy*). Women who dared perform something outside this female repertory were attacked by guild members, as were men who performed without passing the initiation rite. Since punishing them physically was unseemly and since they had no musical instruments to smash, women were subjected to the destruction of their household belongings, the so-called smashing of the cups.[63]

The thought that an entire female subdivision of minstrelsy existed is fascinating, and there is good evidence for it. Mentions of a specific women's repertory are numerous, at least in manuscript. Roman Iaremenko says that he does not know a particular item because it is a women's song. One of Martynovych's unnamed sources mentions songs that are specific to women and gives the titles of five of these, noting that all are now performed by men. This record of the transfer of a women's song to a man is not unique. Various items in the Martynovych manuscripts are parenthetically labelled women's songs, and in the case one of these recorded from a male performer, there is an explanation that he learned it from his wife.[64] The custom of granting men access to the women's repertory, while not permitting women similar access to men's, is symptomatic of the injustice perpetrated on women minstrels. The unfairness is especially poignant since women very much enjoyed minstrel art, including the songs that should have been sung by men only. Wonderful marginalia in the Martynovych manuscripts record female performers' reactions to their own songs and indicate that they certainly derived pleasure from singing, even if they did not receive recognition for it.[65]

It is remarkable that the female subdivision of the profession has so totally escaped scholarly recognition. Perhaps male guild members kept their female colleagues away from collectors because these were seen as an especially good source of revenue. Perhaps scholars themselves ignored women because they assumed that minstrels had to play a musical instrument as well as sing songs. Perhaps women did not draw the attention of collectors because the specifically female repertory that they were allowed to perform in public did not contain enough of the genres that scholars considered prestigious. Whatever the reason, a skewed picture of the tradition emerges if female performers are ignored. An analysis of apprenticeship clearly encourages viewing women as integral to the profession. If beggars could be linked to minstrels on the basis of overlap in repertory and likely common training, then certainly women need to be recognized as part of the tradition.

The Initiation Rite: The Conclusion of Apprenticeship

The initiation rite was the conclusion of apprenticeship and gave the novice permission to earn his living as a minstrel. It was a true rite of passage, something that the elders enjoyed not only for the chance to eat and drink, but also for its beauty and solemnity, and like apprenticeship itself, something that the initiate wanted to get through as quickly and as painlessly as possible. Speranskii says that the initiation tested knowledge of songs and the secret language, yet actual descriptions of the rite reveal little testing.[66] Considering how important knowing songs was to being a minstrel, it is surprising how little minstrels discuss learning songs when describing their apprenticeship. Similarly, it is remarkable how little emphasis the initiation rite put on testing songs, on determining whether a young man about to be accredited as a performer was actually able to sing and play.

Most descriptions of the initiation begin with a call to the brotherhood to gather for the ritual. Sometimes this is done by the master who has a pupil to present for guild approval. Sometimes it is done by the young man who wants to ask men already in the guild to accept him as a fellow minstrel. All of the minstrels in a particular area are invited. In some areas, family members, such as the wife of the initiate's master, are invited; in others, only guild members may be present. Under all circumstances the initiation rite is kept secret from people not connected to the profession in some way. Humeniuk told Kvitka that an initiation rite must always take place at night, to conceal it from the public. It may take place outdoors or in the master's home; but in the latter case, all outsiders, even the wife and children of the master and the guides, must leave. Once the rite itself is over, the lights are turned on, and the family and the guides are invited back. Now all feast and are entertained by the singing and the instrumental playing of the various minstrels present.[67]

During the rite itself, the actors can be limited to the initiate and his master, the rest of brotherhood speaking in unison when appropriate, or the actors can include the initiate, his master, and a small group of other officials. These may be officers of the guild, or people selected for the individual rite, in which case they are assigned titles similar to the titles used for guild offices; or they may be a group of "worthy" elders, as appears in the Zlatarskyi description given below. This special group can be invited along with the rest of the brotherhood, or separately, before the others are issued invitations.

The core of the initiation ritual is a solemn and elaborate ceremony in which bread, or bread and salt, were central symbols. For Ukrainians, as for other East Slavs, bread and salt were tokens of welcome. Bread also suggests the influence of the Eucharist on minstrel ritual. Even more, however, bread and salt were chosen because they were symbolic of sustenance. The various exchanges of bread and salt, the ritual conferring of bread or bread and salt upon the initiate, were a symbolic acceptance of him. The ritual initiated a young man into professional minstrelsy and allowed him to earn his keep, his bread and salt, by singing.

Elaborate, repetitive speech was also important. Because the words of the initiation ritual were so complex, there were provisions to help the initiate through them, especially as his nervousness might cause him to stumble. One of the officers, the master's helper (*pidmaistrovyi* or *molozhyi*), could prompt the young man if necessary.[68] Although the initiate might see repetitiveness as a burden, minstrels already in the guild clearly enjoyed it. To them, the initiation rite was a most solemn occasion, and its verbal ornateness added to its sacred character. The epitome of elaboration appears in a version of the initiation rite that Martynovych collected in Poltava. Here, the various phrases are repeated, not thrice, as in the descriptions which follow, but twelve times. Although the degree of repetition seems excessive to us, the informant praises the Poltava version and calls it the most beautiful one he knows, superior to other rites he witnessed.[69]

While a test of musical ability was not part of the initiation process, there is one mention of a test of singing and playing. It appears in Borzhkovskii's description of a *lirnyk* initiation:

> When the course of instruction is finished, the teacher gathers the elders, and the pupil is examined. Having passed his test, he gets his freedom or *vyzvilka*, and becomes a real *lirnyk*. The exam and the granting of the *vyzvilka* take place as follows. When the elders who have been invited have gathered, then the pupil walks into the house, kneels at the master's feet, kisses them two times, then kisses his hands once; he kisses only the hands of the other elders, and makes his request that they allow him to be a *lirnyk*, that they grant him his *vyzvilka*. Then he treats them to vodka, of which he has to provide about half a pail, depending on his financial circumstances. First he drinks himself, then he gives the master three shots, then he gives a drink to all of the elders in turn. After the drinking, the exam starts: the pupil sings the songs he has learned, plays his *lira*, and recites his prayers. At the end of the exam, one of the senior minstrels, in most cases the teacher himself, gives the pupil a loaf of bread. The pupil cuts three whole pieces from this bread (meaning pieces with crust). He salts one and places it in his bosom. Placing this piece of bread in one's bosom is what constitutes receiving one's *vyzvilka*. This is considered the most important act of the initiation, because after this, the pupil becomes a real *lirnyk*, and no one has the right to destroy his *lira*.
>
> Having given the pupil the bread, the minstrels express their good wishes: "May God grant that you be as healthy as water and as rich as the earth; that you may receive from the water and from the dew. . . . " Then they send him on his way, saying "go in the name of God."
>
> The initiate receives the *lira* either during this rite or afterwards. This is accompanied with the following ceremony. The teacher hangs the *lira* on his own neck. Then he raises the hem of his coat and the pupil covers the *lira* with the hem of his own. Then the teacher takes the strap off his own neck and places it around the neck of the pupil. In this manner, the *lira* is passed on. At the end, the teacher blesses the young *lirnyk*, he throws a few coins into his *lira* for good luck, and lets the young man go to assume an independent life.[70]

Martynovych published an excellent description from *kobzar* Trykhon Mahadyn, in the Lokhvytsia region of Poltava province. Here there is no mention of a test, though there is some concern with the pupil's ability as a musician. It appears, however, that the master determines whether or not the pupil is ready, and the rest of the guild does not question the master's judgement. The master is the main actor in Lokhvytsia. He informs the members of the guild that one of his apprentices is ready to join their ranks, and summons them to the initiation rite. During the ceremony, he addresses the assembled minstrels, requests their permission on behalf of his apprentice, and distributes food and drink to each of them, receiving their blessings in return. The master is attended by his wife, who pours the vodka into a bowl so that the blind minstrels can drink without spilling it, and by the guild key-keeper, who helps distribute the food. Only after the master is finished does the apprentice arise. He drinks to his master, repeats the request to be accepted into the guild, and distributes food and drink. When all have received this second round, the master, on behalf of the guild, accepts the youth as a member and allows him to assume a seat at his side. According to Mahadyn, this rite permits singing only, and if a man wants to have apprentices of his own, he must wait ten years and appeal to the brotherhood for permission to "take on help." This time, the person seeking to advance his status takes the initiative, buys the food and drink, and summons the assembly of guild members. If his petition is accepted, then he can take as many apprentices as he wants. "Once they let you take the first pupil," Mahadyn says, "well, then you can do what you want; you can have twenty pupils if you want to."[71]

According to Zlatarskyi, the apprentice and his master plan for the initiation well in advance. They choose a religious festival as the site and occasion for the rite because holding an initiation in conjunction with a secular event, such as a fair, and in a secular place, such as a tavern, is unseemly.[72] They also save up money, the master permitting his apprentice to set aside some of the proceeds from begging for his initiation costs. As the occasion approaches, three elders are invited to serve as officers during the rite.[73] On the day of the initiation itself, the apprentice is sent to all of the minstrels in the area. He addresses each with an elaborate greeting and an even more elaborate invitation. After all have gathered and are seated, the young man speaks in an ornate dialogue with the guild members present, expressing wishes for peace and requesting that the assembly bless his master. Once the dialogue is complete, the young man asks to join the guild by requesting "permission to approach." Permission is granted, and the young man drinks, then pours a drink for his master, then one for each of those present. More rounds of drink follow and food is distributed, the rite ending with the older members reciting a formula wishing the initiate fame and prosperity.[74]

Speranskii collected a description of an initiation rite from Parkhomenko which contains a test of sorts. It is not a test of the novice's ability to play his *bandura* or to sing, but of the quality of the apprentice's service to his master, and to an extent, of his morals. In Mena, Parkhomenko's guild, the master presents his pupil "for examination" at the annual meeting of the brotherhood. During the ceremony proper, both master and apprentice play important roles, though the master is the primary celebrant. They begin with the pupil handing the master a loaf of bread and "paying respects" by uttering prayers and expressing thanks for the master's instruction and moral guidance. Similar "respects" are paid to the three men designated as "elders" for the ceremony. Afterwards, the master, addressing the entire assembly, recites prayers and requests that his pupil be accepted into the brotherhood. All assembled pretend to ignore the master's prayers and entreaties until he repeats each item three times, at which point they question him about his pupil's behavior. The master assures them that his pupil is worthy, and offers them food and drink which, they accept upon his third try. After the master has spoken and distributed food and drink, the pupil arises, prays, and offers a second round of vodka. If anyone present feels that the initiate has not behaved properly, the assurances of the master notwithstanding, he can refuse to accept the offer and force the apprentice to beg forgiveness. Forgiveness is eventually granted, and all feast, concluding the ceremony with prayers for local and state officials, members of the brotherhood, living and deceased, and especially for the teachers of the past.[75]

A description of an initiation rite collected by Khodorovskyi provides a variation on the one given by Parkhomenko. Here, instead of the brotherhood questioning the master about the pupil's behavior, the master turns to the assembled brethren and says: "Elder brothers and younger brothers, has this pupil offended anyone? Has he stolen from anyone? Has he slandered anyone? Has anyone noticed anything bad about him?" If someone from amongst the brotherhood voices a complaint against the novice, then the novice must ask for forgiveness. If he is forgiven, then the brotherhood requests that the novice give them bread and salt. This means that the novice must buy each person a roll and a fish. The novice then poses a formulaic question, asking all those present if they are satisfied with the food provided. If they are, he asks their blessing to "travel in all four directions."[76]

Even though apprenticeship and the initiation rite might be unpleasant experiences for a young minstrel, both institutions served his interests. Apprenticeship especially, with its division into stages, accommodated his abilities and needs. Structured in such a way that any child whom blindness prevented from farming could enter, apprenticeship prepared those who were musically and verbally gifted to be minstrels. Lack of emphasis on singing in the initiation rite may well have been part of the function of apprenticeship as a safety net for all blind children. If the less talented children never learned songs, there was little point in testing their singing. Similarly, if women were not taught the playing of a musical instrument, then there was little reason to see if they could play. By the same token, it was very much worth marking the transition of all people leaving apprenticeship, no matter how many stages they had mastered, into a special category of person, a mendicant, a person outside the village norm.

Enforcing obligatory apprenticeship can be seen as a way of ensuring that apprenticeship served all who might need it, that it acted as an effective social welfare institution. By making sure that there were no freelancers, perhaps more talented people who might learn a minstrel's art by ear (as Oleksandr Dimnych had done), obligatory apprenticeship actually served society as a whole. It guaranteed that even those who did not need the safety net of the guild were nevertheless its members and would help those, perhaps the less-talented blind people, who could not survive without a special institution. It guaranteed that the blind would be cared for by institutions of the blind, that they would not become a burden on the community. And apprenticeship did teach and enforce submission to the guild; it instilled a firm commitment to sharing, to caring for all guild members, just as initiation articulated brotherhood bonds in a solemn and sacred ceremony.

Chapter 7

Learning Minstrel Songs

S ongs were the heart of minstrelsy. Being able to perform songs,
especially religious songs, was more important than playing one
of the musical instruments after which Ukrainian minstrels were
named. Songs were learned either from the master during apprenticeship or
from fellow minstrels afterward. Information exists about the methods used
to teach songs during apprenticeship and the techniques employed for expanding one's repertory after initiation. From this information, we get a
good picture of the process of Ukrainian song transmission, which, on the
whole, conforms to standard oral theory.[1] The Ukrainian tradition, however,
because of the relatively short length of the songs and their tendency toward
stanzaic structure, is perhaps more stable and less subject to variation than
others. One rather unusual feature of the Ukrainian transmission process is
the privileging of dictation. Although the songs were always sung in public
rather than recited, when minstrels set about teaching songs to each other,
both during apprenticeship and afterward, they favored recitation over singing, dictating the words without musical accompaniment to the person seeking to learn the song text. Preference for the recited or dictated text tied
Ukrainian oral literature to written literature and may have originated in the
practice of literate people trying to teach blind minstrels by reading verses
to them. We will never know whether recitation became prevalent through
efforts to teach from a written text or arose spontaneously within the tradition, before minstrels became affiliated with the church and influenced by
scripture. In any case, the practice of teaching by reciting or dictating allowed Ukrainian minstrels to easily absorb written material.

Patterns of Learning: Apprenticeship

Most minstrels agree that an apprentice should learn the words to songs first
and only then learn the music, though this was not a universal practice. In
the sequence of training given by Iakiv Zlatarskyi, learning the words of a
song and learning its music are given as separate stages (see chapter 6).[2]

According to Mikhail Speranskii, some masters taught the words first, then added the music; others taught the words and the music together. Thus, Havrylo Vovk first made his pupils memorize the text, then taught them to join this text to singing and instrumental playing. Hnat Honcharenko was taught the same way. Babenko and Kutsyi's master, on the other hand, taught the words together with the music. From this, Speranskii concludes that the method is up to the teacher.[3] Outside of Speranskii, we find much the same situation, except that minstrels themselves do not admit flexibility and insist on one method only. Thus, Hrytsko Oblychenko, for example, learned the words and the music together, while most informants agree with Zlatarskyi and say that the words must be learned first and the music afterward.[4] Samson Veselyi told Kharkiv, "First you recite it, then you sing the words; only then do you learn to play."[5]

Either way would make sense in terms of oral theory. Albert Lord's experience in Yugoslavia revealed that some people just could not produce a narrative without musical accompaniment. Others, perhaps the greatest storytellers, were "liberated" by being asked to dictate instead of singing. They produced long and elaborate texts of special beauty.[6] Thus, in the Ukrainian tradition, learning words alone was better for some teachers and pupils, and learning words and music together was better for others. Masters were not flexible enough to vary their methods to suit pupil learning needs, and in all probability, they taught in the same way that they themselves had been taught. The way the tradition developed over time, namely the ease with which written texts were introduced as sources of material, would indicate that learning by reciting the words first and adding the music later was probably the preferred method.

A number of sources specify that a master never taught his pupils all the songs that he knew. When the person being interviewed is speaking from the point of view of the master, he usually presents this as a given of the profession, as Ivan Humeniuk did to Klement Kvitka. Oleksa Horbach heard much the same in Galicia, and Valerian Borzhkovskii, in Eastern Ukraine.[7] When the point of view is that of the apprentice, failure to teach all of the songs is seen as yet another way in which masters exploit their charges. Thus, Drahomanov's source chided master *kobzari* of old for laziness and greed, accusing them of both refusing to teach all they knew and living off the earnings of their apprentices, whom they sent out wherever and as often as they wished.[8]

The most negative descriptions are again in the Kharkiv manuscripts. Here, minstrels accuse their masters of "teaching little and sending me out to beg often." Describing their apprenticeship, they say, "I spent a lot more time travelling and begging than studying." Makar Khrystenko complained to the same collector that his master was "wily" (*z khytrynkoiu*), and taught only two or three psalms, while he himself knew close to one hundred. Ashamed for not having gotten more out of his training, Khrystenko managed to learn more songs after his apprenticeship, and his repertory at the time of collection had grown to thirty religious songs, plus other material.[9]

Speranskii provides an interesting perspective. Speaking in general terms rather than quoting from a specific minstrel, he claims that the master does not teach all that he knows for two reasons: to protect his own financial interests by making sure that his pupils are not his equals and to respond to changes in public taste. Thus, Ivan Kravchenko-Kriukovskyi did not teach as much historical material, including epics or *dumy*, as he himself knew, because he thought that audience demand for it had decreased. Speranskii noted that some omissions were unintentional: a master might forget with time, and become incapable of teaching what he no longer remembered.[10]

The situation is a bit more complicated. True, masters did not teach all that they knew to protect their own interests. Money, which appears as a motive again and again, was surely a motive here, and at least some practicing minstrels took care not to produce someone who could compete with them right away. There was also professional rivalry, as Speranskii postulates.[11] Thus Makar Khrystenko told Kharkiv that he was a better instrumentalist than his master Pavlo Hashchenko because he played with three fingers rather than one and played all of the *bandura*, including the base strings. Hryhorii Kolisnyk told the same collector that he was better at the *lira* than his master Ivan Petryk. Here, the difference was in the turning of the crank: Petryk's was supposedly monotonous, while Kolisnyk's was expressive.[12]

Other factors were at work as well. A gifted performer is not necessarily a good teacher. Some masters may have tried to teach more, but simply did not know how. Veresai, a gifted musician, was probably very bad as a teacher. He had only one pupil, and even that pupil left him.[13] Ivan Kravchenko-Kriukovskyi may also have been an unsuccessful teacher, and he, unlike Veresai, was well liked and highly respected as the revered leader of his guild.[14] Kravchenko-Kriukovskyi was also an outstanding artist. While he himself learned easily and was recognized as one of the greatest of *kobzari* by his fellow minstrels, he seems to have had difficulty with his pupils. As he told Horlenko, "Some of them (the pupils), you repeat it for them twenty times, and they still don't get it." In addition, Kravchenko-Kruikovskyi found it hard to teach the *bandura*.[15] The problem may have been the pupils' lack of talent. But, if Kravchenko-Kriukovskyi had trouble teaching both the texts and the playing of a musical instrument, perhaps the fault lay with his instructional techniques. Perhaps the great artist was not a good teacher.

It is highly likely the master could not have taught all he knew even if he had wanted to do so. Both the nature of apprenticeship, which encouraged apprentices to get out as quickly as possible, and more important, the nature of the material itself prevented the master from teaching a pupil everything. The level of knowledge and artistry achieved by mature minstrels could not be passed on in three years, or even six. It literally took years of experience and practice to play and sing that well. In addition, there were certain things that could not be taught. The artistry of great performers demanded a certain level of maturity and depth of feeling which could come only with time, with living and suffering. Artistry was enhanced by the life experience of the artist.

A phrase from the tradition itself, "attain wisdom" or "mature into wisdom" (*doity rozumu*), encapsulates the above.[16] This is what minstrels were supposed to do as they practiced their profession. Presumably, during the ten years between initiation and becoming a master who accepts apprentices, a man gained the experience and wisdom which made him a better performer and teacher. Even where there were no official strata to mark maturity, minstrels realized that they grew and developed with time. The younger Humeniuk, though not himself a minstrel, put it very well when he told Kvitka that a performer improves throughout the course of his life, learning more and more.[17]

Post-Apprenticeship Learning

Oral Sources

Expanding one's post-apprenticeship repertory was almost a given. Makar Khrystenko learned twenty-seven psalms between completing his apprenticeship and the time that he was interviewed by Kharkiv. Semen Vlasko did not tell what or how much he had learned, but he was quite aware of his primary sources. He got additional texts from two old men, Savko and another man, whose name he had forgotten. He acquired improved instrumental techniques from Korniivskyi, a man who did not sing but played beautifully.[18] Ivan Kravchenko-Kriukovskyi reported that he picked up material from other *kobzari* at fairs. He was especially influenced by one old man, Havrylo Vovk, aged ninety, who could no longer play or sing but was willing to dictate song texts. Kravchenko-Kriukovskyi paid him a quarter gold piece for each song.[19]

Having one particularly influential teacher in the period after apprenticeship seems to have been quite common. Pavlo Hashchenko stated that he learned additional material after he was already an initiated minstrel, and that he was particularly indebted to Dmytrii Trochenko from the Bohod-ukhiv region.[20] In the rather thick folder that Martynovych collected from Khvedir Hrytsenko, he notes the sources of songs consistently. A few of the texts are "from other *kobzari*," but most are listed as being either "from the master" or "from Kocherha," Hrytsenko's main post-apprenticeship source.[21] Kyrylo Kuzmynskyi studied with Ivan Knut, but then picked up significant portions of his repertory from Kornii Hondarenko and Sevotynets Zakharchenko.[22] Ananii Homyniuk reported simply that, after he finished his formal training, he picked up additional material from *lirnyky* he would meet in his travels.[23] Petro Tkachenko, also called Halushka, reported that he filled out his repertory after he completed his apprenticeship and that he was particularly influenced by Terentii Parkhomenko.[24] Prokop Chub, who appears in the literature also as Prokip Dub, tried to respond to public preferences. Chub played the *bandura*, but felt a *lirnyk* repertory was in greater demand. His efforts to learn this type of song were analyzed by Malynka, who called him a transitional minstrel because of his position somewhere between *lirnyky* and *kobzari*.[25] Demian Symonenko actually went through two apprenticeships. From his first mas-ter, Hrytsko Dubyna, he learned religious songs. But Dubyna did not play, and Symonenko wanted to learn the *bandura* to improve his earnings. Thus, after one and a half years of performing without an instrument, he appren-ticed himself to Holienko. Symonenko did not care for Holienko's singing style, but did get the instruction in playing an instrument that he wanted. Symonenko had to pay for both of his apprenticeships. However, he was fortunate enough to run into Mykhailo Kravchenko, a *kobzar* who was unusually generous with both his musical instruments and his knowledge of songs, and Kravchenko taught Symonenko *dumy*, another item he wanted to learn, for free.[26] Kharkiv reported that learning additional instrumental skills, be it playing the *bandura* or the *lira*, occurred routinely in the period after apprenticeship.[27]

One particularly noteworthy pattern reported by Kharkiv is studying with a simple beggar first and then going through an apprenticeship with a min-strel master. According to the *lirnyk* Hryhorii Kolisnyk, some men would first go through an apprenticeship with a beggar elder, a person also called a master (*pan-otets*), just like a minstrel teacher. Such a person could give instruction in the fundamentals of begging: how to live as a blind person, the begging song, and possibly some other songs. The young man going through such an apprenticeship would pay for it by begging and turning over the proceeds to his teacher. As Kolisnyk explained further, if a person who had completed such training later decided that he wanted to learn how to play a musical instrument and become a minstrel, he could go through a second apprenticeship, this time to a minstrel master. Such an apprenticeship would normally be much shorter than if a man went to a minstrel master directly, and would be paid for in cash.[28]

Terentii Parkhomenko made efforts to learn the sort of material that would earn him the most money, and most of this occurred after apprenticeship. He switched instruments, mastering the *bandura*, because the better-paying intellectuals were more interested in it than in the *lira*. He learned *dumy*. In short, he went way beyond the training he had received from his master.[29] Learning after apprenticeship was so much a part of the profession that masters sometimes taught their pupils how to go about this. Tsarko instructed Iakiv Bakhmut: "Afterward, you will learn on your own. Be good to your minstrel brothers, and you will learn from them."[30]

The traditional source for the material that minstrels picked up over their lifetimes was other minstrels. They listened to each other whenever they gathered in large numbers, at religious festivals and fairs. They may have performed for each other at gatherings such as their annual meetings, and relaxed after an initiation rite by playing. Varion Honchar told Kharkiv,

> We travel and we travel, and then, when we get together and drink . . . Well, then one may play and then another may start to play . . . and then someone else, and someone else. And I don't know something. And if I don't know something, he'll tell me, buy me half a glass of vodka and I will teach you. You listen and you learn.[31]

According to Ivan Humeniuk, minstrels even traveled to other parts of Ukraine to hear different renditions of songs and thus improve their own.[32] Kharkiv adds that minstrels learned across instruments, so to speak. Thus, a *lirnyk* might pick up new material from another *lirnyk* or from listening to a *kobzar*. The same was true of the *kobzari*, who learned from fellow *kobzari* and from *lirnyky*.[33]

Minstrels did not tend to share their knowledge readily or make the process of picking up new material easy. Mykhailo Kravchenko seems to have been the only minstrel who gave willingly and without compensation. Everyone else asked for a fee, such as money or alcohol; some refused to pass on knowledge. Kravchenko-Kriukovskyi paid Vovk a quarter gold piece; Bratytsia simply refused to teach new material to fellow minstrels who came to him for instruction. Horlenko attributes this miserliness to Bratytsia's wife, saying that she sent the minstrels away. It is difficult, however, to know whom to blame, especially since Horlenko had a tendency to attribute all behavior of which he disapproved to the wives of minstrels.[34] Parkhomenko heard Kiashko sing the *duma* about Khmelnytskyi at Chernihiv and decided he wanted to learn it. He pleaded. "I begged him and begged him," he says. He plied Kiashko with vodka, but all to no avail. Kiashko would not share his material.[35]

Several scholars reported that on discovering that their texts were being written down, minstrels tried to keep their songs from the collector. Thus, Borzhkovskii reported that the *lirnyk* Nikon was quite upset when he found out his material was being recorded, fearing that having his songs disseminated in written form would somehow diminish their value.[36] Chykalenko had a similar experience collecting from the *lirnyk* Vasilyi Moroz. Chykalenko was busy writing down what he considered to be a particularly interesting version of a song. When Moroz found out that his words were being put on paper, he refused to sing all of the verses, and the collector was left with a fragmentary text.[37] Given the police persecution of minstrels, it is possible that these men suspected the collector was preparing a document to be used against them. It is also possible that they were protecting a valuable commodity and feared that having their songs published would make them less profitable. One priest reported that when his minstrel learned that the material was being written down, he demanded fifty kopecks, a sum much higher than the two or three kopecks usually paid for a song performance and one that was quite excessive for the priest's meager resources.[38]

Written Sources

An interesting new source of material emerged as scholarly interest in minstrelsy grew. Scholars shared material they had collected from one minstrel with other *kobzari* and *lirnyky*. Sometimes they "reminded" minstrels of material they felt that the minstrels should know. They admitted that they sometimes experimented with minstrel learning techniques, trying to figure out how the process of text acquisition worked. Sometimes they were trying to change the course of the tradition. Panteleimon Kulish was one of the people who tried the latter approach, seeking to preserve material that was dying out. Oleksandr Malynka, who did a great deal of solid work, was one of the experimenters. He read minstrels published material and material he himself had collected elsewhere. He reports how he read a variety of texts to the *lirnyk* Evdokim Mokroviz, who showed no interest in epics or *dumy* with historical subject matter but was quite taken with "The Widow and Her Three Sons," an epic song which most resembles religious verse. The minstrel was also attracted to the satirical song "Khoma i Iarema." Mokroviz wanted to add these songs to his repertory immediately, and called in his daughter to help with the process. The reason for calling in the girl, the minstrel said, was that her memory was especially good because of her youth.[39] Malynka had a similar experience with Oleksii Masliukov. He read him several *dumy*, and the *lirnyk* showed no interest; he read him some satirical songs and dance songs, and he became most interested indeed. Malynka left Masliukov some published texts, which, presumably, the *lirnyk* would have some sighted person read to him so that he could learn them. The minstrel was boundlessly grateful for the printed texts.[40]

Minstrels also procured books on their own, often from intellectuals other than folklorists who were trying to help either the particular minstrel or the tradition as a whole. Terentii Parkhomenko used books to learn the *dumy* that his better-paying intellectual customers wanted. He even hired a literate guide so that he could have someone to read new texts to him. Malynka reports that Semen Vlasko had received Shevchenko's *Kobzar* as a gift. It is not clear whether he had already learned any material from it at the time of the interview.[41] Petro Drevnik (also called Drevchenko) got a manuscript of the religious song "Afon hora" (Mount Athos) from an unnamed lady and included it in his repertory. Speranskii checked the repertory of Drevnik's master, Hnat Honcharenko, and confirmed that this song was not part of the material he knew. Speranskii also reports that Honcharenko himself had been given the text of the *duma* "Marusia Bohuslavka," presumably so that he could learn it. Unfortunately, Honcharenko lost the text before he could fulfill his patron's intent.[42]

Pavlo Bratytsia learned from books. Horlenko went to record Bratytsia and discovered that he knew more *dumy* than other collectors had reported, including Khmelnytskyi *dumy*. These were quite rare, and the search for minstrels who knew them had long been fruitless. Thus, Horlenko was thrilled with his discovery—until he learned the source of Bratytsia's knowledge.[43] Bratytsia's perspective on the whole situation is quite interesting. The patron who taught Bratytsia all of his new material used collections published by Kulish, Metlynskyi, and Rusov. The Khmelnytskyi *dumy*, the ones to which Horlenko assigned the greatest significance, were texts recorded by Kulish from the famous minstrel Andrii Shut. Perhaps because Shut was the master of Andrii Beshko, the man who had been Bratytsia's teacher, Bratytsia began to consider himself Shut's pupil.[44] As the interest of intellectuals in Khmelnytskyi epic songs persisted, other minstrels followed Bratytsia's example. Kharkiv reported that Makar Khrystenko added Khmelnytskyi epics learned from books to the religious songs that he had picked up orally.[45]

Books eventually became the sole source of material. The tradition was slowly dying, and significant changes came with the turn of the century. Kolessa found "concert" features in the performance styles of a number of the men he recorded. Parkhomenko, the subject of Speranskii's study, was revamping almost all the aspects of minstrelsy to suit the tastes of intellectuals, the new audience he had identified as being more profitable. Some well-meaning intellectuals like Hnat Khotkevych, a man who eventually learned to perform himself, were changing the tradition even more actively. Charged with preparing a group of representative minstrels to perform at the Twelfth Archeological Congress to be held in Kharkiv in 1902, Khotkevych gathered the group, Parkhomenko among them, and did all sorts of things to "help" them be better performers. Probably the least intrusive thing he did was improve their voices with a mixture of lemon juice and honey, complemented by an improved diet. The more intrusive things would make a modern-day folklorist wince. On the basis of his own musical training, Khotkevych concluded that the tuning of the *bandura* which his charges used was wrong—and so he retuned their *banduras* for them. The men refused to accept the new tuning, and Khotkevych, when he himself learned to play, realized that the minstrels knew what they were doing. Khotkevych also decided that it would be nice to have some ensemble performances in addition to traditional solo singing, and so taught his charges to sing together in various size groups. Here the minstrels did not protest, at least Khotkevych does not record their protests in his notes. Possibly as a result of this, ensembles, especially *bandura* ensembles, became progressively more wide-spread.[46]

Whatever remained of the tradition was wiped out for good in 1939, at the infamous congress in Kharkiv, where Stalin summoned those minstrels who were still left and had them executed. Thus, when the Khrushchev Thaw permitted a revival of minstrelsy, the tradition was dead. The men presented to the public as new Soviet minstrels, men like Ehor Movchan and Fedir Kushneryk, were self-taught. The guilds were but a memory, and training by apprenticeship was no more. Anyone who wanted to be a minstrel, now that this was possible again, had to learn from published sources. The oral tradition was gone.

Soviet folklore played a decisive role in the destruction of oral transmission. The Soviets monitored everything, and folklore was no exception. Where ideology and reality did not coincide, it was reality that was altered. The task of folklorists was not so much to describe what was, as to implement what should be. Instead of collecting the songs that the folk were actually singing and publishing them, folklorists were supposed to teach the people the songs that their new Soviet circumstances required. Thus, we have "Duma about Lenin," a new song, and careful editing of old songs to ensure perpetuation of suitable elements only.[47] The regulation of minstrelsy, even after Stalin, guaranteed that none would have the audacity to learn anything in a purely oral manner, and all would use only texts prepared by Soviet folklorists and carrying official approval. Early Soviet minstrels, men like Ehor Movchan, Fedir Kushneryk, Evhen Adamtsevych, and Avram Hrebin, had at least some sense of the oral text and oral transmission. They had heard the minstrels of the past. Hrebin was Parkhomenko's student. But approved songs existed as written texts, and so these men worked from written material. As for the people who came after them, they probably were not even aware of the possibility of oral transmission.

Written Texts as an Exclusive Source: Pavlo Suprun

Pavlo Suprun, the contemporary *kobzar* whom I have recorded, became a minstrel in the Soviet period, and works exclusively from written texts. Examining his methods of expanding his repertory, along with his techniques for composing new material, provides an opportunity to see first-hand how texts of written origin function in the Ukrainian tradition. Suprun's methods, with the exception of his occasional reliance on Braille, typify all work with written texts, both that being done now and that which was done by men like Parkhomenko and Bratytsia. There is every reason to believe these methods were in use even before the late nineteenth and early twentieth centuries; written texts may have entered the tradition as early as the seventeenth century, and possibly earlier still. Furthermore, teaching by recitation rather than singing, an approach used in the purely oral setting, resembles the methods of Pavlo Suprun.

When adding new songs to his repertory, Suprun takes books and learns the words of the pieces he has selected from these. He uses various standard collections of *dumy* and historical songs. On one of my visits, Pavlo Stepanovych offered to give me several of these volumes. Since they were out of print and very hard to find, I was reluctant to accept the offer, feeling I was going to deprive Suprun of his material. Suprun insisted that this was quite all right—he had mastered all the songs that he wanted out of the various collections. The way that Suprun masters a verbal text is to have someone read it to him. Sometimes he can learn it from the reading alone. If he cannot, he transcribes it into Braille and works on it until it is his. His term for this is "*osvoiity.*"[48] Once a text has been mastered, Suprun does not use the Braille. He does not discard it, but he does not refer back to it, either. Perhaps he passes his Braille texts on to someone, as he passed on his printed texts to me. This is not likely, however, because there are few blind performers now, and Suprun does not have a high opinion of most of them and would be reluctant to give his texts to people he felt could not do them justice.[49]

The standard collections of *dumy* and historical songs that Suprun uses have words only—no music. This does not present a problem. Where he can, he gets the music to a particular piece either from a sound recording or from notes published separately. This, too, he writes down in Braille if he feels he cannot remember it otherwise. Where he cannot get music, he composes his own. Though Suprun has had some conservatory training, making up music is and was a widespread practice.

Suprun's most recent efforts are new compositions. Up until 1990, he took traditional *dumy* and historical songs, such as the *duma* "The Captive's Lament" or the historical song "Baida," and set these to music. During one interview, he talked about his wanting to add other traditional *dumy* to his repertory in response to requests from elementary school students.[50] In 1990, with the collapse of the Soviet Union, Suprun turned to totally new material. The technique he used in creating his new *dumy* was analogous to the one he had used for learning old ones. He took poems that he liked and felt answered the needs of contemporary Ukrainians, composed music for them, and added them to his repertory. "Duma about Chornobyl," from a poem by Mykola Chychkan, is one such creation.[51] Suprun composes on the *bandura*. With his own compositions, he does not write down his music in Braille, and the first time that the notes for "Duma about Chornobyl" were set down on paper was when this piece was transcribed for publication in *Socialist Culture.*[52] Suprun has ten of these new creations.[53]

What Suprun is doing is a direct result of a series of events leading up to the current historical, political, and artistic situation. Yet, it is also similar to traditional learning. Almost ninety years ago, Speranskii, observing Parkhomenko and others working from books, wrote that minstrels take texts and set them to music. Lack of music did not present a problem and minstrels learning from books found the words of a song sufficient for mastering it.[54] Setting texts to music is not as difficult as it may seem, and one does not need conservatory training to do it. The traditional melody is repetitive. Furthermore, a minstrel will have one, or at most, several melodies for his various *dumy*, a similar set of one or several melodies for his religious songs, historical songs, and so forth.[55] Thus, a minstrel has a melody, or a small fund of melodies, to which he performs each of the various genres he knows. All of this underscores the dominance of words over music and tells us that learning a song was virtually the same as learning its verbal text. Suprun is somewhat more innovative in his music— a reflection, no doubt, of his conservatory training.

Suprun's method, with the exception of his use of Braille, resembles the method of late nineteenth- and early twentieth-century traditional *kobzari*. Furthermore, if we look at printed sources more as texts than as something written, then his approach is analogous to learning from a text dictated by minstrels, with no exposure to writing. A text read from a book is very similar to a song without music recited by one illiterate minstrel to another, exactly what happened both during apprenticeship and in the transmission of texts after training. In most oral traditions, the introduction of writing viewed as a sign of impending decay. In the Ukrainian case, exclusive reliance on books and other written texts accompanied the disintegration of traditional minstrelsy which took place under Soviet rule; but because written material was learned in a way virtually identical to the method used in transmitting oral material from one blind performer to another, the reading of texts to minstrels, at least prior to the Soviet regime, did not undermine the tradition but merely continued it. Learning from written texts read by a literate person probably goes back to the time when *kobzari* and *lirnyky* first came under church influence in the seventeenth century.

Suprun's method of creating new songs has interesting implications for what might have happened in the past, under church influence, when literate persons sought to expand minstrel repertory and introduce more Christian subject matter into it. Just as Suprun had sighted friends read contemporary poetry to him so that he could select texts and then turn them into modern *dumy* by setting them to his own music, so in the past, minstrels might have listened to material read by seminarians: scripture, apocrypha, even the seminarians' own compositions, and set these to music using their genre-appropriate sets of melodies.

Evidence that minstrels learned songs using the words alone predates the modern period. Here the documentation is less plentiful, but it includes the example of Ivan Kravchenko-Kriukovskyi, one of the greatest of traditional *kobzari*, who described the transmission of songs by verbal text alone. Havrylo Vovk, from whom he learned a number of songs, was so aged that he was capable only of reciting them, for he could neither sing nor play. This did not stop him from being a good source of material. The arrangement Kravchenko-Kriukovskyi made with Vovk was that the latter would get paid once his client had mastered the desired song. In most cases, this required Vovk to recite the text three to four times. Perhaps even more indicative is the fact that Kravchenko-Kriukovskyi himself was quite ready and willing to recite his own songs. Vasyl Horlenko went to collect from this *kobzar* in 1882. According to Horlenko, he established a relationship with the minstrel quickly and easily. Soon they got down to business, and Kravchenko-Kruikovskyi "willingly dictated" the texts of the *dumy* he knew.[56] Thus, in a purely oral setting, two illiterate minstrels transmitted texts in a way analogous to the method used by Suprun.

Kravchenko-Kriukovskyi possessed the facility to learn from a dictated text and to produce a dictated text for others. It is fascinating to note that one of the minstrels who relied heavily on books, Parkhomenko, had a hard time dictating. According to Speranskii, when asked to "tell" his songs, the minstrel "made errors and omissions; noticing his mistake, he would immediately correct it and restore the text, only this time singing it, having played several chords on his *bandura*, at which point he would recite it correctly."[57] Most likely, then, Parkhomenko could not teach by reciting. It would be useful to know how he did teach his students. Did he recite and resort to singing when necessary, correcting himself with his *bandura* as he did for Speranskii, or did he sing all of his material, making his students learn the words and the melody together? Two other minstrels, Kuzmynskyi and Stupak, are mentioned as people who had to rely on a musical instrument to remember their songs; but we know nothing about how they were taught, how they learned following apprenticeship, or how they taught their own pupils.[58] The example Parkhomenko, and possibly Kuzmynskyi and Stupak, present of learning from recitation yet having difficulty reciting is probably not unique. If it is easier to learn from a recited text than a sung one, then Parkhomenko's case may provide one more explanation of why apprentices did not learn all of the songs of their masters.

Centuries before the tradition started to collapse and intellectuals sought to preserve it by teaching minstrels recorded texts, seminarians and other members of the religious community were no doubt reciting and teaching psalms, scripture, and even their own compositions to *kobzari* and *lirnyky*. Many religious songs are at least partially based on written texts, often apocryphal rather than canonical. At least one popular minstrel song, "To Every City Its Rights and Mores" (*Vsiakomu horodu nrav i prava*), is clearly of written origin, based on a poem by the eighteenth-century philosopher, poet, and former seminarian Hryhorii Skovoroda. It is impossible to establish when these songs entered minstrel repertory, but their written origin is without doubt.

The Art of a Mature Minstrel: "Levels" of Knowledge

Minstrels did a great deal of learning after they had completed apprenticeship. They picked up new material and improved their renditions of the songs they knew. Just as the number of stages completed during apprenticeship and the amount learned during formal training varied, so too there was a great deal of variation in learning success after apprenticeship. The level of knowledge, artistry, and skill could differ significantly from one mature minstrel to the next. In *Kobzari*, his study of Ukrainian minstrels, Fedir Lavrov, following Anna Astakhova, claims that there are three types of mature performers.[59] The first, and the least meritorious artistically, are those singers who are merely tradition bearers. They try to memorize their songs, and repeat them in the same form as they learned them from their masters; their texts vary little over time. The second type are minstrel-improvisors. They do not make up songs, but they do vary them from performance to performance. Sometimes they add elements; other times they omit elements, and sometimes they even alter the personality of the characters. The third and best type of performer, according to Lavrov, is the minstrel-creator. Minstrels of this type can make up their own songs and create new material on topics such as current events.[60]

Lavrov's scheme of minstrel types is one which fits Soviet ideology and Soviet ideas about folklore. As Frank Miller points out in his book about the folklore of the Stalin era, shortly after the Soviet socialist revolution, folklore and folklore scholarship were threatened with extinction. If folklore expressed the problems of the oppressed, then with the introduction of Communism and the classless society, oppression should cease and there should be no need for folklore. If folklore was the art of the uneducated rural population, then with industrialization and with the mass schooling provided by the Communist system, there should be no uneducated rural masses to perpetuate this art. Soon, however, the perception of folklore changed. As its artistic power and its mass appeal were recognized, folklore was seen as an ideal propaganda tool. In the Stalin era, folklore was used as precisely such a tool. What was desired of folklore was that it voice sorrow over the horrors of the situation that had existed before Communism and sing the gratitude of the people for their current blessings. Folk performers were "encouraged" to create "new folklore" with just such content, and folklorists were supposed to help them create this art befitting their new lifestyle.[61] Lavrov, and his mentor Maksym Rylski were among such helpers.

Still, we cannot totally dismiss Lavrov's scheme on the grounds that his performer types fit the Stalinist emphasis on creating new Soviet folklore. Closer examination reveals that he is essentially correct, and that his designation of various levels of achievement is useful. His mistake lies in assigning particular artistic merit to the creation of new songs. The Ukrainian tradition did not value new material. Rather, it prized the ability to reproduce existing narratives well, to perform them in an emotionally effective manner. Performers of Lavrov's "middle tier"—minstrel improvisors who worked to achieve the most moving versions of traditional songs—were the ones most valued by the village audience. Moreover, it is in fact easier to compose and improvise than to reproduce existing songs. Improvisation is not the ultimate skill. It is an intermediate one, acquired on the way to artistic excellence.

The Turkish minstrel tradition has both improvised song and learned song and thus provides a good case study of their relative difficulty. Like the Ukrainian tradition, the Turkish one clearly considers improvisation to be a lesser skill. In his autobiography, the accomplished minstrel Sabit Mudami Yilmaz describes how easy it was for him to improvise, how difficult it was to learn traditional material, and how audience pressure forced him into mastering the latter. Mudami says that his life as a minstrel began with a dream of inspiration, a traditional feature in a Turkish minstrel biography. After this dream, he immediately started to compose songs and set about learning to play a *saz*, the traditional minstrel instrument. As he describes it, in the songs that he spontaneously composed, he sang about objects he saw and people he met. He expressed his feelings and he narrated events. Proud of himself, he decided to perform in front of an audience. The audience was willing to listen to Mudami's own compositions for a while, but soon tired of these and began requesting traditional songs and narratives by the great masters of the past. Mudami could not produce these, and suffered humiliation. It was only after a long apprenticeship that Mudami developed the skills demanded by the audience. Apprenticeship gave Mudami the ability to narrate and to master traditional plots, a process he describes in much the same terms as those used by Kravchenko-Kriukovskyi—namely, listening to a text three or four times and then "sleeping on" a text, taking some time to think through the logic of the narrative.[62]

Mudami's autobiography states clearly that improvised material is considered less valuable and easier to produce and that learned songs are more demanding on the performer and more highly prized by the audience. Ukrainian minstrelsy had no improvisation that we know of until this century, when outsiders (scholars) prompted its introduction. We know of only two newly-created *dumy*, both by Mykhailo Kravchenko, describing a tragic massacre in Sorochintsy which he witnessed. Neither was adopted by other minstrels or entered the tradition. Of course, there was no time for this to happen because of the advent of the Soviet period, but Kravchenko's *dumy* probably would not have become part of the canon anyway.

Under the influence of scholars like Maksym Rylskyi and Fedir Lavrov, other collectors from the Soviet period sought to find evidence of the creation of new texts. Mykhailo Polotai asked Kyrylo Kuzmynskyi if he composed new songs, and the minstrel answered that he did not really, perhaps he could come up with a new verse to an existing song now and then.[63] Kharkiv noted that minstrels would sometimes try to create new material to meet what they perceived as changes in audience taste and to earn more money but that these new songs were often unsuccessful and did not produce higher income.[64] Ukrainian minstrelsy was simply not a tradition that was open to incorporating new narratives into the existing corpus.

While professional *kobzari* and *lirnyky* were not supposed to improvise, there was plenty of improvisation in the Ukrainian folk milieu at a non-professional level. A number of scholars, Filaret Kolessa and Roman Jakobson among them, have pointed out that Ukrainian epics are closely related to laments.[65] These two genres are similar in line length, rhyme pattern, performance style, elegiac tone, and melancholy content. The differences between them are in musical accompaniment, improvisation, and professionalism. Epics were sung to the accompaniment of a *bandura* or a *lira* and had traditional plots, story lines recognized by the audience. Laments were unaccompanied and improvised to fit a particular situation: the death of a specific person, or a particular tragic event. Epic, the learned genre, was performed only by the special group of *kobzari* and *lirnyky*, men who received lengthy formal training. Lamentation was a skill that every woman, not just women trained by minstrels, was supposed to acquire. Every bride was expected to lament during her wedding, and every wife, mother, sister, was expected to wail over the family deceased. All available evidence indicates that every woman did actually lament, though some were better than others, to be sure.[66] Furthermore, in Ukraine, unlike in other Slavic areas, men lamented as well as women.[67] If poetic improvisation was a skill possessed by the entire female population of the Ukrainian countryside and by a number of men as well, it could not have been all that inaccessible, or something achieved only by a few great artists. Rather, producing known songs with a recognized plot was the skill that required apprenticeship, much as in Sabit Mudami's experience. Mykhailo Kravchenko's two new *dumy* on the massacre at Sorochintsy were not the great achievement that Soviet scholars held them to be. Indeed, Kravchenko had merely done what every woman and many men did in times of death and sorrow. It is probably no coincidence that the subject matter of Kravchenko's *dumy* resembles lament. While funeral laments are the category best known to scholarship, laments about tragic events such as storms and other natural disasters were widely sung among the folk themselves. Kravchenko's songs are about man-made rather than natural disasters, but they are about tragic events just like so many traditional improvised laments. Indeed, Kravchenko's creations share features with a category of lament sung for recruits going off to battle.

The relative simplicity of improvisation as an oral performance skill has been obscured by a number of factors. Soviet ideology demanded new folklore and thus assigned special merit to the ability to produce something new. Western culture values "creativity," and this influences our perceptions and those of Ukrainian scholars familiar with Western ideas. Both belief systems foster the idea that if improvisation is particularly good, it must also be particularly rare.

The other part of the problem has been a reluctance to draw too many parallels between something considered a women's art form and minstrelsy. Lament was considered "women's art," even if that label was incorrectly applied. Even in Ukraine, where both women and men lamented, lament, especially ritual lament at funerals and weddings, was seen as primarily a women's genre and thus not related to epic poetry. The most striking example of refusing to connect anything to do with women to minstrelsy appears in the work of Filaret Kolessa. While he drew extensive and striking parallels between epics and funeral laments, citing almost identical wording in very similar lines, his bias against women's art led him to suggest that the origin of epics was not in the funeral laments that he himself had used but in laments sung by captives.[68] Kolessa may have felt that a genre like the heroic epic could only originate in an exclusively male setting such as a Turkish prison or galley. In any case, had there been more extensive examination of the lament-epic connection, it might have been apparent sooner that oral poetic creativity was far from rare and that ordinary women and some non-professional men could compose complex narratives when circumstances demanded.

When it came to professionals, the *kobzari* and *lirnyky*, audiences wanted them to have "learning" (*nauka*). They wanted "songs from the Book," not something "made up." Like Mudami's audience, they demanded traditional material. The success with which minstrels produced traditional material varied a great deal. Lavrov says that performers of his first type, singers who just reproduce what was passed on to them, are few. Here Lavrov is mistaken, for minstrels of lesser skill were actually quite numerous. All oral traditions tolerate numerous poor performers, but the vast majority are not recorded or noted in any way simply because they are bad. Thus they are not known outside the immediate tradition and appear to be insignificant. Poor performers were especially likely in Ukraine. The Ukrainian tradition had an extra incentive for tolerating and paying performers without talent because the reason for support was, at least ostensibly, disability rather than performance skills. Artistry was not irrelevant, but performers were supported as much for religious reasons. Furthermore, the availability of training to virtually all disabled children necessarily produced minstrels with a great range of performance skills, including many with little talent.

Characteristics of Performers with Lesser Skills

Although we do not know a great deal about the lower end of minstrel artistry, bits of information were recorded, indicating that poor performers misunderstood or did not try to understand their material. The problem goes beyond their merely memorizing their material, as postulated by Lavrov; these people did not attempt to make sense of what they were saying. Perhaps they felt that their material was sacred and thus beyond their comprehension. In any case, they produced "nonsense," as disparagingly noted by collectors.

An example of "nonsense" from a prayer published by Hnatiuk is the tendency of certain *lirnyky* to say *vochi nas* (roughly, in our eye) instead of *Otche nash* (Our Father). Hnatiuk notes that he asked what "*vochi nas*" meant, and could not get an answer. Though this is the only example Hnatiuk gives, he claims that he has heard numerous such "twisted words."[69] P. Demutskyi explains that certain religious songs are not well known and are frequently sung in jumbled form.[70] Kharkiv also mentions that *lirnyky* do not always understand what they are saying and can become confused, but does not illustrate his statement.[71] Indeed, material that is considered inferior or defective is seldom transcribed, even though it may be plentiful. The Martynovych manuscripts also give infelicitous expressions. Apparently, when Martynovych questioned Khvedir Hrytsenko about his repertory, Hrytsenko answered that he knew the song "Brav i brava." This expression is nonsense in Ukrainian, but Martynovych immediately recognized the item to be a written poem by Hryhoryi Skovoroda which had entered minstrel repertory: "Vsiakomu horody nrav i prava" (To Each City Its Rights and Its Mores) and informed Hrytsenko. The minstrel apparently responded that, while *nrav i prava* has meaning and *brav i brava* does not, *brav i brava* was, nonetheless, the way the song was supposed to be sung.[72]

Vochi nas is an infelicitous phrase from a prayer, and *brav i brava* are meaningless words introduced into a poem. Similar "nonsense" existed at all levels and in all genres. There were performers whose songs turned out badly—and most of these were simply not recorded. Fortunately, a few were. Malynka collected songs from the *lirnyk* Ananii Homyniuk when he was still a relatively young man of thirty-two and had completed a short apprenticeship of one year. He also had picked up some material following apprenticeship from *lirnyky* he met in his travels. Yet, his artistry was minimal. Malynka noted that Homyniuk mixed things up to the point of nonsense.[73] Another way to characterize Homyniuk's texts would be to say that they have traditional lines but are not traditional songs, for they lack plot. Homyniuk seems to have a sense of how a *lirnyk* repertory should sound and what belongs in it, but he cannot pull this into a meaningful narrative. In terms of the oral-formulaic theory, he has formulas and a few themes, but he has no song. This absence of a plot is revealing and important for expanding our understanding of the oral process. When he wrote

Singer of Tales, Albert Lord assumed that a traditional minstrel had a story to tell and that he then proceeded to do so in song by using poetic building blocks called formulas. What Malynka's work with Homyniuk shows is that knowing the stories of a tradition is not that easy or that automatic. Such knowledge may escape a minstrel even after formal training plus some eight years on the job.

Thus, at the bottom end of the scale of minstrel competence, there were performers who simply did not understand their material. To them, it was mysterious, perhaps because it was religious. It did not make sense, and this fact did not bother them. The crucial characteristic of the bottom end of minstrelsy is this willingness to forego comprehension

Characteristics of the Best Minstrels

Homyniuk's example is also useful for contrast. While the problem of the weakest minstrels was failure to comprehend their material, the best minstrels understood their material very well indeed. Furthermore, while Homyniuk's difficulties with narrative lay in lack of plot structure, a sense of narrative line was the key to a song, for the best performers. Work done with Ivan Kravchenko-Kriukovskyi, a *kobzar* of the highest caliber, provides some excellent examples. Martynovych tried to record as many epic songs, or *dumy*, as he could from this minstrel. When they got to the epic about "Samiilo Kishka," Kravchenko-Kriukovskyi could not produce a complete text. He tried, but said that the thirty years which had elapsed since he last sang the song were just too much. If the thirty years is an accurate number, what Kravchenko-Kriukovskyi did produce is amazing, for he got more than halfway through the narrative with only a few lacunae. The verse portion was complete with descriptive embellishments, dialogues, and all of the other features of the finest, fullest texts. What the *kobzar* gave for the last part of this epic was a prose plot summary. Fortunately for us, Martynovych wrote down the plot summary verbatim, along with the verse portion.[74] The fact that Kravchenko-Kriukovskyi gave the story line where he could not produce verse shows that for him, it was the heart of the song. While men like Homyniuk may not have had a sense of where their songs were going, a clear sense of narrative was what performers like Kravchenko-Kriukovskyi retained, even when other parts of their song were gone.

The plot was the skeleton to which oral compositional features were attached, and even in the prose plot summary Martynovych recorded from Kravchenko-Kriukovskyi, there is evidence of the remnants of such features. For example, the summary is built on scenes, which call Lord's themes to mind. The scene depicting the grave of Samiilo Kishka, though rendered in prose, contains traces of the ornate, formulaic description found in the fullest versions of this *duma*. Thus, it is tempting to think that although the minstrel could not produce under the time pressures applied by Martynovych, he could have reactivated his material, given a few days. After all, Kravchenko-Kriukovskyi had burial and grave descriptions elsewhere in his repertory. He could have drawn on these to flesh out what he remembered of "Samiilo Kishka."

Although in Martynovych's recording of "Samiilo Kishka" the story line is what is left when virtually all else is forgotten, it is likely that the story line was also the first thing learned when Kravchenko-Kriukovskyi acquired new material. It is noteworthy that learning new songs took not only three or four recitations, but two or three days, and Kravchenko-Kriukovskyi's account of learning "Samiilo Kishka" in the first place stresses that it took him several days to master this particular poem.[75] What the minstrel likely did during the several days of learning was contemplate his narrative, make sense out of it, figure out the story line. Once this was done, the addition of descriptions, dialogues, and embellishments from the common fund of epic formulae, skillfully applied to the story learned, could follow.

Martynovych collected from Kravchenko-Kriukovskyi in 1876. In 1882, Vasyl Horlenko went to see the *kobzar* and also tried to record "Samiilo Kishka." What he got is a fragmentary text which cannot be used to determine whether Kravchenko-Kriukovskyi still remembered his story line. A major problem is that Horlenko recorded only verse and did not indicate whether the *kobzar* had an opportunity to produce a prose summary of the *duma* as he had done for Martynovych.

While the evidence provided by Horlenko's recording of "Samiilo Kishka" is inconclusive, there is another text which would indicate that Kravchenko-Kriukovskyi did indeed build his songs around a clearly articulated story line. The *kobzar* told Horlenko that he once knew a *duma* about Taras Bulba. Horlenko was rightly skeptical, for Taras Bulba is a character from written literature, namely, the work of Nikolai Gogol. Also, there are no other recordings of this supposed epic song. Kravchenko-Kriukovskyi insisted that Taras Bulba was indeed a *duma*, and Horlenko took down what the *kobzar* knew. This turned out to be a prose plot summary with four lines of verse in the middle. The scenes or themes of this text resemble Kravchenko-Kriukovskyi's *dumy* much more than they resemble Gogol's tale. While the brief scene at the beginning fits Gogol's story to an extent (Dmytro, the youngest son of Bulba, betrays his father, who then kills him), the main narrative has little connection to the written *Taras Bulba*. It tells of the eldest son Tereshko's hubris and his falling asleep in the steppe, oblivious to possible danger. Tereshko is surrounded, and he must abandon his horse and part of his armor and battle the enemy on foot, with just his sword. Tereshko manages to escape but is grievously wounded. His father questions him about the wound and the missing armor and horse. Here the narrative becomes somewhat like a folktale, and the father offers blessed soil to Tereshko to help heal his wound. Tereshko eschews the magical agent, heals himself without help, recovers his horse and armor, and admonishes the enemy never again to threaten Ukrainian soil.[76] This, in all probability, is not a real *duma*, but to modify Horlenko's comments on it somewhat, a conflation of some heroic epic scenes that were favorites of Kravchenko-Kriukovskyi and a folktale, with a few characters from Gogol thrown in. Whatever its source, it provides further evidence that for Kravchenko-Kriukovskyi, the heart of any song was its story line. Whenever Kravchenko-Kriukovskyi could not produce a full verse text, he felt that he could convey the essence of a song to the collector by giving its plot.

The wide use of recitation is further evidence of the importance of plot. Story structure is probably easier to isolate from a dictated text than from a sung one. If mastering narrative structure is the key to learning, then it would make sense that the method which made this structure the most obvious to the greatest number would be the one in widest use. Kravchenko-Kriukovskyi was one of the greatest of all *kobzari*. He learned from recited texts, and he was willing to dictate to collectors. He also had a very strong sense of plot. His artistry attests that these features go together.

Knowledge of the plots of existing narratives was the mark of professionalism. This is what made *kobzari* and *lirnyky* different from other singers. If everything went well, what they learned during apprenticeship was the plots of at least a few narratives, usually religious songs, plus the technique for picking up additional stories. While professional minstrels did improvise a great deal, improvisation was not a mark of professional status. There is no mention of teaching improvisation as part of training, and up until this century, there is no evidence that minstrels were concerned with improvisation, with improving their ability to vary texts or to compose. Rather, like Kravchenko-Kriukovskyi, they were concerned with plot, almost as if, once the story line was mastered, the verse could be improvised to tell it.

A strong sense of the basic story line seems to have guided even the variation found in the texts of the best minstrels, which following Lord's example, should be studied using multiple recordings of the same song from a single performer. Unfortunately, Ukrainian scholars, like early collectors elsewhere, did not record multiple versions of the same text. Since the narratives sung by folk performers were believed to be imperfect renditions of texts created by educated men, there was little sense of a *kobzar* or *lirnyk* as an artist, and few attempts were made to see what he might do to a song from performance to performance. By the time recording multiple versions became standard practice, the oral compositional aspects of Ukrainian minstrelsy were dead. Still, a few multiple recordings were made. The "Epic about the Widow and Her Three Sons" was collected from Mykhailo Kravchenko in 1902, 1904, and 1908, and the scholar Borys P. Kyrdan analyzed the differences between the three texts. The variation he found was consistent with an effort to achieve the most artistically effective presentation of the plot of this song as Kravchenko understood it. There are changes in the sequence of lines which gradually make the presentation more logical. There are additions and omissions which underscore the contrast between the widow, who dedicates herself to the welfare of her children, and the sons, who neglect and even mistreat their mother in her old age. Some of the variation may have been caused by expansion or contraction in response to perceived audience interest or the personal health or mood of the performer (both discussed by Lord). Information about these possible factors was not available. This problem notwithstanding, Kyrdan was able to find a motivation for almost all changes in terms of improved transmission of story line.[77]

What Mykhailo Kravchenko did to his rendition of "The Widow and Her Three Sons" was what the best minstrels did to their songs: they did not simply repeat what they had learned from their masters or from the sources that they had used after apprenticeship, as Lavrov supposed; but they did not compose new songs either. There was no incentive for them to create new songs and no evidence of their doing so prior to this century. Rather, the best minstrels spent their creative energies on making traditional texts the best they could be, modifying them to achieve the greatest emotional impact. Besides the direct evidence of Mykhailo Kravchenko's texts, this supposition is supported by secondary proof, including minstrel confessions that they aroused audience emotions to get better pay and minstrel boasts that they surpassed their masters.

In the Kharkiv manuscripts, the characteristic of the best minstrels is said to be "grasp" (*hortan*). This term is used to describe fellow minstrels that the informant particularly admires and to complain about one's own shortcomings, when a minstrel is dissatisfied with his performance or his rendition of a particular song.[78] The prevalence of this term, at least in the area where Kharkiv collected, is one more indication that the mark of artistic excellence was comprehension. A minstrel who understood his song, its story line, and its emotional meaning was the best artist—not the minstrel who memorized or the minstrel who created something new.

Minstrels in the Intermediate Range

Kravchenko's modifications to "The Widow and Her Three Sons" appear intentional, and the best of minstrels probably had a keen sense of when they had achieved a good rendition of a song. In addition to the variation aimed at improvement, the Ukrainian tradition tolerated a great deal of variation that met the demands of oral composition and had no specific artistic intent. We can substantiate this from minstrel statements and from the texts themselves. Although written down long before Lord articulated oral theory, a great deal of our information is consonant with the *Singer of Tales.* Slastion asked Mykhailo Kravchenko why he occasionally introduced new words, phrases, and sometimes entire verses which had not appeared in his earlier performances of an epic song. The *kobzar* answered:

> Oh, everyone does this; this is not a (lyric) song, you know. You do it as it is appropriate, you know: sometimes it will be short, and sometimes it will be longer. . . . Everyone does it like that: sometimes you forget and you make up something, or you remember something from somewhere else. A song is supposed to be different; but here, that's how it's done.[79]

Speranskii got similar information from Parkhomenko. In this case, the scholar asked the *kobzar* about differences between his version and those of other minstrels. The answer was, "That way is also possible; everyone sings it according to his own liking."[80] Speaking for himself, Slastion wrote:

> Apparently, in the performance of an epic song, a lot depends on the mood of the singer himself and his immersion in the content of the epic. Even earlier I knew that the points in the text that are recited rather than sung, the high vocalizations, the lament elements, cannot be designated in advance. These are a matter of the performer's mood and even the circumstances of performance.[81]

Martynovych gives many remarks about variation in the margins of his manuscripts. He apparently recorded his songs by having the informant dictate, then read the text back to the minstrel and allowed him to make corrections. When questioned about their corrections, minstrels told Martynovych that both versions were acceptable.[82] They gave whole series of lines, saying that these were alternates for each other and that a minstrel could use one set, if that seemed appropriate, or the other, if he felt it to be more effective.[83] They told him about the possibility of having short versions of songs and turning these into long versions, if the situation demanded.[84] In only one case did a minstrel substitute one line for another and insist that the substitution was the correct line because the other line belonged in a different song.[85]

Martynovych's informants told him that should one forget a word or a line, it was much better to "remember from somewhere else" than to sing nothing at all.[86] They recognized that certain epics and other songs had several valid endings from which a minstrel could choose.[87]

The work of Martynovych, Slastion, Speranskii, and Kyrdan gives us a good sense of the stability and flexibility in Ukrainian minstrelsy. The story line had to be stable, but it could be developed in a variety of ways. Singers could and did seek more-effective ways of rendering the story line. This is evident not only from Kyrdan's analysis of Mykhailo Kravchenko's texts, but also from Ivan Humeniuk's statement that *lirnyky* would travel to various regions of Ukraine to hear other versions of songs, looking for ways to improve their own. In keeping with the sense that a minstrel should produce an emotional impact on his audience, the stable part of a story line was its psychological development, not the physical actions of which it told. Kyrdan found that Mykhailo Kravchenko actually changed the ending of "The Widow and Her Three Sons." In his earlier versions, the widow did not forgive the children who had abandoned her in her old age and did not return to their household. In his final version, Kravchenko had the widow forgive her sons, though she still refused to live with them. While this plot variation represented a significant change in the events of his *duma*, it nonetheless enhanced the existing psychological plot, which turned on the contrast between the goodness of the widow and the meanness of her children. There are other *dumy* and religious songs which have similar variation. In the variants of "The Escape of Three Brothers from Azov," for example, the elder siblings who abandon their youngest brother to die in the steppes are sometimes punished by fate, sometimes by their parents, and sometimes by their own guilty consciences. If we apply Kyrdan's work on Kravchenko to the variation found here, we can say that the plot always has to do with punishment for lack of sibling loyalty and that the changes are attempts to convey this plot with the greatest possible impact. Similar phenomena occur in religious songs. In "Saint Barbara" (Varvara), for example, the heroine is sometimes tortured by her father, who disapproves of her devotion to Christianity, and sometimes by her pagan suitor. One could argue that the variation depends on whether a performer found cruelty by a father or a suitor to have more emotional weight.

In sum, it is indeed useful to distinguish three levels of skill in oral performance. Some singers seem to just muddle through, not really sure of what they are singing. Better performers learn poetic speech—the ability to describe an object, a person, or an event in verse. While poetic speech could produce improvisation, improvisation was not highly valued. It was restricted to situations where material specific to a person or event was needed, such as funeral laments.[88] Among professionals, where improvisation was not desired, the best performers went beyond poetic speech and developed a sense of plot, both knowledge of existing plots and techniques for learning new ones. When they performed, plot structure guided their poetic speech. They improvised, varying the surface elements of the plot, namely its external events, but always retaining, and where possible, enhancing the essential, psychological story line.

Chapter 8

Minstrel Guilds and the Orthodox Church

*K*obzari and *lirnyky* were associated with the church and were generally regarded as spiritual descendants of Christ by way of the Apostles. This belief was substantiated by a legend according to which God first sent Jesus Christ to teach people and to bring them to righteousness; then came the Apostles; and then the mendicants. Thus, spreading the word of God throughout the world fell to the minstrels.[1] According to the *lirnyk* Zakhar Holovatyi:

> God assigned *lirnyky* the job of teaching the people so that they would live according to God's way, so that they would not harm orphans and would be forever mindful of the Last Judgement.[2]

Lirnyky told Kharkiv that their instrument was descended from the lyre of the Biblical David, and that their religious songs were composed by the saints and the Apostles.[3] Variations on the David legend are numerous. One of the fullest versions goes as follows:

> The *lira* is the zither of King David. King David took pity on the disabled and gave them a mountain of gold so that they might mine it and thus support themselves. The son of Solomon said that this was not right, that this was not appropriate to the disabled because then people would kill them for it (meaning the gold). One should give them the "volot" and the "zakharbet" (the horse and the begging bag) so that they might travel throughout the world, walking (sic) from village to village, and from house to house begging for alms. Thus they would support themselves and no one could take this from them. They would go from house to house praising God and thus support themselves.[4]

Because minstrels were among God's servants, each minstrel guild was officially affiliated with a church, and by the late nineteenth century, it did not matter whether this church was Orthodox or Uniate Catholic.[5] Ivan Humeniuk told Klement Kvitka that there were no Catholic-Orthodox differences. He said that minstrels would perform at religious festivals outside of both Orthodox churches (*tserkvy*) and Uniate ones (*kosteli*), and that it was perfectly acceptable for an Orthodox man to sing outside a Catholic church and for a Catholic minstrel to sing outside an Orthodox one. Humeniuk said that minstrels would willingly attend each others' services and that the important distinction was between Christians and non-Christians, not between the Orthodox and the Catholics. Problems arose only when an inexperienced minstrel would accidentally try to perform in the home of a Jewish family. Humeniuk added that even Old Believers, although they did not condone music, were quite generous with alms.[6] Samson Veselyi told Kharkiv that the circle of potential listeners extended to the Baptists and that Baptists were particularly fond of a song based on the Skovoroda poem, "To Every City Its Rights and Mores."[7]

Tolerance of all Christian faiths was not always the case. The Cossack Rebellion of 1648, also known as the Khmelnytskyi Uprising, was a bitter conflict between the Orthodox and the Catholics, which grew to cataclysmic proportions, involving all strata of Ukrainian society and affecting almost all of the Ukrainian lands. It was so important to Ukrainian history that it had a profound effect on all Ukrainian institutions—and it virtually transformed minstrelsy. Presumably, Ukrainian folklore, minstrelsy included, was once similar to the folklore of its neighbors. Yet by the time of the intensive folklore scholarship of the second half of the nineteenth century, Ukrainian minstrelsy was quite distinctive. Practically all of the features peculiar to Ukrainian minstrelsy can be connected to the Cossack Rebellion in some way.

One of these peculiar features is the guild system. While the Russian epic was transmitted by amateurs, people who loved epic singing and performed in their leisure time to entertain themselves and their fellow villagers, the Ukrainian epic was in the hands of professionals, minstrels organized into craft guilds. Furthermore, the Ukrainian epic was not an avocation, but the mainstay of its performers.[8] This radical difference between traditions that probably had a common ancestor can be best explained by the importance that guilds acquired in the conflict between the Orthodox and Catholic churches.

The Cossack Rebellion and the Rise of Church Brotherhoods

The Khmelnytskyi Rebellion of 1648 was officially a fight to defend Orthodoxy from annihilation by the Catholic Church. Prior to the Cossack Rebellion, Ukraine was part of the Polish-Lithuanian Commonwealth, which enjoyed a cultural and economic Golden Age in the sixteenth century, followed by inevitable decline as it reached the limit of its natural and human resources. This decline led to social, economic, and political discontent, especially among those members of the population who felt some degree of alienation, such as the Ukrainians. It was they who saw themselves as victims of the policies adopted to counter decline.[9]

This dissatisfaction was aggravated by a threat to religion. Ukrainians were Orthodox, while the Commonwealth was officially Roman Catholic. State support for the Catholic Church placed it in a position of such dominance that, unable to compete, a group of Orthodox clergy signed the Union of Brest in 1596, thus creating the Uniate Church, a religious body which retained the Eastern rite and Ukrainian as the liturgical language but belonged within the administrative structure of the Catholic Church. With the Union of Brest, the Orthodox Church ceased to exist legally within the borders of the Commonwealth, and the Orthodox hierarchy was disbanded. The burden of the struggle to preserve Orthodoxy fell to the laity, many of whom also were opponents of the Commonwealth's secular policies.[10]

Especially important among the Orthodox laity were church guilds or brotherhoods. They had been officially recognized by the Patriarch of Constantinople, who prior to the Union of Brest, sensed the precarious position of the Church. With the abolition of the church hierarchy, the brotherhoods became the only organized Orthodox body.[11] They became even more important with the Khmelnytskyi Rebellion, where they served as a channel through which the Cossacks reached out to all Ukrainians, from all walks of life. The Cossacks provided the military might for this uprising; but an insurrection of the Cossacks alone could never have been as successful as was the action led by Khmelnytskyi.

The Rebellion of 1648 was an uprising of all strata of Ukrainian society: the peasants, the burghers, the Cossacks, and the Orthodox nobility.[12] Defense of Orthodoxy was its rallying cry, and church brotherhoods were the catalyst that brought the various groups together. In 1620, the leader, or hetman, of the Cossacks, Petro Sahaidachnyi, led the entire Zaporozhian Host to join the Kiev Epiphany Brotherhood. Prior to this action, Cossack demands to the Polish-Lithuanian Commonwealth had focused on their own social and economic issues. After they became brothers (*bratchiki*), however, the Cossacks began to require recognition of the Orthodox Church and repeal of the Union of Brest.[13] With the link between the church and the military established, the action that began in 1648 to address purely Cossack concerns quickly became a major uprising fought in the name of the Orthodox faith. As Khmelnytskyi himself said:

> I will liberate all of the Rusian people from Polish oppression. Before, I fought to avenge the wrongs and misdeeds committed against us; now I will fight for our Orthodox faith. All of the common people will help me; the people in Liublin and in Krakov, all who do not reject it (the Orthodox faith) as I do not reject them (the people), for they are our right hand.[14]

The church brotherhoods which flourished from the sixteenth to the eighteenth centuries and were so important to both the defense of Orthodoxy and the Cossack Rebellion were termed *hurty, tsekhy,* or *bratstva* (guilds or brotherhoods). They were composed mostly of city-dwelling traders and craftsmen, although their charters offered admission to people from all areas and all social strata.[15] Because of the dominance of burghers in the brotherhoods, they bore a strong resemblance to trade or craft guilds. They had considerable independence and were self-policing, exercising control over their members outside the jurisdiction of the normal civil authorities. Their purpose was to uphold the Orthodox Church in every possible way. They provided support for the physical structure of the church with which they were affiliated and money for maintenance and the acquisition of new religious items.[16] They helped each other in times of need, loaning money, providing burial services for deceased brothers and caring for their families. Church brotherhoods also practiced charity in the community at large. They assisted disabled and impoverished parishioners and ran agencies called hospices (*shpytali*), which offered housing and care to the disabled and needy.[17] Church brotherhoods are best known for their educational work; they founded printing presses and established church schools, some of which, such as the Kievan Mohyla Academy, became renowned and tremendously influential. Besides establishing great centers of higher learning, brotherhoods provided education on the elementary level, including subsidized education for children of families with limited means.[18] Sensing that Orthodoxy was in mortal danger and that they were charged with its defense, they put tremendous effort into their philanthropic and outreach activities, the hospices and the schools. These efforts paid off, and the institutions and the brotherhoods themselves exerted a profound influence on Ukrainian culture.[19]

Church brotherhoods had a decisive effect on minstrelsy, and minstrel guilds were patterned on them. Minstrel guilds had the same names as church brotherhoods (*hurty, tsekhy,* and *bratstva*) and each minstrel guild was affiliated with a church or monastery and assumed responsibility for the place of its affiliation. The difference between church brotherhoods and minstrel organizations was one of scale. Instead of giving money to maintain the entire church, minstrel guilds took care of one icon. Minstrel guilds also practiced charity on a smaller scale, for all they could do was help those of their own number who experienced a calamity such as fire. Like the church brotherhoods, minstrel guilds were self-policing, and it can be argued that minstrel guilds engaged in educational efforts. Their large apprenticeship schools were probably patterned on the educational practices of the church guilds, especially if they had the policy of accepting all blind children for at least some form of training (see Chapters 5 and 6). Furthermore, a central tenet of the profession, the belief that minstrels were like the Apostles, disseminating religious information among the people, drew on the proselytizing ideas of the church groups. Finally, becoming a minstrel required knowledge of religion. A novice received not only musical training, but a great deal of training that was religious in nature. This training was considered extremely important and was tested more thoroughly than musical knowledge during the initiation, which itself was very much like a rite of entry into a religious group.

The parallels between church brotherhoods and minstrel guilds are extensive, and by the second half of the nineteenth century, minstrels saw their organizations as something like church brotherhoods, doing the same important religious work. Through the agency of the brotherhoods, Ukrainian minstrels developed a close relationship with the Orthodox church—an intriguing situation, especially considering that, in the eleventh century, the church persecuted professional performers, then called *skomorokhi*, driving them north into Russia, where they found a home, only to be attacked again by religious and state institutions and finally formally proscribed by Tsar Aleksei in 1648.[20] To understand how minstrels came to be linked to the church through the brotherhoods, we need to examine brotherhood structure and function.

Institutions Supported by Church Brotherhoods: The Hospices

Churches routinely had a three-fold structure: the church itself, which served as the place of worship and religious celebration; the church school; and the hospice (*shpytal*) providing housing for the indigent and disabled. The three-fold structure was remarkably widespread. Pavlo Efimenko, who has written an extensive study of Ukrainian hospices, says that in 1732, there were one hundred and eighteen of them in the Chernihiv region alone, and that, for the years 1740–1747, five hundred and eighty nine hospices are recorded in Left Bank Ukraine.[21] Some churches had four parts, and included a monastery (possibly also a women's monastery) in addition to the parts already listed. What was unusual about this arrangement and distinguished the Ukrainian church from even its Russian neighbor was that two parts of this unit were controlled by the laity. The same church brotherhoods that were so important to the defense of Orthodoxy and to the Cossack Rebellion were responsible for both the hospices and the schools. These were associated with the church, and there were never more of them in any one region than there were churches, though there could be less.[22] They were located on church grounds or near the church. They had tremendous social impact and survived for such a long time that, as late as 1883, there were still some hospices remaining, and Efimenko was able to interview people who were living or had lived in these. The hospices and schools were remnants of the efforts that church brotherhoods made in defense of the Orthodox Church, and their locations coincided with the Orthodox areas of the Polish-Lithuanian Commonwealth. Philanthropy was handled differently in the Russian north, where there were no hospices and the poor, who happened to be housed on church grounds, were placed in dining halls (*trapezy*), not in buildings erected specifically for their use. Here there was no effort to set up separate, lay-sponsored and -controlled facilities.[23]

Efimenko informs us that hospices often were structured in two parts, one for men and one for women. Sometimes they were separate cottages or cells; sometimes they were complexes of several buildings, which eventually grew into monasteries; and sometimes monasteries were given the mission to care for the disabled and were founded along with the hospices. Hospices sheltered religious pilgrims, both as they travelled and at their destination, and poor students attending church schools could live there. But mostly hospices housed the disabled and the indigent, especially widows and people without families, including some Cossacks. Efimenko even found a record of a nobleman who fell on hard times and lived out his life in a hospice.[24]

Hospices were founded and supported mostly by church brotherhoods. Sometimes they were established by trade guilds, sometimes by wealthy individuals, sometimes by congregations. A few were established by leading clergy, but more as a private than as a church act. Basically, initiative for them came from outside the church hierarchy. After building a hospice, the brotherhood or individual sponsor would assure its continued functioning by providing an endowment. This could be a piece of land, a forest, a toll bridge, a town, sometimes even a tavern. Sometimes a cash sum was donated at the time that the hospice was opened. and other times a nobleman would designate an allotment to be paid yearly. Brotherhoods would send food to their hospices at Christmas and Easter, and the rich would donate food on various feast days, sometimes sending banquet left-overs. Some hospices were supported lavishly, and their inhabitants received food, clothing, bedding, and fuel. In most establishments, the residents had to fend for themselves outside of feast days.[25]

Within the hospice, the poor were organized according to a pattern resembling the structure of church brotherhoods and minstrel guilds. They elected an elder (*starosta*) from among their number to keep order and to run the practical side of their affairs. Large hospices had their own elders; small hospices would band together and elect an elder among them. This did not pose logistic problems, because before the system started to collapse, there was often a hospice at every church, and scores within a single city. The poor living at the hospice would beg, sometimes near their church and sometimes at the bazaar. With this money they would take care of their food and clothing needs. Although they were not obliged to do so, the poor often collected money from amongst themselves to buy items such as icons and Bibles for their church, which according to Efimenko, were still on display at the time that he wrote his study.[26]

The extraordinarily large number of hospices in the sixteenth to eighteenth centuries would indicate that they housed virtually all of the disabled and poor. This monopoly was fostered by the administrative practices of the hospices themselves. Church brotherhoods encouraged all the disabled and impoverished to live at the institutions which they supported, no doubt so that they could have direct access to a church and be exposed to the Orthodox view on Christianity. They may also have coveted a chance to perform more righteous acts by serving more people, thus insuring themselves a favorable religious position. Yet the financial burden of all of the hospice residents must have been enormous, and the various endowments likely proved insufficient rapidly. In his history of the Ukrainian Orthodox Church, Metropolitan Ilarion tells us that the poor living at hospices were obliged to contribute to their own support by going out and begging under the banner of the affiliated church brotherhood.[27] This policy was probably meant to alleviate the financial burden on the hospice. Instead, it too increased the demand on and for hospices by driving all non-affiliated beggars out of business. It is likely that when church brotherhoods were at the height of their influence and power, beggars affiliated with them shared in their prestige and had much better success than unaffiliated alms seekers. Hospice beggars probably protected their turf from beggars who were not guild members, and this was yet another reason why those outside the church-hospice system did not stand much of a chance. In any case, by the nineteenth century, when our data become more plentiful, there were no beggars who were not guild members. Since beggar guilds were patterned on church brotherhoods and probably came into being under hospice influence, all beggars attested in the nineteenth century were descendants of the hospice system.

Minstrels Prior to Hospice Influence

Something analogous but much more complex happened to minstrelsy. Apparently, the vortex of the church brotherhoods sucked in a part of Ukrainian music and made it the exclusive property of brotherhood clients. While in the nineteenth century there were no minstrels who were not guild members, prior to the heyday of the church brotherhoods, sighted professional free-lance performers who played the *bandura* for a living did exist. They were not members of guilds, and they were not mendicants. They were not affiliated with the church, and their behavior may have been less than pious.

Interesting documentary evidence from the second half of the eighteenth century exists for what must have been the very last of the non-brotherhood minstrels. Here we learn about sighted performers, *bandura* players (*bandurysty*) who were affiliated not with the church but with the remnants of the Cossacks. The most detailed information is the personal deposition of Danylo Bandurko, given in 1761 at the Elizaveta fortress, where he had been brought for trial on charges of banditry and theft. Bandurko was born in Kiev, presumably in 1738, because his age at the time of his trial is given as twenty-three. His family name was Rykhliivskyi, but he received the appellation Bandurko from his craft, which he learned by studying with a master in Bohuslav. He claims to have gone for training at the age of ten and studied for one year. Upon completion of training, he became a court bard of sorts in the home of the governor of Kiev, a certain Leontiev, where he was favored for his musical abilities. The governor died three years later, and Danylo went home to live with his mother. Soon he turned up in the Sich, the headquarters of the Zaporozhian Cossacks, where he worked as a musician, entertaining the Cossacks and earning clothes and money in payment. He was also given odd jobs such as plowing and guarding the herds and the goods of the Cossacks. Soon Bandurko started joining various raiding parties of the *haidamaky*, groups of Cossacks who made their living as brigands. Bandurko's deposition accounts for the goods in his possession by describing several raids into Polish territory. He also tells of entertaining the *haidamaky* during their travels and being rewarded with clothing, horses, and other prizes for his artistry. Bandurko paints a colorful picture of the cordial reception that the *haidamaky* received in Ukraine, even though in one village, they accidentally burned down some five or six houses during their drinking and revelry, and in another, they managed to set fire to the home of their host. But the charges against Bandurko were not for forays into Polish territory or the accidents that occurred on the way; rather, they were for banditry in the Elizaveta province, a Ukrainian region, and to these he pleaded innocent, asserting that here he never caused any physical harm or stole anything except for some crackers to complement his *horilka* (vodka). We do not know what ultimately happened to Bandurko.[28]

The fate of three other *bandurysty*, Prokip Skriaha, Vasyl Varchenko, and Mykhailo Sokovyi Ziat is more certain. According to the record (*Kodenskaia kniga*) of the trials and executions that took place following the Koliiv-shchina, the 1768 uprising against the Poles, all three were sentenced to death.[29] Both the record and the trials on which it was based are fascinating in a gruesome sort of way. The proceedings began in Kodnia, and hence "Kodenskaia," and the punishments meted out would have made any medieval executioner proud. They included drawing and quartering, flaying, and excision of various body parts. Apparently, the screams and moans of the accused were so horrible that the ruler of Kodnia, Glembotskii, ordered the proceedings out of town so as not to disturb law-abiding citizens. Consequently, the trials were moved to Troianov, and then again to Tetiev, where they continued until the whole process ended in 1772. The book in which the proceedings are recorded consists of six hundred and eight pages and covers the years 1769 to 1772. The pages were apparently sewn together at random, and they are not arranged chronologically, so that the materials belonging to one trial are sometimes scattered in several places. There may also be material missing from the record. What exists gives evidence that three minstrels (*bandurysty*) were tried and sentenced. One, Prokip Skriaha, must have been sighted, because he is accused of participating in murder and pillage along with the Cossacks whom he was serving as a musician. At least one of the men pleaded innocent. Mykhailo Sokovyi Ziat claimed that all he had done was play music and that he did not participate in robbery or the murder of two Jews, although the crimes did occur in his presence.

Evidently, nineteenth-century presuppositions about minstrels led the author of the article about the *Kodenskaia kniga* to read the trials of the three *bandura* players as dreadful tortures inflicted on innocent "men of God." If we judge by Danylo Bandurko, however, these men may not have been innocent and godly. They were probably somewhere between minstrels like *skomorokhi*, who may indeed have been guilty of some of the pilfering and philandering of which they were often accused, and minstrels who had to be blind, church-affiliated, and pious. Furthermore, the above records suggest there was probably an intermediate step between minstrels like *skomorokhi*, who were affiliated with no one except each other, and nineteenth-century *kobzari* and *lirnyky*, who belonged to minstrel guilds officially tied to churches. During this intermediate stage, which ended with the close of the eighteenth century, sighted musicians evidently could find work only in the military. This supposition would explain the lack of sighted *kobzari* and *lirnyky* in the nineteenth century, for when the Zaporozhian Sich was liquidated and the Cossacks and *haidamaky* were disbanded, sighted minstrels like Danylo Bandurko and Prokip Skriaha also ceased to exist. If the military was the only place that sighted performers could work, then its demise would mean their demise also. In the civilian sphere, blind minstrels like those who monopolized the profession in the nineteenth century were already well established, and there was no room among them for the sighted. Nineteenth- and early twentieth-century guilds controlled access to their territory and denied performance opportunities to all non-affiliated singers. Similar attacks on persons who did not fit the hospice and brotherhood profile likely occurred when the Sich was disbanded and sighted *bandurysty* like Bandurko became relics of the past.

There is documentary proof that blind, non-military performers affiliated with churches and hospices were well established long before the nineteenth century. An arrest warrant for a blind, church-connected minstrel dates to the first half of the eighteenth century. Queen Elizabeth of Russia had a taste for music in general, and probably under the influence of her paramour Rozumovskii, Ukrainian music in particular. She imported the *kobzar* Hryhorii Mykhailovych Liubystok in 1730, but apparently the minstrel did not reciprocate Elizabeth's affection for him and his music, and a year later, he tried to flee. Elizabeth's edict that he be captured and returned to court was distributed to places where Liubystok would have tried to find shelter: churches, monasteries, and their hospices. The edict provided a description of Liubystok as fair, of medium height, and blind. By the time he was found, he had managed to travel from Moscow to Kiev, where he had taken shelter at the Lavra Monastery, no mean accomplishment for a blind person travelling alone. He was removed from Kiev under guard on August 10, 1731, and returned to Moscow. After this, Liubystok apparently accepted his fate. Records indicate that he remained at Elizabeth's court until 1749. At that point, a group of Moscow gentlemen bought his freedom. His subsequent fate is not entirely clear, but he seems to have received some lands and become relatively prosperous.[30]

Thus, the few sighted *kobzari* we know about in the eighteenth century were being tried and executed. By the nineteenth century, sighted *kobzari* and *lirnyky* were simply not tolerated, though many people played minstrel instruments and sang for their own pleasure. Borzhkovskii quotes a peasant as saying that her daughter could sing "Konovchenko," a popular but long and complex epic poem.[31] Only people with a disability, however—people who would have qualified for residence in a hospice—were allowed to enter minstrel guilds and make money from this type of music.

The Influence of the Church Schools

Church schools, the other philanthropic institution sponsored by the brotherhoods, can give us some clues to the process by which minstrelsy was restricted to the church milieu. Schools were probably the agency that encouraged hospice residents to sing and gave them material to perform. In their efforts to spread Orthodoxy, church schools likely reached out to those nearby, the people living in the hospices, and taught them whatever liturgical material they could. Songs were probably a high priority among such material, possibly even for reasons like the ones articulated by Nadiia Suprun, namely a belief that the downtrodden and the blind are particularly predisposed to musical expression. Once hospice residents began singing religious songs for money as part of their efforts to secure alms, they took singing away from other potential performers, much as church beggars eliminated beggars with no church affiliation. Church schools are also important to minstrelsy because they are relatively well documented. In the records of the church schools and in the biographies of their students we can find confirmation of minstrel phenomena, some of which can otherwise only be surmised.

Pavlo Zhytetskyi discusses church schools and their connection to minstrelsy as an explanation for the origin of the Ukrainian epic songs, *dumy.* While his argument for the origin of the epic in the writings of seminarians is not convincing, he brings up a number of points that are important to minstrelsy in general, as well as to the epic in particular. One is that schools served virtually everyone who wanted an education, a phenomenon that would explain both the wide availability of minstrel training even after the hospice and church school system had collapsed and the villagers' tendency to easily accept minstrel claims to knowledge of scripture. Schools were as plentiful as hospices, and were often built right along with a new church. Thus they were available in practically every village and were not the exclusive privilege of the wealthy. The rich educated their children more comfortably. They could hire a deacon as a private, live-in tutor. If they chose, those who were better off could send their children to a school in the city instead of using the local institution, which was probably more poorly equipped and staffed by a teacher with less extensive training. Rich children who had to live away from home during their schooling could live in an apartment and receive food and money from home; they did not have to live in hospices or fend for themselves. Yet poor families could educate their children as well. Payment in kind was quite acceptable to the schoolmaster, and Zhytetskyi cites the tale of how pleased school residents were when the payment for the education of one of their number was a pig. Life at school for poor children may have been difficult, but an education was possible, and according to Zhytetskyi, the hunger and privation were made tolerable by the hope of social betterment. Clergy positions were not hereditary in Ukraine, and a poor boy who mastered his lessons could become a deacon, or even "claw his way up to (being) a priest."[32]

In order to make it through the difficulties of life at school, students tried to earn a bit of money any way that they could. During the academic year, they would go out to beg in the town or city where they were studying, sometimes even in groups, singing and chanting and requesting support. These are activities that might well have set the pattern for other hospice residents, such as beggars and minstrels. In the summer, students would head out to the villages, trading their knowledge for money, or food, or clothing—anything that the villagers could spare. Some of the more adventuresome would head out to the Zaporozhian Sich, where their knowledge of writing came in handy and where they could find work as regimental scribes. Zhytetskyi points out that some of the students who left in the summer to earn money never returned, and remained Cossack scribes. Many found the abundance of life in a village so much better than the privation at school that they stayed, earning a living with their meager knowledge. Zhytetskyi quotes a poem written by a pupil at a church school which is virtually a panegyric to village food:

> Oh, beloved village, when will I see your delicious dishes?
> Cabbage and peas, turnips and beans, all cooked in bacon?
> Oh, happy evenings! Oh, blissful nights!

With sentiments like these, it is little wonder that many chose life in the village over further schooling. Some even wrote poems urging acceptance of fate and renunciation of school. Privation was not the only problem. Corporal punishment, especially in conjunction with grammar lessons, gave many an incentive to leave. Zhytetskyi includes a satirical poem about how each letter of the alphabet was not only taught to students, but literally beaten into them.

> The teacher (*bakaliar*) told me to say "Az, Az" (alpha)
> And when I didn't, he hit me, "Bam! Bam!"
> He yelled at me a second time, "Say buki!" (beta)
> But before I had a chance, he got his hands on me.
> Then he yelled a third time for me to say, "Vide!"
>   (the Cyrillic v)
> And his itchy fingers were already reaching for my hair.
> Then the fourth thing he said was "Say zhyvite!" (not delta,
>   but zh, the next letter in the Church Slavonic alphabet)
> "Okay, boys, lay him down on the bench and spread him out!"
> I begged; I prayed; I became even more terrified.
> And they gave me such a beating that I was senseless.

Especially bad were the Saturday exams, with their "reinforcement" of the grammar covered during the preceding week.[33] Hryhoryi Skovoroda, a widely known and respected Ukrainian philosopher and poet, supposedly left the school in Pereiaslav because of just such instructional practices and wandered the countryside, seeking God and writing. These incentives to quit school produced a pattern of people leaving at various points in their training, much as with minstrel apprenticeship, and using whatever they knew to support themselves.

The instruction that students received at school and then traded for a crust of bread began with grammar. They learned how to read and write, and afterwards came religious instruction. While not part of the curriculum officially, the arts were very important, and church school students wrote serious and satirical poetry, painted, and sang. In sum, the students acquired knowledge on a variety of subjects that could be sold to various potential employers. Zhytetskyi claims that the art produced by church school pupils was in special demand, and says that when government schools were introduced by Catherine the Great, they failed precisely because they did not meet the aesthetic needs of the populace.[34] The value placed on artistic services again links phenomena observed in church schools to minstrelsy.

Zhytetskyi's point that all levels of knowledge were acceptable, or at least marketable, is very significant. While the completion of training and appointment as a deacon or priest were highly desirable, failure to complete training was not a disaster. All forms of knowledge were honored and prized in their own way. Zhytetskyi illustrates this through the inclusion of Ilia Turchynovskyi's autobiography from the first half of the eighteenth century. Turchynovskyi was the son of the Lieutenant (*sotnik*) of Berezan. He studied in the local church school, then went on to the Academy in Kiev, where he completed the lower forms, only to be withdrawn by his mother, who needed his help at home. After a while, Turchynovskyi left home "to see the world and get more education." He served as a scribe, then decided to journey to the city of Mohilev, but quarreled with his travelling companions and would have lost his books, clothes, money, and perhaps even his life, had he not been rescued by the head of a military regiment stationed nearby. The hetman, a friend of the author's father, made Turchynovskyi his personal scribe; but Turchynovskyi, not one to stay long in any place or any position, soon requested permission to proceed to Mohilev to further his education and learn Latin. In Mohilev, Turchynovskyi studied in both Orthodox and Jesuit schools, eventually attracted the attention of an Orthodox bishop with his singing, and was asked to join the choir at the Church of the Epiphany. Turchynovskyi likely had a quarrelsome personality, for he was soon at odds with the choirmaster, who during the all-night service leading into Easter Sunday, threw him over the railing of the choir balcony. As Turchynovskyi writes:

> If I had not happened on the heads of the women, I surely would have fallen to my death on the marble floor. And the heads of many of the women were injured, and the head of one old woman was completely broken, and she died three days later.[35]

Turchynovskyi's autobiography continues in this same manner. Although his education was limited and he tended to involve himself in altercations, Turchynovskyi gradually advanced through the church hierarchy. He fled Mohilev and the vengeful choirmaster, and became regent at the monastery in Shklov, where he served for four years and staged a particularly successful play (*intermediia*), only to become embroiled in another controversy. This time, he fled to Chernihiv, almost drowned on the way, but survived and became a deacon. He then travelled to his homeland, and found his parents still living. After staying with them a while, he headed for Pereiaslav, where he continued to sing and served as a regent. For his services in the choir, he was appointed a priest back in his native Berezan. He married in 1718, the year of his appointment. As priest, Turchynovskyi offended a powerful woman by refusing to accept her confession. It is telling that when the woman turned to the bishop and sought to oust Turchynovskyi, the latter supported the newly appointed clergyman and even wrote that if the petitioner "did not want to kiss (Turchynovskyi's) hand, she could kiss him somewhere else." Failing to get satisfaction from the religious hierarchy, the woman turned to civil authorities and the last extant sheet of the autobiography describes Turchynovskyi under arrest, travelling in a cart, and involved in yet another accident.[36]

Turchynovskyi introduces his autobiography with the statement that he is writing to instruct his children and grandchildren. What the author was trying to teach his descendants is not clear, because his life is hardly exemplary of Christian virtue. It does, however, show that success was possible even if one knew as little as, judging by the grammar and punctuation errors in the autobiography, Turchynovskyi did. Considering that Turchynovskyi was repeatedly recognized and rewarded for his artistic abilities, his singing and his playing, this text also shows that art was a good way to compensate for limited scholastic knowledge.

Zhytetskyi does not draw a direct connection between *kobzari* and *lirnyky* and mendicant "scholars" like Turchynovskyi, but parallels certainly exist. The crux of the matter is, again, that all levels of "church knowledge" were valued and rewarded, and that singing was particularly prized. People with some knowledge of scripture could travel the Ukrainian countryside and make a living in the eighteenth century, much as mendicant minstrels did in the nineteenth and twentieth. Turchynovskyi, a man with limited book learning but a fine voice, could make his way in the world; and minstrels who knew some psalms, some prayers, and a few saints' lives were also honored and compensated for their artistic and religious services. Next to defending Orthodoxy, educating the people was the main goal of church brotherhoods, and those who had acquired some of this education were esteemed; those who sought to share their knowledge and educate others were doubly honored. In many senses, minstrels were like mendicant scholars because they were not ordained clergy, yet possessed knowledge and disseminated it among the people. Very likely, minstrels saw a parallel between themselves and mendicant scholars, especially as agents for dispensing religious information. This may be where they got the comparison between themselves and the Apostles and the idea that their *lira* came from the lyre of David. With all the similarities and links between minstrels and wandering seminarians, it is no coincidence that a frequent component of minstrel repertories was "To Every City Its Rights and Mores," a song based on a poem by the former seminarian Skovoroda.[37] It is also possible that many minstrel songs, as Zhytetskyi proposes, came from compositions written by seminarians far less well-known than Skovoroda, but we cannot establish this for a fact because the written versions of these songs are no longer available.

Minstrelsy's Dual Heritage: Links to Beggars and Links to Church Brethren

What we have, then, is a link between minstrelsy and the two parts of the church complex controlled by the brotherhoods, the hospices, and the schools, under the influence of which minstrelsy probably achieved the form in which we know it. We do not have the data to reconstruct a precise sequence of how hospices, church schools, and Ukrainian folk music came together, but there are clear indications that hospices were the starting point and that *kobzari* and *lirnyky* were all descendants of hospice clients. The criteria for becoming a minstrel were derived from the criteria for admission into a hospice. Of course, the primary qualification for minstrelsy was blindness, and talent was not a consideration. Physical disability, without regard to any other traits, is precisely what would have made someone eligible for admission into a hospice. Our knowledge of hospice admission criteria comes from charters that routinely state that the purpose of the hospice was to serve people with physical disabilities.[38] Statements minstrels made to folklorists about who could and who could not be a minstrel sound exactly like the hospice charters in that they said that a man had to be disabled (he had to be a *kalika*), but did not specify that he had to be blind.[39]

Kobzari and *lirnyky* had a great deal in common with beggars, the other descendants of the hospice. Earlier we noted evidence that beggars and minstrels studied together and that ordinary beggars were people who did not complete the full course of minstrel training. Other ties exist as well. Beggars knew the secret language (*lebiiska mova*) used by minstrels. The terminology applied to beggars in ordinary speech was frequently applied to minstrels as well. While beggars were never called *kobzari* or *lirnyky*, minstrels, like beggars, were called *zhebraky*, a term derived from the verb "to beg, to request alms," the activity that those living in hospices needed to perform to support themselves. Minstrels and beggars both were called "elder" (*did* and *starets*), terms that linked them to the church, and as we shall see, possibly also to pre-Christian religious activity. Both beggars and minstrels organized themselves into guilds, a practice both inherited from church brotherhoods. There is evidence that beggars had apprenticeships and that their teachers were called "master," just like minstrel teachers, and that a man could study with a beggar master and then continue his education with a minstrel.[40] If beggars could sing, they were allowed to do so for money, like minstrels. There was probably once a continuum of musical knowledge, a pyramid with minstrelsy at its apex. At one point, perhaps in the sixteenth century, when brotherhoods first rose to prominence, this pyramid was whole; but eventually; the apex broke off into a separate category, that of the professional minstrel.

While minstrels shared the hospice heritage with beggars, they were not beggars but professional craftsmen. The way that minstrels broke away and became professionals probably had a great deal to do with church schools. Schools and hospices were very closely linked to each other. Not only were both sponsored and controlled by church brotherhoods, they also had many internal ties, and certain of the church school pupils lived at the hospice. Hospice residents and church school students ate together, attended services together, and sang together. During a service, they both assumed low-ranking duties within the church. Church school students even did some begging, like the residents of the hospices.

The mission of the church schools was to act as a conduit, channeling learning, both secular grammar and religious scripture, down to the people. At the same time, they were supposed to elevate the people by preparing them to fill the depleted ranks of the clergy. Surely schools must have exercised some of this social dynamism on the hospice. Presumably, with the admissions policies of the schools, hospice residents, not just those who used the hospice as a dormitory, but the poor who were permanent hospice dwellers, could study at the schools. Furthermore, those who were able to succeed academically could leave the ranks of the poor and become deacons or priests, just like anyone else. There are indications that the disabled indeed participated in school life. Almost all of the material in minstrel repertories, except for epic and possibly historical poetry, is probably of school origin. Skovoroda's "To Every City Its Rights and Mores" is a scholastic poem, and the abundant scriptural and apocryphal material which P. Demutskyi found in *lira* songs may be derived from similar poems.[41] Writings by and for church school pupils are voluminous and contain modifications on scripture and apocrypha, just like minstrel songs. We cannot know whether the minstrel material came from these writings directly or was orally produced on the pattern of scholastic poetry; but in either case, the influence of the school is manifest.

Yet with all of their ties to the church schools, the disabled, especially the blind, could not become priests or deacons. The blind could, however, sing, chant, and recite, which did not require writing. Turchynovskyi advanced his career quite far on singing, and for the blind, there was the possibility of singing professionally. As professionals, minstrels were not clergy, but they resembled something as good or better: they were craftsmen, like the members of church brotherhoods. At some point, minstrels must have drawn the analogy between themselves and the members of the church brotherhoods (*bratchyky*), claiming for themselves some of the prestige afforded brotherhood members. Many other things contributed to minstrelsy's stature. Music was considered pleasing to God. Zhytetskyi claimed to have a manuscript in his personal archives which says that Adam was created to please God by making music for Him.[42] Khotkevych discussed various legends about the divine source of music.[43] Music was considered an especially effective way to disseminate religious knowledge to the common people and fulfill the educational mission of the church brotherhoods.[44] Music was perhaps considered especially suited to the disabled because of the belief in their musical aptitude.

An interesting manifestation of the combined heritage of the hospices and the brotherhoods is that nineteenth- and twentieth-century minstrels were viewed as both passive, like the clients of the hospices, and active, like church brethren. The sorry state of the blind was supposed to serve the divine purpose by arousing pity and prompting people to charity, an act pleasing to God. Minstrels were conscious of this and utilized it in their begging songs, which explicitly called on the hearer to contemplate their disability, to show compassion, and to donate money, food, or cloth. They also relied on sad music to stir the emotions and produce pity (*zhalist*), almost like the wounds and deformities which beggars displayed to get sympathy and money.[45] Veresai claimed that he could turn on pity (*zhalist*) at will, unless perhaps he was incapacitated by illness: "It seldom doesn't work—maybe if I'm sick. But if I want to get to somebody, then I'll put a lot of sorrow in my voice, so much sorrow that it goes right to the heart."[46]

Yet many minstrels did not want pity and did not want to do God's work passively by displaying their suffering. They saw themselves as active agents, just as the church brethren had once been. After all, they made donations to their churches, just like the brethren, and bought church supplies, artifacts, and gifts. Minstrels felt that they, too, disseminated knowledge of religion, and, in fact, might be the most efficacious distributors of religious information because they were divinely chosen for this mission, like the Apostles. Singers and village dwellers alike believed that minstrel prayers were especially effective and that *kobzari* and *lirnyky* had an obligation to pray for the salvation of their audiences and the eternal rest of the departed. Veresai said that minstrel prayers were more powerful than the prayers of others, adding rather undiplomatically that minstrel prayers ascended to God more directly than the prayers of the nobility. He reassured the collector by saying that he prayed for all those who had given him alms, especially those who had rewarded him with particularly nice gifts or particularly large donations.[47]

Thus, mendicants attributed a cosmic significance to their very existence, which, they felt, brought salvation not just to the individuals who offered them charity and to their ancestors, but to the world as a whole. As V. Danyliv heard outside the Lavra monastery in Kiev, they believed that the end of the world was coming, if not in their lifetime, then during the next generation, and that as Christ suffered on the cross for the salvation of mankind, so before Armageddon, "the poor will suffer torture and torment, in the name of Christ." The following legend, told by a blind man, assigns mendicants an essential place in the natural order.

> Frightening times are approaching. It is written at the end of the Bible that a time will come when the nobles and the priests and the merchants will say, "We don't need the poor anymore. Let's drown them all or slay them, every one." And they will want to drown or kill us. Maybe this won't happen to us, but it will surely happen sooner or later. Then a person will come forth, maybe the ruler of a foreign kingdom, and he will say to our king, maybe not the current king, but whoever is king at the time, "Sell me all the poor from throughout your kingdom." And what will our king do? He will go and sell the poor. He won't care. And they will gather the poor from all over the land and send them over to a different land, the land of the king who bought them. And there will be no more poor people left on Russian soil at all. And then all of the nobles and the priests and the merchants will start to live happily and to rejoice that they have no more poor people and that they don't have to

worry about them or give them alms. They will start to drink and to celebrate. And they will keep on drinking until a great famine comes to the Russian land. Then they will start to die, but they won't know why the famine has come. Then someone will tell them about us, or maybe they will remember themselves, and the nobles and priests and merchants will say, "Where are our poor? Why aren't we giving them alms. Why are they not wishing us good health? Why are they not praying for our departed? Maybe that is why our crops have failed." They will remember that they sold the poor to a foreign land, and will want them back. But it will be too late. The Lord Jesus Christ will take the poor up to Heaven and will Himself descend to earth with His heavenly angels to punish the wicked.[48]

Ukrainian traditional society, then, took care of its disabled in a most effective way: it not only gave them an explanation for their plight and a purpose to their existence, it let them work. A disabled person could rise above his disability. A blind person could become an active worker for social and moral good, and did not have to settle for accepting charity. He did not have to be a good-for-nothing (*darmoiid*). As a minstrel, he could perform a valued service. The wisdom exhibited by traditional Ukrainian society was not conscious, but the result of the quirks of Ukrainian history. It was the threat to Orthodoxy that prompted church brotherhoods to action, and their efforts on their church's behalf that gave the blind who entered minstrelsy not just an explanation to ease the acceptance of their fate, but that all-important potential for action.

The fight to preserve Orthodoxy had a profound effect on Ukrainian culture but did not do much for the Orthodox Church. The Cossack Revolution failed. Ukraine could not sustain a constant state of war, and Khmelnytskyi was caught between official submission to Poland and alliances with the Crimean Tatars, Moldova, Transylvania, and other small states. Eventually, in 1654, he accepted a treaty with Moscovy, but Russian protection did not bring peace or protect the Ukrainian Orthodox Church. Khmelnytskyi died three years later, in 1657, and factional fighting among his successors and potential successors grew worse in the years that followed. Ukraine was partitioned. In the east, the Hetmanate created by the Pereiaslav Treaty with Russia survived as a semi-independent protectorate for a while, but was eventually absorbed by Moscovy. Its religious institutions met the same fate as its political ones, and the Ukrainian Orthodox Church was subjugated to the Moscow Patriarchate. West of the Dnieper, the situation was far worse. The western part of Ukraine suffered a period of virtual depopulation appropriately called The Ruin (*Ruina*). Needless to say, the Orthodox Church did not fare well in this area.

But Orthodoxy did survive, and bore surprisingly few grudges against Catholicism. As stated at the beginning of this chapter, by the nineteenth century, there was next to no Orthodox-Catholic animosity. Even in the eighteenth century, Turchynovskyi crossed fairly freely from Orthodox churches and schools to Catholic ones, and back. Part of the reason may be that the hospices and schools were essentially western institutions borrowed by the Orthodox from the Catholic Church. In their efforts to fight Catholicism, the Orthodox church brotherhoods patterned their behavior on Catholic practices. Thus, while intended to ward off Catholicism, the hospices and schools of the Ukrainian Orthodox Church may actually have made it more like the Catholic one and eventually brought the two churches closer together, at least on Ukrainian territory.

There may be another factor at work as well. The Ukrainian national consciousness was shaped by a struggle against a non-Christian enemy, the Moslem Turks and Tatars. The distinction between Christians and non-Christians may have been so thoroughly ingrained that it overrode all subsequent ones. It is interesting and indicative that in the epic songs based on the period discussed in this chapter, the *dumy* about Khmelnytskyi, there is not a word about fighting Catholicism. The Poles are the enemy in many songs, but nothing is said about their religion. Often, antagonism is transferred to a non-Christian enemy, and Jewish agents of the Poles are supposed to be the real villains, the real oppressors of the Ukrainian people. In the next chapter we will look at the Khmelnytskyi *dumy* and the other serious songs in a minstrel's repertoire. The fact that a whole new cycle of song developed as a result of the Cossack or Khmelnytskyi Rebellion is further proof that this period affected minstrelsy profoundly, both the songs sung by minstrels, and minstrel institutions.

Chapter 9

Minstrelsy and Martyrdom: The Influence of Religious Song on Epic

*T*he Khmelnytskyi Rebellion transformed minstrelsy and limited it to blind performers who were organized into professional guilds patterned on church brotherhoods. It would appear that this important historical event also took two groups of musicians that had once been separate, the *kobzari* and the *lirnyky*, and joined them into one professional cadre. Up to this point, *kobzari* and *lirnyky* have been examined as one unit: Ukrainian professional minstrels. And indeed, in the period from which we have our data on performers, they were one group.[1] Different terms were applied to them, depending on the instrument they played; but other than that, there was little to distinguish *kobzari* from *lirnyky*. Their repertories were virtually identical; they belonged to the same guilds, knew each other and interacted with each other.[2] They even learned from each other, both during apprenticeship and after initiation, when minstrels would fill out their repertories by picking up additional songs.[3] Parkhomenko, for example, learned both the *bandura* and the *lira*. He taught his pupils both instruments, and his most famous pupil was not a *kobzar*, like Parkhomenko himself, but the *lirnyk* Avram Hrebin.

Kobzari and *Lirnyky* As Distinct Categories

At some point in the past, however, *kobzari* and *lirnyky* were most likely separate categories of musicians. The immense difference between their two instruments points to separate origin and separate evolution until some cataclysmic event like the Cossack Rebellion. The *lira* and the *bandura*, along with its predecessor, the *kobza*, look different, sound different, require different playing techniques, and even encourage different singing styles. The *bandura* is a strummed and plucked, asymmetrical lute, while the *lira* is a crank-driven hurdy-gurdy that produces a continuous drone. Oleksandr Malynka and later Filaret Kolessa noted that the *lira* made its players sing in a louder, more forced voice and did not allow the subtlety and expressiveness permitted by the *bandura*.[4] With all of these differences, the *bandura* and the *lira* could not possibly be related, and the musicians who used them were probably also once distinct.

It appears also that specific song genres were once associated with each instrument. While there was very little difference in repertory in the late nineteenth and early twentieth centuries, probably the *bandura* was originally the instrument of epic, while the *lira* was the instrument of religious song. The *bandura* and the symmetrical *kobza* resemble the instruments used to accompany epic in other Slavic and even non-Slavic traditions. Although it is asymmetrical and very distinctive in appearance, the *bandura* is, after all, a lute, just like the Central Asian *domra*, the South Slavic *gusle*, the Turkish *saz*, and other epic instruments.[5] Documentary and historical evidence links the *bandura* to the epic and its subjects. The military musicians who appear in court records and who were probably the last sighted minstrels were all *bandura* or *kobza* players. The Cossack Mamai of a widely disseminated folk picture always holds a *kobza* or a *bandura*. The geographical distribution of *kobzari* in the nineteenth and early twentieth centuries corresponded closely to the boundaries of the Hetmanate, the Cossack state left after the Khmelnytskyi Rebellion and the Treaty of Pereiaslav. *Kobzari* could be found in the regions of Kiev, Kharkiv, Poltava, and Chernihiv, but not in Galicia or Western Ukraine.[6] The distribution of epic poetry was virtually identical to the distribution of *kobzari*. In Galicia and Western Ukraine, where there had been no Cossack state and there were no *kobzari*, there were also no epic songs, or *dumy*. *Dumy* were a phenomenon strictly of Eastern or Great Ukraine. Even in Eastern Ukraine, where *kobzari* and *lirnyky* existed side by side and both knew epic songs, it was slightly more likely that a *kobzar* would know *dumy* than a *lirnyk*.[7]

While the *bandura* was the instrument of the epic, the *lira* was the instrument of the mendicant and of religious songs. The court records of *bandura* players predate references to the *lira*, although Hnat Khotkevych mentions a painting in a thirteenth- or fourteenth-century psalter, where the Biblical David holds a Ukrainian folk *lira* in place of the classical lyre.[8] Because of the dearth of written records, the *lira*'s heritage must be inferred from its uses outside Ukrainian territory. Also called the *lera* and the *relia*, the *lira* existed in Russia and Belarus, and possibly also in Moldova and Ukraine's other neighbors to the west. Here, just as in Western Ukraine, it was the instrument of the mendicant, although not all mendicants knew how to play it. The repertory of these mendicants partially coincided with that of Ukrainian *lirnyky*, in that they performed religious songs and begging songs.[9] Perhaps they also played dance tunes and satirical songs like Ukrainian *lirnyky*, but there is not enough information about the private and less solemn part of their repertory to state this with certainty. Outside of Ukraine, *lira* and *relia* players did not know epic song, and this genre was acquired only by those Ukrainian *lirnyky* who worked on the same territory as *kobzari*.[10] It would be useful to show that in Eastern Ukraine, religious songs were more closely associated with *lirnyky*, just as epic songs are more closely associated with *kobzari*. Unfortunately, collectors preferred *dumy* and simply did not record religious songs in numbers great enough for us to say that they were more characteristic of one type of minstrel than the other.

As *kobzari* were once the minstrels of the military, so *lirnyky* were probably always mendicants and always the minstrels of the church, the musicians associated with disability and begging. There is no way of knowing when they acquired this position. Perhaps it was when church brotherhoods first started taking over the care of the disabled and indigent, perhaps earlier. While we have court records, geographical distribution, and *dumy* to link *kobzari* to the military, we have little that specifically links *lirnyky* to the church. There was, however, one feature: large schools of minstrelsy similar to church schools were found among *lirnyky* only.[11] The fact that only *lirnyky* had large schools indicates that their affiliation with the three-fold complex of church, school, and hospice was one of long standing and that *kobzari*, the poets of the Cossacks, were a later addition to the system.

From Separate Existence to Union: The Assimilation of the *Kobzari*

How *kobzari* came to be one with *lirnyky*, how epic songs came to be part of the same repertory as religious songs, and how, on Ukrainian territory, epic singing came to be restricted to mendicants are important questions. They help us understand the history of Ukrainian minstrelsy, and the folk interpretation of minstrelsy as a phenomenon. The usual answer to these questions is that when the Cossacks were disbanded, at least some of their minstrels—the disabled and possibly also those who were extremely poor and without relatives—went to live in church hospices. Once there, they shared their songs with the *lirnyky*, performers already in residence, and these, sensing the superiority of epic poetry, added it to their repertories to the extent that they were able. Actually, the situation is considerably more complicated, and it is useful to examine data and repertory together to help understand Ukrainian minstrelsy.

Examining the contrast between scholarly terminology and the names used for songs by the minstrels and the folk, it would appear that epic song did indeed pass from *kobzari* to *lirnyky*. At the same time, it appears that the epic was not viewed as the superior genre. That distinction belonged to religious song. *Duma*, the term used for Ukrainian epic, is of scholarly origin.[12] *Kobzari* and *lirnyky* called epics either Cossack or captives' songs, or Cossack or captives' psalms (*kozatski* or *nevolnytski pisni* or *kozatski* or *nevolnytski psalmy*).[13] The latter term is particularly indicative because *psalma* is the word used for religious song. Thus, epics songs were interpreted as the Cossack equivalent of religious songs. Most likely, the time when such an analogy was made was when the Cossacks were considered defenders of the Orthodox faith and were thus linked to the saints and martyrs described in religious material, the period of the Khmelnytskyi Rebellion. We know that this period generated new *dumy*, songs about Khmelnytskyi, and so it is probable that it affected other aspects of minstrel repertory.

Something similar seems to have happened to the minstrels themselves. As the Cossacks became more and more involved with the church, their minstrels, the *kobzari*, became interpreted as the Cossack equivalent of church singers, the *lirnyky*. Prior to their entry into the church system, *kobzari* were probably men like the *skomorokhi* or Danylo Bandurko: professional musicians with no special, distinguishing traits, who would entertain anyone who would pay them. *Kobzari* were most frequently hired by the military, and it is easy to see how they might follow the Cossacks as they became more and more involved with the complex of church, school, and hospice. After Petro Sahaidachnyi led the Zaporozhian Host into the Kiev Epiphany brotherhood, or possibly before, Cossacks routinely acted like lay brethren. Regiments could and did affiliate with and give financial support to a specific church, just as a church brotherhood or a minstrel guild might do.[14] Interestingly, this behavior is documented in *dumy*, which describe the Cossacks dividing their booty and allotting a portion for church upkeep.

> And they burned the galley,
> And divided the gold and silver into three parts:
> They took the first part and dedicated it
>   to the church,

To the church of the Savior of Mezhihorsk,
To the Trekhtemyrivskyi monastery,
To the Mother of God of the Sich they gave
      their money,
To the places built long ago with Cossack
      treasures,
So that, as they arose and as they retired for
      the night,
People would pray for them;
And the second part (of the booty) they divided
      amongst themselves,
And they took the third part,
And they sat by the roadside,
And they drank and made merry,
And fired off their cannons.[15]

Cossacks performed charitable acts. Efimenko cites a number of charters for hospices founded by Cossack regiments. Needless to say, these often specify that the mission of the particular hospice be to care for disabled or elderly Cossacks left without a family.[16] About the only thing Cossacks did not do was sponsor educational efforts; they spread Orthodoxy by more violent and forceful means. Presumably, their minstrels, the *kobzari*, were affiliated with churches and church brotherhoods as part of their attachment to Cossack regiments. If *kobzari* did more singing than fighting, as Bandurko and the other minstrels listed in court records claim, then they might have been more like lay brethren than their employers precisely because they were craftsmen rather than warriors.

Disabled and elderly Cossacks were supposed to live at hospices, and according to Efimenko, they in fact did.[17] As hospice residents, they learned religious songs and psalms by participating in church services and possibly by studying at the schools. They were encouraged or required to beg to help with their own support, and those among them who could sing, perhaps the erstwhile military *kobzari*, used singing as part of begging. In this scenario, it is easy to understand how Cossack *kobzari* might add religious material to their repertory and how this type of minstrel might end up knowing both historical song and religious song.

But historical, military material also passed from the *kobzari* to the *lirnyky*. Heroic poetry, the *dumy*, became a part of the repertory of those *lirnyky* who had contact with *kobzari*. Scholars do not discuss this process because they assume that it was a natural phenomenon, requiring no explanation. They hold that *dumy* were artistically superior to all other genres and that minstrels, sensing this, naturally picked them up as soon as they heard them. But even if epic was superior to religious song, artistic excellence was not a primary motivation in Ukrainian minstrelsy. Earnings were only secondarily based on artistic merit, and entrance to the profession did not depend on artistic abilities. Here, too, artistic excellence was probably not the driving force: it is more likely that minstrels viewed *dumy* as sacred material, a form of religious song suitable for church-affiliated singers. *Dumy* were considered sacred material because their heroes, the Cossacks, as champions of Orthodoxy, acquired the mantle of Christian martyrs.

Suffering and Holiness in Religious Song

A very important martyrdom marker in both *dumy* and religious songs is the physical suffering of the hero. This is extreme and gruesome, yet it cleanses the hero's soul and makes him or her ready for an afterlife in heaven. It is almost as if physical suffering in this life guarantees salvation from suffering in the hereafter. Good deeds and virtue are not obligatory to attaining the kingdom of Heaven, as long as this life contains sufficient torment. A very popular religious song called "Lazar" (Lazarus) or "The Two Lazars" (*Dva Lazaria*), tells of the extreme physical suffering of a hero who performs no good deeds but merely endures great physical and psychological tribulation, and as a result, is rewarded with the kingdom of Heaven. It is the tale of two brothers, one of whom is healthy and wealthy, while the other is poor and afflicted with a horrible illness which leaves his body covered with open sores. The poor Lazar begs his brother for help, but is rejected and, in some versions, thrown off the premises of the rich brother's estate. As he lies in the gutter, his brother's dogs lick his open wounds. The scene with the dogs, usually used in pictorial representations of this song, is interpreted in two ways. Sometimes it is seen as the ultimate degradation of the afflicted brother. Sometimes it is used to show that unlike the rich man, the dogs understand the value and goodness of Lazar. In this version, the poor man's goodness draws the dogs to him, and they try to relieve his pain. Eventually, the two brothers die. The poor Lazar ascends into heaven and sits at the right hand of God. The rich brother is cast down into Hell and subjected to torments, such as being suspended by his left rib from a meat hook. In his misery, he prays to the poor brother, asking him to intercede with God.[18]

Another popular religious song is the one about St. Varvara (Barbara). Varvara is a beautiful maiden who refuses to give up her Christian faith. The initial episode of her story differs from version to version. In some, her father tries to make her renounce Christianity; in most, a pagan king asks for her hand in marriage, and she refuses on religious grounds. What follows is essentially the same in all texts. Varvara's suitor or her father tries to force her to change her mind by subjecting her to torture. She is made to walk or lie on broken glass; she is boiled in pitch or in oil. From each assault on her body she emerges more beautiful than before. Then the king or father has her buried alive, and forgets about her. Thirty years pass. The king or father remembers Varvara and orders her bones dug up and strewn in the fields. When the grave is opened, Varvara emerges, as fresh and lovely as ever. Lightning strikes the evil tormentor, and his soul descends to Hell, while Varvara's soul is assumed into Heaven.[19]

"Oleksii, Man of God" (*Oleksii Bozhyi Cholovik*) is something like a male version of the song about Varvara, only without graphic description of the hero's torments. For the love of God and in rebellion against his father, Oleksii refuses to consummate a marriage. He leaves home and spends thirty years in the wilderness, and when he returns, his skin is so blackened by exposure that no one recognizes him, and he is so weak that he dies immediately upon revealing his identity.[20] Oleksii, too, goes to heaven. Though forceful enough to stand up to his father, like Lazar and Varvara, he, too, practices passive rather than active resistance, and his virtue seems to be enduring the privation of life in the desert. The latter theme is more directly presented in the story of Onufrii, where the hero is explicitly praised for forsaking the palace and loving the desert. Onufrii's reward is that animals come to serve him, their final labor being digging his grave. The narrative ends with a statement that the hero, having suffered, is a good intercessor between man and God, and asks Onufrii to pray for all sinners.[21] The idea that the prayers of those who suffer are particularly effective recalls the belief that minstrels, having endured blindness and hardship, can utter especially powerful prayers.

A topic as popular as the agony of various saints, and possibly the basis for the idea that suffering is itself a virtue which purifies, is the Passion of Christ. Quite a few religious songs tell about Christ's travail on the cross. Some treat the Passion from His point of view, emphasizing Christ's torments and adding a briar belt and slivers of willow driven under His nails to the Biblical nails and crown of thorns. Others view the events through the eyes of the Virgin Mary, and focus on her tribulations. Sometimes descriptions of suffering are not motivated by the plot and are present for their own sake. Thus, one song not only describes the anguish that the Mother of God experiences as she beholds her son upon the cross, but talks about the pain she endured when she gave Him birth. The couplet about the birth pangs is repeated three times, an unusually high number even for religious songs. The whole song ends with a string of alleluias and the line, "Glory unto

your suffering, oh, Christ!"[22] As if to imply that anguish must occur somewhere, if not in this life, then in the next, those songs which do not describe
the suffering of the living focus on the torments of the deceased. The
torments of the damned are listed and described at length in the various Last
Judgement religious songs and in the ones that warn the listener to lead a
righteous life, lest facing death also mean facing eternal damnation.[23]

"The Orphan Girl" (*Syritka*) is not a religious song, but rivaled "Lazar"
in popularity.[24] Like the songs summarized above, it turns on the theme that
the misfortunes endured in this life guarantee salvation. The song has similarities to folktale in that a poor girl's mother dies, and her father remarries.
The unhappy girl then looks for her mother's grave.[25] Although God urges
her not to seek her mother, she persists, and finds the grave with God's
help. When the girl begs her mother to let her join her, the mother, from
beneath the earth, describes worms eating away at her body and her flesh
rotting. She sends the girl back to the stepmother, first to have her hair
washed and then to have a shirt made. The stepmother fails to care for the
girl, inflicting various, usually undescribed, horrors instead. The orphan girl
dies and is taken into Heaven, while the stepmother also dies and is banished to Hell.[26]

Suffering and Martyrdom in Epic Songs

Dumy offer equally graphic accounts of suffering and torment, depicting
deaths as gruesome as that of Lazar and entombment similar to that of St.
Varvara. In many epic songs, heroes lie dying on the field of battle. On their
bodies are cuts so deep that blood gushes from them with each heartbeat,
revealing the "yellow bone" underneath. They have been shot, and stabbed,
and slashed, and as they suffer their death agony, there is no one to bring
them water. Thus, *dumy*, like religious songs, focus more on what the hero
endures than on what he or she does. Though termed "epic," *dumy* are not,
on the whole, centered around military conflict, and the heroism of their
characters consists not in demonstrating great courage or outstanding fighting skills, but in enduring agony.

Songs about Death

An excellent example of an epic song devoted entirely to an agonizing
death is "The Three Brothers by the River Samarka" (*Try braty Samarski*).
The brothers lie dying in the field by the river of the title, and the number
and severity of their wounds is described at length. The eldest turns to the
middle brother to ask for a drink. The middle brother says that he is as

grievously wounded as his sibling and unable to rise. They then turn to the youngest brother. He too, it turns out, is as badly wounded as the others and cannot fetch them a drink. The elder two then ask the youngest if he will at least play and sing for them. He answers that he would be happy to, but he does not want the Turks and Tatars to hear him and attack once more, or worse yet, carry them off to captivity. The *duma* ends by saying that the three brothers died by the river Samarka and that their souls ascended into Heaven.[27] Description of the battle in which the three brothers were wounded and of heroic action is lacking, and suffering alone makes the brothers heroes and earns them the Kingdom of Heaven.

Other *dumy* describe deaths from battle wounds similar to the ones suffered by the three brothers. In "Death of a Cossack in the Kodyma Valley" (*Smert kozaka na dolyni Kodymi*), the hero dies with no one to minister to his needs. In addition to his physical misery, he suffers the mental anguish of having earlier lost his best friend and his faithful horse.[28] The deaths of Fedir, the Man Without Kin (*Fedir Bezridnyi*) and Ivas Konovchenko are less lonely, but no less painful. Both heroes die from grievous saber and bullet wounds, like the three brothers near the Samarka.[29] Ivas Konovchenko is pictured as a successful warrior, though prone to celebrating his victories with alcohol. But military prowess is not the focal issue. What matters is that the hero die in physical or psychological distress, or both, and Konovchenko's fighting skills merely compound the tragedy of his death by emphasizing that the other Cossacks will suffer the loss of their champion, much as the Virgin Mary had to bear the loss of her son.

If one adds to the gruesome deaths in *dumy* the ones described in historical songs, there emerges an inventory that is truly macabre. Morozenko's beating heart is removed and shown to him while he is still alive. Baida is suspended by his rib cage from a meat hook, much like the rich Lazar. In some versions, after enduring his agony for three days, he manages to trick the Turks into shooting him full of arrows and ending his suffering. In others, he has to wait until the hook works its way into his heart.[30] Baida has some similarities to St. Varvara in the sense that he refuses to marry someone not of his religion; but as in religious songs, it is not this action that makes these heroes heroic. Valor, efforts on behalf of Orthodoxy, or fighting skill is not what distinguishes the warriors of historical song. Rather, as in religious song and epic, heroes are heroic because they die in gruesome ways.

A different twist on physical and psychological suffering and painful death is presented in the *duma* about the "The Escape of Three Brothers from Azov" (*Utecha trokh brativ z Azova*). Here the emotional trauma of being rejected by one's own kin is added. The narrative begins with the two elder brothers escaping from Azov on horseback, while the youngest is on foot. The youngest brother tries valiantly to keep up with his siblings, leaving a bloody trail where his feet are cut by the stones, tree roots, and sharp grasses. Every so often, he catches up to the two men on horseback and begs them to give him a ride. They refuse, citing either their own safety or their unwillingness to throw away their booty, or both. In many versions, the youngest brother then begs his siblings to kill him so that he will not have to face a slow death in the steppes. The elder brothers refuse again, because they cannot strike down their own flesh and blood. Eventually, the youngest brother succumbs to weakness, starvation, and dehydration (*bezkhlibbia, bezviddia*). He climbs the Savur burial mound and dies slowly, watching the wolves and the eagles gather to rip apart his flesh.[31] What is unique to the epic about "The Escape of Three Brothers from Azov" is the motif of rejection by siblings. The youngest brother's continued proper behavior and concern for his elder siblings intensifies the pathos of the situation. Most versions include a scene where the youngest brother sees bits of clothing left by the middle one to mark the path for his foot soldier sibling. The hero worries that these are not trail markers, but the remnants of a Turkish attack on his brothers and that he failed them in their time of need.[32]

Songs about Captivity

A different sort of agony is described in the various *dumy* about Turkish captivity, where there is no death in sight and no hope that the torment will end. This suffering is analogous to Varvara's tortures and entombment and Oleksii's thirty years in the wilderness. Like Oleksii, the captives described in the epic songs suffer exposure, and like Varvara, they are subjected to multiple assaults on their bodies and are beaten until their flesh is "cut to the yellow bone." Often the cruel Pasha asks that his henchman first beat the captives with whips, to open up wounds on their backs, then with "bitter grasses," so that the wounds will sting and burn. The men are kept shackled, and the irons on their hands and feet have worn the flesh down to the "yellow bone." Kept in deep dungeons or chained to their seats in galleys so that they do not see "God's sunlight for three and thirty years," the captives, like Varvara, are deprived of light.[33] Here, again, what makes the imprisoned Cossacks "heroic" is suffering. Even in the songs about escape, the real hero is often the person who sacrifices his or her life to cover the flight of the others, as Marusia Bohuslavka does in the epic that bears her name. Not surprisingly, the bulk of the narrative describes physical and mental agony.

The idea that the suffering of the body cleanses the soul was, then, very important to minstrel songs and to Ukrainians. In other epic and historical song traditions, those who have suffered are not seen as morally better merely because of torment or deprivation. In *dumy* and religious song, suffering, even in the absence of good deeds or displays of virtue, leads to salvation. Perhaps this concept originated in the reinterpretation of the Passion of religious songs: just as Christ's torments expiated human sin, so the suffering of any man atones and purifies. This notion was certainly important to mendicants who saw their own suffering as a way, passive though it might be, to serve the divine purpose.[34] Following this line of reasoning, if the Cossacks suffered on the field of battle, enduring painful wounds, exposure, deprivation, and possibly even death, then their stories could be joined to religious material.

Songs about Everyday Life

The so-called "*dumy* about everyday life" appear to exist solely to serve as panegyrics to physical torment and psychological anguish. Most Ukrainian epics can be connected to a known historical figure, an important event, or at least a specific period, and their purpose is partially to serve as an oral record of the past. The *dumy* about everyday life have no such connection to history. They name no geographical features. The heroes are not assigned proper names as in many of the other *dumy*, and are called simply "brother," "sister," "widow." They deal with battle only obliquely by mentioning that someone leaves home. But while the plots of these *dumy* are different from others, they, too, center on suffering, which here is mostly psychological and occurs as a result of conflict between family members.

The most popular of the *dumy* about everyday life, in fact the most widely collected *duma* of all, is the one about "The Widow and Her Three Sons" (*Udova* or *Udova ta Try Syny*). It tells about a woman who is left alone to care for three boys. She literally wears her fingers to the bone, but manages to keep her boys at home, earning enough money on her own to support them, and thus sparing her sons the ordeal of serving as hired help.[35] The boys grow to maturity, and are prosperous and successful: they have a nice home, wealthy friends, and they marry well. Ashamed of their mother, who is haggard from physical exhaustion, the brothers ask her to leave. In some versions, they say that her ill health and her constant coughing might disturb their guests and frighten their children. In others, they tell her that she is a burden and that her appearance is an embarrassment. The mother leaves, and blinded by her tears, stumbles, causing the sons to laugh and accuse her of drunkenness. A neighbor finds the old woman, takes her home, and cares for her. As a result, the household of the neighbor prospers, and the household of the three errant sons is struck by crop failure, marital discord, and other misfortune. Eventually, the three sons realize the cause of their problems and beg their mother to come home. She returns, in some versions, but not in others. Though there is no mention of the mother dying and going to heaven, as in the religious songs, almost all of the versions of this *duma* close with an admonition about the power of a mother's prayers to insure salvation or bring on damnation.[36]

> He who respects and honors his elderly mother,
> Him God helps,
> Him God sends luck and good fortune
> In the fields and in the house and on the paths
>   and byways.
> God bless the people,
> God bless the Christian people,
> God bless all who have listened,
> For many years
> And until the end of time.[37]

The song about the "Widow and Her Three Sons" largely focuses on mental anguish, the suffering of the mother when her sons, for whom she sacrificed her health, reject her. The second most popular *duma* from this group, "Sister and Brother" (*Sestra ta brat*), centers on mental torment almost exclusively, and expresses a woman's pain at being separated from her family. When she requests that her brother come and visit, he refuses, and the rest of the text is a cry of anguish with many similarities to lament.[38] The remaining *dumy* in this group tell of psychological and physical suffering as the result of family problems. In "Cossack Life" (*Kozatske zhyttia*), the husband rides off to war, leaving his wife with the impossible task of caring for the household and the children alone. She fails, and he beats her as soon as he returns. Like the youngest brother of the three escaping from Azov, instead of punishing her husband for his brutish ways, the wife protects his reputation and makes excuses for her black eyes so as not to dishonor him before their neighbors.[39] In "The Farewell of a Cossack to His Kin" (*Proshchannia kozaka z rodynoiu*), a young man goes off to war, having been kicked out of his home by his stepfather. He endures rejection, and will suffer the deprivation of travel and the hazards of war. The song includes a poignant lament by the youngest sister which very much resembles the expression of grief in "Sister and Brother."[40]

Many scholars have trouble with the *dumy* about everyday life because they are "unheroic" and have so little to do with Cossacks and armed conflict. Kateryna Hrushevska and Borys Kyrdan consider these the most recent addition to the genre and place them at the end of their collections. Filaret Kolessa includes them with his first group of *dumy*, the ones about battling the Turks and the Tatars, on the assumption that they told about what occurred at home while the men were gone to war. Pavlo Zhytetskyi tries to tie *dumy* about everyday life to a historical period when the number of widows increased.[41] What these *dumy* share with other epic songs is not military subject matter, but depictions of suffering, which, of course, is precisely the element that *dumy* about captivity and the aftermath of battles have in common with religious songs. The fact that suffering is the theme shared by all of this material indicates that this was a primary marker of subject matter suitable to minstrels. It is probable that religious songs first made the theme of suffering important and that *dumy* about war were joined to religious song because they too told of physical pain and mental anguish. In that case, *dumy* about everyday life would indeed be the most recent addition, one that extended the realm of those who suffer from martyrs to ordinary folk who suffered in their family relations, the kind of people who would listen to a minstrel at a religious festival. It is interesting that the *dumy* about everyday life do not specifically offer salvation as a reward for suffering, though salvation is at least implied, especially in "The Widow and Her Three Sons." This would indicate that the theme of suffering had acquired importance in its own right, apart from its value as a path to redemption.

While scholars had problems with genre definitions, such issues were not a concern of the folk, who equated *dumy* about everyday life with epics about death on the field of battle and religious songs. A text collected from the *lirnyk* Dorokhtei Karnaukhiv and published by Borzhkovskii shows that minstrels blended genres. The song begins by chastising people for quarreling and not respecting their family members, as do many religious songs. The bulk of the narrative, however, is dominated by a post-battle death scene typical of Ukrainian epic, where three dying brothers claim that their predicament is due not to the strength of their enemy's attack, nor to the bullets and sabers that have wounded them, but to the curses that their parents uttered. The final scene comes from epics about everyday life, and depicts a sister mourning the dead brothers and asking when they will return—the answer, of course, being never.[42]

Of course, depictions of suffering and death characterize all epic poetries. Siegfried, of the German *Nibelungenlied*, is treacherously slain by Hagen, and the Nibelungs all perish in the struggle with Etzel/Attila. Roland, of the French epic, literally blows his brains out when he uses his horn Oliphant to summon help. Beowulf defeats Grendel, but succumbs to the bite of the fire-breathing dragon that attacks in the second half of the epic. In the epic poetry of the Russians, the closest neighbors of Ukraine, Vasilii Buslaev dies after he shows disrespect to a skull, Ilia tragically slays his own son, and Sviatogor dies slowly because he cannot free himself from a magical coffin. Ukrainian epic poetry is unique not in its plentitude of death scenes, but in its elevating death, and particularly a slow, agonizing death, to the position of prime importance. Though the deaths of heroes enter into other epic poetries, these also devote many lines to describing battles and heroic deeds. Siegfried slays a dragon. Roland and the French battle the Saracens, and their mighty blows receive ample treatment in the narrative. Beowulf is victorious in his battles with Grendel and Grendel's mother, and even the description of the battle with the fire-breathing dragon focuses more on the actual struggle and Wiglaf's eventual triumph than it does on Beowulf's death. Ilia, of the Russian epic, defeats the mighty Idolishche and chases him from Constantinople and his conflict with the monster is depicted in detail. In Ukrainian epics, by contrast, the death scene is the focus, and sometimes the entire song can be devoted to its description. There are some depictions of battle in Ukrainian epics, and not all of these end with the death of the hero, but military prowess and valor are not as important as the suffering of the protagonists. In Ukraine, epic song accommodated itself to religious song, and the role of the Cossacks as defenders of the faith came to take precedence over their accomplishments as warriors. The Cossacks of minstrel song were important not because they fought well, but because they died like martyrs.

Other Links Between Epic and Religious Song

Other features indicate that epic song came under church and religious song influence. Adherence to Christianity motivates the action in a number of stories; and while religious conflict appears in many, if not most, epic traditions, defending Orthodoxy in the Ukrainian context acquired special meaning, because Cossacks were elevated to the status of martyrs. The hero invariably sacrifices something dear, sometimes his or her life, for the sake of religion. In the story of Ivan Bohuslavets, the hero loses his wife. A Turkish widow falls in love with the captive Ivan and offers him freedom and wealth if he will marry her. Ivan agrees, on the condition that the Turkish lady not disparage his Christian faith. She obeys, until after drinking too much alcohol, she boasts that Ivan rejected his faith for her and the luxury of the Turkish court. When the hero hears these words, he becomes enraged and renounces his beloved. She apologizes profusely, but too late. Ivan returns to the Cossacks, and leads them on a midnight raid of his wife's palace, during which he himself kills the woman he had loved for, to him, love of the faith takes precedence over love for a person.[43] Marusia Bohuslavka makes an even bigger sacrifice than Ivan. Although she seems happily married to a Turkish Pasha or Sultan, she cannot forget that she is a Christian. She steals her husband's dungeon keys, and on Easter Sunday morning, she releases all of the Cossack captives from prison, an act that will probably mean her execution.[44] Marusia and Ivan do not go as far as St. Varvara of religious song, who completely refuses marriage to someone of a different faith. Nonetheless, they value their religion more than their non-Christian spouses.

Religious feelings can prompt people to risk losing prosperity and security. In the song about Samiilo Kishka, the captives obtain their freedom because Buturlak, a convert to Islam, cannot forget his Christian roots. Even though he is happy among his new Turkish or Tatar compatriots and achieves a high position there, Buturlak feels an irresistible attraction to the Christian Cossacks. Buturlak, we might note, is a problematic figure. He is often called "The Pole" (*Liakh*), and as such, he would be Catholic. Perhaps because he is not Orthodox, his allegiance to the Cossacks, and thus to the faith, is not as unquestioning as that of Marusia or Ivan. In some versions, he hesitates to free the captives, and Samiilo Kishka must get him drunk before he will hand over the keys. In other versions, he escapes with the Cossacks and even helps them cover their tracks, but then wavers when he sees his former Turkish masters, and Samiilo Kishka must kill him before he can betray the Cossacks.[45]

While conflict between people of different religions is not peculiarly Ukrainian, the prayers for the faith that appear at the end of many epics are unique and probably more directly influenced by the church. Many *dumy* end with a prayer that asks for life in the Christian world.

> Liberate us, oh, God, (so that we may go)
> To the happy land,
> To the baptized world,
> To the land of the bright star,
> To the Christian cities.
> Health be to all the Christian world,
> For many years to come.[46]

Although such prayers are thematically appropriate only to songs about captives, they can be found at the end of virtually any epic.

Dumy promote Christian virtues, another feature not necessarily typical of epic traditions and one very closely linked to religious verse. Religious songs typically list sins or virtues. In "The Guardian Angel" (*Anhelu Khranyteliu*), the angel awakens the lazy and sinful soul and tells it to go to church, lest it be sent to Hell after death. The soul, having missed virtually all of the services, requests protection, but the guardian angel says that it is too late, and offers a list of sins, mostly of neglect: failure to go to church, failure to buy wax for church candles, failure to offer alms to the poor and comfort to the sick and needy.[47] Catalogues of sins appear in the many songs about the Last Judgement.[48] One version of the Last Judgement, also called "Archangel Michael" (*Arkhistratihu Mikhailu*), lists the sins in a very interesting form: the souls of the damned curse their parents for failing to teach them the right things to do, for neglecting to take them to church, to teach them prayers, to show them how to observe the fast.[49] The emphasis on teaching recalls the role of minstrels as men who disseminate religious knowledge and the importance of church schools to the institution of minstrelsy. In the song called "Archangel Gabriel" (*Arkhanhelu Havriilu*), the narrator confesses that if he knew when death was to come, he would have prepared for the afterlife. He then lists the proper preparations, and these include attending church, reciting prayers, and offering alms—a positive list, but one corresponding to the above-mentioned sins of neglect.[50] In the Ukrainian folk version of "The Prodigal Son" (*O bludnomu synovi*), the young man forswears his parents and their guidance and spends his time drinking, behavior which dooms his soul to damnation. Other versions of this song have the young man committing other sinful acts, including blasphemy and adultery.[51]

Epics are also characterized by lists, and the sins given are virtually identical to those above. The treatment here is an interesting variation on religious song material. Rather than being the cause of damnation, in epic songs, sins are the reason for the mortal peril of their heroes. In a number of texts, heroes on the verge of death realize that their plight resulted not from the enemy's fighting skill or fearsome weapons, but from their own sins, or the curses their parents uttered in reaction to their sins, or both. As the heroes themselves put it:

> It is not the sharp sword, oh my brothers, which has cut us,
> And not the quick bullet which has shot us,
> It is our father's and our mother's prayers punishing us,
> Because, as we left for the volunteer army,
> We did not bid farewell to our father and our mother,
> We did not honor our older brother as our elder,
> We deprived our close neighbors of their bread,
> We rode past the church, past the holy cathedral, and we did not
>   take off our hats,
> And we did not cross ourselves,
> And that is how we lost our happiness and our good fortune.[52]

The hero or heroes are sometimes saved from death once they confess their sins and promise to behave better in the future. This is especially true of the songs about the sea. In these, a terrible storm threatens to capsize the Cossack ships, killing all aboard. In the songs about "Oleksii Popovych," the commander of the Cossack troops either calls upon all men to confess their sins or asks that the man with the most heinous sin step forward.[53] This turns out to be Oleksii, the son of a priest, and the regimental scribe—a person who according to his own words, should be schooling the men in "all good and righteous things." His sins, it turns out, are an expanded version of the list given above, for he also trampled small children with his horse, kicked his sister, and spilled Christian blood. Oleksii Popovych saves his comrades either by offering to be sacrificed on their behalf or by having his pinky cut off and feeding his blood to the stormy waters, actions which immediately calm the seas.[54] In the epic about "The Storm at Sea" (*Buria na mori* or *Buria na Chornomu Mori*), the Cossack ships already have been destroyed by the storm, and two brothers who confess their sins and ask their parents for forgiveness are saved, while a man who has no parents to whom to address prayers of atonement perishes.[55]

Where lists of sins do not appear, the plot often conveys the message that the hero's problem is not the enemy's strength, but his own misdeeds, usually a transgression against a family member. The sons in the song "The Widow" are punished explicitly for mistreating their mother. The elder brothers in "The Escape of Three Brothers from Azov" suffer because they abandon their youngest sibling. Punishment is avoided in only one version, a song that is quite short and differs significantly from the others. Here, there are only two brothers, the older of whom leaves the younger to die. Even in this version, the older brother escapes punishment by atonement, for he sacrifices the wealth that he brought with him to the well-being of his parents.[56] In "Ivan Konovchenko," the hero successfully fights hundreds of the enemy single-handedly; clearly it is not their numbers or skills that kill him, but his mother's curse. The hero incurs his mother's wrath because he disobeys her request that, as her only remaining son, he not join the army. Thus, unlike Oleksii Popovych and the heroes who almost die at sea, he is not guilty of a multitude of sins. Perhaps because he is merely disobedient and motivated by noble desires to serve his homeland, Ivan holds off the effects of the curse for quite some time. It is only when he celebrates his victories with an excess of alcohol and then forgets to pray for his mother's or his colonel's blessing that the curse takes effect.[57]

Thus, if the religious songs with catalogues of sins urged the audience to avoid these for fear of purgatory, the epic songs with similar lists urged avoidance on pain of death. They warned that not even the mightiest person could withstand divine wrath. It is significant that it is precisely in epics that one finds the topic of not relying on brute force, the Ukrainian heritage of Cossack warriors and rule by force notwithstanding. This topic appears occasionally in religious song and in some versions of "Lazar," in which the rich brother foolishly hopes to avoid divine retribution and death by force, deploying his armies.[58] But the dominance of divine powers over all earthly ones is perhaps most effectively expressed in epic.

Martyrdom was the central element shared by religious and epic song. The marker of martyrdom, be it that of a saint or a Cossack warrior, was cruel and painful death. Suffering was a meaningful topic not only for the church and those affiliated with it, but for ordinary people, who would make up a minstrel's audience. For them, descriptions of suffering like their own, such as the descriptions found in "The Orphan Girl" and the epics about everyday life, probably had the therapeutic effect discussed by Nadiia Suprun.[59] They provided a vehicle for expressing, and thus healing, pain and sorrow. For the Ukrainian nation, which suffered numerous historical disasters and was never truly independent, the *dumy* may have offered similar consolation and healing.[60] It was important that those who sang about suffering be people who themselves knew pain, as did the blind *kobzari* and *lirnyky*. And in the eyes of the Ukrainian people, their suffering, like that of the heroes of epic and religious songs, brought them close to God and carried the promise of salvation.

Chapter 10

Epic and Lament: The Influence of Kobzari on Lirnyky

*T*he Orthodox church exerted a tremendous influence on Ukrainian minstrelsy. The traits of those singers originally associated with the church, the *lirnyky*, were extended to other serious professional performers, the *kobzari*, and by the nineteenth century, all minstrels had to be blind and affiliated with the church through their guilds. The sighted minstrels of the eighteenth century, who sought their own affiliations and frequently ended up working for the Cossacks, men like Danylo Bandurko, were no more. Religious songs influenced epic poetry, and *dumy* came to treat subject matter found in religious verses, so that the *dumy* recorded from the nineteenth century describe how the Cossacks died like martyrs and speak more of moral transgressions and atonement than of hubris or military prowess. Yet the influence did not go in one direction. There are many pre-Christian elements in the songs sung by minstrels and in the institution of minstrelsy itself. Indeed, some, such as veneration of sightlessness, may have found their way into the Ukrainian version of Orthodoxy. These elements are clearest in epic poetry, and they were probably preserved in a non-religious institution, the military, and by the minstrels of the military, the *kobzari*. Of course, pre-Christian ideas entered Orthodoxy independent of Cossack influence, but the elevation of Cossacks to the status of defenders of Orthodoxy, and the linkage of the *kobzari* with the *lirnyky*, provided an extra impetus for this process. Some notions about minstrels found in their songs, including the special position assigned to blindness, may have their origin in Turkic, rather than Slavic, paganism. These surely were introduced by the Cossacks, because it was they who had extensive contact with the Turkic peoples.

The Unquiet Dead

A prolonged and agonizing death is important as a marker of martyrdom. In epic, however, descriptions of dying Cossacks may also serve to prevent the consequences of an untimely death. Cossacks were men who died young and violently. In East Slavic belief, people who die before their time and especially people who are killed, who die by unnatural means, become unquiet dead, beings who cannot rest and are forced to roam the earth until their allotted time in this world is complete, often causing harm to the living.[1] By all rights, Cossacks, who perished on the field of battle, should have become unquiet dead, yet they did not. What prevented their becoming unquiet dead was most likely a special ritual or a set of special rituals, and *dumy* may well be remnants of these funerary and commemorative rites.

The idea of a specific time allotted to each person (*srok*) was developed by Dmitrii K. Zelenin using Russian and Ukrainian material and focusing on *rusalky*, the spirits of young women who die young and violently, often by their own hand. Accordingly, a person who died having completed his or her allotted time rested quietly in the earth. This was a good death, and the body of such a person united with the earth, while the soul was accepted into heaven. A person who perished prematurely did not rest. This soul could not make a proper transition to the land of the dead, and retained a bond to the place of its untimely demise, haunting it and bringing misfortune to the living. There was apparently a way to prevent those who died in an untimely manner from becoming unquiet dead beings. (Zelenin does not discuss this because his interest is in presenting various manifestations of the unquiet dead, primarily the *rusalky*.) A special funeral ritual called the "wedding of the dead" could be performed, at least for an unmarried person, to bring peace to the deceased and insure that he or she rested quietly in the grave.[2] A permutation of the death-wedding, wedding as a metaphor for death, occurs frequently in *dumy* and historical songs. More important, if even one ritual to counteract the possible bad effects of an untimely death survives, perhaps there were once others. Perhaps there was a special rite for young men who fell on the field of battle, and perhaps *dumy* evolved from songs either performed during this rite or subsequently, or some combination of the two. Perhaps also *kobzari* conducted these special rituals themselves or were descendants of priests who did so.

Theories of Epic Origins

Scholarship on Ukrainian epic songs seldom touches on death, dispatching the soul to the afterlife, and praying for the deceased. The most prevalent theory on the origin of *dumy* claims that they were composed close to the time of the events that they describe. Accordingly, there exist two epic cycles: the Turko-Tatar *dumy*, dating roughly from the fourteenth to the seventeenth centuries, and the Khmelnytskyi songs, from the second half of the seventeenth century. (The *dumy* about everyday life, as we noted, present classification difficulties.) This explanation contends that *dumy* were composed by eye-witnesses to the important events which are their subject matter. Their purpose was to record these events in song, and by singing of heroic deeds, to instill courage in the Cossacks, urging them on to greater success in battle. Kateryna Hrushevska notes that this theory was first proposed by Izmail Sreznevskyi and has little to no basis in fact.[3] As she explains, early scholars, Sreznevskyi included, projected the ideals of the school to which they adhered onto epic song. Nonetheless, Sreznevskyi's theory has become a kind of metafolklore, taken as truth and repeated from scholar to scholar, many of whom take it as obvious and do not bother to cite Sreznevskyi.[4]

The misconceptions about the Ukrainian epic stemming from Sreznevskyi's theory do indeed create an attractive picture. We see a man with a *bandura* at the head of the assembled Cossack host, issuing a call to battle. After the battle, the same man, or perhaps another, glorifies the heroism of the combatants. Yet this hardly conforms to reality. It would be insanity to carry a *bandura* or a *kobza* into battle. Both are heavy and cumbersome instruments, antithetical to the light cavalry fighting style of the Cossacks. More important, actual *duma* texts contain few descriptions of valorous deeds and so are clearly not a pattern for behavior in battle or a blueprint for military success. Most tell about the death of the hero, something a soldier would rather avoid than emulate. Finally, the adherents of this theory have a great deal of trouble explaining nineteenth-century performers of *dumy*. If *dumy* originated among the Cossacks, how, then, did they come to be performed exclusively by blind mendicants who had nothing to do with the military? The usual answer is to posit a gradual process of transition from the Cossacks to the ranks of mendicants. According to Sreznevskyi and his followers, *dumy* were originally performed by participants or eye-witnesses, *bandura* or *kobza*-playing combatant Cossacks. Later, specialization occurred, and Cossacks who wanted to remain with their regiment but could no longer fight because of injury or old age, or because they had been blinded by the Turks while in captivity, earned their keep by providing musical services, and thus became the first professional *kobzari*. Once a link between disability and music had been established, *dumy* could pass to the disabled, which supposedly happened when the Cossacks were disbanded. This sequence of events has some correspondence to the facts of minstrelsy, but presents many problems.

Toward the end of the nineteenth century and in the first decades of the twentieth, information about *kobzari* and *lirnyky* finally became abundant enough for scholars to question this theory. Pavlo Zhytetskyi, for example, emphasized the link between minstrels and the church and between religious songs and *dumy*, and he discussed the moral messages of the latter. He proposed that the creators of *dumy* were not Cossacks, but beggar minstrels much like contemporary *kobzari* and *lirnyky*, who received their information about Cossack life from wandering deacons (*mandrovany diachky*) like Turchynovskyi (see ch. 9). These deacons served many employers, working as Cossack scribes and then returning to the church to serve as choirmasters or to assume other positions. While in the church, they had contact with minstrels, and as men trained in letters who composed verse themselves, they gave mendicants the verse patterns which yielded the *dumy*.[5] In the brief period between the advancement of this argument and the Communist disruption of scholarship on *dumy*, Zhytetskyi's theory acquired one important adherent. Citing the complexity of the *dumy*, Kateryna Hrushevska argued that they could not have been composed by the Cossacks, because witnessing important historical events did not automatically confer artistic talent or knowledge of compositional techniques. *Dumy* must have had their origin amongst professional minstrels, people with special training in song.

Filaret Kolessa took issue with Zhytetskyi. He claimed that *dumy* were of purely folk origin and not based on written church literature but on oral laments. To support his point, Kolessa cited similarities in musical form and verse form between laments and epics and gave very convincing examples of parallel imagery. In the *duma* about "The Cossack's Farewell," there is a passage of some ten lines in which one of the sisters asks the departing young man to tell her the direction from which he will return. Will it be from the open field, or from the Black Sea, or from the Zaporozhe, she asks. At least one recorded lament contains a passage with nearly identical questions and wording. The implied answer in both texts, of course, is that the person addressed will never come back.[6] Even more extraordinary are parallels between a passage of some twenty lines which comes from the *duma* about "A Sister and a Brother" and another lament. Here the question is when the brother or the deceased will return, and the answer, which is a poetic expression of never, goes as follows:

> Sister, dear sister,
> My beloved relative!
> Expect me as your guest when the rivers freeze over on
>   St. Peter's Day,
> When the rowan tree blooms in the field on Christmas.

Go, sister, go to the quiet Danube,
Take, sister, some sand in your white hand,
Sow, sister, sow the sand upon a rock:
When the sand sprouts upon the white rock,
When it blooms with blue flowers,
When it covers the white stone with periwinkle in
    the form of a cross,
When it decorates the rock with colored blossoms,
Then, sister, I will come to visit you. . . . [7]

On the basis of parallels between epic songs and songs that were purely oral, such as laments, Kolessa concluded that *dumy* must be a product of oral tradition, and cannot be a verse form which evolved from church writings. Thus, Kolessa argued, *dumy* were created by the Cossacks rather than by mendicants.

Kolessa was dealing with the first sound recordings of *dumy* and had the additional advantage of having done some of the recording himself. Thus he had access to the most accurate available data. His observations about the parallels between *dumy* and laments are highly credible, and his assertions were subsequently corroborated by Roman Jakobson, who showed that a link between epic and lament is a Slavic phenomenon: "in all three Slavic areas where these genres exist (Russia, Ukraine, and the Balkans), the epics and the laments prove to be closely interconnected structurally (and, in particular, in their metric form)."[8]

Kolessa felt that the earliest *dumy* were the laments of captive Cossacks held in Turkish captivity and that the genre was then extended to voice other pain: death in battle, the loss of loved ones.[9] Here his arguments are less convincing. Within the genre of lament itself, "lyrical laments," or songs which bemoan a sad situation, are secondary. As ritual songs first and foremost, laments are an integral part of funerary ceremonies. Furthermore, death rather than captivity is the primary topic of *dumy*. *Dumy* did indeed originate in laments, but they were laments performed for the dead, not laments sung by captives.

Links Between Epics, Laments, and Funerals

Epic songs have much in common with laments sung at funerals. In funeral laments, a narrative rendition of the death was a way to make it "proper," to put the death into the context of the culture and to say that the death occurred in an acceptable way. It freed the soul from its bonds to this world so that it could journey to the next, and a description of this journey was another frequent component. This content indicates a ritual and a psychological function: to take care of soul of the departed and to help the living cope with loss. The lament tradition thus provided a way to express the conflicting emotions that people feel when someone dies: longing and aversion, anger and grief.

Many *dumy*, just like laments, narrate how the dead person perished, place the death in context, and present conflicting emotions such as sorrow at the loss of someone and pride in his or her noble death. A number of epic songs are death scenes almost in their entirety (for example "The Three Brothers by the River Samarka" and "The Death of a Cossack in the Kodyma Valley"). "Fedir, the Man Without Kin" also describes the death of its hero. In addition, it stresses the importance of proper funerary ritual. As Fedir lies mortally wounded, he calls his servant, and being without kin, passes his horse and his battle gear on to him. After assuring himself that the servant can properly assume his gear, and presumably, his place in battle, Fedir has him ride out to the river, tells him how to correctly greet the Cossacks, and requests that the servant have the Cossacks arrange for proper burial. Everything is done as Fedir requested, and the *duma* concludes with a panegyric to his glory.[10]

There are a number of longer *dumy* which tell about events surrounding the death of the hero, but whose focus is nonetheless the hero's death scene. "The Escape of Three Brothers from Azov" tells about the flight of the three brothers and the youngest brother's many calls for help and then presents the poignant scene where the youngest brother finally dies from thirst and hunger and exposure. Almost all versions of this *duma* also have a post-death episode where the two older brothers have to deal with their parents and their own feelings of guilt.

The *duma* about Ivas Konovchenko describes the events leading up to his death at length and details the contradictory emotions felt by his mother. The hero is the only surviving male in his mother's family, his father and his brothers having been killed in battle. Ivas is in the fields one day when a Cossack colonel rides past, calling all men to join the Zaporozhian Host in a new campaign. His mother, fearing that he will suffer the same fate as his father and brothers, does not want Ivas to go. A long argument ensues, Ivas insisting that fighting is the only path to honor and glory, and his mother maintaining that farming is equally honorable. When Sunday comes, the mother goes to church, and Ivas searches the house for his father's weapons, hidden earlier by his mother. The mother returns from church, discovers the weapons and her son gone, and curses him, an action which she immediately regrets. She is so sorry, in fact, that she sells what little she has and buys a horse to send to her son, to help him in battle. Meanwhile, Ivas joins the Cossack Host, and in spite of his youth and lack of training, turns out to be an excellent warrior. He battles three hundred of the Tatar enemy single-handedly, then defeats six hundred. After each victory, he drinks to celebrate. When Ivas rides into battle for the third time, he is so drunk that he forgets to pray for his mother's blessing. Immediately her curse takes effect, and in the pivotal scene of the epic, the hero is shot and stabbed and lies bleeding from wounds that show bone between gushes of blood. Ivas asks his comrades to tell his mother that he took a Turkish woman as wife, that their match-maker was the sharp sword, their bed—the damp earth, their pillow—the hard rock, and their coverlet—the green grass. The mother's reaction varies from version to version. Sometimes she under-stands the metaphor right away; sometimes she does not realize what has happened until she sees the riderless horse. The *duma* ends with a wake, a feast that the mother gives to celebrate Ivas' memory.[11]

The death of the hero is central in the *duma* "The Death of Bohdan Khmelnytskyi" and in a number of historical songs, such as "Morozenko" and "Baida," which are essentially descriptions of death. "The Widow of Ivan Sirko and Her Sons," sometimes classed as a *duma* and sometimes as a historical song, shares elements with the story of Ivas Konovchenko. The sons go to seek their father, who has disappeared, against their mother's wishes, and join the Cossack Host. They do not heed the warnings of the elder Cossacks, and are careless. As a result, the groom of the older brother is captured by the Turks. He buys his freedom by promising to deliver his master to the enemy. The Turks manage to kill not only the elder of the Sirko brothers, but also the leader of the Cossacks. Apparently something happens to the younger brother as well, because the song ends with the mother expressing her sorrow that her husband and her elder son are dead, while the other son is dying.[12]

Even *dumy* where death is not the central core contain panegyrics to the hero or heroine and prayers for the souls of the living and the dead, which are analogous to elements found in funerary ritual and probably derive from eulogies and posthumous prayers. Many narratives stress the particular im-portance of having the parents pray for salvation, and some attribute extraor-dinary powers to such prayers. In "The Storm at Sea," for example, two brothers saved from drowning witness the death of one of their comrades. This convinces the brothers of the importance of honoring one's mother and father, because they were able to pray to their parents for forgiveness, while the poor dead man had no kin to address in prayer.[13] A general prayer for ancestors and all Christian people concludes this epic song. In "Marusia Bohuslavka," Cossacks kept in Turkish captivity for three and thirty years escape, thanks to the efforts of the heroine. She does not go with them, claiming that she has become too accustomed to Turkish luxury. This statement should not be taken at face value, but understood in the same vein as Ivas Konovchenko's marriage: Marusia sacrifices herself to let the Cossacks escape.[14] She will die when her deed is discovered, and this song, too, ends with prayers for the living and the dead.

Dumy reflect Ukrainian funerary practices not only in structure, with their descriptions of how the deceased met his or her end and their concluding prayers, but in content. The striking scene from the *duma* about Ivas Konovchenko where the hero equates his death to marriage is based on actual ritual. Deaths of young men and women who died unwed were indeed celebrated as weddings to avert the return as unquiet dead of those who left this world before their time. The death-wedding has been best documented for Ukraine's neighbors, but is amply attested in Ukraine.[15] A variation on the death-wedding, death as marriage to a foreigner, appears in historical songs as well as epics, and it may be that this metaphor was so widely used, it could be read in reverse.[16] Thus, if someone married a foreigner, that person was as good as dead to the people he or she left behind. Marusia Bohuslavka's marriage to a Turkish Pasha seems to make her equivalent to a dead person. Presumably, Marusia herself was once a captive and was forced to wed a Turk. She may not have wanted this union, but her feelings are never mentioned, because intent matters far less than ritual. Once married, whether for love or out of necessity, Marusia can never return and assume a normal role in Ukrainian society. No Ukrainian would ever have her as wife, and the only possible place for her might be in a hospice, living life as a marginal person. This being the case, Marusia's choosing physical death may just be the inevitable consequence of the symbolic death which she has already suffered.

Dumy often describe funerary ritual. Under normal circumstances, the body of someone who had died was washed and dressed and laid out on a bench in the icon corner of the house. Relatives and friends would then lament the dead person. Often special rituals were conducted with water, food, and soil. A coffin was prepared, usually by neighbors or friends of the deceased, and after three days, the body was removed from the house for burial.[17] To the funeral rite in the household, the introduction of Christianity added a church service during which the body was blessed and then interred in the sanctified ground of the graveyard. The soul was dispatched to the afterlife by means of the service and by individual prayer. The final step of the funeral was a wake: a party with food, drink, and often music and folk drama. For the deceased, it was a celebration of his or her arrival in the world of the dead. For the living, it was a way to release the tension of loss and grief, and thus permitted a return to a normal, neutral existence.

Burial on the Field of Battle

In the steppe, all of this was impossible. There was no church, no grave-yard, and no family to prepare the body and lament the soul. This does not mean, however, that there was no ritual. In Ukrainian belief, all souls deserved to be helped on their way with the proper rites. Only the greatest sinners, people who were believed to have lost their souls by committing such heinous acts as killing their neighbors or setting fire to their neighbors' homes, did not deserve lamentation.[18] Souls that were in danger of wandering after death, of being "unquiet," such as the souls of young men who died violently, were the ones most insistent on proper ritual. It was believed that they literally pestered the living, demanding proper burial and refusing to leave the living in peace until the rites were duly performed.[19] Thus, in the steppe, there were alternate funerals, funerals patterned on regular burial ritual with appropriate modifications.

Ukrainians were apprehensive whenever there was a possibility that the proper burial rites might not be performed. Many *dumy* voice concern that the steps of a funeral be executed properly. Often the hero begs that someone attend his death (*smert dohliadaty*) and bury his body. The elder two of the three brothers dying by the river Samarka want their youngest sibling to play his trumpet precisely because they are looking for someone to attend them. They are hoping that the Cossacks will hear them and then summon their relatives to bury them properly. The death of the three brothers is shown to be all the more distressing and painful because any sound is likely to yield the opposite of the desired result. As the youngest brother says, in all probability it will be the enemy who will respond, and desecrate the bodies.[20]

Fedir, the man without kin, even while in agony, makes sure that his groom, his kin substitute, arranges for proper burial. The burial duplicates the steps of a normal funeral to the extent that the circumstances of the steppe and Cossack life allow.

> Then the hetman of the army,
> He did as he should,
> On Saturday, he selected fifty Cossacks from
> the seven hundred,
> And on Saturday, toward Sunday,
> At four o'clock in the morning,
> He sent them to the Bazaluh plain.
> And they arrived in the plain,
> And they found the Cossack's body,
> And they put it on red silk,

> And they washed the brave Cossack body,
> And with their swords they dug the soil,
> And carried it in their hats and the skirts of
>   their coats,
> And they erected a high burial mound,
> And set a flag at the head,
> And celebrated the glory of the wise knight.
> They remembered him
> With what they had—
> Stale military bread![21]

A burial like Fedir's is described in a number of *dumy*. The picture of the Cossacks digging the hard ground with their swords and carrying the soil for a high, high burial mound with their hats and coat skirts appears in most versions of "Ivas Konovchenko." It is found in some versions of "The Death of a Cossack in the Kodyma Valley" and most versions of "The Death of Bohdan Khmelnytskyi."[22]

Dumy speak of concerns that reflect the special circumstances of death on the field of battle, yet are in keeping with general Ukrainian belief. In Ukraine, as in most of the East Slavic areas, there was a belief in the connection between body and soul. The body had to be preserved, and all parts of it had to be buried for the soul to be able to successfully separate from it. Missing body parts and missing organs were not tolerated, for fear that the deceased would return in search of them. In *dumy*, many heroes are worried that they will not be buried at all and that their bodies will fall prey to scavengers. The youngest brother escaping from Azov repeatedly requests that his siblings not leave him to be devoured by wild beasts (*Zviriuptytsi na potalu ne podaite*) and that they make sure he is interred (*U chystomu poli pokhovaite*).[23] The same request is expressed in other *dumy*, using virtually the same words.[24] In "The Escape of Three Brothers from Azov," the contrast between the elder siblings' refusal to respond to the hero's requests and the hero's fear that his brothers have died and he has failed to bury them underscores that sibling duties include helping one's brother when he is alive and burying him when he is dead. According to *duma* texts, caring for the body and soul of a dead family member is as basic as feeding and aiding a living one.[25]

Variations on the theme of proper burial serve to emphasize its importance. In some versions of the *duma* about "The Escape of Three Brothers from Azov," nature does what the elder brothers fail to do. The wind blows the grasses and reeds that grow on the Savur mound, and thus keeps the animals away from the youngest brother's corpse.[26] In some, the animals perform the burial and cover the scattered bones.[27] Where human beings take care of someone, they go to great lengths to bury all body parts. In many versions of the *duma* about Ivas Konovchenko, he is already dead by the time the Cossacks arrive on the field of battle, and either his whole body or a part of it is missing. In some, the hero's body has been carried off by the Turks, who toy with it to tease his comrades. The Cossacks do not choose safety and do not concede Ivas' body to the enemy; they mount an expedition to retrieve it. In those versions where the Turks have decapitated Ivas, the Cossacks conduct a gruesome search among the bodies of the fallen until they retrieve his head. The search for the head is sometimes described as lasting thirty days.[28] All in all, such importance is assigned to proper burial that the possibility that one's death might not be properly attended becomes terrifying. As the *dumy* themselves say, one of the most frightening things is to die far away from one's kin.

> Oh, as hard as it is for a bird or a beast
> To be without the field or the forest,
> As hard as it is for a fish or a pike to be on
>   dry land,
> Oh, as hard as it is to lift a heavy stone
> From the damp earth,
> So it is hard to die in a strange land, without
>   one's mother and father:
> To have no beloved family at one's side![29]

It was even more frightening to leave the soul unattended. In *dumy*, as in funeral rites, the soul was cared for verbally, by lament, though usually not the normal lament by a family member that would be performed at a funeral. In a number of the versions of "The Escape of Three Brothers from Azov," wild beasts scatter the bones of the youngest brother, and only the skull is left on the Savur mound. A cuckoo (*zozulia*) comes and sings over the skull. The bird's song is compared to a lament, and the bird herself is compared to a sister, or mother, or both.

> From somewhere a grey little cuckoo bird came,
> And sat at the head (of the deceased),
> And she cooed mournfully;
> She lamented him as a sister would her brother,
> Or a mother would her son.[30]

> And she cooed as if she were speaking with words:
> "Oh head, oh head, oh Cossack's head!

You used to drink and to eat,
You used to travel in comfort,
You used to journey in foreign lands,
You knew all of the Cossack customs well,
Now you care about nothing
Except wanting God's righteous judgement
    for yourself."[31]

Posthumous Prayer

Sometimes the cuckoo flies to the parents' home and sings to them, letting them know that their youngest has died. This is one variant of an extremely important motif: relatives must be informed of a death so that they can care for the soul of the departed. Of course, it is best to care for both body and soul immediately after a person's demise; but where this is impossible, it is necessary to provide care at least for the spirit. Posthumous prayer is extremely important. Such prayer has not received the emphasis it deserves, because funeral rite studies tend to focus on death and burial and the acts and words which accompany these, sometimes adding information about omens that presage death.[32] But posthumous prayer occurs in both epic poetry and practice, where major church services forty days after death, and annual commemorations, are routine.

In *dumy*, desire for a posthumous prayer to soothe the spirit motivates those scenes where someone or something informs the Cossack's kin of his death. In the *duma* about Ivas Konovchenko, informing the mother about the hero's death is a climactic moment. Her reaction, holding a wake, confirms that relatives who learn of a death immediately perform ritual acts. There are a number of historical songs which are variations on the ending of the Ivas Konovchenko *duma*. A Cossack is dying alone in the steppe, horse standing over him. The young man speaks to the horse and instructs him to go home and tell the man's mother what has happened, usually using the metaphor of marriage to a foreign woman. The Cossack dies, and the horse gallops home, arrives at the gate, and in most versions, actually speaks to the mother, conveying the son's message.[33] The mother reacts much like the mother of Ivas Konovchenko. The reason why Marusia Bohuslavka insists that the escaping Cossacks tell her parents not to bother ransoming her is, no doubt, because having someone care for the soul is so important. It is hard to believe that she wants to inform her parents that she has accepted Islam and the Turkish way of life. It is much more likely that, like Ivas Konovchenko, she is using a metaphor to convey her death to her parents so that she can be properly mourned.

The best indication that *dumy* have a great deal to do with praying for the dead is fact that the death of the hero is mentioned even in songs about successful ventures, where one would expect a happy ending. Instead, the few *dumy* where the hero is not killed in battle or while escaping captivity conclude by informing the listener that the hero died, while his glory lived on, and pray for the hero, the audience, or all Christian people. In the *duma* which bears his name, Samiilo Kishka escapes from Turkish captivity with all of his men. He even manages to inflict losses on the enemy in the process, and the narrative proper ends with the Cossacks congratulating Kishka. Instead of concluding on a positive note, however, the congratulations are followed immediately by a statement of the hero's death.

> They (the Cossacks) drank and feasted,
> They fired their long pistols,
> They congratulated Samiilo Kishka:
> "Glory," they said, "Glory to you, Samiilo Kishka,
> Hetman of the Zaporozhian Sich!
> You did not perish in captivity,
> You will not perish with us, the Cossacks, in freedom."
> Gentlemen, Samiilo Kishka laid down his head
> In the Kiev-Kaniv Monastery . . .
> But his glory will not die and will not perish!
> His glory will be great
> Among the Cossacks,
> Among his friends,
> Among the knights,
> Among brave young men!
> Sanctify all of the people, oh God,
> Sanctify all of the Christian people,
> And the Zaporozhian and Don armies,
> And all of the simple people in the Dnieper region,
> For many years,
> And until the end of time![34]

There are a few satirical *dumy* which have nothing to do with armed conflict, yet conclude with the death and prayer formula. In "Fesko Hanzha Andyber," the hero successfully teaches a group of Polish gentlemen a lesson. Andyber shows up in a bar wearing shabby Cossack clothes and is treated badly by the Polish patrons. He leaves and returns in fine raiment, and the gentlemen start to fawn all over him. Andyber then reveals his identity and chastises the Polish dandies for honoring the clothes rather than the man. Many versions of this narrative end by saying:

And then Fesko Hanzha Andyber,
Hetman of the Zaporozhian Sich,
Although he died,
His Cossack fame will not die and will not perish!
From this day forth,
Sanctify and support, oh Lord,
Sanctify all the people,
The Christian people,
For many years.[35]

The same is true of several of the *dumy* from the Khmelnytskyi cycle and from the cycle about everyday life. The *duma* about Khmelnytskyi and Barabash, for example, tells how the hero successfully tricks the scheming Barabash into turning over documents he had concealed. Although the body of the narrative tells about an action with a positive outcome, the closing in many versions is similar to those translated above: it tells the listener that Khmelnytskyi died, and then eulogizes him and offers a prayer.[36] The *duma* about Cossack life, the story of a husband who leaves his wife to go to war and then punishes her for not maintaining the household and the farmstead in his absence, would hardly seem to warrant a conclusion alluding to the protagonist's death. If anything, the couple seem to be relatively young and their death a long way off. Nonetheless, the closing about death and glory, followed by a prayer, is found in versions of this song also.[37]

The Question of Male Lament

Dumy express the earnest wishes of the hero to be properly buried, to be lamented, and to be cared for by his kin. In real life, this was not possible. A dying Cossack was attended by his comrades, who washed his body and buried him in the steppe. But did they also lament? The *dumy* themselves describe Cossacks doing the washing and performing the burial, but do not tell of lamentation, except when it is done by a cuckoo, an animal substitute for human mourners. Laments, like other ritual songs, often describe the actions of the ritual, a feature which probably served as a mnemonic device, but do not mention the act of singing itself. Thus, funeral laments might describe the arrival of the mourner in the house of the person who has passed away, her speaking to the family and viewing the body, but they will not mention her singing over the deceased. Failure to mention singing in *dumy* cannot be construed as evidence that Cossacks did not lament.

More problematic is the fact that lament, at least in the context of a ritual, is considered a women's genre. Jakobson states categorically that in all three Slavic areas where both epic and lament are performed—Russia, Ukraine, and the Balkans—"the former genre has a string accompaniment and is monopolized by men, while the latter is performed by women only."[38] If laments were "performed by women only," then warriors should not sing laments. Probably the association between funeral lamentation and women prompted Kolessa to think that laments about captivity, rather than funeral laments, were the origin of *dumy*. But although lamenting was more common among women than among men, for Ukraine at least, Jakobson's categorical statement does not apply. Men did sing laments. In fact, funeral laments by men have been recorded as recently as the turn of the century.[39] In all probability, laments, and specifically funeral laments, were once performed by men as well as women among all of the Slavs, and all Slavic epic song is connected to lamentation.[40] This cannot be established for a fact; but recent emphasis on Ukrainian material makes this supposition appear a great deal more likely than it had previously. Furthermore, if there is ample evidence that male funeral lament was an active oral form in Ukraine, then there is every reason to believe that Cossacks, too, sang funeral lamentations.

Nonetheless, lament is more closely linked to women than to men. Most of the Ukrainian laments that have been published were recorded from women. In addition, when someone sings a funeral lament in the *dumy*, it is a female being, like the cuckoo in "The Escape of Three Brothers from Azov," and the human mourners that she is supposed to replace are women: the sister and the mother. This fact does not argue against Cossacks performing lament. Even if lament was more of a woman's than a man's genre, just as men took over other women's functions while out in the steppe and living in an all-male society, so they probably took over lament. In a normal funeral, women washed and dressed the body for burial, and men prepared the coffin and performed the actual interment. In the steppes, men performed both the men's and the women's parts of the funeral rite. This is attested in *dumy* which describe Cossacks ritually washing the deceased. If Cossacks could perform one ritual act that was associated with women, namely washing the body, there is every reason to suppose that they could assume other ritual functions, such as lamenting the dead.

Hrushevska presents another problem with regard to Cossacks singing funeral laments: could it be that ordinary men were able to sing songs so lengthy and complex? Folklore tells us that the answer is yes, with qualifications. In areas where the tradition still exists, everyone who is supposed to lament actually can do so. In most of the cultures for which we have information, lament is a women's genre, and this means that all women know how to lament. Westerners have a hard time believing that the entire population, or at least its female half, can compose verse, but that is, in fact, the situation.[41] Oral composition is not as difficult as it may appear to outsiders. Abundant data exist on weddings, which were supposed to be accompanied by lament. It was a given that every woman, when she became a bride, could and would perform wedding laments; and apparently, all did.[42] Thus, it is conceivable that all Cossacks could sing over the body of a fallen comrade, should the need arise.

The crux of the matter is that in traditions where everyone sings and everyone composes, some do it much better than others. There is a great range in quality, but outsiders see only the best because collectors record the finest singing by the best performers. Outsiders, therefore, have the misconception that all singing must be of a high level. An analogy from material culture can be useful. Where embroidery is traditional, all women embroider, but not every hand-embroidered blouse is a masterpiece worthy of becoming an heirloom. Where wood-carving is traditional, all men carve, but not every hand-carved utensil is an object of beauty. What tends to be preserved, whether by outsiders or by members of the group, is the excellent: the finest cloth items, or wood items, or laments. The level of artistry of the best singers or craftsmen is inaccessible to others, but this does not prevent the less talented from engaging in song or craft. As an informant stated to Ivan Bordenyi, "It is an honor to lament well, but it is not a disgrace to lament badly."[43] Thus, when a Cossack died in the steppe, he probably was lamented by his comrades. Some laments were no doubt memorable, and others far less so. Those Cossack laments that were of high artistic quality and had an appeal beyond the immediate situation may well have been the basis of *dumy*.

Kobzari as Remnants of a Pagan Priesthood

Lamentation, though universal, has a tendency to become professionalized. Kolessa speaks of professional mourners.[44] There were professional mourners in Russia, and when folklore became an important political vehicle in the Stalin era, certain of them achieved virtual celebrity status by composing laments for Lenin and later Stalin.[45] Professionalization is a consequence of varying levels of artistry. Oftentimes, people may want a higher level of artistry than they can achieve themselves; and while all could lament, it may have seemed more effective to dispatch the soul of the deceased, especially of a problematic dead person who could prove unquiet, with a lament sung by someone who was particularly adept. In the steppe there were probably some rank-and-file Cossacks who were outstanding singers. There were also professional musicians, the *kobzari*. If *kobzari* were asked to lament, and in all probability they were, perhaps they produced good laments consistently. *Dumy* may well come from the laments of professional *kobzari* as well as the laments of the best non-professional singers.

There is other evidence that *kobzari* led the Cossacks in celebrating the funerals of their dead. In addition to religious songs and *dumy*, traditional Ukrainian minstrels also performed dance melodies and playful, satirical songs. This happy material is totally out of line with the rest of minstrel music, which emphasizes seriousness and solemnity, and with all of the minstrel functions examined so far—unless one views it as music appropriate to a wake. Wakes did include music and even satirical ritual drama, and the tone of this material and perhaps some of its content was similar to minstrel satirical songs.[46] Thus the consistent presence of both serious and satirical material in every minstrel repertory may indicate that *kobzari* once worked a funeral from beginning to end, from laments for the deceased, sung while the body was laid out for viewing, to the wake after burial. It may indicate that they were not just musicians for hire, but spiritual functionaries.

Russell Zguta has argued that the *skomorokhi*, the Russian professional minstrels whom early, sighted *kobzari* most nearly resemble, were remnants of a pagan priesthood; and with the probable role of *kobzari* as celebrants at funerals, it is tempting to link them to pre-Christian priests also.[47] Whether or not Ukrainian minstrels were actually descendants of pagan religious functionaries, in the songs that they sang and in the legends told about them and other mendicants, there is abundant imagery dealing with crops and human sacrifice, the supposed concerns of pagan priests. Issues of crop fertility appear in Ukrainian epic poetry. Misbehavior is punished by crop failure, as in the *duma* about "The Widow and Her Three Sons," where the sons' refusal to respect their mother leads to a series of bad harvests. Even more pertinent is the song about Ivas Konovchenko, which contains a long debate between the hero and his mother on the topic of crop fertility and how it can best be achieved: by working the land or fighting over it. The mother argues that the direct approach, actual farming, is best, and Ivas argues that the land must be defended before it can be worked. Ivas also raises issues of honor and the standing in the community of one who farms as opposed to one who fights. When Ivas is killed, he becomes a sort of sacrifice on behalf of the community, a point that is emphasized by the fact that the mother adds a sacrifice of her own, spending all of the money she had so zealously guarded on a wake in memory of her son.

At some level, all Cossacks who died were seen as sacrifices on behalf of the rest of the citizenry. Martyrdom, especially martyrdom linked to Christ's crucifixion, implies dying for the sake of others, and many *dumy* end with prayers for the community as a whole: "Sanctify all of the people, oh God,/Sanctify all of the Christian people."[48] According to N. N. Veletskaia, human sacrifice for the sake of community well-being and especially crop fertility was at one time a wide-spread practice among the Slavs.[49] Writing about the Slavs in general, but drawing heavily on Ukrainian data, she hypothesizes that in the past, two types of death existed, much as they do now, but the value assigned to them was different. The preferred death was a ritual one, called a "red death." Under normal circumstances, it was bestowed upon an elder, a person around the age of sixty who was of sound mind and body and thus a worthy gift to the world of spirits. He was taken out to a special tree, mound, clearing, ravine, or other designated place and either left to die or killed with a special pillow or a ritual blow. Those who died a "red" or ritual death were especially honored and were believed to maintain contact with the living and to intercede on their behalf with the gods. Such intercession guaranteed crop fertility and favorable disposition of the spirits toward the community. People who were not given a "red death," and died of old age, disappeared and had no special powers. When the practice of ritually killing elders was discontinued, the two categories of dead remained, but the labels applied to them were inverted. Those who died naturally became the "good" dead, while those who died violently and before their time became the unquiet dead. Like the ritual dead, they maintained contact with the living, only they caused harm instead of bringing good. This is precisely the situation earlier described by D. K. Zelenin. The implication of Veletskaia's work is that Cossacks, as men who died violently and before their time, might be seen as potentially unquiet dead now; but at some point in the past, they were men who were sacrificed for community good and for crop fertility.

Most of Veletskaia's work deals with the elderly and draws on evidence such as legends collected in the nineteenth and twentieth centuries which tell why the practice of killing old people was discontinued. Interestingly, like Ivas Konovchenko's mother, they offer alternative ways to secure good crops. In one such legend, a man who is supposed to give his father a "red death" is reluctant to do so, but is pressured by his neighbors because they fear that if he does not, crop failure will ensue. He pretends to take the old man out for a ritual death, but instead brings him back home and hides him in a root cellar. The following summer there is a serious crop problem: drought, or frost, or too much rain. The man fears that his refusal to kill his father is the cause and tells the old man, who counsels his son on how to counteract the weather emergency. The son then saves his own crops and those of his neighbors. This happens again the following two summers, at which point the village begins to wonder about the source of the hero's wisdom. Pressured, he reveals that he learned everything from his father, whom he did not kill as he was supposed to do. The village then recognizes the value of old people and discontinues the practice of dispatching the elderly to the other world.

While she mostly deals with the elderly, Veletskaia claims that under special circumstances, the ritual killing of young people was considered appropriate. The killing of elders was essentially a family matter and a routine practice, done no matter what the weather and the condition of the crops. In time of severe crop problems, however, sacrifices of large numbers of people, and particularly the vigorous young, needed to be performed. Group sacrifices were done not by family members, but led by pagan priests (*volkhvy*).[50] Cossacks too died in large numbers, and they died for others. Thus they were precisely like the people sacrificed in times of crisis, and those attending them, the *kobzari*, may have had something in common with the *volkhvy*.

Veletskaia's work provides another link between minstrels and pre-Christian spirituality. If military *kobzari* were like pagan priests who officiated at group sacrifices, the handicapped minstrels we encounter in the nineteenth and twentieth centuries may have had some connection to the elders dispatched by means of a "red death." Veletskaia suggests that in the period when ritual death was practiced, the disabled were treated like the elderly and killed for crop fertility at the first indication that their disability would incapacitate them.[51] In nineteenth- and early twentieth-century data, there is no evidence that the disabled were sacrificed, but there are indeed links between them and the old. Mendicants are called grandfather (*did*) or elder (*starets*), regardless of age, and considered wise, like the elderly. They considered themselves intermediaries and felt that they could affect crops. In the legend collected by Danyliv (see Chapter 8), mendicants say that people need them to pray for the dead and that when the foolish king sells them to the ruler of another land, the result is crop failure and famine.[52] What is perhaps most intriguing is that Ukrainians believed that mendicants were absolutely necessary to pray for the dead.

In a version of the begging song (*zhebranka*, see Part II, pp. 214–15), the versified request for alms is followed by a prayer for the peace and happiness of the departed.[53] Beggars who knew nothing else knew the begging song. While travelling from house to house, a minstrel sang at least the begging song, and other songs followed only if the audience was so inclined.[54] The presence of a prayer for the deceased in this most basic of songs would indicate that the legend collected by Danyliv was implemented in minstrel practice: what minstrels and other mendicants did, first and foremost, was pray for the dead.

Minstrels and mendicants in general were so good at praying for the dead that when people were dealing with problematic dead, persons who died violently and before their time, they needed the prayers of minstrels. The text of a begging song recorded by Kharkiv from the *lirnyk* Varion Honchar offers prayers specifically for such persons:

> I ask you, my mother, my caretaker,
> Not for silver and not for gold, and not for
>   costly clothing,
> I ask you for a bit of cloth in the name of Christ.
> If we can obtain just one scrap of cloth,
> Then we will remember your sinful relatives,
> Those who died from death,
> And those who received death suddenly,
> Those who were killed by (falling) trees,
> And those who were drowned in water,
> And those who were burned in fires,
> And those who lay down their heads in battle,
> Who shed their blood for the whole Christian world.
> For their sake, have pity and apportion to us
> A scrap of cloth in the name of Christ.[55]

Later in the same interview, the informant says, "and if this does not help," meaning if the person addressed still offers nothing to the minstrel, "then you add:"

> Is it possible, my mother, my caregiver,
> That no one in your family has died,
> Not even a small child,
> That you do not wish to remember (that child),
> That you do not want to give us alms?

Again, the emphasis is on a death that occurred earlier than it should, implying that expressly in such a case, the help of a minstrel is needed. In a begging song collected by Martynovych there is a similar passage:

> My father and my mother, you should give
> Either a kerchief, or a shirt, or a piece of towel
> So that I could wipe my dark (clouded) eyes;
> Do you begrudge, my father and my mother,
> To part with one penny,
> So that you could earn the heavenly kingdom
>   for your soul?

> Then each day, my father and my mother,
> We would gather up scrap upon scrap of cloth,
> To be made into a shirt,
> And we would remember your difficulties,
> And we would praise merciful Christ for your
>   sake.
> Then we would make (create) a prayer and
>   remember your relatives,
> Those who died before their time,
> Who laid down their heads in battle,
> Who shed their blood for the Christian world,
> For all of us Orthodox people.
> And as for you, do not throw that scrap (of cloth)
>   into the trash,
> Do not trample it under foot,
> Do not burn it in a flame.
> You need to think about your eternal kingdom
>   and prepare for it,
> That which you give away with your own hands,
> You will see in the other world, in God's house.[56]

Especially significant here is the fact that men killed in battle belong among the problematic dead who need the prayers of mendicants.

The belief that mendicants were the best intermediaries between the living and the unquiet dead is voiced by the general population. In the material published by Hnatiuk, one of the informants states:

> If a dead person continues to walk about in this world, you need to give something to the poor: a shirt or a kerchief; or you need to give money to mendicants (*didy*) for the sake of his (the dead person's) soul. You need to continue to do this until the dead person stops walking.[57]

It is difficult to trace a straight line from pagan priests, to military *kobzari*, to minstrels as they were attested in the late nineteenth and early twentieth centuries. Nonetheless, ideas of sacrifice for the well-being of a community, of having professionals conduct such sacrifices, of praying for those who met untimely deaths, are all linked to minstrelsy or the minstrel repertory in some way. Even if minstrels were not descendants of *volkhvy*, they assimilated much of the imagery connected with pre-Christian spirituality.

Dealing with Loss

In material collected from and about them, *kobzari* and *lirnyky* are presented as praying for the deceased long after the latter's interment. They are not shown as lamenting over a body, but as singing for someone dead for quite some time. It would appear, then, that posthumous prayer was as important as lamentation and that such prayer, along with laments, may have been the source of *dumy*. A closing formula about the death and glory of the hero, followed by a prayer for a group—all those listening, all Christian people, or all Ukraine—is added to virtually every *duma*, whether or not this is in keeping with the plot. *Dumy* themselves present prayers for the departed as very valuable. The pleas by Marusia Bohuslavka, Ivas Konovchenko, and other heroes who ask that their relatives be informed of their deaths, are all requests for posthumous prayer. Minstrels themselves considered praying for the dead one of their main functions, and if Veletskaia is right that those who met ritual deaths served as intermediaries between this world and the next, helping the living, then prayers to and for these victims of sacrifice must have been extremely important. Probably individuals could pray to and for their family dead. But in extreme circumstances, the prayers were led or performed on behalf of the group, by priests. Praying for the departed might have been another pagan priest function linked to *kobzari*. This connection between *kobzari* and *volkhvy* is, of course, tenuous; but it is clear is that *kobzari* were associated with spiritual things even before they became officially bound to the church through their minstrel guilds. In fact, the existing tie between *kobzari* and spirituality may have been another reason for joining them to the church and equating them with minstrels already affiliated with Christian religion, the *lirnyky*.

It is even possible that the mandate that minstrels be blind is linked to the themes of suffering and martyrdom expressed in epic and to Cossack experience. Because blindness caused so much physical and psychological pain, it produced men who themselves knew suffering and could present it convincingly in song. But other disabilities were also horrible, yet not considered appropriate to minstrelsy. Blindness may have been selected because darkness was associated with Turkish captivity, that other form of Cossack suffering, that intermediate state between life and death. Captivity was portrayed as life in darkness, life without light. Since the intermediary state of captivity was darkness, then perhaps mediators, too, needed to experience a life without light. Blindness was such a life, as begging songs so often state, and those who were blind were between life and death, just like captives, and thus suitable intermediaries.

It is easy to demonstrate that being captured by the Turks or Tatars was a state somewhere between life and death, a "living Hell," as Kolessa calls it. Captivity was what a Cossack feared most. It was worse than death, as the *duma* about the three brothers by the river Samarka tells us, for it meant agonizing punishments and being deprived of one's humanity, treated like an object and not a person. In the fourteenth to seventeenth centuries, taking captives was not just a way to reduce the number of the enemy's fighting men; it had economic benefits. Captives were literally booty, a commodity like the horses, jewelry, and clothing captured in a raid, which could be used or sold.

Turkish captivity was pictured as dark. The *dumy* tell us that Cossacks do not see the sun for "three and thirty years." The Ukrainian word for dungeon is *temnytsia*, literally, a dark place, and Cossacks were kept in the sunless underground. The darkness imagery used to describe Turkish captivity probably has a number of sources. Captives may literally have been deprived of light; between being kept in dungeons and galleys, they may have been in darkness for the duration of their imprisonment. Another source may be ancient Ukrainian belief, which equates life and light. This world is light (*svit*); death is darkness, existence under ground. If captives were like the dead and existed in the "other," Turkish world, then their experience should have been one of darkness and their existence should have been beneath the surface of the earth.

There is another side to the world of the dead, however. The world of the dead is the world of the spirit, and it is no coincidence that those who sought to renounce this world and to seek a spiritual life, the monks of Kievan Rus, went down into the earth and into darkness, digging the Kievan Cave Monastery (the Pecherska Lavra) and the other underground monasteries. The monks of Kievan Rus were trying to recreate the wilderness experience of the Bible, but went beneath the soil rather than to the desert probably not only because life under the earth would be one of deprivation, but also because it was akin to death.[58] The parallels between the monastery cave experience and Turkish captivity probably did not pass unnoticed and may have lent captivity a sacred quality. Being a captive was somewhat like being a monk, even though one was forced into the position, instead of assuming it voluntarily. Thus, those who suffered captivity, even though they were passive, were imbued with some of the sacred aura of monks and of the Cossacks who died for Orthodoxy. This may well be the reason why stories of men and women in captivity were felt to belong together with the narratives about Cossacks dying like martyrs on the field of battle.

Blindness may have been selected as the disability which marked a man as a potential minstrel largely under the influence of the imagery of Turkish captivity. This made the blind into men of God (*Bozhy liudi*). There is even a legend linking the blindness of *kobzari* to Turkish captivity, which tells that the Turks blinded their captives and that the *kobzari* came from the ranks of blinded, captive Cossacks. This legend circulates widely in oral and popular literature but has little basis in fact and does not appear in scholarly writings except those of Lavrov.[59] Military *kobzari*, like Danylo Bandurko, were sighted, and it is unlikely that Turks would have lowered the economic value of their captives by blinding them. While the legend does not present fact, it beautifully encapsulates Ukrainian belief: from the death-in-life experience of Turkish captivity came the idea that blindness, imposed life without light, marks a sacred person, a person who can serve as a mediator between the living and the dead.

While it is unlikely that Turks created blind minstrels, it is possible that Turkish notions about sight influenced Ukrainian ones. The Turks place extreme value on eyes and on sight. A beloved person is called "my eye" (*gözüm*), and a set expression compares someone or something especially dear to the pupil of one's eye (*göz bebeği*). It may be that Ukrainians in Turkish captivity learned from their captors a special reverence for eyes and sight.

In discussing the links between *kobzari* and *lirnyky*, the military and the church, we have touched on all parts of minstrel repertory except the *dumy* of the Khmelnytskyi cycle. These are an anomaly in many senses. Their tone is satirical rather than elegiac. They do not speak of physical suffering and death with the frequency of other *dumy*. In fact, their plot, to the extent that they have one, has a positive outcome: the battle is won, the oppressor is punished.[60] Being so out of line with the rest of minstrel repertory, Khmelnytskyi songs disappeared from the tradition around the middle of the nineteenth century. Scholars were very interested in Khmelnytskyi *dumy* because they referred to relatively recent events and contained many references to people, places, and battles that could be connected to historical fact; but minstrels and the rural audience were not interested in these songs.[61]

Khmelnytskyi *dumy* died out because they were so different from the rest of the tradition. But why were they created in the first place? The Khmelnytskyi uprising was the period when the church, the Cossacks, and the common people all came together. It may be that in this period of union, seminarians or other church servants created songs about the Cossacks which for a time, entered the oral tradition. Kolessa suggests that Khmelnytskyi *dumy*, unlike the others, were of written rather than oral origin.[62] If, then, minstrels were used as propaganda agents to spread Orthodoxy to the common people, they may also have been used by deacons and seminarians to solicit support for the defenders of Orthodoxy, Khmelnytskyi and the Cossacks. The relative plentitude of historical fact in

Khmelnytskyi *dumy* may be the sign of a learned hand, and the favorable outcome of most of the plots may well be a remnant of attempts to instill a positive attitude toward the Cossacks and their uprising. If the scenario proposed here is true, then the satirical tone of the Khmelnytskyi *dumy* would have been added later, when the rebellion collapsed.

It is also possible that Khmelnytskyi *dumy* always had a satirical tone. The Khmelnytskyi Rebellion raised hopes of independence and prosperity, and when the rebellion collapsed, these were killed as brutally as the Cossacks who were shot and stabbed and died slowly of their wounds in the *dumy* of the Turko-Tatar cycle. While the contrast between the playful tone of the Khmelnytskyi *dumy* and historical reality was still apparent, it accentuated the pathos of the real-life situation. At that point, these *dumy* helped deal with the pain of dashed hopes, much as other *dumy* helped deal with the pain of death. As the hopes were forgotten, the satire lost its effect, and Khmelnytskyi *dumy* disappeared. The satirical tone may have had a literary origin, but a folk origin is also possible. Using satire to deal with death is not as unusual as it may seem, and satirical songs likely already existed along with solemn historical and religious material in minstrel repertory, just as satirical songs performed at wakes were part of solemn funerary ritual.

It is appropriate to end with Khmelnytskyi *dumy*, as a wake might end with satirical songs. The balance that satire provides to pathos serves as a reminder that pathos, too, helps heal. As gruesome as the subject matter of *dumy* and religious songs may have been, it did not encourage pessimism and distress, but rather helped the audience overcome negative emotions. *Dumy* were not descriptions of glorious deeds which were supposed to inspire the listeners to perform similarly heroic acts. At the same time, *dumy* actually did help Cossacks face combat. They articulated grief and fear and helped Cossacks recover from the horrors of battle, the way that laments help people express and overcome loss and pain and return to normal life. *Dumy* empowered the Cossacks and the Ukrainian nation, but not by singing of military glory. Rather, they helped by "singing out" suffering and pain. *Kobzari*, men who sang *dumy*, were men who helped heal the spirit. It was only natural, then, that they became associated with the ultimate healer of the spirit, the church.

Conclusion

*U*krainian minstrelsy was probably always linked to the sacred. In its beginning, *kobzari* helped care for the souls of those who died violently and had the potential of becoming unquiet dead. They were most closely connected to the Cossacks, the men who sacrificed their lives for the Ukrainian land, its inhabitants, and its crops. They sang laments and prayers out of which *dumy* probably grew, and they surely told stories and sang and played many other musical forms. When the Cossacks declared themselves to be the defenders of the Orthodox church, *kobzari* became linked to the Christian definition of the sacred and were merged with the minstrels who already served the church, the *lirnyky*. In the process, the repertories of the two types of minstrels blended, and Ukrainian epic acquired many features of religious song, the genre of the *lirnyky*. In the nineteenth century, when *kobzari* and *lirnyky* were one category of performer, they were still associated with death and often violent or untimely death, but their primary function seems to have been offering songs and other forms of posthumous prayer.

Minstrelsy was also a social welfare institution. In the nineteenth and early twentieth centuries and possibly earlier, minstrelsy was a way to take care of those who could not farm and thus support themselves in the same way as the majority of Ukraine's rural population. But it was not a path open to all disabled or indigent persons; minstrelsy was available only to the blind. The reason for this restriction was probably that minstrelsy was associated with the sacred just as much as it was a practical solution to disability. Beliefs about the nature of the sacred and about spirituality demanded that the performers of sacred song be blind. Sightlessness was associated with the other world, with death, with an existence beneath the soil. The blind were also people who suffered, and suffering in this life was a mark of spiritual purity, a guarantee of salvation after death.

The songs that minstrels sang were their exclusive property. Others knew these songs but were not allowed to sing them in public or for pay. This restriction had a practical side and helped guarantee that the people who needed to make money by singing were the ones who in fact did. It also had an important spiritual function. Minstrels were a path to God, and restricting the most beautiful of songs to people who were not physically beautiful was a way of helping ordinary citizens experience the divine mystery. One had to overcome a certain discomfort in the presence of the physically deformed to enjoy the beauty of their songs. Yet, the songs were such that this is precisely what happened. And making the jump from a certain degree of revulsion to joy in the art was something of a divine encounter. It allowed one to see the beauty of all of God's creatures, even the ones who appear less than perfect. Going back to my own experiences of listening to Pavlo Suprun, I can attest that I had forgotten that his misshapen eye, his dented skull, and his shrapnel scars are quite disconcerting, that dealing with a person who is blind is disorienting, until I introduced him to my husband and my son.[1] In the Ukrainian countryside at the time that traditional minstrelsy flourished, people dealt with not just one Pavlo, but many. They regularly experienced the juxtaposition of beauty and deformity.

Conversely, offering art to the handicapped to help them escape their plight provides a useful perspective on social welfare. Traditional practices, such as Ukrainian minstrelsy, did not attempt to ignore the fact of deformity and to integrate the disabled into society as if they were ordinary citizens. Blind minstrels did have a normal component to their lives: at home, in the village where they owned a house and a plot of land and raised their families. But when they functioned as minstrels, the blind were no longer ordinary. They were integrated into society, only in a totally different capacity. Their socially useful function, their work, drew precisely on their handicap, playing on the contrast between disability and art. By recognizing disability and incorporating it into the profession, traditional minstrelsy let the blind be something more than ordinary citizens. Perhaps this might prove instructive in the current settings as we attempt to integrate the disabled by trying to overlook their disabilities. The blind are not "visually challenged." If they are like Pavlo and Nadiia Suprun, they cannot even see the difference between night and day. The blind do not want us to act as if they are not there and they do not want us to pretend that they are not different from sighted people. A profession that uses the difference to constructive ends, as traditional minstrelsy did, is a good solution that helps both the disabled person and the group. In fact, the stigma attached to being a mendicant is probably a concession to the group, one that recognizes the awkwardness people feel around a disabled person and permits expression of this discomfort.

It is also instructive that in the traditional setting, the callings reserved for the disabled were artistic ones. Art has the power to heal the injured, be the injury physical or psychological, or both. As we look at performers who were physically and psychologically in distress, as Ukrainian minstrels were, we come closer to seeing if there is a factual basis for this widespread belief. This is not to romanticize the folk artist, but to recognize that art is a special, multifaceted activity, perhaps an activity with a practical side as well as a spiritual one.

There is something missing from minstrelsy as it is being revived in Ukraine today, where anyone can pick up a *bandura* and sing whatever he or she pleases. Traditional Ukrainian minstrels may have been named after their instruments, but it was not the instrument which defined the artist. The restrictions placed on traditional minstrelsy, the restrictions that permitted only blind people to become minstrels and kept ordinary folk from performing a certain set of songs, did not inhibit the profession. Rather, they contributed to its artistic power and especially to its spiritual effectiveness. When I see the restaurant owner discouraging Pavlo Suprun from singing traditional minstrel songs because they are too melancholy, or Suprun slighted in favor of minstrels who are sighted and easier to deal with because they are not disabled, I cannot help but think that Ukraine, which longs for spiritual sustenance, is overlooking one of its traditional sources.

An unknown *lirnyk* and his guide, with village children in the background. The photograph was taken in 1910 near Poltava.

An unknown *lirnyk* and his guide. Photograph taken in 1905 along the roads of the Volodar region.

Note: Except for the last, all the photographs are from the private collection of Ivan Honchar. They were rephotographed for reproduction by Volodymyr Fedko.

Two unknown *lirnyky* brought in to perform in a folklore ensemble in Kiev in 1939.

Two adult mendicants, one carrying a *lira*. In all probability, one of the men had limited vision and acted as the guide. The photograph is from the Kiev region, date not known.

An unknown *lirnyk* and his family. The photograph is from the Romen region, dated 1925–30.

An unknown *lirnyk* with his guide. The lirnyk is from the village of Maly Pavlovtsi, Okhtyrskyi region. He was born in the village of Hryn, same region. Date of the photograph not known.

Ostap Veresai and his wife Kulyna.
Photograph taken in 1873 when
Veresai was performing at the Ar-
cheological Congress in Kiev.

Kobzar Stepan Artemovych Pasiuha in his old
age. Photo taken in 1910.

The *kobzar* Tereshko and his wife Odarka. Photo taken in the Romen region, 1950.

Kobzar Demian Symonenko with his guide, Stolnyi region, 1915.

Kobzar Nykonor Onatskyi with his guide, 1910.

Kobzari (from left to right) Stepan Pasiuha, Ivan Kuchuhura-Kucherenko, Pavlo Hashchenko, and Petro Drevchenko.

Kobzar Ivan Kuchuhura-Kucherenko with two sighted amateurs. Photo taken 1929.

Kobzar Ivan Kuchuhura-
Kucherenko, 1922.

At the Historico-Ethnographic concert in Kiev in 1929. The *lirnyky* in the photo are from left to right Kuprian Moskalenko, Semen Zelinskyi, Ivan Martynenko, and Mykhailo Radievych. The two *kobzari* are V. Potapenko (left) and Pylyp Kulyk (right).

Kobzar Ehor Movchan with his sister, 1969.

Ehor Movchan with the sighted performer Hryhoryi Tkachenko, 1966.

Performers and scholars photographed in 1930. Front row, left to right: *kobzar* Ehor Movchan, the Russian singer of epic and lament Marfa Kriukova, *kobzar* Fedir Kushneryk, and *lirnyk* Dodatko. Standing in back row, left to right: the composer Kozytskyi, the writer Petro Panch, Academician Sokolov, the poet and scholar Pavlo Tychyna, and the composer Vekyrivskyi.

The Kiev Ethnographic *Kobzar* Ensemble. Front row, left to right: Petro Hudz, Ivanenko, Ehor Movchan. Back row, left to right: Volodymyr Perepeliuk, Pavlo Nosach, and Oleksandr Markevych.

Kobzar Ivan Petrenko, Romen region, 1956.

Kobzar Evhen Adamtsevych, 1950.

Kobzar Okelsienko
(Adamtsevych's teacher),
Romen region, 1930.

Kobzar Oleksa Chupryna, performing at the grave of Taras Shevchenko in Kaniv, 1979.

Pavlo Stepanovych Suprun performing in Kiev, 1995. Photo taken by Michael Naydan.

Part 2

Minstrel Rites and Songs

"If the people listen to you sing a song all the way through, if they listen to your singing, then tears come to their eyes. Then they give you alms. And then I stop."

Texts

A Religious Festival

The Description of a Religious Festival Given by
Valerian Borzhkovskii in His Article "Lirniki"

Just this year (1889) I was at an *otpust* in Brailiv.[1] This *otpust* is celebrated at a nunnery and a Uniate Catholic church. An enormous number of people and *lirnyky* gather here. Of the latter, there were at least fifteen. Some of the *lirnyky* were in the town, some were in the fields, and some were on the roads outside of Brailiv—near the church itself there were none. There were three at the railway stop. The first one I met was a *lirnyk* from Zinkov, named Bernatskyi. I asked him to sing the *panshchyna* song.[2] "Why do you want it? I don't know it." I did not believe him, and later I confirmed that he indeed knew the song. Be that as it may, I requested the song about Saint Nicholas. Around us gathered a group of worshippers from the Iampil region. Some of them gave the *lirnyk* a piece of bread, others gave him a roll with filling (*pyrih*), others gave him a kopek. The peasants listened to the song very attentively. Just then, a noble woman drove past us and looked with disdain in our direction.

"She's grinning," an old peasant said to me in a whisper, "and she doesn't realize that in the eyes of God, this blind man is probably a hundred times more worthy than she is, or than we are."

The song is over. We walk further. [. . .] I strike up a conversation with the old peasant about mendicant elders (*didy*). His opinion of them is high.

"And who do you think is more charitable to *lirnyky*?" I ask.

"The peasant, of course. Would a mendicant ever teach you something bad? As he works for his bread, he sings God's songs; people listen to him, and maybe it will move their hearts, maybe it will bring them to their senses."

In Brailiv itself, in the town and around the monastery, there were masses of worshippers; I estimate there were some ten thousand people. The crowds move constantly. In the monastery compound, by the wall, people are resting in groups by village. From the gates to the monastery are two rows of peddlers (*sydukhy*). They are selling smoked fish, bread, rolls, candy, and the like.

Lirnyky are scattered throughout the entire courtyard. Around each is a dense crowd of listeners. They are peasants of all ages and both sexes. Some of them make themselves more comfortable by sitting down right on the ground next to the *lirnyk*. Silence reigns in the crowd, broken now and again by a listener's remark. If someone requests a song, he pays three kopeks. But at the end of a song, and often during it, others give also; one will give a kopek, another, a roll. Having listened to one *lirnyk*, people head over to another one and their places are taken by new arrivals. If a *lirnyk* is left without an audience for a period of time, he gets up and walks over to a different place. I noticed a young man who was walking from *lirnyk* to *lirnyk*.

"Do you like these songs?" I ask him.

"Of course I do. I could listen to them for twelve hours straight. It's such a shame that there are no *lirnyky* in our town of Shaphorod."

Just at this moment the *lirnyk* was singing:

> Brother is enemy unto brother,
> And sister wants to curse sister. . . .

"And isn't that just how it is in this world, just as the mendicant sings it," one could hear in the crowd.

I walk over to the next group and hear weeping, which sometimes grows louder, sometimes fades to quiet sobs. Most of the listeners here are women and girls. Who knows, maybe there are orphans among them, like the orphan about whose difficult life the *lirnyk* is singing:

> Although the orphan works and works,
> Work does her no good—
> Her stepmother keeps on saying:
> The orphan is a lazy good-for-nothing.

Two noblewomen have joined this group. But it is obvious that the song "The Orphan Girl" does not have the same effect on them as on the rest of the listeners, and the noblewomen's smiling faces are in stark contrast to the rest of the scene.

In another group, the peasants are asking the *lirnyk* to sing the song about Iva the most blessed, but he does not know the song.

One peasant complains, "I have already asked five [*lirnyky*] and not a single one knows it; and I haven't heard this song in so long! Okay, mendicant, sing me the song about the Pochaev Virgin, but do it the way that it is written in the book."

"This is a real calamity for us. Here and there people have gone and learned from books and have started to take our bread away from us."

Within the monastery compound, in addition to the *lirnyky*, there were many other beggars. Near the gate sat a beggar who placed his own blackened leg bones on a cloth before him. He was begging in the name of God. An old blind man with a pleasant face was "teaching" the Akathistos.[3] Many were begging and "Oh charitable people . . . " could be heard on all sides. Blind beggars formed groups and sang the "begging song" (*zhebranka*) or "The Twelve Fridays."

There were some who read the Akathistos from a book. People gave money to them, just like to the those who begged in the name of God. I was particularly fascinated by one old man. He had glasses on the tip of his nose and stood in one place all day reading the Psalter. Like every other poor person, he had a bag by his side for receiving alms. But it seems that no one had given him anything for quite some time. Finally, he turned to the passersby in desperation and said:

> Give me alms, oh Christians,
> Give me whatever is your pleasure,
> Give me a slap on the neck, if you want to,
> I will say thank you even for that.
> Just let me know that I am not standing here
> for nothing.

I walk up to a *lirnyk*. He is surrounded by listeners. He is singing "Oleksii, Man of God." I listen to the conversation which ensues when he finishes.

"It's a good thing you didn't ask me to sing it, because I would not have," says the *lirnyk*.

I ask what is going on. The women tell me that they were trying to get the young men to get together five kopeks and ask the *lirnyk* to sing the song about Konovchenko.

A person near me explains, "While this is a very nice song, mendicants sing it only on secular holidays and not during church festivals."

I later asked the *lirnyk* Zoria about this. He explained that it may well have been that the *lirnyk* at the monastery did not know "Konovchenko," just like the other man may not have known the *Panshchyna* song. Nuns forbid the singing of both of these songs only within the monastery. Otherwise, Konovchenko is very popular, and according to Zoria, during holidays, people make you sing it in virtually every house.

Source: Kievskaia Starina, Vol. 26, 1989, pp. 662–65.

The Minstrel Initiation Rite

The Eastern Version of the Rite
Supplied by the *Kobzar* Trykhon Mahadyn

When a master has taught a boy to play and the latter is about to leave the master and go earn his own bread, then the master informs the brotherhood of the poor, saying, "I have a boy who has learned to play well—it is time to let him earn his own bread [literally: give him bread]; come join us for the initiation rite." In order to celebrate the initiation rite properly, in order for there to be many members of the brotherhood of the poor in attendance, they pick a convenient time—a fair.

Toward the end of the fair, in the evening, the brotherhood slowly gathers at the master's. On the way, they buy food and vodka. They gather at a tavern until it gets completely dark. At that point, the master's wife, or a hired girl, or one of the guides, will pour some vodka into a bowl, will cut some bread and some fish and will give each person a spoon.[1] Then the brotherhood sits down at the table. In the summertime, this is done outdoors. Then the master takes bread into his hands, walks up to the assembled company and says, "With prayers to the Holy Father, our Lord Jesus Christ, Son of God, have mercy upon us." The assembled company answers as a group, "Amen." "Peace be onto our conversation." In unison they say: "May Christ God Himself come in peace and bless us." "A kopek invites you to drink vodka, but I summon you to honor, to love, and to the initiation rite."[2] The master then puts the bread on the table; next to him is the key-keeper with the bread.[3] The master then gives everyone a glass and invites the assembled group to partake of the bread and salt. Everyone in the group comes up individually and says to the master, "With prayers to the Holy Father." The master answers, "Amen." (Then the person who has approached the master says) "May God bless the master for his holy Amen, for Jesus' prayer, for the word from the Bible, for his godly greeting, for his teaching as a master. We bow before you with bread and with salt." Then the master places the bread in that person's hands, saying: "Take this bread and salt, and accept us into your honor." Each person approaches in this manner; when he gets his bread, he sits down in a row. Then the master stands up, takes a glass, pours a shot of vodka and says, "With our prayers." Everyone answers, "Amen." The master thanks them for the Amen. (Then he) asks, "Has everyone, gentlemen elder members and junior members, received a glass of vodka from the master?" "Thank you, we have all received a glass." Then the master sits down and the pupil stands up in the middle of the circle (sic), raises a glass and says, "With prayers." He is answered, "Amen." He thanks them for the Amen. "Please bless me that I may offer a glass of wine to my master."[4] The group says, "May God bless." The master takes the glass in his hands and says, "With prayers." Then he continues, "Give me your blessing, gentlemen members, to drink a glass of wine from my pupil." "May God bless." Then the pupil gives a glass (of vodka) to each of those present, saying, "With prayers." At the end he asks, "Gentlemen members, have you all received a glass of wine?" "We humbly thank the master and you; we have all received a glass." Then the pupil puts down his glass and says, "With prayers." Then he bows and says, "Gentlemen members, whatever bread and salt you have amongst you, give me the same bread also." Then the master stands up and says, "With prayers. Gentlemen members and the entire assembly, bless me so that I may give this boy his bread and salt." "May God bless." Then he hands the boy the bread and salt and sits down. Then the boy says, "I most humbly thank you, gentlemen masters, for this bread, for this salt, and for your guidance." They say, "With prayers." "Give me your blessing, gentlemen, to pass out my master's bread, piece by piece." "May God bless." Then he cuts the bread, piece by piece. He gives a piece to the master, then to each of those present, until everyone has a piece. Having passed out the bread, he says, "With prayers," and then, "Did all of you gentlemen receive a piece of the master's bread?" "We humbly thank your master and you; we all have a piece." Then two elders take him (the pupil) by the hands and seat him next to the master. Then all celebrate until the party breaks up.

Mahadyn continues:

About ten years after finishing an apprenticeship, a man gets the right to take pupils himself. He buys a pail of vodka, perhaps half a pail; he summons the brotherhood and asks them to allow him to take on help: "Allow me, gentlemen members, to get some help for myself." Once they let you take the first pupil, well, then you can do what you want; you can have twenty pupils if you want to.

Source: Recorded by Martynovych, July 3, 1876, and published in *Ukrainski zapisi*, pp. 76–77. In the text, there is some confusion between the word "master" meaning the teacher of the initiate and "master" meaning any man who is a professional minstrel. This is avoided in the translation and "master" is used for the teacher only. Since this is an oral text, written down from dictation, other apparent contradictions are also present. The minstrels are said to gather at the home of the master. Later it is unclear whether they are at a private home or a tavern. The confusion probably came about because in Eastern Ukraine, minstrels could conduct the initiation rite in either place.

The Eastern Version of the Initiation Rite
Supplied by Terentii Parkhomenko

The pupil and the teacher arrive at the gathering, which takes place either in a home or outdoors, together. Then the following dialogue takes place:

Pupil: With prayers to the Holy Father our Lord, Jesus Christ, Lord God . . . .

Teacher: Amen.

Pupil: I humbly thank you for the blessed Amen, for the word from the Bible, for your teaching as a master. I bow before you, lord father (insert the name of the teacher), with bread and with salt, with a low bow and with wishes for good health. God grant me permission to greet you. I have the honor to greet you on this holy evening (or morning, or day, or holiday, if the event takes place on a holiday).

Teacher—takes the bread which the pupil gives him and says: May God grant that as this bread is pure and good, that you too be pure and good among the people of the Christian world and among the members of the brotherhood. May God bless you [to go] in all four directions.

Pupil: I humbly thank you for your good words.

At this point the pupil approaches each of the three masters present [apparently, there need to be three elders, three people in addition to the teacher, who are accredited as teachers, present] and addresses each with the same words he had just used to address the master; this is called "paying respects." When respects have been paid to all of the masters, then all sit down at the table. Usually, the elder minstrels [the ones who have achieved master status] sit at the table and the younger ones sit wherever they can. At this point the teacher recites a prayer: With prayers to our Holy Father, Lord Jesus Christ, Lord God . . .

All are quiet.

The teacher repeats: With prayers and so forth.
All are silent.

The teacher says a third time: With prayers and so forth.

At this point all say: Amen.

Teacher: I humbly thank you for your holy Amen, for the word from the Bible, for professional instruction. I bow before you with the request that you, oh brotherhood of Christ, elder brethren and younger ones, will agree to give my pupil (insert name of pupil here) bread and salt.

All: Was he good to you? Did he carry you on his finger (meaning, did he beat you)? Did he greet people properly? Did he thank them for the alms he received? Did he learn any evil ways?

Teacher: No, he was a good lad.

All: If he was a good lad, then may God help him, that people may respect him. We agree. We agree. If he was a good lad, then we must accept him and give him bread and salt [meaning the right to earn his living as a minstrel].

At this point the teacher gives out the bread and fish which was provided ahead of time by the pupil and says: With prayers to the holy Father . . .

All are silent.

Teacher repeats: With prayers . . .

All are silent.

Teacher says a third time: With prayers . . .

All: Amen.

Teacher: I humbly thank you for your holy Amen, for the word from the Bible, for professional instruction. A kopek invites you to drink vodka, but I summon you to honor, to love, to a glass of vodka.[5] Would you like to drink a glass of vodka provided by my pupil?

All: Let that which is baked and boiled not stand [Let prepared food not go to waste]. If it has been said, if he has been accepted, then it cannot be undone. Let us drink.

The teacher drinks. Then he passes the glass to the pupil. Then all drink.

Pupil: With the prayers of the holy fathers . . .

All plus the teacher: Amen.

Pupil: I thank you, master (name of teacher), for your blessed Amen, for the word from the Bible, for professional instruction. A kopek invites you to drink vodka, but I summon you to honor, to love, and to a glass of vodka. I invite you to drink a glass of vodka provided by me, just as you drank a glass supplied by my master.

If the pupil has behaved himself well, then all drink. If he has behaved badly, then they say, "We don't want your vodka." But eventually they take pity on the pupil and forgive him, and then accept the drink.

Pupil: With the prayers of the holy fathers . . . Have you all had a drink, oh brotherhood of Christ? Perhaps someone has not had enough. Please let me know. I ask you, I question you, are you pleased with the bread and salt and the ceremony?

All: We are pleased.

Pupil: Thank you.

All: Thank you.

After this, the banquet continues. At the end, all get up, walk away from the table, line up and say a prayer. The prayer ends with their singing long life to the tsar, the local officials, the brotherhood, and all Christian people. At the very end, they pray for the dead and for teachers of the past.

Source: Speranskii, pp. 113–15. Parkhomenko was trained as a *lirnyk* and probably went through his initiation as a *lirnyk*, though by the time Speranskii collected from him, he was a *kobzar*. This version of the rite is practiced in Mena. Parkhomenko does not describe how the members of the guild are summoned to the rite, giving only the words spoken as part of the initiation. He does say a few words about the celebration that follows the initiation proper. The parenthetical remarks are those made by Parkhomenko, unless they are placed in square brackets.

The Western Version of the Initiation Rite
Supplied by the *Lirnyk* Iakiv Zlatarskyi

When a pupil has put in his three years or whatever, then he is sent out on a practicum [that is, to beg], so that he will get to know people, so that he will gain wisdom, so that he can save up a bit (because you have to have some money for the initiation rite), so he can earn some money for clothes, so that he can put away a bit of money and have it ready. Then they decide at which religious festival to have the initiation. (It is always celebrated next to some monastery or other; it can be a Russian one [Orthodox] or a Polish one [Catholic]; that does not matter.) The people who are invited to an initiation are not just anybody, only the ones who are worthy; three are invited, not more. If the person invited is married, then the wife comes too. The rite itself is performed in the open square near the monastery; you are not supposed to do it in a tavern. They usually gather in the evening, when the public has left. Also, they are careful that no one should see them; and if someone does see them, they just sit down and wait until that person goes away and there is no one to know what is going on amongst them. After they have come to that religious festival and after the evening prayers, the master sends out his pupil to summon the *lirnyky* and the plain beggars and instructs him: when you come to him [the person], if he says, "Praise be to Jesus Christ," then you answer, "There is a meeting."

The pupil comes to a learned *lirnyk*, as is the custom, sent by the master and in obedience to the master. He comes to him and he says, "Praise be to Jesus Christ." He takes him by the hand and tells him: "The favor of God is with you at the meeting and in trade. God favors you with health and in all things when Christ shows the way. The master has sent me and I myself am summoning you to honor and to love, to the initiation rite and to a bit of vodka (or drink)." Thus he asks each one. And that one answers: "I humbly thank your master and you, my friend, I humbly thank you for the honor and the love." Then he asks, "Where, my son, will the meeting take place?" "It will be at the master's place; the location has been chosen; there we will gather and there we will have God's meal, and at that place we will pray to God, and then there will be time for drinking." Then they gather at the square next to the monastery. This is done in Chirvonohrad and Lashkivtsi, Vokitsi (near Russia), on the Khreshchatyk and in Bukovyna and in Husiatyna—where else, I don't know; I'm telling about the ones I know. There they spread a tablecloth on the ground and have their meal. They provide bread and salt, and some kind of drink, either beer or vodka, whatever you can get. They also try to provide garlic or some kind of cucumber or pickle; if times are bad, they provide cheese for dessert, not a lot, just a small amount, not so that you could fill up on it, but so that everyone can have a taste. After the pupil has seated everyone, he begins to pronounce his initiation. He walks up to the master and stands next to him, and a helper pours him a little bit of liquor. He holds a kerchief in one hand and the drink in the other and says, "Peace be unto you, my fathers." They answer him, "Come in peace." Then they say it a second time. "Peace be unto you, my fathers." "Come in peace." Then they say it a third time. "Peace be unto you, my fathers." "Come in peace." Then he says, "May God greet all those who are seated." They answer, "And may God greet those who pass by." Then they say it a second time. "May God greet all those who are seated." They answer, "And may God greet those who pass by." A third time he says, "May God greet all those who are seated." They answer, "And may God greet those who pass by." Then it goes like this: he says to them, "By the prayers of our holy fathers, Lord, Jesus Christ, Son of God, have mercy upon us." They answer him, "Amen." He says to them, "Thank you for the amen, for the word of God, the word of the angels." This they say three times. Then he says three times, "Bless my father [meaning the master]." They answer him three times, "With God's prayers." Then he says, "Allow me to approach." They say, "Please do, please do." Then he drinks the liquor that he has been holding in his hand all this time. Then he gives the glass to his master [and the master drinks]. Then he sends the glass down the line, only he takes it from each person himself and passes it on to the next. That is how they do the first round. After that, they just pass the glass to each other. They pour their own liquor and drink. After that, they pray to God and then thank the master and the pupil: "We thank God on high that God helped you learn, and we thank you, master, for your teaching, for the bread and salt, for the honor and the love, for the bit of liquor. As for you, our comrade, may you be well known and prominent among the nobles, and among the clergy, and among the people, and among the members of the brotherhood of the poor. May you be known throughout the world. May you lack neither bread nor salt nor anything good." With this, they each go their own way.

Source: Hnatiuk, pp. 4–5. The parenthetical remarks, unless marked by square brackets, were made by the *lirnyk* himself.

Songs

The Begging Song and the Song of Gratitude

The begging song (*zhebranka*) was performed when a minstrel arrived at someone's home. It also was sung at religious festivals and fairs. If the audience responded favorably, then the minstrel would sing additional material, such as religious or historical songs. The song of gratitude (*blahodarinne*) was sung after a minstrel had received alms. If the minstrel sang the begging song only, he could conclude it with a prayer, as in the first example below. If the minstrel sang other genres, a song of gratitude was the appropriate conclusion to the performance.

The Begging Song of a *Lirnyk*

The Son of God, my mother,[1]
The Holy Spirit, my flower,
Dwells in your home,
And comes to your aid.

My dear mother,
My dear father,[2]
Beloved of God,
Descendants of Jesus Christ!

Thus having, my mother,
Thus having, my flower,
In your pitying heart,
In your blessed house,
A shirt, my mother,
A shirt, my flower,

Or pants for my sinful body,
To cover my nakedness.

Please cover, my mother,
Please cleanse, my flower,
From both dirt and from filth,
The way the Lord himself covers:
The tree with bark,
The earth with grass,
The sun with the moon,
The water with darkness,
The fish with scales,
The sky with clouds,
The bird with feathers,
The mountains with cliffs,
The bird with feathers,
The mountains with cliffs,
The shore with sands,
The sky with clouds.

In this world, my mother, before you have much of a chance,
In this world, my mother, before you have much of a chance,
You have to fold your hands before Christ,
You have to surrender your soul to God.
So remember, my mother,
So remember this:
That this world, and the sky and the earth are His!
And what you get are four oaken boards,
With a layer of damp earth on top.

I'm not asking, my mother,
I'm not asking, my flower,
For either silver or gold, or fine raiment,
Or for a princely ransom.

I only ask and weep,
With a low bow,
With the word of God and the Angels,
In the name of Jesus Christ.
So, my mother, if you have,
So, my flower, if you have,

A towel or a coin,
In praise of God,
To be collected for a shirt,
Then I will, my mother,
Walk the wide earth,
And gather coin upon coin,
And pray to the Lord for your sake.

So if you have, my mother,
So if you have, my flower,
Oh righteous one, a cowl,
In praise of God,
To be collected for a shirt,
Then I will, my mother,
Then I will, my flower,
Walk the wide earth,
And gather cowl upon cowl,
And pray to the Lord for your sake.

Because this world, my mother,
Is like the blossom of a poppy,
It blooms brightly,
And no one plucks it,
But the damp earth devours it.

So if you have, my mother,
So if you have, my flower,
A towel or a kerchief,
To wipe Jesus Christ,
Then I will, my mother,
Then I will, my flower,
Wipe my stricken eyes,
And pray to the Lord for your sake,
For your health, dear mother,
For a long life.

So if you have, my mother,
So if you have, my flower,
A penny or two,
In praise of God,
To be collected for a coat,
Because the winters are so cold!

Then I will, my mother,
Warm my body,
And pray to the Lord for your sake day and night.

Don't pass me by, my mother,
Don't pass me by, my dear one,
Don't be miserly, my flower,
And don't be miserly, my flower.
And don't cast me in the dirt,
And don't trample me with your feet,
But seek the heavenly kingdom,
But seek the heavenly kingdom for your soul.

Mother, as you have loved the Lord in heaven,
So, mother, love the poor man on this earth.
It will not be a great expense,
You will be compensated by the Lord God.
You will be compensated by the Lord in Heaven,
Where body and soul most need to be.

Do not behave, my mother,
Do not behave, oh Christian people,
Like the rich man Ilion behaved,[3]
Who had gold and silver aplenty,
But gave nothing to the churches and the chapels.

But behave, my mother,
Like the Virgin Mary behaved.
She had but one cloak,
But she divided it into three pieces.
And the first piece, my mother,
And the first piece, my mother,
She gave to Saint Basil to protect him,
And with the second piece she covered the poor,
And the third piece, my mother,
And the third piece, my mother,
She gave to the churches and the chapels,
And she inherited the Kingdom of Heaven.[4]

We praise you, oh Lord God, and pray for the eternal rest of all our
departed relatives, those registered and those not registered, who rest in

their graves.[5] Remember them, oh Lord, in your heavenly kingdom, in eternal rest, in bright Paradise. Remember them, oh Lord, during the evening prayers, and the all-night vigils, and the morning prayers, and the Holy service, and grant them, oh Lord, the Kingdom of Heaven, and eternal rest, and bright Paradise, where all the Saints repose and sing the songs of angels. May God have mercy upon you and lead you to salvation; may He grant you health and good fortune and long life from now and forever. Amen.

Source: Borzhkovskii, "Lirniki," pp. 655–57. Borzhkovskii does not give the name of the performer, but it was probably Andrii Dovhaliuk, also called Zoria, the source of most of Borzhkovskii's material. The line and stanza divisions of the translation repeat those of the original.

The Begging Song and the Songs of Gratitude Sung by the *Lirnyk* Mykolai Doroshenko

The Begging Song

Only Son, Holy Ghost, Righteous Mother of God!
Send, oh Lord, send your Guardian Angel to this honest
    and worthy home.
Do not be, oh, my father, oh, my mother, like the rich
    man Ilion.[6]
He had plenty of silver and gold,
He did not allot any of it for the holy churches
And he did not apportion any of it for the humble poor
    folk.
Oh, be, father and my mother, like the most holy St. Mary,
Who had but one mantle,
And even that she divided into three pieces:
And the first pieces she gave to the Savior for curtains
    (she donated it to the church),
With the second piece she covered St. Basil (she gave it
    to the poor),
And the third part she used to cover her own self.
Cover, oh father and my mother, cover my sinful body,
Like our Lord covers the water with mist, the fish with
    scales,
The earth with grass, the tree with leaves and bark,
The sky with clouds,
And the sinful person with clothes.

Source: Recorded by Porfyrii Martynovych, IMFE fond 11–4/589, ark. 17. The parenthetical remarks were made by the *lirnyk* himself. They appear in Martynovych's manuscript as notes between song texts. Explanatory parenthetical remarks not found in the
manuscript appear in square brackets. The capitalization and the division into lines and
stanzas is that of the original. The punctuation is that of the original where possible.

Songs of Gratitude

(This is performed when you are leaving the house, when you are tired.)

> May God accept your fasting and your prayers, you who
>   have given alms.
> May your alms provide a bridge to the heavenly kingdom,
> to the Son of God, to the throne of the cherubim.
> May the Lord see you at the second coming.
> May God count your alms towards bright Paradise,
>   toward blissful repose.
> May God accept your gift as praise of the Heavenly King.
> In accordance with God's Akathistos,[7]
> In accordance with Christ's customs,
> And may God in his Kingdom remember
> His most worthy servants [meaning the alms givers],
> May God recall the bread and salt,
> Given in Christ's glory,
> May the Lord grant you mercy
> and health for all ages,
> And the salvation of your soul.

(The one below is performed if they give you a towel.)[8]

> Remember, God, the bread and salt given in Christ's
>   glory.
> My mother, your alms are apparent before God and
>   before the merciful Lord.
> They are accepted as a humble offering.
> Your alms will not sink beneath the waters
> And they will not burn in a fire,
> They will become a help to you in every hour of need.
> They will pull your soul up from the bottom of the sea
> and lead the whole world to the heavenly kingdom,
> and lead your body and soul to the heavenly kingdom,
> to health and to salvation,

to many years in God's help,
to receiving happiness and joy from the Heavenly King.
Your alms, oh father and my mother,
Are covered by a mantle.
[Give] pants or a shirt,
To be worn by the poor,
Or give a scrap of a towel,
To be used for a sleeve,
Oh that scrap,
Oh father and my mother,
Will not make you poor, will not make you impoverished,
It will not make your children suffer,
That scrap which you give to the poor in this lovely world.
Let it be, father, oh my mother,
either a kerchief or a shirt,
or a towel to wipe my darkened eyes.
Let it be, oh father and my mother,
a single penny, to make change,
to let you secure a place for your soul in the Heavenly
    Kingdom.
Then we will, oh father and my mother,
Gather scrap upon scrap,
Gather scraps for a shirt;
we will walk in our travails
And turn to the merciful Lord on your behalf.
We will utter prayers
And remember your kin,
Those who died from misfortune,
Those who laid down their heads in battle,
For the sake of the Christian world,
For the sake of all of us Orthodox people,
Who spilled their blood for our sake.
And you will not throw that scrap away.
You will not trample it under foot,
You will not burn it in a fire.
That which you give with your own hands,
You will see in the next world,
At God's second coming
You will see it, my mother, before your soul.

Source: IMFE fond 11–4/589, ark. 18.

The Begging Song
Sung by the *Kobzar* Pavlo Hashchenko

God's greetings to you,
Most merciful mother,
Most merciful mother, my nanny,
May you behave in this righteous world,
So that Christ in Heaven,
So that you may be beloved by God.
Please cut me a piece of towel,
For the sake of Christ,
So that I may collect [cloth] towards a shirt,
As one needs to in this world,
As was done by two poor brothers,
In the name of Christ.
And it will be apparent, it will be clear,
What you give on the damp earth for the sake of your
  soul.[9]
I ask you, my nanny, my mother,
Not for silver and not for gold and not for costly clothing,
I ask you for a scrap of towel in the name of Christ,
Because we will gather scrap upon scrap,
And we will remember those of your relatives who have
  been sinners,
Those who have died before their time,
And those who were killed by falling trees,
And those who drowned in waters,
And those who were burned in fires,
And those who laid down their heads in battle,
Who shed their blood for the whole Christian world.[10]
For their sake you should allot us, you should provide us,
A scrap of cloth in the name of Christ.
Then the merciful Lord will cover you, oh my mother,
At the second coming, at the arrival of Christ,
He will cover you with the holy mantle that does not
  decay, with the protective hem of his coat,
And protect you from eternal torment and from most
  horrible fear,
From the inextinguishable flame,
The Lord will protect you and have mercy upon you,
Don't place your trust, merciful father,

And you, my merciful nanny, oh my mother, in your
    neighbors or your siblings,
Or in beautiful, multi-colored clothing,
Or in this bright, in this appealing world.
Because this world is like the flower of a poppy,
It blooms and it blossoms and then it falls to the damp
    earth.
Therefore know, my merciful father,
And you, my merciful nanny, oh my mother,
That we live and we dwell in this bright world,
And we do not know when the hour of our death will
    come,
Perhaps we will be alive in the evening,
And in the morning we will have to lie in a coffin,
And we will be able to take nothing with us.
The only thing that we will be able to take, that we will
    bring along,
Will be a deep, deep measure of earth,
A measure of earth deep and wide,
And that will be our only wealth.

(If the above doesn't work, if you don't get alms having sung the above,
then you can add the following.)

    Oh my nanny, oh my mother,
    Did you never have a child that died,
    Did you never have a small child,
    That you need to have remembered,
    That you can afford not to give alms?
    Cover, oh my mother,
    Cover my sinful body upon this earth,
    Like the Lord Himself covers,
    The tree with leaves and with bark,
    The earth with grass,
    The fish with scales,
    The birds with feathers,
    And the sky with clouds,
    And the sinful person with the blankets of Christ.

Source: Collected by Kharkiv, IMFE fond 6–4/161/4, ark. 22. The parenthetical remarks are those made by the minstrel himself. Explanatory remarks not found in the manuscript are in square brackets.

Religious Songs

Religious songs were the most important part of a minstrel's repertory, and the goal of most minstrels was to know as many of these as possible. There was no occasion where a religious song was not appropriate. Religious songs could be sung in a home, if the hosts were willing to listen and to pay for more than the begging song. They could be sung at religious festivals and fairs, or while begging on the street in a city. While satirical songs and historical songs were considered unseemly under certain circumstances, no one ever reprimanded a minstrel for singing religious material. Several songs included toward the end of this section ("Justice," "The Orphan Girl," "Misery") are not strictly religious songs, but, like religious songs, they were deemed suitable for all performance occasions.

Lazarus (*Lazar*, also called *Dva Lazaria*)

Oh, there has been more than one rich person,
Who always lived in luxury.
He had enough gold and silver,
And never admitted any of the clergy into his household,
He did not recognize his brother Lazarus as a brother.
Oh, in that household there was not a single soul,
Not a single compassionate soul,
Who would approach the sickly Lazarus,
And bring him food and drink.
Only the rich man had two fierce dogs,
They would always go under the table,
They would gather the tiny crumbs,
They would bring them to the sick Lazarus, sitting in the filth,
They would drip water on his parched lips,
They would lick his painful wounds,
They would lighten and support his body and soul.
Oh, when the rich man caught sight of the two fierce dogs,
He ordered his servants to chain them with iron chains,
To punish them with iron whips:

So that they would not go to the sickly Lazarus,
So that they would not use up his possessions,
Would not carry away his gold and his silver. . . .
"Oh, brother, my brother, you are rich and powerful!
But it looks like you think you won't die,
Because you do not care to make preparations for the
      hereafter."
"If I start to die, then I will buy my way out of it;
If I can't buy my way out if it, then I will fight my way
      out,
I will not submit to all of the Holy ancestors in Heaven
And I am not afraid of the Lord God Himself . . . "
"Oh, Lord, God, Savior, divine mercy is Yours!
Lord, hear my prayers:
Accept my body and soul, according to Your divine
      mercy!"
And the Lord listened to his prayer,
"Go, Angels, go fetch his soul.
Descend, Angels, go very quietly,
And gently take Lazarus' soul into your hands.
And seat him to the right of Abraham,
In the heavenly Lord's bright Paradise!"
Then the Angels and the Archangels sing a song,
They cheer up the sickly Lazarus.
Oh, after some time, after an hour, after a little bit,
A desire to go out, to ride in the open field seized the rich
      man. . . .
Oh, the rich man rode out from his household, from his
      new gates,—
And his entourage followed him, his sumptuous troops,
And he saw that there was no more brother Lazarus and
      nothing to worry about.
The rich man rode past the second set of gates,
And a black illness came out after him:
It took the rich man and started to beat him against the
      earth. . . .
It finally occurred to the rich man to pray to God:
"Oh, Lord God, Savior, divine mercy is Yours!
Oh, Lord, do not be angry with me now!
Did I not eat, did I not drink, did I not walk,
That I have angered the Lord God unto eternity.

Oh, Lord God, Savior, divine mercy is Yours!
Oh, Lord, hear my prayer:
Take my body and my soul, take them where Lazarus is!"
And the Lord heard his prayer,
And he sends the servants of Hell to fetch his soul:
"Go, servants of Hell, go quickly to the earth,
And take the soul of the rich man into your hands. . . . "
The servants of Hell have not yet reached his household,
And yet they have already turned his wealth to ashes,
    scattered far and wide:
They chased away his ready entourage,
They took away his gold and his silver,
They took the rich man's soul out with a hook.
They hung the rich man from his left rib:
"Tell us, oh, rich man, where is your wealth,
Your ribbons, your towels and your fine carvings
Your gold, your silver, your ancient coins?"
Oh, they carried the rich man high into the sky,
And they dropped the rich man into Hell, way below:
"Swim, swim, oh rich man, there is plenty of room
    here,
Look up at Heaven, see how high God is!"
The rich man looked up to Heaven with his eye,
And he cried with his voice unto his brother Lazarus,
He pleaded and cried and he even called him his dear
    brother:
"Oh, brother, my own dear brother!
Couldn't you please exercise your will—
Couldn't you dip your pinky finger into the sea,
Couldn't you quench the fires of Hell just a bit?"
"Oh, brother, my own dear brother!
I could exercise my will,
But I do not want to anger the Lord God;
Even if I dip my pinky finger into the sea,
I can never quench these fires of Hell."
"Oh, brother, my own dear brother!
One mother bore us, she carried us under the same
    heart,
But she did not give us the same fate:
She gave you, my brother, great poverty,
And she gave me, my brother, great wealth.

You earned the heavenly kingdom with your poverty,
And I inherited Hell through my wealth.
Oh, brother, my own dear brother,
Pray to God for me once more;
Ask Him to let me return to the world once more;
Then I will know how to prepare for this world:
If I have gold and silver, I will hand it out to the poor,
Every Sunday, every holiday, I will go to God's temple
And I will pay for the services and the reading of the
    Psalter,
And I will always recognize you, brother, as my kin;
I have five more brothers, and I will teach them. . . . "
"In that world there are sacred, spiritual writings:
Let them read the sacred writings,
And may your five brothers come to understand."

Source: Recorded from Adrian Kravchenko, village of Okhmatova, Tarazhanskii region and published in Demuts'kyi, *Lira i iii motivy*, pp. 52–54.

Saint Barbara (*Varvara*, also called *Varvara Velykomuchynytsia*)

Oh, a star rose in the middle of the sea,
Oh, it was not a star—it was the blessed Varvara.
The king himself took a liking to the Blessed Varvara,
Oh, and he commanded his servants to gather gold,
Oh, and he commanded his servants to gather gold,
To send the Blessed Varvara a present.
The Blessed Varvara did not accept the present,
Because she did not want to sin in this world.
Oh, and the king ordered that glass be broken into fine
    slivers,
And that the Blessed Varvara be led over that glass.
The Blessed Varvara was not afraid,
She fell on her knees before the Lord.
God sent an Angel from the Heavens:
"Go, Varvara, walk on the glass because you must!"
"Lord, God! You send me torment,
Don't torture me, God, if I am without fault!"

Oh, and the king ordered oil to be heated,
And for Varvara to be placed in the oil.
The Blessed Varvara was not afraid,
She fell on her knees before the Lord.
God sent an Angel from the Heavens:
"Go, Varvara, enter the oil because you must!"
The Blessed Varvara stepped into the oil,
It had no effect on her body.
The king ordered a tomb to be dug,
And the Blessed Varvara to be buried in the tomb alive.
The Blessed Varvara was not afraid,
She fell on her knees before the Lord.
God sent an Angel from the Heavens:
"Go, Varvara, lie in the tomb because you must!"
"You give me, God, you give me death,
Do not let me die if I am innocent!"
The king went to a far-away war,
He did not return soon—after twenty-three years.
The king came back from the far-away wars,
And he peacefully lay down to sleep:
The Blessed Varvara came to him in a dream,
More beautiful in her tomb than she had been
        in this world,
"Servants, my servants, you did not serve me faithfully:
You fed the Blessed Varvara while she was in the tomb."
"Sir, our king! The Lord fed her:
He did not let Varvara die just yet."
"Go, then, you servants, dig up the tomb,
Take the bones of the Blessed Varvara and scatter them!"
Oh, the servants went and the dug up the tomb . . .
And all bowed before the Blessed Varvara.
Oh, you are not holy, you are a sorceress,
That no harm can have any effect upon you.
Oh, and the king ordered a scaffold to be erected,
And the Blessed Varvara to be sent to the executioner.
The Blessed Varvara was not afraid,
She fell on her knees before the Lord.
"Lord God, you let me die,
Do not let me die without a confession!"
The Blessed Varvara ascended the scaffold,

No harm befell her body.
The executioner did not have time to swing his sword,
When the executioner and the king were struck by bright
    lightning.
The lightning struck from under the bright sun. . . .
It struck down the executioner and the king, sitting next to
    the window.
You, oh king, go to suffer in Hell,
You, Blessed Varvara, come to rule in Heaven!
Grant us Christians, Lord, life in this world,
Let us praise the Blessed Varvara and the Holy Trinity!

Source: Recorded from Pr'okhor Hulka and published in Demuts'kyi, pp. 27–28.

The Passion of Christ (*Strastiam Khrystovym*)

Across the wide field,
Across the deep sea,
There walked the most pure one,
The most pure one, the Virgin Mary.
She meets three Angels,
Three Angels, three Archangels,
"You Angels, you Archangels,
Have you seen my Son?
Have you seen my Son,
My Son, your God?"
One answers, "I did not see Him,"
And the other says, "I did not behold Him."
And the third one says, "I was there myself,
As the Jews took Him, as they crucified Him on the cross,
As they nailed His hands with nails,
As they placed the wreath of thorns upon His head,
As they put a belt of brambles around His waist,
As they drove willow slivers beneath His fingernails,
As they pierced His ribs with a spear,
As they pierced His ribs with a spear,
As they spilled innocent blood."
St. Peter stands and St. Paul stands also,

And also his Virgin Mother.
"Oh, my Son, my Savior,
You are experiencing great torments,
You are suffering wounds, you are accepting pain,
All at the hands of the Jews,
You are suffering wounds, you are accepting pain,
All for the sake of Orthodox Christians."
"Don't stand there, Mother, don't grieve,
And do not look upon my wounds.
Take, Mother, take your keys,
Open, Mother, open Heaven and Hell,
Release the righteous souls,
The righteous souls and the sinful ones;
Only don't release those souls,
Who sang songs on Fridays,
Who did not wash on Saturdays,
Who ate early on Sundays,
Who made their mother and their father angry,
Who quarreled with their elder brothers,
Who made merry during Lent,
Who prepared their souls for Hell."[1]
Alleluia, alleluia,
We praise you, oh most pure one,
We praise you, oh most pure one,
Oh, most pure one, the Virgin Mary.

Source: Demuts´kyi, p. 1; performer not given.

Guardian Angel (*Anhelu Khranyteliu*)

An angel awakens a sinful soul from sleep:
"Get up, sinful soul, awake from your sleep,
And gaze upon the Angel of God!"
Oh, Angel of God, oh, my savior,
You, oh sinful soul, be not proud:
Soon God will call you to judgement!
And there God will question you:
"Where have you been hiding, oh sinful soul,
That you did not hurry to join God's kingdom,
That you did not attend morning and evening prayer,

That you did not hold prayer services for the dead,
That you did not buy incense for the churches,
That you did not give gifts to God's throne,
That you did not get wax for His candles!"
At that point the sinful soul roused itself.
When you stand at the pearly gates, oh soul,
They will bind your hands, oh soul, and your feet,
They will cast you down, oh soul, to rest in Hell,
To rest in Hell, to suffer fire and torment!
You will burn, oh sinful soul, from now and forever.
At that point the sinful soul roused itself.
It called out unto the Angel with its voice:
"Oh, Angel, oh Angel of God, my savior,
Do not let me be cast into fire and torment!"
Then the Angel answered solemnly:
"And where have you been hiding, oh sinful soul?
That you did not listen to the morning and the evening
        prayers,
That you did not pay for services or prayers for the dead,
That you did not give wax for the candles,
That you did not invite distant travelers into your home,
That you did not visit those who were ill or those in
        prison,
That you did not help support orphans and widows,
That you spent your time in great luxury,
That you enjoyed sweet drinks and liquors,
That you fell into Hell and eternal torment!"

Source: Recorded from an unnamed *lirnyk*, town of Vynohrad, Zvenihorods'kyi region; Demuts'kyi, p. 22. [The punctuation is that of the original.]

The Prodigal Son (*Syn bludiashchyi*)

Oh, he who comes into the world,
In this day and age,
Every such person must sin,
Oh, this miserable age.
And, as he sins, he thinks to himself:
"Oh, I am still young,
I will have time to repent before I die,

And I will not go to Hell!"
But on Sunday, in the morning,
Do not drink wine:
There is much sin in wine,—
It will make you lose your senses.
A group stopped by an inn,
To have a drink and a bite,
And having done so, they lost their senses,
They had to sin.
The prodigal son's father and mother come to him,
They try to teach him some sense, for they pity their child;
And he, he flees from them like an animal,
He despises their words;
And, drunk, he sits there naked,
And shakes his fist,
And evil faith follows him,
And evil faith seduces him,
And leads him
To sin, to fornication, to theft,
"When I stop sinning,
God will forgive me."
God gave the prodigal son,
God gave him early death:
The sinner lies in his coffin,
He is plagued by misfortune.
The sinner races through Hell and through fire,
He is confused;
He spies his father and his mother,
He begs them to save him:
"Rescue me, I am your babe, oh father, oh mother!
How long will you let me scream and cry in these
        flames?"
"Run, son, run through Hell and through fire:
This is what you deserve;
I tried to lead you to your senses,—
But you didn't like it.
Run, son, run through Hell and through fire,
Run night and day,
Because you did not heed your father, nor your mother,
Nor righteous people!
Son, your soul will perish in Hell,

Until Jesus Christ Himself comes
To save all souls."
Rescue God, rescue, oh Creator,
Save this soul from torment,
Hand not this body and soul into the Devil's grasp!

Source: Recorded from Veresai by Lysenko and published in "Kharakteristika muzykal'nykh osobennostei," pp. 390–92.

The Hermit and Paraskovia Friday (*Pustelnyk i piatnytsia*)

Oh, a hermit was toiling in the wilderness,
He did not have the use of one arm and he did not have
    the use of one leg.
Friday appeared as an apparition to him in a dream,
The most holy Paraskovia,
The one who held a cross in her right hand,
And in her left she held a triple candle.
She blessed him with the cross,
She illuminated him with the candle,
She perfumed him with dark incense,
She awakened him with God's words:
"Oh, arise, servant of God, rouse yourself!
Oh, arise, servant of God, and say a prayer!
Then go, servant of God, go throughout this world,
And speak, servant of God, say unto this world:
"Oh, you men who would be blessed, women who would
    be saved,
Do not work three days out of the week,
On Friday do not get your garments dirty,
And, on Saturday, do not work with a saw,
And do not card hemp,
And do not sweep up soot;
And on Sunday go to the church;
Fathers and mothers, do not curse your children,
Do not call them Jews, do not call them your enemies,
Because the Jews are cursed in the cross,
They crucified Jesus Christ,
They put a wreath of thorns on His head,
They hammered nails into His hands and feet.
They pierced His ribs with a spear,
They spilled His most blessed blood.

Jesus Christ suffered the wounds and the torments,
For the sake of all Orthodox Christians,
Jesus Christ suffered His torments and His passion,
May He preserve us from all misfortune!"
He who copies this verse,
He who sings this verse through,
Oh, him the kingdom of heaven awaits!
And we, we give voice to this verse:
Alleluia, alleluia,
We praise you, Christ our Lord!

Source: Recorded from Veresai by Lysenko and published in "Kharakteristika muzykal'nykh osobennostei," pp. 398–99.

Justice (*Pravda*)

There is no justice in this world, justice cannot be found!
These days justice has gone to live with injustice.
Now justice is held captive in the noblemen's prison,
And injustice visits in the noblemen's drawing room!
These days justice must wait at the doorstep,
And injustice dines with the noblemen at the head of the
    table!
Justice is trampled underfoot by the nobles,
And injustice sits among them and keeps them company.
Now justice is stepped upon and crushed,
And injustice is feted with wine and with liquor!
Now justice is in deep trouble with the nobles,
And injustice is granted free rein!
Well now justice,—justice is dying,
And injustice is devouring the whole world!
Well now justice,—justice is dead,
And injustice has smothered the whole world!
There is no justice in this world, justice cannot be found . . .
The only justice in this world—is your father and your
    own mother!
And where can justice be found? It cannot be bought and
    it cannot be earned,
You can travel the whole world and not find justice.

Once there were children; now they have become orphans;
They have nowhere to turn for help,
They cry and they cry; they cannot hang on,
They cannot forget their own dear mother:
"Oh, mother, oh falcon, where can we find you?
We cannot buy you and we cannot earn you;
You can travel the whole world and not find justice."
If only we had the wings of angels,
Then we would fly and we would gaze upon you;
Because the end of the age is approaching,
And you have to be wary of even your own brother!
Because even when you stand with him in court,—you
    will not find justice,
All you will find is the need to placate the nobles with
    gold and with silver.
Whichever man can still carry out justice,
Him God will reward daily with Heavenly grace.
Because God Himself—He is divine justice,
He will conquer injustice; He will vanquish pride,
He will raise up the blessed,
From now and forever!

Source: Recorded from Veresai by Lysenko, pp. 388–89.

Misery (The song sung by people who live in misfortune—*Pisnia, shcho po neshchastiu zhyvuchi na sviti spivaiut'*)

Oh, it is misery, misery to live in this world,
But save us, God, from death,—
For then God will judge us.
While a person is healthy, everyone loves him;
But when misfortune comes upon him, then even his kin
    forsakes him.
When all is going well, people call you friend and sworn
    brother,
And when the hour of need comes, then no one is there,
    not even your relatives.
An elderly mother was dying in sorrow:

"Children, my children, it was I who fed you! . .
As hard as it is to swallow a stone,
So it is hard to keep one's children fed!"
And the children's reaction to this—no, they pay no
   attention,
And they wound their father and their mother,
Even more cruelly with their words.
Whom God tries in this world, him He also rewards,
And for hurting one's father and mother, the son of God
   wreaks vengeance.
If we wish to live in the Heavenly Kingdom,
We must remember not to show disrespect to our father
   and mother;
If we wish to abide in the Kingdom of Heaven,
We need to remember not to embitter our father and our
   mother!
Oh, Jesus, Jesus of Nazareth,
Comfort and have mercy on the Christian people!
Oh Jesus, oh sacred Jesus,
Comfort and have mercy on all of the Orthodox lands!

Source: Recorded from Veresai by Lysenko, pp. 389–90.

The Orphan Girl (*Syritka*)

A strange time has come, by God's will,
And more than one orphan has been left by his mother.
The mountains rustle and the rivers murmur,
Oh, a mother has died and the children are left behind. . . .
Children, you are now orphans forever!
The father will find himself a new wife; they will live as a
   couple;
And the poor orphans will have to go and become
   servants.
The ones who are bigger will go and work;
The ones who are smaller will go and perish.
When the son of a father works, his work prospers;
When an orphan works, he is always considered lazy.
No matter how an orphan works, his work is for nothing:

The stepmother will always say that the orphan is a
    sluggard.
An orphan girl went wandering out into the world—
She went out to search for her own dear mother.
The Lord meets her and begins to question her:
"Where are you going, orphan?" "To find my mother."
"Go back, little orphan, you will wander far through the
    world,
And you will not find your mother, ever or never,
Because your mother is on top of a high mountain,
Because your mother rests in a coffin house."
The little orphan girl went to that coffin to cry,
And her mother answered her tears:
"Oh, who is that crying atop my coffin?"
"It is me, Mommy, take me in there with you!"
"Oh, as hard as it is to take the sun down from the
    heavens,
So it is even harder to take you in here with me.
Here, my little orphan, there is nothing to eat or to drink,
Because God has willed that I rot in the grave.
Why don't you go, little orphan, go ask your stepmother,
If she would not be merciful, if she would wash your
    hair."
But the evil stepmother did not wash her hair,
She broke the health of the unfortunate orphan. . . .
"Why don't you go, little orphan, go ask your stepmother,
If she would not be merciful, if she would sew you a
    shirt."
But the evil stepmother did not sew a shirt,
She dressed the unfortunate orphan for her funeral. . . .
God sends an Angel from the Heavens:
"Come, then, little orphan, come to the clear heavens;
As long as you obey God's will,
You will rule with the saints in heaven.
And as for you, evil stepmother, you have prepared
    yourself for Hell,
You had orphaned children and you did not take care of
    them.
Open up, Hell, and in it will burn
The one who would not take care of orphaned children."

Source: Recorded from the *lirnyk* Rydka, village of Bohatyrets, Tarashchinskyi region, and published in Demuts'kyi, pp. 54–56.

Misfortune (*Bida*)

"Misfortune" was something like a cross between a religious song and a satirical song. Like a religious song, it complained about the pervasiveness of misfortune. Like a satirical song, it contained word play and slap-stick elements. Because of its satiric qualities, "Misfortune" could not be performed at religious festivals and might provoke censure in other public places. In this song, Misfortune is both a condition that befalls mankind and a personified being which walks the earth.

> Oh, in a deep ravine,
> There stood a high thorn bush,
> And from that thorn bush
> Emerged young Misfortune.
>
> Oh, whoever does not know Misfortune,
> Let him ask me:
> Because my house is at the edge of the village,
> Because I know every Misfortune,
> Because spent the night in the home of Misfortune,
> Because I got to know Misfortune in all her forms,
> Because I supped at the home of Misfortune,
> And so I know Misfortune well.
>
> Misfortune has been gone for a whole seven years,
> Misfortune's fame has spread worldwide;
> From Kharkiv to Krakow,
> Misfortune is the same everywhere;
> From Kremenets to Kremenets,
> There is no end to accursed Misfortune anywhere;
> From Ruzhyn to Ruzhyn,
> She has smothered seven fields of wheat.
>
> Little Misfortune, small Misfortune,
> She was pestering a poor man. . . .
> "Where were you born, oh, Misfortune,
> That you latched onto me?"

"I was born in Odessa,
I was baptized in Kiev,
I grew up in Vasylkiv,
In Khmilnyk I got married,
In Khmilnyk I got married,
And I found you here."

Here, Misfortune, sit on this goat,
I will even show you the way,
I will even show you the way,
I will take you to the devil.
Misfortune visited Bohak,
There they hung her up on a hook;
As soon as she escaped from the hook,
She ran from Bohak as fast as she could.

Along came Veremii,
He whipped Misfortune with a belt;
Along came Opanas,
He pummeled Misfortune on the forehead.
Along came Denys,
He hit Misfortune on the shoulders;
Along came Martyn,
He grabbed Misfortune and threw her against a
    fence!
Down under our spring rye,
Lies Misfortune, silently furious;
Then she sold herself in Braslavets,
And she dressed herself up in fox fur.

But there the people are quite savvy,
They fancy foxes a great deal;
And they chased the fox and grabbed her,
And they beat her to a pulp.

Misfortune walks around beyond the Dniester,
There she walks around with oxen and an oar;
Along comes Misfortune with a cart,
In it are pudding and sour mash;
Women step up and surround Misfortune,
They buy her pudding, they buy her mash,

They buy her pudding, they buy her mash,
They punch poor Misfortune in the ribs.

And in Kiev, in Trostiantsi,
She gave the mendicants each an egg,
But she gave me two,
Because I sing to Misfortune.

On a green hill,
Misfortune herded sheep for seven years;
Misfortune went to pick up her pay
And she started with the outermost house.
Misfortune went to Hryhor's house,
From Hryhor's house she came out naked.
Misfortune went to Dymian's house,
From Dymian's house she came out drunk.
Misfortune went to Denys' house,
From Denys' house she came out bald.
Misfortune went to Andrykha's house,
There they boxed Misfortune's ears.
Misfortune went to Peter's house,
There she burned her feet,
Misfortune went to Khvedir's house,
From Khvedir's house she came out sick.
Misfortune went to the priest's house,
They beat Misfortune like a sheaf of wheat.
Misfortune went to the deacon's house,
And there too they gave her a beating.
Misfortune went to the school,
They beat Misfortune to their hearts' content:
They struck Misfortune across the shoulder,
"Don't try to get up on the stove, Misfortune!"
They hit Misfortune in the breasts,
"Don't try to get up on the furnace, Misfortune!"
They struck Misfortune across the shoulder blades,
"Don't try to get up on the bench, Misfortune!"
Misfortune went to the miller's house,
There they gave her a dumpling;
Misfortune went to Luka's house,
There they gave her some flour;
Misfortune went to Busyn's house,
There they gave her some cheese in a vat;

Misfortune went to Havril's house,
There she cooked up some of her own food.

Misfortune went to the tailor's house,
There they gave her some fiber;
Misfortune sat down on a chair,
And she wrinkled up the floor mat,
Misfortune put her hands on her hips,
They dragged Misfortune across the floor;
Misfortune walks along, moaning,
They gave Misfortune a pair of bast shoes:
Misfortune is herself surprised,
That she will soon be shod so well!
Misfortune walks any old which way,
And she's lost her walking shoes.

The gypsies were changing horses,
And they recognized their Misfortune,
They beat Misfortune with staffs:
"Don't you dare follow us, Misfortune!"
They beat Misfortune with green twigs:
"Don't stand there, you wasp, you troublemaker!"

Misfortune sits under a bridge,
People carting brush are driving over;
Misfortune decides to play a game,
And breaks all the people's wheels.

The mendicants were standing around in a group,
They found Misfortune under a wagon;
They beat Misfortune with their staffs,
"Don't trail after mendicants, Misfortune!"

And there Misfortune died,
And there Misfortune perished,—
Her horns rolled down the hill,
She stuck her hooves up in the air.

Along came Iakov,
And he lamented Misfortune;
Along came Herasim,

And he also wailed for her;
Along came Iaryna,
And she said the "Lord's Prayer" over Misfortune;
Mother Kateryna came along,
And she brought a shirt.

The Devil brings along Marta,
And Marta brings a quart of vodka. . . .
And there Misfortune died,
And there Misfortune perished,—
Her horns rolled down the hill,
She stuck her hooves up in the air.

But she had a daughter,
That daughter went around the world;
That daughter went around the world,
And came back to us. . . .
The Devil will be and will exist,
One will die,
And ten will take its place.

Source: Recorded from the *lirnyk* Rydka and published in Demuts´kyi, pp. 56–58.

Epics (Dumy)

Epic songs were considered serious and suitable for public performance. A minstrel could sing them, along with religious songs, in a home, at a fair, or even at a religious festival. Some of the clergy, and those who defined a minstrel's repertory more narrowly, might insist that they not be performed on certain holidays or in the vicinity of a church or monastery. (See, for example, the discussion of where and when "Konovchenko" could be sung in Borzhkovskii's description of a religious festival, above.) But most people considered epics solemn, uplifting fare, and were eager to listen to and willing to pay for them under all circumstances.

No epics from the Khmelnytskyi cycle are included among the translated samples below because they died out somewhere around 1875 and were not normally sung by the minstrels described in this book.

A number of the texts have switches in tense, from present to past and back again. This is a stylistic feature of the *dumy* and not an error.

Duma about the Storm on the Black Sea
(*Buria na Chornomu Mori*)

Oh, on the Black Sea,
On a white stone,
Oh, there sits a bright, white-eyed falcon:
He has bent his head down low,
And sorrowfully he cries and he intones,
And he looks up with concern
At the blessed heavens,
At the dark sea.
Because in the blessed heavens,
Upon the Black Sea, all is not well.
Upon the blessed heavens all the stars have been obscured,
And half the moon has faded into darkness;
On the dark sea, all is not well;
From the bottom of the sea a powerful wave arises,
It breaks the ships of the Cossacks, the brave youths, into
    three parts.

It separated the first group of ships,
And carried them up the quiet Danube River;
It separated the second group of ships,
And carried them to the Arabian lands,
Into Turkish captivity;[1]
It separated the third group of ships,
And started to drown them in the dark sea.
There in that third part were two true brothers,
Pale as two turtledoves,
And they were drowning,
And they saw no hope of escape anywhere.
They swam one toward the other,
And they spoke with words,
And they cried bitterly,—
They asked for forgiveness,
They confessed their sins before All-merciful God.
Between them was a third man, a stranger and a loner,
A man without a job, without kin and without help,
A man who could not hope for salvation from anywhere.
Well, he swims toward them,
And he speaks with words,
And he cries bitter tears,[2]
And he begs for forgiveness;
Before God the All-merciful
He confesses his sins.
Well, the two brothers speak with words,
And they cry many bitter tears:
"This, brothers, is not a strong sea wave that is
      drowning us;
This is our father's prayer, and our mother's
Which is punishing us
Because, as we were preparing to join the volunteer forces,
We did not ask our father and our mother for forgiveness,
And our old mother, we pushed her away from us, pushed
      her away with our stirrups;
Because we had overbearing pride:
We did not recognize our older brother as our sibling,
We showed great disrespect to our middle sister,
We deprived our close neighbor of his bread and his salt;
Because we had overbearing pride:
When we rode past God's church,

We did not remove our hats from our heads,
We did not place the sign of the cross upon our faces,
We did not turn to the All-merciful Creator for help,
And we made our horses prance along the streets;
And we took no heed of people that we met,
Small children, we trampled them with our horses,
We spilled Christian blood upon the damp earth!
Oh, brothers, if only our father's and our mother's prayer
    could free us from here,
Then, surely, we would know well,
How to honor our father's prayer and our mother's,
How to respect our older brother as if he were our father,
How to honor and respect our middle sister,
How to behave towards our neighbor as if he were our
    own brother!"
As they began to utter these words,
As they began to remember their father's and their
    mother's prayers,
Then God, the All-merciful, began to help them,
The Black Sea began to calm down;
And it became so calm
That it seemed there had never been a storm.
And the two brothers began to swim to the shore,
They started to grasp the white stone with their hands,
And they began to emerge from the sea,
Onto the happy land,
Amidst the Christian people,
Into the Christian cities,
And they came as guests to their father and to their
    mother.
And the father and the mother came out to greet their sons,
And they asked their sons and questioned them:
"Oh, sons, oh you brave youths!
Did things go well for you on your journey?"
"Oh father and mother, it was good to venture onto the
    Black Sea,
But it was not good, father and mother,
For a stranger and a loner who drowned in the dark sea:
He had no one from whom he could receive forgiveness,
And he had no one to rescue him in a foreign land!"
Oh, God, hear our prayers and our supplications,

The prayers of the tsar's subjects,
The prayers of the Christian people,
All the heads that bow obediently,
Now and forever,
And till the end of time.

Source: Recorded from Veresai by Lysenko, pp. 369–72.

The Escape of Three Brothers from Azov
(*Utecha Trokh Brativ z Azova*)

Oh it was not clouds of dust forming
And it was not the fog arising,—
As from the city of Azov, from terrible captivity,
Three brothers were escaping:
Two were on horseback, and the third was an infantry
    man, on foot:
He was like a stranger and an outcast,
He had to run and he had to race. . . .
It was as if his white feet were starting a fire,
And his blood was washing away his footprints!
And he caught up to his brothers,
He ran between their horses,
He said with words,
He cried with bitter tears,
He grabbed them by the stirrups:
"My elder brothers, my dear owns,
Pale as turtledoves!
Won't you stop and graze your horses just a while,
And wait for me, your younger brother;
Or else turn back,
Take me upon your horses,
Give me a ride for just a small part of the way,
Help me know how to flee, how to find the way,
To the Christian cities,
To our father, to our mother, to visit them?"
"Oh, younger brother, our dear one,
Pale as the turtledove,
Then we won't be able to escape, ourselves,
And we won't be able to rescue you, either;

For from the city of Azov
A great and fearsome search party will pursue us;
This way you can hide amidst the thorns and in the gullies,
And the search party will chase us,
They will shoot at us and they will strike at us,
Or they will try to take us alive and take us prisoner."
"Oh, my elder brothers, my dear ones,
Pale as turtledoves!
You have with you shining swords . . .
Strike my head from my shoulders,
And take my Cossack body, my brave body,
Bury it in the open field,
Let it not serve as fodder for the birds and the beasts!"
Then the brothers spoke with words,
Their eyes flowed with bitter tears:
"Oh, our younger brother, our dear one,
Pale as the turtledove!
Even though we do have bright, shining swords,
Our Cossack hearts, our brave hearts would never dare,
And our Cossacks hands, our brave hands would never
    rise up,
And our bright swords would never strike off your head:
They would crumble to dust!"
"Oh my elder brothers, my dear ones,
Pale as turtledoves!
As you ride along the paths,
Cut branches from the thorns with your swords,
Mark the green gullies,
Leave branches along the path, that I, the youngest
    brother, the foot soldier,
Might have a Cossack token,
That I might know how to flee,
To the Christian cities,
To arrive as a guest at the home of our father and mother."
Well, the brothers rode along the path,
And they chopped branches from the thorns with their
    swords,
And they marked the green gullies,
And they left markers along the path,
To serve as Cossack tokens.
As they rode out onto the steppe, the Murav Steppe,

There were no more thorns or green branches to be found.
Oh, then the middle brother spoke with words:
"Oh, my elder brother, my dear one,
Pale as the turtledove!
Oh, let us stop and graze our horses for a while,
Let us wait awhile for our younger brother;
Either that, or let us turn back,
Let us take him on our horses,
Let us give him a ride for just a little way,
That he may better know,
The way to the Christian cities,
To our father's and our mother's house."
Then the older brother spoke with words,
His eyes were flooded with bitter tears:
"Oh, my younger brother, my dear one,
Pale as the turtledove!
Hasn't Turkish captivity made enough of an impression on you,
Hasn't the rawhide eaten deeply enough into your wrists,
That you would consider going back,
That you would linger even a day,
That you would risk drawing attention to our horses?!
He will be fine and he will be well,
He will make it to the Christian cities,
To our father's house and our mother's, even on foot!"
Well, that middle brother reacts with great care,
From under his coat he pulls red silk,
He rips it and scatters the scraps,
He leaves them to mark the path
For the youngest brother, the infantryman on foot.
Oh, then the youngest brother, the infantryman on foot
He runs and he catches up. . . .
He runs so fast, it's as if his white feet were starting a fire,
And his blood was washing away his footprints! . .
He arrives at the Murav Steppe,—
He sees no thorn branches marking the path for him,
All he sees is the red silk;
So he comes up to the red silk,
He takes it in his hands, he presses it to his heart,
He speaks with bitter words:
"Oh, so this means that the Azov horde achieved a great
      triumph,

First it passed me by,
Then it caught up with my brothers,
It shot them and it slashed them,
And maybe it captured them alive! . . .
Oh, Lord, my God!
If only I could know,
Whether my brothers were shot,
Whether they were slashed,
Whether they were captured alive;
Oh, then I would go and wander through the thorns and
    through the gullies,
I would search for their Cossack bodies, their brave
    bodies,
I would take their Cossack bodies, their brave bodies,
And bury them in the open field,
I would not let them become fodder for the beasts and the
    birds."
Oh, the youngest brother approaches the Savur burial
    mound,
His first problem is lack of water,
And his second is hunger,
And his third problem is no road to follow;
Oh, he approaches the Savur burial mound,
And he lowers his head upon the Savur burial mound,
He cries bitter tears.
Oh, and upon him came the pale-winged eagles,
They approached his black curls,
And started to remove his eyes from under his forehead.
Oh, then the infantryman, the man on foot,
Lonely as the stranger,
He spoke with words,
He shed copious and bitter tears:
"Oh, you my guests, my unwelcome, unbeloved guests,
Oh, stop a minute, wait a while,
Wait till the Cossack soul, the brave soul,
Departs from the white body.
Then you can pick the flesh from the yellow bones,
Then you can remove the eyes from under the forehead."
It was not a black cloud that approached,
It was the Cossack soul, the brave soul
Which was departing from the white body.

And the pale-winged eagles attacked,
They picked the flesh from the yellow bones,
They removed the eyes from under the forehead.
Then also the pale-maned wolves,
They came running from the steppe,
They ripped the bones from their joints,
They scattered them through the thorns and the gullies.
Oh and also the stormy winds blew,
They covered the yellow bones with reeds.
Oh and the Cossack was not mourned by his father
    or his mother,
It was a pale cuckoo who came flying over,
And who sat at his head,
And who cooed mournfully:
"Oh head, oh Cossack head, oh brave head!
You did not drink your fill and you did not finish eating,
And you did not celebrate well;
And here you are being forced to just lie here,
To become fodder for the beasts and for the birds!"
And as the two brothers,
They started to enter the Christian cities,
They started to approach the churches,
And to curse and berate the Turkish land:
"Oh, land, oh Turkish land,
Oh, Moslem faith,
Oh, Christian separation!
You separated brother from sister,
And husband from wife,
And friend from friend!
And you give the poor captive no rest, no rest ever!
Oh land, oh land,
You are truly cursed!
Only the Turk, the stone-hearted Turk
Is rich with gold and silver!"
Hear, oh Lord, the requests and the prayers,
Of the tsar's people, the Christian folk,
Of all those who are listening,
For many years into the future,
Until the end of time!

Source: Recorded from Veresai by Lysenko, pp. 372–77.

Kanivchenko (also called Konovchenko)

Oh, near the city of Cherkassy
There lived a widow named Hrytsykha,
And her married name was Kanivchykha.
She had a son Ivas Hrytsenko,
And his last name was Kanivchenko.
Well, she raised him to maturity,
She never let him go work as a hired hand,
She did not let strangers abuse him,
She wanted to have fame and glory through him,
She wanted to live with him in her old age.
Before long Ivan Kanivchenko grew to be a young man,
He started going to the market,
He started playing with a black mace and a cudgel,[3]
He started calling to the wine-makers and the beer
    brewers,
"Oh, young Cossacks, brave gentlemen,
Who among you wants to stop brewing vodka in the
    wineries?
Who among you wants to stop making beer in the
    breweries?
Who among you wants to stop delivering wood to the
    tavern maid,
To trade for a glass of vodka?
Let him follow me to join Khvylon Korsunskyi,
Let us join his forces,
Let us win the glorious kingdom for ourselves.
Oh, Widow Hrytsykha, oh, my aged mother!
If you would like to do me a great service,
Then you would buy me a raven horse,
This would please my brave, young Cossack soul
    mightily."
"Oh, my son, Ivas Kanivchenko,
We have four strong oxen,
And two raven horses;
If you would take them to the field and plow,
Then all of the farmers and all of the Cossacks would
    honor you."
"Oh, Widow Hrytsykha, oh, my aged mother!
I don't feel like sowing seeds in the furrows,

I don't want to fill my clothing with dust,
And I don't want to use my brave Cossack voice
To call to the oxen,
And even more I don't want the farmers and the Cossacks
To call me a buckwheat sower."
On Holy Sunday, early in the morning,
The Widow Hrytsykha went to God's morning service,
And she locked all the doors with three locks each.
Well, Ivas Kanivchenko awoke from his sleep,
And he walks around the household,
And he is mightily distressed,
That he has no raven horse,
That he has no Cossack armaments.
He walks into the room,
He knocks off all of the locks,
He takes his father's sword down from its peg,
He straps it to his waist,
He sets off on foot and hurries to join the battle.
And the neighbors saw what was going on,
They let the Widow, they let Hrytsykha know:
"Oh, Widow Hrytsykha, here you are in church,
        praying to God,
And you have no idea what has befallen you,
You do not know that when you get home,
You will not find the brave knight Ivas Kanivchenko."
Well, the Widow Hrytsykha listened to God's morning
        service till the end,
Then, like a pale dove, she flew back to her home,
She arrives at her household,
She falls to the ground,
She sheds copious tears,
She blames and she curses her Ivas Kanivchenko.
"Oh, Ivas Kanivchenko, in your first engagement,
May the first bullet not miss you,
For you did not want to feed me,
To give me bread and salt in my old age,
And you went off to battle to satisfy your own desires."
And as she cursed him,
Then she thought and then she pondered.
She bought a raven horse,
The kind that would please his brave Cossack soul.

And she hired a Cossack,
And she paid him twenty rubles and bought him a weskit.
And that Cossack behaved well,
He caught up with the regiment,
He summoned Ivas Kanivchenko from the encampment.
Well, Ivas Kanivchenko emerged from the encampment,
He crosses himself,
Then he tightens the Cossack saddle straps,
He mounts his horse and says,
"Praise be to you, Lord God,
Praise to my mother's, my father's prayers.
I had thought that my elderly mother was scolding and
    cursing me,
And here she has done me, willful man that I am, a great
    service."
Then he mounts his horse,
He crosses himself,
He rides up to Sir Khvylon Korsunskyi,
He rides beneath his banners.
"Sir Khvylon Korsunskyi, my colonel,
Let me go into battle and play a while,
Let me win the glorious kingdom for myself."
"Ivas Kanivchenko, my son,
You are still a young child.
If you go to play in battle,
The Turks will defeat you."
"Sir Khvylon Korsunskyi, my colonel,
What if you take two ducks, an old duck and a young one,
Take them and let them swim in the water,
Will not the young duck swim as well as the old?"
"I will bless you, Ivas Kanivchenko,
I will bless you to go into battle."
Then he mounts his horse,
He tightens the saddle straps,
And when he went into battle, he did not win much,
He attacked and he slew three hundred souls,
And another seven hundred he took captive,
He delivered them under Colonel Korsunskyi's banner.
Colonel Korsunskyi is full of joy,
He calls Ivas Kanivchenko a glorious knight.
"Sir Khvylon Korsunskyi, my colonel,

Allow me to take mead, and wine, and pure vodka,
Let me take as much as I want and drink my fill.
And then let me ride drunk into battle."
"My son, Ivas Kanivchenko,
Under my command, mead, and wine, and pure vodka are
    not forbidden,
Take as much as you want and drink and enjoy,
But I will not allow you to ride drunk into battle,
Because vodka is treacherous,
May it not remove you from this world."
Well, Ivas Kanivchenko does not pay heed,
He takes as much as he wants, he drinks and enjoys,
And on Sunday, early in the morning,
He pokes elderly Cossacks with his staff,
And then he rides to battle and he does not conquer much,
He attacked and he slew three hundred souls,
And he took seven hundred captive,
And he started to lead them to Khvylon Korsunskyi,
To lead them under his banner.
From out of nowhere a Turk appeared,
He approaches from the side,
He aims his sword at Ivas Kanivchenko.
Well, he did not inflict a great wound,
He almost cut Ivas Kanivchenko in half.
Well, the horse knew what to do,
He broke his silken tethers,
He escaped and ran back to his own Christian
    encampment.
And Sir Khvylon saw him,
And he collapsed on the spot.
"Oh, my son, Ivas Kanivchenko,
It is not that I forbade you to drink mead, and wine, and
    pure vodka,
To drink as much as you wished,
It is that I ordered you to lie down in rest under my
    supervision,
And now tell me where you want your brave Cossack
    body buried.
Do you want it sent back to the city of Cherkassy,
Or do you want it buried somewhere here?"
"Sir Khvylon Korsunskyi, my colonel,

I do not want my brave Cossack body
To be sent back to the city of Cherkassy,
I do not want great sorrow inflicted on my mother, the
    Widow Hrytsykha,
I order that my body be buried here somewhere."
Well, he ordered the first regiment to dig a grave,
And he ordered the second regiment to make a coffin,
And as for the third regiment,
He ordered them to use their hats and their coat hems to
    erect a high burial mound.
They buried Ivas Kanivchenko,
They read the twelve gospels over his body,
That his fame may be known throughout Ukraine.
On the night before Easter Sunday,
The Widow Hrytsykha had a dream.
And around noon she came out of her house,
She recounted it to the old women.
"Old women, tell me the meaning of my dream.
I dreamt that my Ivas Kanivchenko married a Turkish
    woman,
A woman proud and haughty,
She walks by your home and she won't even glance in
    your direction,
She wears fine clothing and sweeps up her footprints with
    her train,
It's as if a knife was piercing my heart."
Well, the neighbors understood this dream well enough,
But they did not tell the Widow Hrytsykha the truth,
"Don't cry, oh widow, and do not pine,
God will let him return from battle,
Will let him care for you in your old age."
Just then, from the hills, three regiments descended,
The first regiment approaches,
It sounds like the humming of bees;
The second regiment approaches,
It seems to bloom like a field of poppies,
The third regiment approaches,
It leads Ivas Kanivchenko's horse by the reins.
And the Widow Hrytsykha saw this,
And she collapsed on the spot,
She fell upon the earth,

She spoke with words,
She shed copious tears,
She blamed and she cursed Sir Khvylon:
"May it befall you, Colonel Khvylon Korsunskyi,
That you have no kingdom and no rule[4]
Because you sent my Ivas Kanivchenko into the other
    world."
From out of nowhere a Cossack came running.
He had a black box in his hands,
He tries to cheer up the woman Hrytsykha,
"Don't cry, oh Widow, and don't be sorrowful.
The Lord did not punish him for going off to war,
But the Lord punished him because he arose early Sunday
    morning,
Because he drank mead, and wine, and pure vodka,
Because he poked old men, old Cossacks with his staff."
Well, she invited all three regiments into her home,
She celebrated Ivas' wedding and his funeral together,
That his fame may be known throughout Ukraine!
Grant us, oh Lord, grant the nation of the tsar,
Grant the Christian people,
And grant unto you, all you Orthodox Christians,
Grant health and long life.

Source: Recorded from Fedir Hrytsenko-Kholodnyi by Martynovych; IMFE fond 11–4/592, ark. 58–60.

Marusia Bohuslavka

On the Black Sea,
Upon a white rock,
There stood a stone prison,
And in that prison seven hundred Cossacks were
    languishing,
Seven hundred Cossacks, poor captives.
They had been in captivity for thirty years,
Their eyes had not beheld God's light or the righteous sun.
To them comes the captive girl,
Marusia, the priest's daughter, Bohuslavka,

And she speaks to them with these words,
"Oh, Cossacks,
Oh, you poor captives,
Guess what day it is in our Christian land today."
The poor prisoners heard this,
They recognized the captive girl,
Marusia, the priest's daughter, Bohuslavka,
By her voice,
And they spoke with words,
"Hey, captive girl,
Marusia, the priest's daughter, Bohuslavka,
How can we possibly know
What day it is in our Christian land today?
For we have been in prison for thirty years,
Our eyes have not beheld either God's light or the
 righteous sun.
And we cannot know
What day it is in our Christian land today."
Then the captive girl,
Marusia, the priest's daughter, Bohuslavka,
She heard this,
And she spoke to the Cossacks with these words,
"Oh, Cossacks,
Oh, you poor captives,
Today, in our Christian land, is Holy Saturday
And tomorrow is the blessed holiday, that fateful
 day—Easter."
Then the Cossacks heard this,
They fell with their white faces upon the damp earth,
They chided and they cursed
The captive girl,
Marusia, the priest's daughter, Bohuslavka,
"Oh, captive girl,
Marusia, the priest's daughter, Bohuslavka,
May you have neither luck nor good fortune,
For you have reminded us of the great holiday, that fateful
 day—Easter!"
Then the captive girl,
Marusia, the priest's daughter, Bohuslavka,
Then she heard this,

And she spoke with words,
"Oh, Cossacks,
Oh, you poor prisoners,
Don't blame me and don't curse me,
When our Turkish lord departs for the mosque,
Then he will hand his keys to me,
To the captive girl,
To Marusia, the priest's daughter, Bohuslavka,
Then I will come to the prison,
And I will unlock the prison,
I will let you, all you poor prisoners, out into freedom.
Then on the great holiday, that fateful day—Easter,
The Turkish lord departed for the mosque,
And he turned the keys over to the captive girl,
Marusia, the priest's daughter, Bohuslavka,
He gave the keys into her hands.
Then the captive girl,
Marusia, the priest's daughter, Bohuslavka,
She behaved well —
She came to the prison,
She unlocked the prison,
She let out all of the Cossacks,
All of the poor prisoners,
She gave them freedom,
And then she spoke with these words,
"Oh, you Cossacks,
You poor prisoners,
Listen carefully and pay heed,
Flee to the Christian cities,
Only I beg of you, do not pass the city of Bohuslav by,
Please let my father and my mother know,
Let them behave well,
Let them not send money and a big ransom,
Let them not try to amass a great fortune,
Let them not try to buy me,
Me, the captive girl,
Marusia, the priest's daughter, Bohuslavka,
Let them not ransom me out of captivity.
Because I have become Turkicized and Islamized,
For the sake of Turkish luxury,
For the sake of accursed temptations!"

Oh, free us, God, free us poor prisoners,
From hard labor,
From the Islamic faith,
And deliver us to the bright horizon,
To the calm waters,
To the Christian land!
Hear, God, hear our earnest requests,
Hear our miserable prayers,
The prayers of us poor prisoners!

Source: Recorded from Ryhorenko (first name not known) and published in Hrushevs´ka, vol. I, p. 21; first published in Panteleimon Kulish, *Zapiski o iuzhnoi Rusi*, vol. I, p. 210.

About the Widow and Her Three Sons
(*Udova*, also called *Pro Udovu i Trokh Syniv*)

Oh, on Sunday, early in the morning,
Very early, at the time of twilight,
It was not the pine forest rustling,
And it was not the green glade talking with the wind,
It was a poor widow, an old woman,
Pale as the turtledove,
Speaking to her children, the widow's sons.
She had three sons,
Bright as young falcons,
And she raised them from a young age to maturity,
And she did not send them to work as hired hands,
She did not let strangers abuse them,
She was hoping to achieve fame and glory through them,
She was hoping to live with them throughout her
    declining years.
Quickly her sons grew and they matured,
They began to take young wives,
They began to disdain the old widow,
They began to chase her from her own household.
"Go, old widow, go from us,
Go live in another household,
For we will have our friends and our comrades as guests,
They will come wearing fine coats and fine jackets,
They will invite us to their own houses, to fine banquets
    in return,

And you, old mother, you will be left standing at the
     doorstep.
And you, old mother, you will be left standing at the
     doorstep."
The widow heard this,
She spoke to her sons with these words,
She fell to the ground,
She shed copious tears,
She stood on her knees before God.
"Oh, my sons, my young children,
How I worried and worried over you,
And look what I have gotten from you in return!
Where am I supposed to go now to await death?
Where am I supposed to rest my head now?
Where am I supposed to rest my head now?"
A close neighbor hears all this,
And he speaks to the widow with these words,
"Oh, don't cry, you widow, don't cry old woman,
Come, come and live in my household.
You can guide my life
And I will respect and honor you, old widow."
Well, the old widow lived in a strange household,
From dusk to dawn, she knew not a care,
Yet, every day she shed copious tears,
Yet, every day she shed copious tears.
Friends and comrades came as guests to the home of the
     sons,
And as they left, they chided the sons,
"How is it that we have eaten and drunk at your house this
     many times,
And we have never set eyes on your aged mother?
Have you given her away?
Have you sold her?"
The oldest brother hears this,
And he speaks to the younger brothers with words,
And he also cries bitter tears,
And he also cries bitter tears.
"My dear younger brothers,
Bright as young falcons,
Let us go to the other household, let us fall down,
Let us ask our aged widow,

We will call upon her to come back to her old house.
Because people have begun to judge us,
And God has begun to punish us.
He has begun to reduce the grain in our fields and in our home,
He has begun to reduce the grain in our fields and in our home."
Then on Easter Sunday, early in the morning,
All three of the widow's sons entered the other household,
They fell down before her,
Tearfully they begged and implored:
"Come, come, old widow,
Come back to live in your own household,
It is better that you restrain our wives,
That you instruct our young children,
That you instruct our young children,
And that you guide us,
And we will honor and respect you till the end of your days."
Well, the widow heard this,
And she spoke to her sons with words,
And she stood on her knees before God,
And she also shed copious tears,
"Oh, holy God, oh God most mighty,
What has come to pass in this world,
That a father or a mother no sooner marries her children,
Than those children start denying her sustenance,
Than those children start denying her sustenance.
Whatever person
Honors, respects, and venerates his father's and his
    mother's prayer,
That person will be saved from sin by the prayer of the
    mother and the father,
The prayer will guide him into the heavenly kingdom,
That prayer will help him in business, and in the field, and
    on the sea,
It can rescue him from the bottom of the ocean!"
Grant, oh God, to the land of the tsar,
To the Christian people,
And to all you Orthodox Christians,
Grant health and long life.

Source: Recorded from Hrytsenko-Kholodnyi by Martynovych IMFE fond 11–4/592, ark. 6–7.

The Stepfather (*Otchym, Vidchym*)

Oh on Sunday, very early in the morning,
It was not all of the church bells ringing,—
It was the mother and the father talking in a
    house at the edge of the village,
The father and the mother were talking,
They were sending their son off to foreign
    lands:
"Go, son, go among the people:
Things will be better for you there!"
"Oh, mother, somehow I have no desire
To go and live in a strange land:
When people meet me,
They will call me a stranger!"
Well, the oldest sister leads his horse
    by the reins,
And the middle sister brings his armor,
And the youngest sees her brother off,
She speaks with words:
"Oh, my dear brother,
Pale as the turtledove!
From which direction will you return?
In which direction should I look?
Will you return from the fierce battlefield, or
    from the open field,
Or will you return from the Cossacks in the
    Zaporozhe?"
"Oh, sister, do not look for me,
Do not expect me from the fierce battlefield, or
    from the open field,
Or from among the Cossacks in the Zaporozhe;
Take, sister, take yellow sand,
And sow it upon a white rock;
And arise early in the morning,
And water the sand often,
In the morning and in the evening twilight!
Water it with your many fine tears!
Then, sister, when the rivers freeze on
    St. Peter's day,

And when, on Christmas, the rowan tree in the meadow is
    covered in white blossoms,
And when it bears fruit on the Day of St. Basil,
When the yellow sand upon the white rock begins to
    sprout,
When it becomes covered in blue blossoms,
When it covers the stone with green periwinkle,
Then, sister, then I will come to visit you!"
"Oh, my dear brother,
Pale as the turtledove!
Oh, as long as I have been in this world,
I have never heard old people say:
That the rivers could possibly freeze on St. Peter's day,
That the rowan tree in the field could bloom on Christmas,
That it could bear fruit on St. Basil's day,
Or that yellow sand could sprout upon a white stone,
That it could bloom with blue blossoms,
That it could cover a stone with green periwinkle,—
Or that a brother should only then visit his sister."
"Well, sister, if it is so
That you cannot figure this out,
Then I will tell you that rivers never freeze on St. Peter's day,
Just as the rowan cannot bloom at Christmas,
And cannot bear fruit on St. Basil's day,
And yellow sand cannot sprout upon a rock,
It cannot cover the rock with periwinkle.
And so for me, sister, being a guest in your house
Is out of the question."
"Oh, brother, it is good to know,
And it is good to keep this knowledge,
That when you are in a strange land and you wear
    expensive garments,
Then people will recognize you and treat you well,
They will call you bosom friend and sworn brother,
But when, brother, things start to go wrong in a foreign
    land,
When the evil time comes,
When the hour of misfortune arrives,
All those who have called themselves your family will
    forsake you,
All the bosom buddies and the sworn brothers,

And all of the true companions."
Oh, as hard as it is for a fish on dry land,
For a beast or a bird without the field, without the forest,
So it is hard for a person to live in a foreign land,
Without his kin, without his beloved family.
Oh, as hard as it is to remove a stone,
From out of the damp earth,
So it is hard, so it is difficult to die,
In a strange land, without one's kin, without one's
    beloved family!
Hear, oh Lord, hear the requests and the prayers
Of the tsar's people, of the Christian folk,
And of all those who are listening,
For many years into the future,
And until the end of time!

Source: Recorded by Lysenko from Veresai, pp. 380–82.

Historical Songs

Closely related to epic in content, historical songs differed from them in form and tended to have couplet rhyme. Minstrels and their audiences were minimally aware of these structural differences, and historical songs, like epics, were items suitable for most performance occasions.

The Dying Cossack and His Horse
(*Pomyraiuchyi Kozak i Kin*)

Three years and three weeks,
Elapsed in Ukraine,
Since the Tatars mortally wounded a Cossack,
And placed him beneath a sycamore tree.
Under the green sycamore tree,
Lies a young Cossack;
His body has turned black.
It has become covered with scabs from the wind.
His horse, standing over him, pines in sorrow,
He has stamped his feet (so hard) that he has sunk into the
      earth up to the knee.
"Don't stand over me, my horse,
I see your true devotion!
Run through the steppe and through the groves,
Through the valleys and through the ravines,
To my dear family,
To my faithful wife!
Strike the gateway with your hooves,
Jingle your harnesses.
My brother will come out and be sad,
My mother will come out and be sorrowful,
My beloved will come out and rejoice,
Then she will stop, look, and swoon!"
"Oh, horse, where did you throw your master?
Tell me, horse, has he perished?"

"The Turks caught up with me,
They took my master off my back,
They shot him and they chopped him,
They celebrated near the Dniester River!"
Oh, Mother, don't be sad!
Because your son, he has married:
And as a wife he took
The green valley,
And the steep grave. . . .
Take, Mother, a handful of sand,
Sow it upon a stone:
When that sand sprouts and grows,
Then your son will come home from battle!

Source: Antonovich and Dragomanov, *Istoricheskie pesni malorusskogo naroda*, vol. I, pp. 270–71.

Baida

In Istanbul, at a market,
There Baida drinks mead and vodka;
Oh, Baida drinks, not a day, and not two,
Not one night and not one hour;
Baida drinks and then he nods,
And he looks at his squire,
"Oh, my squire, my young one!
Will you be faithful to me?"
The Turkish king sends for him,
He calls Baida to his side:
"Oh, you, Baida, you fine young man!
Be my faithful knight,
Take my daughter as wife,
And you will rule over all of Ukraine!"
"King, your faith is accursed,
And your daughter is a pagan."
Oh, the king screams at his servants:
"Take Baida, seize him well,
And hang him by his rib from a meathook!"
Oh, Baida hangs not a day, and not two,
Not one night and not one hour.

Oh, Baida hangs and Baida ponders,
He glances at his young squire,
He glances at his black horse.
"Oh, my squire, my young one!
Give me a bow, a tight one,
Give me a tightly strung bow,
And a handful of arrows!
Oh, I see three doves,
And I want to shoot them for his (the Turkish king's)
    daughter.
If I have hope, then I can survive,
Here I hang heavy; with arrows I can fight,"
Oh, he shot, and he hit the king,
And he hit the queen in the nape of her neck,
And he hit the princess in the head.
"Those shots, oh king,
Are in retaliation for Baida's punishment,
So that you will know,
How to punish Baida:
You should have severed Baida's head,
And buried his body,
And ridden on the black horse,
And won the affection of his servant."

Source: Antonovich and Dragomanov, vol. I, pp. 145–46.

Satirical Songs

Opportunities for performing satirical songs were relatively few. Because they were considered frivolous, they were seldom sung in public and most often performed in private homes, to entertain guests at weddings and on other joyful occasions.

The Noblewoman (*Dvorianka*)

A husar's wife lived by her senses,
And according to her senses she behaved,
She celebrated with mead and wine,
And she called her husband to her,
She called him her beloved:
"Oh, my dear one, oh, my darling,
Pale as the turtledove,
Please sell the oxen, the field oxen,
And buy me red boots,
Red boots and green booties!
Please sell the bullocks, the small ones,
And buy me some shoes,
That I may not walk around barefoot,
That I may not scratch my little feet;
Because I come from a noble family,
I have not gone barefoot since I was born.
Sell, my darling, sell the stallion and the mare,
Buy me powder and buy me rouge,
That I may not be sullied by the dust,
That I may not be burned by the sun,
That I may not be blackened by the wind.
And, darling, please also sell the calf,
And buy me two shirts,
And also, darling, sell the cow,
And buy me a silken skirt;
So that I can act like a lady,

And celebrate with mead and wine,
And also keep some vodka,
And invite guests to our house,
And give you your share, too."
The woman started to live like a lady,
To celebrate with mead and wine,
And to keep vodka,
To summon guests to the house,
And also to "honor" her husband,
To make rude gestures right under his nose.
"Oh, my darling, oh, my dear one,
Pale as the turtledove!
Don't shove quite so hard,
You might hurt your own nose,
You might become a laughingstock,
And you wouldn't want to do that,
Because you come from a noble family,
And you have not been in such a position
        since birth."
The woman sat around like a lady,
She used up all the wood in the house,
There is nothing to heat the house with,
There is nothing to cook borshch and
        porridge with,
So as to feed one's husband dinner.
The wife turns to her husband,
She tells him of their great need,
And asks him to go to the forest for firewood.
The husband hears this,
He takes the brace,[1] and off he goes,
He arrives in the forest,
And he gathers dry wood,
Piling it up in his brace,
He hoists the brace up on his shoulders,
And he carries his burden home;
He sits down on the bench and rests,
And he looks at his wife,
He sees that she is walking around looking well,
She is handsome, she is plump,
Her skin is white and her brows raven-colored.
Well, the dear wife thinks and ponders,

She goes and heats the house,
She puts borshch and porridge on the stove
    to cook.
The husband thinks and the husband ponders,
He bends the shaft bow,
He fixes the oaken clasps,
He prepares the harness,
He plaits a thick whip,
And he fixes the wagon,
He attaches the shaft,
The carved shaft,
And the plaited ropes,
And the shining sword.
Just then the wife comes outside,
She calls him to supper.
Well, he hides everything,
So that he will not frighten his dear wife,
So that he will be able to approach her,
And harness her to the wagon,
And drive her to the forest for firewood.
Well, he enters the house,
And he sits down to supper,
And he says to his dear wife:
"Oh, my dear wife, oh, my darling,
Pale as the turtledove!
Please eat quickly, do not dally,
We are going to a ball, please get dressed!"
Well, the dear wife hears this,
And quickly she thanks God,
And she puts shoes on her feet,
And she puts on her dress,
And she applies rouge and powder,
And she gazes in the mirror,
To make sure that she looks nice.
Soon the husband thanks God quickly,
He grabs his dear wife by the braids,
And he pushes her outside,
And he drags her to the wagon,
And he places the collar upon her,
And he hitches her to the harness:
"Stand still, dear one, and don't put on airs,

And get into the harness properly,
So that you do not damage my wagon,
For you are from a noble family,
And you have not pulled a wagon since the day
    you were born."
The dear husband arrives in the forest,
His dear wife looked worse than a beast,
He unhitched her from the wagon,
And tied her to an oak tree:
"Graze, graze, my darling,
But don't break the oak tree,
Because you are from a noble family
And have not grazed at a tree since you
    were born."
Well, the dear husband chops and cuts wood,
And he keeps glancing at his dear wife,
And he keeps telling his dear wife:
"Oh, stand still, my dear one, and don't bend
    your back,
Because I have lots more wood to cut,
And, darling, it is already late,
And we still have too little firewood."
As he cuts down an oak tree,
He loads it on his wife's back.
And as he approaches a hill,
He jumps up on the wagon himself,
And he uses his oaken switch:
"Oh, my dear wife, hurry on along,
That I may not lag behind other people,
That I may not be frightened by the beasts
    in the field;
Because, dear one, it is no longer early,
And the sun is already low in the sky,
And it is still far to our house."
And as he drives down the hill,
He strikes her in the buttocks,
And as he approaches town,
He speaks out and says to an old man:
"Old man, please be careful,
Make sure you do not spook my dear wife,
Because my dear wife is quite skittish,

She has not pulled a wagon since the day
    she was born,
And I want to make sure she does not break
    the wagon,
Does not cause me any damage."
As he arrives at their house,
He unhitches his dear wife,
And as the dear husband comes home,
He unloads all of the logs.
The dear wife walks into the house,
She sits down on a bench and she rests,
And she thinks and she ponders,
What she should call her husband,
How she should honor her husband,
How to live out the rest of her days.
"Oh, my dear one, oh, my raven-browed one,
Please sell my red boots,
And please buy oxen, buy field oxen,
Please sell the dainty shoes,
And buy bulls, buy small ones,
That I need not pull the wagon any longer,
That I no longer be a laughingstock before
    the people,
Because if I have to pull a wagon,
I will not live long."
Please sell the powder and the rouge,
And buy a horse and a mare,
I will be fair even without powder,
I will be rosy-cheeked even without rouge,
And I will not forget you, my beloved,
    for eternity,
I will not forget you as long as I live in this world,
In truth, I will not forget,
By God, I will not forget!
Please also sell my dresses,
And buy me two calves,
And sell also my silken skirt,
And go and buy me a cow:
I will arise early in the morning,
I will chase it out to pasture,
So that it will not walk around all of the yards,

And will not bother all the neighbors,
So that it would not make strangers laugh.
I see that I have had enough of the good life,
Enough celebrating with mead and wine;
I will get up early in the morning,
And I will earn blessed bread,
I will feed you,
I will honor you,
I will call you my turtledove,
I will spread a white bed for you,
I will lie down close to you,
I will embrace you nicely,
And kiss you seven times a night.

Source: Recorded from Veresai by Lysenko, pp. 402–7.

Khoma and Iarema

Khoma and Iarema are brothers,
Khoma and Iarema wear the same clothes,
Khoma has on a coat and Iarema has on an overcoat,
Khoma's is threadbare and Iarema's is the devil
    knows what,
Khoma's has no sleeves and Iarema's is torn!
Khoma tears his clothes and Iarema wears his out.
Khoma and Iarema spent a day in Buh.
They went to Buh and they ate meat.
Khoma flavored his with radishes and Iarema with garlic,
Khoma's innards were upset and Iarema's gut was sick.
"Iarema, my brother, only born not of the same mother,
Brother, we should not live this way!
We should, brother, take up commerce and sell wares;
We should gather salt and make a profit."
Khoma gathered a wagon load of salt and Iarema got
    a barrel,
Khoma stood among the merchants to sell his and Iarema
    stood in a corner.
Khoma showed his wares off with a pot and Iarema with
    a ladle.
No one buys from Khoma and no one does business
    with Iarema;

People steal all of Khoma's wares and they take Iarema's
    without paying for them.
Well, then they got mad and then they got angry.
They joined one another and started to cry,
They started to cry and to bawl like children.
And then they made another decision:
"Dear Iarema, my own brother, only not born
    of the same mother,
Brother, we are not meant to live like this,
We should not be selling these kinds of wares!
Here's what we should do and here's what we should sell:
Let us plait bast shoes and take them to the marketplace."
Khoma pulled lots of linden bark and Iarema got
    a whole bundle,
Khoma plaited shoes and Iarema made baskets,
Khoma stood in a shop and Iarema stood in a stall.
No one buys from Khoma and no one does business with
    Iarema.
People steal all of Khoma's wares and they take Iarema's
    without paying for them.
Well, then they walked outside and then they got angry,
They walked into a corner and started to cry,
They started to cry and to bawl like children.
And then they made another decision:
"Dear Iarema, my own brother, only not born
    of the same mother,
Brother, we are not meant to live like this,
We should not live like this and we should not sell these
    kinds of wares!
We should gather nuts and we should make a profit."
Khoma gathered nuts and Iarema got a whole bushel.
Khoma stood up on top of a hill and Iarema stood
    at the bottom,
No one buys from Khoma and no one does business
    with Iarema.
People steal all of Khoma's wares and they take Iarema's
    without paying for them.
It broke Khoma's heart and he broke what wares
    he had left.
Well, then they walked outside and then they got angry,
They walked into a corner and started to cry,

They started to cry and to bawl like children.
And once again they made a decision:
"Dear Iarema, my own brother, only not born of the same
    mother,
Brother, we are not meant to live like this,
We should not live like this and we should not sell these
    kinds of wares!
We should get some oxen and we should start plowing,
We should grow grain and make a profit."
Khoma paid five coins and Iarema paid three,
Khoma added five loads of grain and Iarema added nine.
Khoma bought a deaf ox and Iarema bought a lame one;
Khoma harnessed his animal and Iarema hitched his,
Khoma calls to his ox and Iarema prods his,
Khoma's doesn't pull the plow and Iarema's just won't go:
Khoma killed his beast and Iarema gave his a thrashing.
"Dear Iarema, my own brother, only not born of the same
    mother,
Brother, we are not meant to live like this,
We should not live like this and we should not sell these
    kinds of wares!
We should go into the fur trade, we should trap rabbits
    and sew white coats."
Khoma bought a staff and Iarema got a stick.
Khoma strikes out with his and Iarema beats the bushes,
Khoma's weapon does no good and Iarema's is useless;
Khoma broke his into pieces and Iarema took his apart.
Khoma catches a dog by mistake and Iarema catches the
    devil himself.
Well then they got upset and then they got angry,
They walked one over to the other and they started to cry,
They started to cry and to bawl like children,
And once again they made a decision:
"Dear Iarema, my own brother, only not born of the same
    mother,
Brother, we are not meant to live like this,
We should not live like this and we should not sell these
    kinds of wares!
What we should do is rob people and make a profit that
    way."
Khoma got an oaken club and Iarema got a leaden one.

Khoma hid in back of a bush and Iarema under it.
Along came a nobleman's son,
And he struck Khoma with the oaken club and Iarema
    with the leaden one;
Khoma ran off screaming and Iarema escaped silently,
"Brother, we are not meant to live like this,
We should not live like this and we should not sell these
    kinds of wares!
We should go work in a church and pray to God."
Khoma went to the nave and Iarema went to the apse,
Khoma got the books and Iarema brought the raiments,
Khoma started to read and Iarema started to dance;
Along came a sexton,
He kicked Khoma with his toe and he hit Iarema,
Khoma ran off screaming and Iarema escaped silently,
Khoma jumped out the window and Iarema went out the
    door:
Well then they got upset and then they got angry,
They walked one over to the other and they started to cry,
They started to cry and to bawl like children.
And once again they made a decision:
"Dear Iarema, my own brother, only not born of the same
    mother,
Brother, we are not meant to live like this,
We should not live like this and we should not sell these
    kinds of wares!
What we should do is plait fish nets and catch fish,
We should catch fish and thus support ourselves."
Khoma got into a boat and Iarema got into a dingy
Khoma caught a perch and Iarema got a bass.
Well, then they rejoiced!
And just then their boat capsized!
Khoma sank to the bottom and Iarema followed him!
They pull Khoma out like a sheatfish and Iarema like a
    barrel:
Whatever business you pursue,
That's the death that will be yours!

Source: Recorded from Veresai by Lysenko, pp. 407–11.

Secret Songs

At the conclusion of the annual meeting of the minstrel guild and after initiations, when no one other than a guild member could hear, minstrels sang secret songs. Only Porfyrii Martynovych was able to collect a secret song, and it has remained unpublished.[1] Minstrels were accused of singing scandalous songs when they were by themselves. The text which follows has no scandalous elements, and is questionable only in the sense that it was considered a charm.

Zhachka

Oh, you Zhachka, oh enlightened one,
Taught in all the schools,
Inform us, Zhachka, what is One?
There is one Son of Mary
The Son in Heaven,
The Son on Earth,
The Son who rules,
The Son who reigns
Over us,
Over us.

Oh, you Zhachka, oh enlightened one,
Taught in all the schools,
Inform us, Zhachka, what is Two?
There are two masters, two chief Apostles,[2]
Two tablets of the Law.[3]
There is one Son of Mary,
The Son in Heaven,
The Son on Earth,
The Son who rules,
The Son who reigns
Over us,
Over us.

Oh, you Zhachka, oh enlightened one,
Taught in all the schools,
Inform us, Zhachka, what is Three?
There are three masters, three Patriarchs,[4]
Two tablets of the Law.
There is one Son of Mary,
The Son in Heaven,
The Son on Earth,
The Son who rules,
The Son who reigns
Over us,
Over us.

Oh, you Zhachka, oh enlightened one,
Taught in all the schools,
Inform us, Zhachka, what is Four?
There are four Evangelists,
There are three masters, three Patriarchs,
Two tablets of the Law.
There is one Son of Mary,
The Son in Heaven,
The Son on Earth,
The Son who rules,
The Son who reigns
Over us,
Over us.

(What happened was that there was a deacon, and the devil was questioning
this deacon and saying:)[5]

Oh, you Zhachka, oh enlightened one,
Taught in all the schools,
Inform us, Zhachka, what is Five?
Five were the wounds inflicted on Christ,
Endured by our innocent Lord,
There are four Evangelists,
There are three masters, three Patriarchs,
There are two masters, two chief Apostles,
Two tablets of the Law.
There is one Son of Mary,
The Son in Heaven,

The Son on Earth,
The Son who rules,
The Son who reigns
Over us,
Over us.

Oh, you Zhachka, oh enlightened one,
Taught in all the schools,
Inform us, Zhachka, what is Six?
There were six great gifts
Upon most blessed Mary;
Five were the wounds inflicted on Christ,
Endured by our innocent Lord,
There are four Evangelists,
There are three masters, three Patriarchs,
There are two masters, two chief Apostles,
Two tablets of the Law,
There is one Son of Mary,
The Son in Heaven,
The Son on Earth,
The Son who rules,
The Son who reigns
Over us,
Over us.

Oh, you Zhachka, oh enlightened one,
Taught in all the schools,
Inform us, Zhachka, what is Seven?
There are seven sacraments of the Lord,
There were six great gifts
Upon most blessed Mary,
Five were the wounds inflicted on Christ,
Endured by our innocent Lord,
There are four Evangelists,
There are three masters, three Patriarchs,
There are two masters, two chief Apostles,
Two tablets of the Law.
There is one Son of Mary,
The Son in Heaven,
The Son on Earth,
The Son who rules,

The Son who reigns
Over us,
Over us.

Oh, you Zhachka, oh enlightened one,
Taught in all the schools,
Inform us, Zhachka, what is Eight?
There are eight mountain ranges rising high,
There are seven sacraments of the Lord,
There were six great gifts
Upon most blessed Mary,
Five were the wounds inflicted on Christ,
Endured by our innocent Lord,
There are four Evangelists,
There are three masters, three Patriarchs,
There are two masters, two chief Apostles,
Two tablets of the Law.
There is one Son of Mary,
The Son in Heaven,
The Son on Earth,
The Son who rules,
The Son who reigns
Over us,
Over us.

Oh, you Zhachka, oh enlightened one,
Taught in all the schools,
Inform us, Zhachka, what is Nine?
There are nine wisdoms of the Lord,
There are eight mountain ranges rising high,
There are seven sacraments of the Lord,
There were six great gifts
Upon most blessed Mary,
Five were the wounds inflicted on Christ,
Endured by our innocent Lord,
There are four Evangelists,
There are three masters, three Patriarchs,
There are two masters, two chief Apostles,
Two tablets of the Law.
There is one Son of Mary,
The Son in Heaven,

The Son on Earth,
The Son who rules,
The Son who reigns
Over us,
Over us.

Oh, you Zhachka, oh enlightened one,
Taught in all the schools,
Inform us, Zhachka, what is Ten?
There are ten choirs of Angels,[6]
There are nine wisdoms of the Lord,
There are eight mountain ranges rising high,
There are seven sacraments of the Lord,
There were six great gifts
Upon most blessed Mary,
Five were the wounds inflicted on Christ,
Endured by our innocent Lord,
There are four Evangelists,
There are three masters, three Patriarchs
There are two masters, two chief Apostles,
Two tablets of the Law.
There is one Son of Mary,
The Son in Heaven,
The Son on Earth,
The Son who rules,
The Son who reigns
Over us,
Over us.

Oh, you Zhachka, oh enlightened one,
Taught in all the schools,
Inform us, Zhachka, what is Eleven?
There are eleven Prophets,
There are ten choirs of Angels,
There are nine wisdoms of the Lord,
There are eight mountain ranges rising high,
There are seven sacraments of the Lord,
There were six great gifts
Upon most blessed Mary,
Five were the wounds inflicted on Christ,
Endured by our innocent Lord,

There are four Evangelists,
There are three masters, three Patriarchs,
Three tablets of the Law,
There are two masters, two chief Apostles,
Two tablets of the Law.
There is one Son of Mary,
The Son in Heaven,
The Son on Earth,
The Son who rules,
The Son who reigns
Over us,
Over us.

Oh, you Zhachka, oh enlightened one,
Taught in all the schools,
Inform us, Zhachka, what is Twelve?
There are twelve Apostles,
There are eleven Prophets,
There are ten choirs of Angels,
There are nine wisdoms of the Lord,
There are eight mountain ranges rising high,
There are seven sacraments of the Lord,
There were six great gifts
Upon most blessed Mary,
Five were the wounds inflicted on Christ,
Endured by our innocent Lord,
There are four Evangelists,
There are three masters, three Patriarchs,
Three tablets of the Law,
There are two masters, two chief Apostles,
Two tablets of the Law.
There is one Son of Mary,
The Son in Heaven,
The Son on Earth,
The Son who rules,
The Son who reigns
Over us,
Over us.

Oh, you Zhachka, oh enlightened one,
Taught in all the schools,

Inform us, Zhachka, what is Thirteen?
The thirteenth is the Lord Himself,
And there are twelve Apostles,
There are eleven Prophets,
There are ten choirs of Angels,
There are nine wisdoms of the Lord,
There are eight mountain ranges rising high,
There are seven sacraments of the Lord,
There were six great gifts
Upon most blessed Mary,
Five were the wounds inflicted on Christ,
Endured by our innocent Lord,
There are four Evangelists,
There are three masters, three Patriarchs,
There are two masters, two chief Apostles,
Two tablets of the Law.
There is one Son of Mary,
The Son in Heaven,
The Son on Earth,
The Son who rules,
The Son who reigns
Over us,
Over us.

Oh, you Zhachka, oh enlightened one,
Taught in all the schools,
Inform us, Zhachka, what is Fourteen?
The fourteenth is the King of the East,
The thirteenth is the Lord Himself,
And there are twelve Apostles,
There are eleven Prophets,
There are ten choirs of Angels,
There are nine wisdoms of the Lord,
There are eight mountain ranges rising high,
There are seven sacraments of the Lord,
There were six great gifts
Upon most blessed Mary,
Five were the wounds inflicted on Christ,
Endured by our innocent Lord,
There are four Evangelists,
There are three masters, three Patriarchs,

There are two masters, two chief Apostles,
Two tablets of the Law.
There is one Son of Mary,
The Son in Heaven,
The Son on Earth,
The Son who rules,
The Son who reigns
Over us,
Over us.

Oh, you Zhachka, oh enlightened one,
Taught in all the schools,
Inform us, Zhachka, what is Fifteen?
The fifteenth one I don't know,
I have not read it in the Psalter,
The fourteenth is the King of the East,
The thirteenth is the Lord Himself,
And there are twelve Apostles,
There are eleven Prophets,
There are ten choirs of Angels,
There are nine wisdoms of the Lord,
There are eight mountain ranges rising high,
There are seven sacraments of the Lord,
There were six great gifts
Upon most blessed Mary,
Five were the wounds inflicted on Christ,
Endured by our innocent Lord,
There are four Evangelists,
There are three masters, three Patriarchs,
There are two masters, two chief Apostles,
Two tablets of the Law.
There is one Son of Mary,
The Son in Heaven,
The Son on Earth,
The Son who rules,
The Son who reigns
Over us,
Over us.

Oh, you Zhachka, oh enlightened one,
Taught in all the schools,
Inform us, Zhachka, what is Sixteen?

The sixteenth is the rooster who crows
And strikes the Devil in the temple,
The fifteenth one I don't know,
I have not read it in the Psalter,
The fourteenth is the King of the East,
The thirteenth is the Lord Himself,
And there are twelve Apostles,
There are eleven Prophets,
There are ten choirs of Angels,
There are nine wisdoms of the Lord,
There are eight mountain ranges rising high,
There are seven sacraments of the Lord,
There were six great gifts
Upon most blessed Mary,
Five were the wounds inflicted on Christ,
Endured by our innocent Lord,
There are four Evangelists,
There are three masters, three Patriarchs,
There are two masters, two chief Apostles,
Two tablets of the Law.
There is one Son of Mary,
The Son in Heaven,
The Son on Earth,
The Son who rules,
The Son who reigns
Over us,
Over us.

(The Devil was trying to discover the secret. And then the deacon hit him in the temple with a Psalter and so he perished there. The Devil was questioning the deacon. And the deacon hit him in the temple.[7] If you start this song, you have to finish it. It is bad to stop without finishing.[8])

Source: Recorded from Hrytsenko-Kholodnyi by Martynovych and stored in IMFE, fond 11–4/592, ark. 47–52. Although Zhachka is used as a name here, it probably derives from the word *zhak*, meaning student, which came into Ukrainian from the French Jacques via Czech. In all probability, this song was a composition written by a student at a church school and was used as both a mnemonic device and for self-aggrandizement, because the *zhak*'s knowledge is said to defeat the devil himself. From the commentary in the margins, it appears that the song was performed with another minstrel, Roman Iaremenko, and that the minstrel's blind wife was present. Most of the commentary to the song was made by the minstrel's wife, Hanna Nynychynovna Iaremenkiva. The performer tells Martynovych to write this song down separately from the others, and the woman tells him that the song's purpose is to chase the devil away.

Bibliographic Essay

Early Ukrainian Folkloristics:
Interest in the Text Rather Than the Performer

The roots of Ukrainian minstrelsy go back hundreds of years. Unfortunately, data on minstrels come from the middle of the nineteenth century on, and we can only speculate about and try to reconstruct what went on prior to that time. While some texts were collected as early as the beginning of the nineteenth century, the performers themselves generated very little interest. Scattered bits of information appear in sources that predate 1850, but nothing extensive and nothing systematic was written before interest in ethnography began to develop. Scholars became interested in *kobzari* and *lirnyky* in a roundabout way. They were first attracted to the poetic narratives that minstrels sang, and especially the *duma*, the indigenous Ukrainian epic. Only after some fifty years of *duma* collecting and publication were the performers of *dumy* recognized as worthy of study in their own right. It has taken even longer to understand that Ukrainian minstrels sang and told many things in addition to epic, and that to them and their village audiences, epic was not the most important genre.

The nineteenth century was an important time for folklore scholarship the world over. The early part of the century was the period of romantic nationalism which continued the Romantic interest in the simple, natural man and the preoccupation with the past, the rural, and childhood. It also included the culturally specific, one's own past, and tended to idealize this past as the true manifestation of the culture in question. Attention to the folk and their lore was a natural outgrowth. The nineteenth century saw the appearance of the Grimm Brothers' *Kinder und Hausmärchen*, the assembling of other folktale collections, the beginnings of folklore archives, and the first definition of the term "folklore." In Russia, Kirsha Danilov's collection of epics was published in 1804 and was popular enough to appear in a second edition in 1818.[1] It is possible, as the eminent folklorist Kateryna Hrushevska has speculated, that the reaction to Kirsha Danilov's work prompted folklore collecting and publication in Ukraine.[2] While there may have been some work done by Vasyl Lomykovskyi prior to the influence of Kirsha Danilov, the first collection of Ukrainian epic that we can attribute and date with certainty, Mykola Tsertelev's *An Experiment in Collecting Little Russian Songs* (*Opyt sobraniia malorossiiskikh pesnei*), published in 1819, could easily have been inspired by the success of the Russian work: its date of publication is very close to the republication of Kirsha Danilov and Tsertelev belonged to a circle of Ukrainian gentlemen who met to discuss literature and culture.[3] They would have been aware of the Danilov book and interested in assembling a Ukrainian counterpart. Of course, there was so much interest in folklore the world over, and in Ukraine in particular, that Tsertelev could have begun his project without prompting from outside.[4]

After Tsertelev's book, other collections of Ukrainian songs followed in a regular fashion. Mykhailo Maksymovych published one work in 1827, another in 1834, and a third in 1849.[5] Izmaiil Sreznevskyi assembled a set of three volumes, which appeared between 1833 and 1838.[6] Panteleimon Kulish prepared a book of songs which was published in 1843.[7] All of these works were true to the understanding of folklore prevalent in their time. They focused on *dumy* because these were considered a particularly high and noble form of narrative, yet also contained historical and other songs, often mixing what we now consider separate genres. Even the idea of "historical song" was rather different from what it is now, and included anything from material that dealt with known historical figures to songs reflecting the mores or lifestyles of the past, to songs simply believed to have originated long ago. Thus, *dumy* appeared alongside lyric songs about Cossack life, ballads, and even songs that were connected to various rituals deemed to be primitive.

The early scholars were primarily interested in texts and in history, and so their collections contained hardly any mention of the minstrel from whom the songs were recorded. Lomykovskyi noted one performer, at least by first name, but his work was not published until late in the nineteenth century and was not widely known or influential. Tsertelev, the collector whose work set the pattern, referred briefly to his sources in a separately published article, and even more briefly, in the introduction to his text collection. The information he provided lacked names and biographical data and merely mentioned that he encountered two blind mendicants.[8] Maksymovych, Sreznevskyi, and Kulish in *Ukraina* (Ukraine) pretty well ignored performers. Some scholars, like Mykhailo Maksymovych, largely republished the work of others and thus may have lost awareness of the minstrels who were the real sources of the texts. Others, like Sreznevskyi, apparently had contact with performers, but considered them unimportant.[9]

Treatment of the Oral Text by Early Scholars:
The Belief That Texts Are Shaped by History
Rather Than by the Performer

The compilers of the early books of Ukrainian epic and song felt no compulsion to preserve the exact words of their performers, and felt free to alter the texts of songs they published to produce what they considered to be a more "correct" version. Sreznevskyi, in all three of his volumes, and Kulish, in his 1843 *Ukraina*, were especially notorious for reworking folk texts and even inventing songs that did not exist in the folk tradition, to produce what "should" have been there. Of the early collections, the ones closest to what *kobzari* and *lirnyky* actually sang were probably Lomykovskyi's, which remained in manuscript, and the first edition of Tsertelev. Comparison of the various editions of Tsertelev shows that he altered his texts for republication, and this casts doubt on the accuracy of his first edition. It is nonetheless likely that Tsertelev intruded least into the texts he published, before he came under the influence of reworkers like Sreznevskyi, whose work, at least at first, was hugely popular and successful.[10]

The assumptions that governed early works on Ukrainian folklore and prompted the approaches described above included a belief that there is an irresistible human impulse to record events of historical significance in some manner. This belief assigned a great deal of importance to songs with a historical content, especially to *dumy*, the material with the greatest length, the most complex form, and associations, through Homer, with high art and great world literature. If history was thought to dictate the contents of epic songs, then the performers of *dumy* had little creative or artistic input; if they did what they were supposed to do well, then they conserved the historical content of their genre. But they themselves played no artistic or creative role; they were merely conduits for historical information.

The belief in the importance of history led to collections that tried to give a history of Ukraine in song. These collections used *dumy* where they existed on a particular historical event, and included historical songs, ballads, or lyric songs where *dumy* were lacking. This is the structure of Sreznevskyi's three-volume work and of two of Kulish's publications.[11] It remained the guiding principle in arranging texts well into the nineteenth century, governing even as sophisticated a collection as the two-volume, multi-variant work prepared by Volodymyr Antonovych and Mykhailo Drahomanov in 1874.[12] An interesting variation on this principle was Lukashevych's *Little Russian and Red Russian Folk Epics and Songs* (*Malorossiiskie i Chervonorusskie narodnye dumy i pesni*) which was arranged by historical figure. This collection tried to provide at least one song for every major historical personage—again, *dumy* where these existed, and other songs elsewhere.[13]

Thus, in collecting *dumy* in the first part of the nineteenth century, assembling historical data was the primary goal and the bearers of these data, the minstrels who sang the songs in which historical material was found, were of little interest. Sreznevskyi's rationale for using folk materials as a historical source exemplifies this attitude. In the preface to his *Zaporozhian Antiquities* (*Zaporozhskaia starina*), he explains that because of the lack of written documents, oral materials must serve as a source of historical information. Oral materials in verse are especially useful because, "being subordinated to music and repeated almost word for word, they have been less affected by the passage of time and have preserved their original content better."[14] This quote would make it appear that to Sreznevskyi, *kobzari* and *lirnyky* were not creative artists but people who merely repeated that which they had learned. Furthermore, Sreznevskyi's description of what he found desirable, namely fidelity to historical fact, provides a key to his assessment of performers and shows that artistic intrusion by a performer was, in his eyes, not desirable and produced a less valuable text.

Ukrainian scholars did not feel as strongly as their Western counterparts that any major form of literature, such as the epic, must have originated in writing. Western scholars seem to have assumed that writing, the manner in which they themselves created texts, was the means by which all literature came into being. Perhaps because the Ukrainian tradition lacked the medieval manuscripts of western Europe and Ukrainian epic was still alive as an oral tradition in the nineteenth century, Ukrainian folklorists did not insist that *dumy* began as written poems which then passed to illiterate oral performers. In fact, this explanation for the origin of Ukrainian epic poetry was not argued until late in the nineteenth century. Ukrainian scholars did feel, however, that a song about an event must originate chronologically close to that event, coming into being shortly after the event had occurred. In any case, all scholars felt that *dumy* and other oral narratives had originated long ago and had been passed down to contemporary minstrels. *Kobzari* and *lirnyky* maintained this poetry, but in imperfect form, for in their hands, it was spoiled by faulty memory and forced to disintegrate with the passage of time. The rather unusual poetic form of the *duma* reinforced this belief. Tsertelev, looking at the irregular lines of Ukrainian epic poetry, felt that *dumy* were a dying genre and that what was available in his time were "the ruins which testified to the beauty of the collapsed building."[15] The uneven line length, varying from three to sixteen syllables, and the irregular dimensions of *duma* "stanzas," led scholars to assume that epic had begun with the even lines and symmetrical stanzas considered good form in the poetry of their day and then devolved to the very uneven verse in which they recorded it from contemporary performers.

Maksymovych, in the introduction to his 1827 collection, mentioned various oral processes by which songs "gradually departed from their original form." He said that songs were sometimes not sung all the way through; sometimes individual verses or whole sections were forgotten; and sometimes two songs were confused with each other. While he did not consider it possible to reconstruct the original, he did feel obliged to correct any material he published, be it texts he was republishing from other printed collections or newly collected material sent to him by friends. He characterized what he had done in the preparation of his edition as comparing texts and making them "agree," sometimes combining two versions into a single text, sometimes discarding extraneous material, always trying to produce what was logical and best captured folk outlook and folk language.[16] Borys Kyrdan, in a book on the collectors of Ukrainian folklore in the early part of the nineteenth century, compared Maksymovych's texts with his sources, or where these are not known, with contemporary collections. He found that Maksymovych consistently produced a more regular line of more even length.[17] By the time he was preparing his 1834 collection, Maksymovych, according to his own introduction, had some two-and-one-half thousand songs, some in as many as five variants, which permitted him "to observe clearly those changes which occurred from their (the songs') being sung over a long period of time and incorrectly and partially from the inventiveness of their singers, thus I was able to present many songs in corrected form."[18] Presumably, Maksymovych used his many variants to remove all of the inventiveness and all of the incorrect forms and to produce texts as he believed they should be.

Kulish, in a letter to Maksymovych, compared his own work as editor to clearing the underbrush from a forest, making it into a grove where one could walk with pleasure and without difficulty. His goal, he stated, was to give lovers of folk poetry a book containing the best of folk songs, without distortions or lacunae.[19] With these attitudes toward the texts that they recorded from minstrels, it is clear that to early nineteenth-century scholars, contemporary performers were imperfect transmitters of a poetry that had been created by someone else long before.

Information about Performers: Growing Understanding of the Oral Process and the First Study of a Specific *Kobzar*

At the very middle of the nineteenth century, Hryhorii Bazylevych, a priest working in a village called Aleksandrivka in the Chernihiv region, recorded *dumy* and other historical songs from a performer called Andrii Shut, whose name and partial biography he included in an article.[20] Why Bazylevych broke with the tradition of ignoring the performer is not clear. We can speculate that he was not part of the scholarly circles that had perpetuated the idea that *kobzari* were only imperfect bearers of someone else's art. Perhaps it was because he was writing an ethnographic article, a form of scholarly work rapidly developing at the time.[21] Thus he gave not only song texts, but a description of a place and its interesting inhabitants, namely Shut. Perhaps it was because Shut himself was a powerful personality, as collectors like Kulish and Amvrozii Metlynskyi, who followed Bazylevych to Aleksandrivka, attest, and he demanded recognition as an individual. Again, it is possible that the atmosphere of the time was such and that scholarship was developing in such a way that eventual focus on a contemporary performer was inevitable.

As important and influential as Bazylevych's article was and as impressive as Shut must have been, it took almost twenty-five years for attention to minstrels to become a regular feature of scholarly work. One of the remarkable things that emerges from Kyrdan's 1974 book on nineteenth-century collectors is that they continued to consider *kobzari* and *lirnyky* unimportant even as they interacted with them more and more and became progressively more cognizant of the nature of oral performance. Thus Kulish, Maksymovych, and Sreznevskyi all made statements about the nature of orality and performance which sound remarkably modern and accurate, and they urged others to write down oral texts word for word, altering nothing; yet, as Kyrdan shows, they themselves doctored their materials with impunity. Furthermore, while they displayed increasing recognition that *dumy* and other songs are oral literature, created and existing in performance, they still refused to acknowledge the central role of the performer. The information they provided on the performance that was the source of the text they printed included only the name of the collector and the time and place of collection. Occasionally, they included a note that the material was from "a *kobzar*." But awareness of the oral process and of performance was growing, and it was probably inevitable that a mainstream scholar and someone dealing with folklore rather than ethnography would finally turn his attention to an actual minstrel.

Even prior to Bazylevych, namely in 1832, Mykola Markevych gave an accurate albeit brief description of a performer in a note to his poem "Bandurist."[22] Markevych's note escaped notice, and like Lomykovskyi's collection, it exerted no influence. It was Bazylevych who finally focused attention on a minstrel and opened a floodgate of scholarly activity. Other collectors, such as Kulish and Metlynskyi, went to record Shut's songs and to write down information about him as a person and an artist. Even so, early work on minstrels was not always accurate or published in a timely manner. Kulish, who seems always to have been looking for the *au courant* thing to do, followed Bazylevych to Aleksandrivka in the same year the latter's article was published. In a letter to O. Bodianskyi, dated September 18, 1853, and published much later in the journal *Kievan Antiquities* (*Kievskaia Starina*), he reported recording twelve long *dumy* from Shut and commented on their historical, artistic, and moral merit.[23] He apparently also met Andrii Beshko, a minstrel who had been Shut's apprentice, and recorded material from him. In 1854, in Poltava, he collected from a different sort of performer, the *lirnyk* Arkhyp Nykonenko. Kulish also recorded material from Mykola Ryhorenko, of the Kharkiv district, and he even seems to have met Ostap Veresai, who is mentioned as "*kobzar* Ostap" in the second volume of his *Notes about South Russia* (*Zapiski o Iuzhnoi Rusi*).[24] Unfortunately, Kulish's focus on performers did not rid him of his tendency to embellish and enhance. In his account of "*kobzar* Ostap," for example, he added the stock "dark and stormy night" to the description of a scene at the roadside inn where he supposedly met Veresai. He also attributed to Veresai a narrative that was not part of his repertory. Kulish totally neglected to mention Beshko in print, so that we know of him only from manuscripts and from the work of others, yet he used texts recorded from Beshko to flesh out the songs of his master, Shut.[25] It is not surprising, therefore, that Kulish has been accused of inventing Nykonenko and attributing to him material that had really been recorded from Veresai.[26] Kulish seems to have sought especially to enhance his own persona. His description of his encounter with Shut contains the much-quoted scene of the impression the collector made on the folk performer. It recounts how awed Shut was that a man from St. Petersburg, a man outside his tradition, knew more about it than he himself. It describes Shut's agitation, appreciation, and wonder as Kulish retold *dumy* and other historical texts.[27]

As annoying as *Notes about South Russia* may be, with its unnecessary embellishments, its self-praise, its self-righteous judgments of the moral and personal qualities of the performers, it is an important book. It is also very different from Kulish's previous work. Even the nature of Kulish's self-aggrandizement is different. Whereas in *Ukraine* Kulish sought to put together a Ukrainian *Odyssey*, thus making himself a Ukrainian Homer, in *Notes from South Russia*, he tried to promote himself, not as a literary figure, but as a scholar. *Notes from South Russia* is not just an assembling of texts; it is a book presenting historical narratives *and* their context, including information on performers. Several of the headings in the list of contents give the full names and whereabouts of minstrels; one section is about performers in general; another discusses mendicants as the principal bearers of poetry and philosophy.

Interestingly, recognition of the artistic role of the contemporary minstrel led to a different attitude toward the song text, whether of a *duma* or other historical song. Early scholars had seldom bothered to record more than one version of a particular text, be it from the same performer, or even from different performers, because they assumed that all versions would be similar to each other, being corruptions of a single original text. Even when they did record more than one version, they knit the multiple versions together into a single song on the assumption that one performer had forgotten certain parts, and another performer others—the combination of the two best reflecting the original. After Bazylevych, collectors no longer shunned writing down texts that had already been published; they were willing to record the same text from several performers and from the same performer more than once. Only twenty years after Bazylevych's work, Antonovych and Drahomanov sought to bring all available versions together into one scholarly edition.

Antonovych and Drahomanov's *The Historical Songs of the Little Russian People* (*Istoricheskie pesni malorusskogo naroda*) is the best of the text collections of the nineteenth century.[28] It represents the culmination of the interest in text and the interest in history. Arranged by historical period, it includes texts only, with no discussion of performers or performance. While this collection developed directly out of the orientation that had prompted a neglect of performers, its inclusion of multiple variants showed recognition of the nature of the oral process. And recognition of the characteristics of orality led Ukrainian folklore scholarship from a focus primarily on texts to an interest in minstrels and minstrelsy.

Early Information on Minstrels

The period shortly after the publication of *The Historical Songs of the Little Russian People* saw some of the most important collecting of information on Ukrainian minstrels. Interest in orality prepared the way for this work, as did other developments. In 1854, Amvrosii Metlynskyi published *South Russian Folk Songs* (*Narodnye iuzhnorusskie pesni*).[29] This book is noteworthy for annotating a number of the *duma* texts published, giving the name of the collector who recorded the text and often the place of recording and the name of the performer. For the lesser genres, such as historical and lyric songs, Metlynskyi noted only the place where the item had been collected. Even more important than the notes to texts is the inclusion of two very forward-looking pieces by Mykola Bilozerskyi: a guide for collectors interested in recording *dumy*, songs, tales, legends, and so forth, and a list of *kobzari* and *lirnyky*. Both pieces are very short and were apparently cut further by Metlynskyi.[30] The list of performers does not try to do much more than direct potential collectors into areas where they might find *kobzari* or *lirnyky*, and consists mostly of a list of regions. Sometimes the names of performers are cited; sometimes Bilozerskyi says merely that a region is rich in singers. Meager as this may be, it is still an important step in the direction of gathering information on folk performers.

Kobzari and *lirnyky* aroused the interest not only of scholars whose focus was primarily philological and historical, but also of people interested in music and art. Mykola Markevych prepared *South Russian Songs with Voices* (*Iuzhnorusskie pesni s golosami*), a collection of song texts and melodies, including the *duma* about a Cossack's departure.[31] The melodies were for accompaniment on a piano, hardly a folk instrument; however, the mere notation of music was another step toward the recognition that dumy and other folksongs and narratives were not just attempts at preserving historical fact, but complex artistic works. Treatment of folklore as art was another development that led to the recognition of minstrels as artists. Furthermore, Markevych's efforts at recording folk music in general and the music of professional minstrels in particular laid the groundwork for the studies written by the composer and musicologist Mykola Lysenko and the ethnomusicologist Filaret Kolessa, whose transcriptions and studies of *dumy* and other folk forms retain their value to this day.[32]

One peculiar development of the interest in performers is the artist Lev Zhemchuzhnikov's fascination with Ostap Veresai. Though Veresai was hardly representative of Ukrainian minstrelsy, Zhemchuzhnikov was thoroughly taken with him and introduced him to various intellectuals, even having him appear at an Archeological Congress in Kiev in 1873. At this meeting, Veresai was observed not only by Ukrainian intellectuals, but by scholars from foreign countries, specifically the Frenchman Rambaud.[33] As the first minstrel these men saw, he set the pattern for their conception of what it meant to be a *kobzar*. Unfortunately, Veresai, as an anomaly within the tradition, made it seem that the tradition itself was not a complex and well-established institution, that it was on the verge of extinction. Rusov even wrote an article describing Veresai as the last of the *kobzari*.[34] If Veresai was the last minstrel, then there was no reason to look for other performers. All one needed to do was study Veresai—as Rusov, Lysenko, and others in fact, did.[35]

The Major Studies of *Kobzari* and *Lirnyky*

The Late Nineteenth Century: The Work of Martynovych and Other Scholars

The late nineteenth century, the period that popularized Veresai, also produced some remarkable folkloristic work. Out of it came marvelous and extensive collections of epic, lyric, and ritual poetry, as well as proverbs, sayings, and folktales. This period yields most of our data on performers.

As dominant as the image of Veresai may have been, not all folklorists succumbed to the idea that this man was the last representative of a dying tradition. Porfirii Martynovych took Veresai at his word when the latter said that the *kobzar* Ivan Kravchenko-Kriukovskyi was a better artist and performer, sought Kravchenko-Kriukovskyi out, and recorded part of his repertory and his striking and moving autobiography. Kravchenko-Kriukovskyi's songs truly were excellent, characterized by both unusual length and high artistic quality. The reason Martynovych did not record all of his repertory was that it was just too extensive to be written down in the time the collector had allowed. Martynovych also recorded Trykhon Mahadyn, from whom he collected several *duma* texts and an account of the *kobzar* initiation rite.

Martynovych sent his materials to Mykhailo Drahomanov on the assumption that the latter would publish them in the continuation of *The Historical Songs of the Little Russian People*. But Drahomanov had to leave the country for political reasons, and he took Martynovych's materials with him. They remained unpublished for nearly thirty years, coming out in shortened form in the journal *Kievan Antiquities* in 1904 and in more complete form in *The Ukrainian Notes of Porfirii Martynovych* in 1906.[36] Fortunately, Martynovych, though discouraged, continued to collect, contributing to the discovery of another outstanding *kobzar*, Fedir Hrytsenko-Kholodnyi, making extensive recordings from *lirnyky*, and writing down a sizable body of folktales, legends, and other prose.

Martynovych was perhaps the best collector ever of information on minstrels. He recorded biographical information on performers and hundreds of texts, including not just the epics that other scholars so favored, but the full range of minstrel repertories—their begging songs, their religious verses, their lyric songs and prose narratives. He seems to have enjoyed the trust of minstrels in a way that no other collector did, and he was able to record material that was secret and inaccessible to virtually everyone else outside the profession. These unique materials include transcriptions of initiation rites, the texts of magic songs, which were supposed to keep the devil at bay, and dictionaries of the secret minstrel language (*lebiiska mova*).[37]

Martynovych seems to have written down everything that his informants said. Thus we have their commentary on their own performances, including both critiques and statements about the emotion which a particular piece aroused in the performer. There are remarks about female performers and what seem to be whole reams of texts collected from women. Martynovych's materials remain largely in manuscript form, and the later manuscripts present special problems because the handwriting is very difficult and attribution is sporadic. Thus it is often hard to decipher the text, and the source of a particular text or comment is difficult or impossible to determine. Even so, Martynovych remains the best single source for information on Ukrainian minstrels.

Some of the Martynovych manuscripts did see publication. Kateryna Hrushevska published his epics in her full, scholarly edition of texts, a collection that was supposed to be an update of Antonovych and Drahomanov's work and was timed to mark the fiftieth anniversary of *The Historical Songs of the Little Russian People*, but she left out all of Martynovych's other materials because they did not fit the aim of her compendium. Nor did the work of Mykola Bilozerskyi, who gave us a list of performers and a guide for collectors, and Vasyl Horlenko, who also collected a significant volume of material, see publication, except for the texts of epic songs that entered Hrushevska's work.

A number of articles on performers appeared, mostly in the journal *Kievan Antiquities*. These included pieces by Oleksandr Malynka, K. F. Ukhach-Okhorovych, Mykola Sumtsov, Valerian Borzhkovskii, P. Tykhonovskyi, Krist, Porfirii Martynovych, and Vasyl Horlenko, among others.[38] Malynka deserves special mention, though he never produced a book and is not widely known. He was an excellent folklorist, and his articles are probably the second-best source for information on minstrels after Martynovych. Malynka, too, collected a variety of information, including biographical data, song texts of all sorts, and information about training methods and women performers. He recorded the songs of poor singers as well as good ones, and gave us the means for identifying the range of performance extant in Ukraine and also the qualities of a good, versus a poor, singer.

The Early Twentieth Century and the Twelfth Archeological Congress

While publishing activity at the end of the nineteenth century was restricted, the intensive collecting of that period laid the groundwork for the significant events that occurred at the beginning of the twentieth. These include the Twelfth Archeological Congress, held in Kharkiv in 1902; the collecting work of Opanas Slastion, Lesia Ukrainka, and Filaret Kolessa; and the publication of Mikhail Speranskii's book on performers.

The preparations for the Twelfth Archeological Congress prompted intense collecting and scholarly activity, including Slastion's recording of materials from Mykhailo Kravchenko, a performer of unusual ability and artistic merit.[39] The presentations at the Congress included papers specifically on *kobzari* and *lirnyky*, among them V. Ivanov's discussion of performer guilds and a paper on minstrels by Hnat Khotkevych.[40]

The Congress probably affected minstrelsy itself no less than it did the study of minstrels. Following the precedent set by Ostap Veresai's appearance in Kiev and in Petersburg, the organizers of the Congress planned to have traditional performers included in their program, in alternation with scholarly papers. But instead of inviting only one minstrel, the conference organizers planned to include many, and placed Hnat Khotkevych in charge of this part of the program. To make the minstrels appealing to an educated and sophisticated audience, Khotkevych essentially decided to alter the tradition. His notes on selecting and preparing the minstrels would make a modern folklorist cringe in horror.[41] For one thing, Khotkevych decided that the men should perform in ensembles, as well as singing the traditional solos, and chose minstrels who would harmonize well, rather than those who were especially gifted or representative of the tradition. Probably preparations for the Kharkiv conference introduced the idea of group performance to the minstrels themselves. In the traditional village setting, *kobzari* and *lirnyky* simply did not perform in groups. They may have gathered in large numbers and performed for one another, as during initiation rites, but even at these large gatherings, there was no choral singing; individuals played and sang in turn. Some duets are attested—two men who would regularly travel and perform together, or a minstrel and his wife, usually with just one of them playing a musical instrument. Duets, however, were the exception rather than the rule; the typical performance was by one man accompanying himself. Furthermore, the traditional lifestyle of minstrels made it impossible to support groups of a size larger than two. In all likelihood, Khotkevych's organizing of the folk performer ensemble that appeared at the Twelfth Archeological Congress began the trend toward the folklore ensembles and *bandura* ensembles which so characterize popular art and music both in Ukraine and among American and Canadian Ukrainians today.

Even prior to the Twelfth Archeological Congress, there had been a general tendency toward the introduction of more Western performance styles and musical arrangements. This occurred not only because Western things were seen as better and more advanced, but also because the folk performers were beginning to find the urban, Westernized elite to be a more appreciative and better-paying audience. As Kolessa noted during his collecting activities, a transition occurred sometime early in the twentieth century. In the late 1880s, when Borzhkovskii was collecting his materials, the villager was still a more sympathetic listener than a member of the nobility. By the first decades of the twentieth century, the opposite was true, and the urban elite was the social stratum interested in *kobzari* and *lirnyky*. Professional performers were recognizing this change and making adaptations to please their new public. *Kobzari* playing their *bandury* together and harmonizing in an ensemble could have resulted from this Westernizing tendency alone, but the appearance of such a group at the Twelfth Archeological Congress gave the ensemble phenomenon a legitimacy and prestige that might have encouraged its perpetuation.

Another aspect of the activity of Khotkevych and Slastion, unrelated to the Congress of 1902, probably affected the course along which minstrelsy developed in Ukraine. Both Slastion and Khotkevych became *kobzari* of sorts, playing the *bandura*, and singing *dumy* and some of the other songs in the traditional repertory of a minstrel. Neither, however, was of the folk, and both were sighted and educated. Khotkevych was a musicologist who became an important author and playwright. Slastion was trained as a painter and developed an interest in folklore by accompanying Martynovych on collecting expeditions. Slastion, curiously, was even among the performers analyzed by Kolessa in his work on the music of Ukrainian *dumy*. Thus, Slastion acted as a scholar, helping Kolessa make the recordings he used in his analysis, and a folk performer, providing some of the material to be analyzed. In all probability, Slastion's and Khotkevych's activity as performers was very beneficial to their scholarly work, giving an understanding of performance, learning techniques, and oral text that scholars of the past could not approximate. In a sense, their becoming one with the subjects of their scholarly work was the ultimate recognition of the value of the minstrel and the minstrel's art and was the culmination of the process begun by Bazylevych. At the same time, the activity of Slastion and Khotkevych was a sign of the deterioration of the tradition as it had existed in the nineteenth century. Minstrelsy was no longer the occupation of poor, blind peasants exclusively and was becoming a means of musical expression suitable to anyone, even gentlemen such as Khotkevych and Slastion. *Bandura*-playing was eventually to be seen as suitable for well-bred young women, who today form the majority of most *bandura* ensembles both in Ukraine and the West.

The Work of Speranskii

Speranskii's book of 1904 is the best published study of minstrelsy to date.[42] Though dedicated to Parkhomenko, it discusses not just him, but all Ukrainian minstrels, and provides information on lifestyles, daily routines, apprenticeship, training, and initiation rites. It includes statistics on the age when a person went blind, the age when he became an apprentice, how long that person trained with a master, the size of the performer's repertory, and data on earnings and family life. It retains its value and was extensively used by Fedir Lavrov and by Kyrdan and Omelchenko for their major books on performers of 1980.[43] Speranskii's book included *dumy* and other texts recorded from Parkhomenko, but subordinated the texts to the data on minstrels. The fact that the texts were placed in the background and presented primarily to help the reader understand minstrels, is indicative of the switch that had occurred in scholarship: as texts had taken precedence over performers in the nineteenth century, so performers took precedence over texts in the twentieth.

Sound Recordings from Kobzari and Lirnyky

The other major event of the beginning of the twentieth century was the making of the first sound recordings of minstrel performances. These recordings were done on wax cylinders, and the cylinders and the whole recording mechanism apparently presented great technical difficulties.[44] Only a very small amount of data could be entered on one cylinder, and many of the songs had to be recorded in fragmentary form for lack of space. Playing the cylinders for transcription meant wearing the wax down and making the recording progressively more scratchy and difficult to hear. Yet with all these problems, the wax recordings are invaluable, for they permitted the first accurate and extensive treatment of the music of minstrels. They give a glimpse of a traditional performance style that was soon to disappear.

The recording project was largely initiated by the poet Lesia Ukrainka, who found the ethnomusicologist Filaret Kolessa in then separate Western Ukraine and convinced him to undertake the work. She helped finance Kolessa's travels and the purchase of recording equipment; the actual recording was done by Kolessa, by Lesia Ukrainka and her husband Klement Kvitka, and by Opanas Slastion. Slastion deserves some credit for initiating this project, for he was the first to become interested in the possibility of sound recordings, and he brought the first wax cylinder equipment from Petersburg to Ukraine.[45] This project yielded Kolessa's two-volume study which included transcriptions of both verbal text and music, and data on the performers.[46] It, of course, also yielded the actual recordings which have now been copied on both record and tape and are available at the Library of Congress of the United States.

The Last Great Period of Ukrainian Folkloristics Prior to Stalin

In Western Ukraine, Volodymyr Hnatiuk, Kyryl Studynskyi, Ivan Franko, and others contributed valuable studies. In the early nineteenth century, Western Ukraine, or Galicia, did not attract much scholarly attention because this region lacked the epic texts deemed the only material worthy of study. Once attention shifted to the performers themselves, this area began to receive the attention it deserved. Studynskyi published a series of articles, including material on minstrel schools and on the secret language of minstrels.[47] Franko published studies of texts, often of genres previously considered secondary, such as lyric songs and historical songs. Hnatiuk, who was perhaps the most prolific collector of Ukrainian folklore ever, collected everything from prose texts to data on rituals; he, of course, collected data on minstrels as well. The lengthy study of Iakiv Zlatarskyi and the other *lirnyky* of Western Ukraine belongs to him.[48] Together with Sventsiitskyi, he produced a collection of Ukrainian laments and data on funerary ritual which allows us to see the parallels between laments and epics and gives valuable insight into folk ideas about the nature of the soul and about the character of life after death.[49]

In Eastern or Great Ukraine, scholarly work continued into the 1920s and early 1930s. During this period, Hrushevska's complete scholarly edition of all *duma* texts was published, and Kvitka, a musicologist, put together a questionnaire and field-work guide to be used in the collection of data about performers.[50] This guide was part of a general effort by the Academy of Sciences to record all of the genres and types of folklore in an organized way. Kharkiv collected both song texts and information about performers. But in the mid-1930s, folklore scholarship for the most part ceased. Hrushevska was unable to add to the two volumes already in print, and Kvitka himself was the only person to use his guide. Kharkiv's material was relegated to archives and reappeared only in 1972, when Borys Kyrdan published the non-fragmentary texts of *dumy*.[51] The famine in Ukraine, Stalin's liquidation of Ukrainian minstrels, and the Second World War made survival everyone's concern, and scholarship an unaffordable luxury.

The New *Kobzari*

By the time scholarship resumed during the Khrushchev Thaw of the late 1950s, the tradition had changed. Kolessa had noted the beginnings of a change in minstrelsy at the start of the twentieth century; this process was complete by the 1950s. Performer guilds no longer existed, and learning through apprenticeship was a thing of the past. As Ehor Movchan told the folklorists who interviewed him in 1958, the information about guilds and initiation which he provided was not based on first-hand knowledge; it was what he had heard from the older generation of performers, not what he had experienced. The rather plain, declamatory, recitative style of singing was also gone. The actual words of *dumy* and other minstrel songs were preserved, having been extensively recorded and published throughout the nineteenth century, and these published texts served as sources for the new *kobzari*. But the manner of presentation of these words was different, and the music was invented fairly freely, usually along more Western, conservatory-style lines.

The relative numbers of *kobzari* and *lirnyky* changed. Prior to the break in tradition caused by the Soviet Revolution and the Second World War, *lirnyky* had been more numerous than *kobzari*. The possible reasons for this are several. The *lira* is a simpler instrument to make and to play. The *bandura*, especially toward the end of the nineteenth century and the beginning of the twentieth, was getting quite complex, with the addition of more and more strings. Also, prior to the use of metal strings, the *lira* was an instrument that could produce a much louder sound than a *bandura*, making it more adaptable to uses other than accompanying a single voice. If a performer wanted to play at weddings or other places where people might dance, the *lira* was suitable. When minstrelsy was revived in the 1950s, *kobzari* far outnumbered *lirnyky*. By then, the *bandura* was a more prestigious instrument. Scholars, at least, valued it above the *lira*, not only because of its complexity, but also because they associated it, through its antecedent *kobza*, with the Cossack milieu in which they theorized high genres, such as the *duma*, originated. People taking up singing at a time when scholarly opinion took precedence over traditional practice naturally gravitated toward the instrument preferred by scholars.

The studies published in this period were monographs about individual performers, such as works on Evhen Adamtsevych, Ehor Movchan, and Fedir Kushneryk, who, while traditionally trained or familiar with traditional minstrels, nonetheless functioned in the very different circumstances of the Soviet milieu.[52] The interviews upon which these studies were based may yield valuable information about the oral process and about a transitional period in minstrelsy. The published materials are of limited usefulness because all of the biographies are so similar—they seem based on Soviet formulas for a proper minstrel life rather than on the real lives of performers.

Very important recent publications on minstrels which seek to combine general information about performers with biographies of individual minstrels are the studies by Fedir Lavrov and Borys Kyrdan and Andrii Omelchenko.[53] Kyrdan and Omelchenko in particular draw on archival sources and the various articles published in the nineteenth century. Kyrdan's work on the scholars of Ukrainian folklore is of major significance, as are his efforts to compare folk texts. Kyrdan's study of several versions of an epic song from a single performer, Mykhailo Kravchenko, is also valuable, as are his efforts to continue Hrushevska's work by publishing archival texts.[54]

Appendix

Tables and Charts

Table 1

List of Married Men

Bilokarpatskyi
Blokha, Trokhim Fedotych
Bratytsia, Pavlo Savych
Chub, Prokip Mykhailovych (also called Dub)
Dimnych, Oleksandr
Dovhaliuk, Andrii
Drevchenko, Petro Semenovych
Dudka, Nykifor
Homyniuk, Ananii Savvovych
Honcharenko, Hnat Tykhonovych
Humeniuk, Sydor
Iaremenko, Roman
Ivanytskyi, Antin
Khrystenko, Makar
Kornienko, Andrii Panteliemonovych
Kravchenko, Mykhailo Stepanovych
Kravchenko-Kriukovskyi, Ivan
Kuchuhura-Kucherenko, Ivan
Kulyk, Pavlo
Kushneryk, Fedir
Merezhka, Ivan Kherlamovych
Mokroviz, Evdokim Mykytych
Moroz, Vasylii
Nikon (no last name given)
Parkhomenko, Terentii Makarovych
Perepelytsia, Efim

Petryk, Ivan Mykhailovych
Riadkov, Arsenii Danylovych
Romanenko, Ivan
Shuga, Musii
Shut, Andrii
Skubii, Ivan Mykolaiovych
Slastion, Opanas Hryhorovych
Symonenko, Demian Havrylovych
Tkachenko, Hryhorii Kyrylovych
Tkachenko, Petro
Veresai, Ostap Mykytovych
Vlasko, Semen Sydorovych
Zlatarskyi, Iakiv

Chart I

Apprenticeship

Minstrel name	Age at beginning of apprenticeship	Years of study
Blokha, Nazar		2.5
Doroshenko, Mykolai	11	2.5
Dovhaliuk, Andrii	3	
Dub, Prokip	16	
Dubyna, Mykola	1	
Dudka, Nykifor	13	3.0
Harasko, Petro	2	
Homyniuk, Ananii	23	1
Honcharenko, Hnat	20	1
Hovtan, Vasyl	14	6
Hryshko, Oleksandr	2	
Hrytsenko, Fedir	15	5
Huz, Petro	2	
Ivanytskyi, Antin	15	2
Khrystenko, Makar	1	
Kravchenko, Mykhailo	17	9
Kravchenko-Kriukovskyi, Ivan	18	
Kuzminskyi, Kyrylo	3	
Mokroviz, Evdokim	15	1
Moroz, Vasylii	6	
Movchan, Ehor	8	2
Okhremenko, Iahor	10	2
Parkhomenko, Terentii	15	1
Pobihailo, Oleksii	25	
Skubii, Ivan	3	
Slastion, Opanas	20	
Symonenko, Demian	17	
Veresai, Ostap	15	1
Vlasko, Semen	3	
Zlatarskyi, Iakiv	7?	6

Note: This information was extracted from a variety of sources. As Speranskii and others point out, minstrels will give different information on different occasions. Speranskii notes the contradictory information he received from Parkhomenko, and Studnytskyi reports similar problems with the *lirnyky* he interviewed.

Chart II

Apprenticeship (Speranskii's data)

Minstrel name	Age when minstrel became blind	Age at beginning of apprenticeship	Years of study
Babenko	14	17	2
Bohyshchenko			1 yr., 2 mos.
Butenko	7	16	
Dub	4	14	
Dubrova	5	12	2
Harasko			1 yr., 6 mos.
Homyniuk	5	22	1
Kaliberha	2	2	
Kornienko	10	3	
Kutsyi	12	17	3
Mokroviz	10	15	1 yr., 2 mos.
Okhremenko	birth	10	2
Parkhomenko	10	15	1
Prikhodko	5	15	1 yr., 6 mos.
Veresai	15	3	
Zozulia	18	22	

Source: Speranskii, p. 116. See also note to Chart I.

Chart III

Minstrel Earnings

Babenko	20 to 40 kopeks per day, sometimes 60
Butenko	30 kopeks to 1 ruble per day
Dubrova	20 to 49 kopeks per day, 50 at fairs
Dudkin	30 to 40 rubles per month
Kaliberha	20 to 60 kopeks per day
Netesa	up to one ruble per day
Okhremenko	up to 10 rubles per month
Parkhomenko (while he worked in villages only)	200 rubles per year
Petryk	3 to 7 rubles per week
Riadkov	25 to 50 rubles a month
Vlasko	200 rubles per year
lirnyky in Chernihiv	40 to 50 rubles in a 6 to 7 week trip
lirnyky in Podile	20 kopeks to 1 ruble per day

Notes

Notes to Preface

1. Kateryna Hrushevs'ka, *Ukraiins'ki narodni dumy*. 2 vols. Kharkiv-Kiev: Derzhavne vydavnytstvo Ukraiiny, 1927–31.

2. Boris P. Kirdan, *Ukrainskie narodnye dumy*. Moscow: Nauka, 1972.

3. For a discussion of Soviet folklore and its authenticity, see Frank J. Miller, *Folklore for Stalin: Russian Folklore and Pseudofolklore of the Stalin Era*. Armonk, New York, and London, England: M.E. Sharpe, 1990.

4. Albert B. Lord, *Singer of Tales*. Cambridge, Massachusetts and London: Harvard University Press, 1960, pp. 18–20.

5. Both blind minstrels and beggars are called *did*, meaning "old man," "grandfather," and *starets*, meaning "old person," "elder."

6. Scholars simply did not collect minstrel material, such as folktales, that was known also by non-professionals. Porfiryi Martynovych is one of the few collectors who gathered such texts. See his archives (fond 11–4) in the Ukrainian Academy of Sciences Institute of Folkart, Folklore, and Ethnography (*Institut mystets'va, fol'kloru, ta etnografii imeni Ryl's'koho*, henceforth IMFE). The Martynovych manuscripts indicate that were was also a category of magical texts which minstrels simply did not reveal to anyone except someone close to themselves, like Martynovych.

7. M. Speranskii, *Iuzhno-russkaia pesnia i sovremennye ee nositeli (po povodu bandurista T.M. Parkhomenka)*. Kiev, 1904. B. Kyrdan and A. Omel'chenko, *Narodni spivtsi-muzykanty na Ukraiini*. Kiev: Muzychna Ukraina, 1980. Fedir Lavrov, *Kobzari, Narys z istorii kobzarstva Ukraiiny*. Kiev: Mystetstvo, 1980.

Notes to Chapter 1

1. *Duma* about the Strus brothers, dated 1506, as described in Hrushevs'ka, vol. I, p. XIII.

2. A number of scholars argue that minstrelsy must have come into being at a date close to the dates of the earliest historical events reflected in minstrel songs. See, for example, P.D. Pavlii's introduction to *Ukraiins'ki narodni dumy ta istorychni pisni*. Kiev: Vydavnytstvo akademii nauk ukraiins'koii RSR, 1955, pp. 52–56.

3. Filaret Kolessa, *Melodii ukraiins'kykh narodnykh dum*. Kiev: Naukova Dumka, 1969, pp. 311–16.

4. Vil'am Noll, "Parallel'na kul'tura v Ukraiini u period Stalinizmu." *Rodovid*, 1993, no. 6, pp. 37–38.

5. The nature of the Sovietization of culture has been described by many. See Noll, above, and Miller, *Folklore for Stalin*, pp. 3–24, for Stalinist alterations as they apply specifically to folklore. Miller also discusses the composition of new material on Communist topics.

6. My interviews, dated October 21, 1987 and November 21, 1987. Total blindness means loss of all sight, including the ability to distinguish between night and day. Total blindness frequently has health consequences such as insomnia and headaches, problems that affect Nadiia Suprun and are reported in the accounts of nineteenth-century minstrels.

7. June 1 and June 15, 1994.

8. June 1, 1994.

9. June 1 and June 15, 1994.

10. November 21, 1987.

11. October 21, 1987.

12. November 21, 1987.

13. August 28, 1990.

14. Telephone conversation, December 30, 1995.

15. N. Kononenko, "Duma pro Chornobyl: Old Genres; New Topics." *Journal of Folklore Research*, 1992, vol. 29, no. 2, pp. 133–54. Suprun expressed his displeasure with pressure to sing only happy songs on June 15, 1994 and again on December 30, 1995.

16. When I visited the Supruns in August 1993, I was rather startled by the fact that a television set now stood in the living room of a blind couple. Nadiia Suprun explained that the news on television was different from the news on radio and that she and her husband listened to both so that they could keep their neighbors better informed.

17. During the tense *perestroika* period, the difference between Suprun and sighted performers was quite striking. All of the sighted singers were afraid of foreigners and attempted to protect themselves in some way: by refusing to see Americans, by feigning illness, or by arranging meetings where a party operative could be present to vouch for their loyalty to the Soviet state.

18. One example is a blind family—mother, father, and teenage boy—I saw singing at a car auction in 1994. They did not play any musical instruments and were primarily beggars, not performers. They were willing to sing amidst the din of auctioneering and car repairs because artistry was not their primary goal. This family can best be compared to the mendicants who functioned alongside minstrels in nineteenth- and early twentieth-century Ukraine.

19. See, for example, the list of *kobzari* and *lirnyky* in V.I. Domanitskii, "Kobzari i lirniki Kievskoi gubernii v 1903 godu." *Pamiatnaia kniga Kievskoi gubernii*, 1904, no. 4, pp. 17–65.

20. V. Iastrebov, "Gaidamatskii bandurist." *Kievskaia starina*, 1886, vol. X, pp. 378–88.

21. For published texts collected from a woman performer, here Iavdokhia Iukhimivna Pylypenko, see Kolessa, *Melodii*, pp. 216–26.

22. IMFE fond 11–4.

23. Baida is probably Dmytro Vyshnevets'kyi, executed in 1563, *starosta* of Kaniv and founder of the Cossack stronghold that laid the basis for the Zaphorozhian Sich. Semen Palii was leader of the Right-Bank Cossacks in the 1702–3 uprising against the Poles. Ivan Sirko was a late seventeenth-century leader of the Left-Bank Cossacks known for his courage.

24. In the Martynovych manuscripts, there are lyric songs and prose narratives, alongside the genres usually associated with a minstrel's repertory.

25. Hryhorii Polunets told Martynovych that there were different types of begging songs and that a special type was to be used at fairs. IMFE fond 11–4/903, ark. 21.

26. See Valerian Borzhkovskii, "Lirniki."*Kievskaia starina*, 1889, vol. IX, pp. 662–65 for the most complete description of a religious festival available (translated in Part 2

of this volume). Borzhkovskii reports that at least one minstrel refused to sing the epic about Konovchenko at a church festival because he feared that he would be attacked for singing something other than religious verse. He reports a similar reaction to a request for "Panshchyna," a song about Polish domination that could be interpreted as a song of social protest.

27. See, for example, Mykola Lysenko's transcription of the dance tunes in the repertory of Ostap Veresai, in *Kharakterystyka muzychnykh osoblyvostei ukraiins'kykh dum i pisen' u vykonanni kobzaria Veresaia*. Kiev: Muzychna Ukraina, 1978, pp. 81–90.

28. IMFE fond 6–2/23(2), ark. 55 and 64.

29. Hrushevs'ka, vol. I, p. viii. The minstrel in question is Ryhorenko who was forced to sell his *bandura* to make ends meet.

Notes to Chapter 2

1. For a discussion of the poetics of begging songs and a list of published sources, see Volodymyr Shchepot'ev, "Starechi prokhannia." *Etnohrafichnyi zbirnyk*, 1928, vol. 6, pp. 30–34. What Shchepot'ev views as a single line should, I believe, be seen as two lines of verse. Pages 35–39 provide begging song texts.

2. Borzhkovskii, "Lirniki," pp. 655–57.

3. Compare the begging song published by Borzhkovskii already cited to the one he gives on pp. 660–61 or to the one published by V. Danilov, "Sredi nishchei bratii." *Zhivaia starina*, 1907, vol. IV, pp. 204–6 and Shchepot'ev, cited above.

4. Borzhkovskii, pp. 656, 655; IMFE fond 6–4/161/4, ark. 22 (begging song collected from *lirnyk* Varion Honchar by Volodymyr Kharkiv).

5. Borzhkovskii, p. 655; Kharkiv, ark. 22; IMFE fond 11–4/589, ark. 18, collected by Martynovych from the *lirnyk* Doroshenko.

6. These statements appear in all the begging songs already listed and also in IMFE fond 11–4/715, collected by Martynovych from the *lirnyk* Ivan Peresada; and in IMFE fond 11–4/940, ark. 1–2, collected by Martynovych from the *kobzar* Kuchuhura-Kucherenko. The parts about dying or rotting in the womb are from Borzhkovskii, p. 661.

7. Borzhkovskii, p. 655; Kharkiv, ark. 22.

8. Borzhkovskii, p. 657; Martynovych from Kuchuhura-Kucherenko and from Doroshenko. The Paraskovia version is from Kuchuhura-Kucherenko, ark. 2.

9. IMFE fond 6–2/23, ark. 51.

10. IMFE fond 11–4/589, ark. 18.

11. The renewed importance of ritual cloths in connection with baptisms, weddings, and funerals is attested by the posting of a fee schedule on the door of St. Volodymyr's, the largest church in Kiev. The fee schedule lists two prices, one if the celebrant provides his or her own ritual cloth (*rushnyk*), and one if he or she needs to borrow a ritual cloth from the church. Personal communication from Anne Marie Ingram, June 1995.

12. Martynovych from Doroshenko, IMFE fond 11–4/589, ark. 18; Borzhkovskii, pp. 655–57; Kharkiv, IMFE fond 6–4/161/4, ark. 22. Kharkiv's informant says that if the standard begging song does not prompt the audience to give alms, the singer may add a special appeal to those who have lost young relatives: "Don't you have someone who has died, any relatives, any small children, anyone who needs a mendicant's prayers?"

13. For two texts of songs of thanks, see Martynovych, 11–4/589, ark. 18.

14. P. Demuts'kyi, *Lira i iii motivy*; zibrav v Kyiivshchyni P. Demuts'kyi. Kiev: Notopechatnaia i drukarnia I.I. Cholokova, 1903, p. vi.

15. Demuts'kyi, pp. 8–9.

16. Demuts'kyi, pp. 43–46.

17. Demuts'kyi, p. 1. The fact that the Virgin releases sinners from Heaven as well as Hell may be a remnant of a pre-Christian belief system which had a single place where all people, no matter how they had behaved on earth, went after death. If all the dead went to a single place, it would make sense that the Virgin could then separate out the righteous and restore them to life.

18. Demuts'kyi, pp. 39–42.

19. Demuts'kyi, p. 22.

20. Demuts'kyi, pp. 52–54.

21. Demuts'kyi, pp. 15–20.

22. Demuts'kyi, pp. 23–25. The song about St. Nicholas was so popular that it existed in two versions, a longer one called "The Greater Nicholas" and a shorter one called "The Lesser Nicholas." The latter was one of the so-called women's religious songs (see chapter 4).

23. Demuts'kyi, pp. 54–56; Borzhkovskii, p. 664.

24. D. Revuts'kyi, *Ukraiins'ki dumy ta pisni istorychni.* Kharkiv/Kiev: Derzhavne vydavnytstvo Ukraiiny, 1930, pp. 157–58.

25. Amvrosii Metlinskii, *Narodnye iuzhnorusskie pesni.* Kiev: Universitetskaia tipografiia, 1854, pp. 359–60.

26. For Varvara, see Demuts'kyi, pp. 27–29. Baida is in V. Antonovich and M. Dargomanov. *Istoricheskie pesni malorusskogo naroda.* Kiev: Izdatel'stvo russkogo imperatorskogo geograficheskogo obshchestva, 1874–75, vol. I, pp. 145–48. "The Death of Perebiinis" is in the same collection, vol. II, pp. 42–46, and "Danylo Nechai" is in vol. II, pp. 55–75, 13 variants.

27. Antonovich and Dragomanov, vol. I, pp. 270–73, four variants.

28. Antonovich and Dragomanov, vol. I, pp. 85–88 (the sisters) and 286–91 (mother and daughter).

29. An example of a historical song about Mazepa can be found in Revuts'kyi, pp. 165–66. Mazepa (1639–1709) was the hetman of the Left-Bank Cossacks. He was a close advisor to Peter the Great and succeeded in joining Right-Bank to Left-Bank Ukraine. Feeling betrayed by Peter, and militarily threatened, he led an unsuccessful revolt against Moscow in 1708.

30. Roman Jakobson, "Slavic Epic Verse: Studies in Comparative Metrics." *Selected Writings.* The Hague and Paris: Mouton and Co., vol. IV, 1966, pp. 414–63.

31. Kharkiv, IMFE fond 6–2/23(2), ark. 52; Martynovych, IMFE fond 11–4/714, labels various items as *rozkaz*. Some are verse and some are prose; all have serious subject matter.

32. "Dve lirnitskie pesni,"*Kievskaia starina*, 1889, vol. XII, pp. 637–40.

33. Lysenko, *Kharakterystyka muzychnykh osoblyvostei*, pp. 66–67.

34. Borzhkovskii, "Dve lirnitskie pesni," pp. 640–42.

35. Kharkiv, IMFE fond 6–2/23(2), ark. 51 is one example.

36. Lysenko, *Kharakterystyka muzychnykh osoblyvostei*, pp. 70–77.

37. See the epic Ivas' (or Ivan) Konovchenko in Hrushevs'ka. vol. I, pp. 12–106, 42 variants, and Kirdan, *Ukrainskie narodnye dumy*, pp. 224–57, 6 variants, for an example of defeat in battle as a result of a mother's curse. See the epic "The Widow" (*Udova*) Hrushevs'ka, vol. II, pp. 233–76, 42 variants, and Kirdan, pp. 346–84, 14 variants, for crop failure which comes when sons mistreat their mother.

38. Satirical songs may have been part of a wake (see chapter 10). This may have been the situation in the nineteenth and twentieth centuries as well as earlier, but documentation is not available.

39. Demuts'kyi, pp. 56–58.

40. See Kharkiv, 6–2/23(1), ark. 71, IMFE fond, for a discussion of memory (*hortan*).

Notes to Chapter 3

1. Such annual meetings may, in fact, have occurred. See, for example, P. Efimenko, "Bratstva i soiuzy nishchikh." *Kievskaia starina*, vol. VII, pp. 314–15.

2. *Powiesci Jozefa Dzierzkowskiego*, vol. II, "Krol dziadow," Lwow, 1875 as quoted in Kyrylo Studyns'kyi, "Lirnyky, Studiia," *Zoria*, 1894, p. 257.

3. The translation is from Studyns'kyi's "Lirnyky," p. 258. His references are "Dziadowska biesiada," "Dziadowskie rody," "Niespodziewany koniec" in Dzierzkowskii, Series IX, pp. 273–82. Lazarus, referring to the figure in religious song, is emblematic of the righteous, disabled sufferer.

4. IMFE fond 11–4/594, ark. 3.

5. V.P. Gorlenko, "Kobzari i lirniki." *Kievskaia starina*, vol. VIII, 1884, pp. 24–25.

6. IMFE fond 3–6/356, ark. 70.

7. N.F. Sumtsov, "O pokrovitel'stve kobzariam i lirnikam," p. 402; A. Malinka, "Kobzari i lirniki Terentii Parkhomenko, Nikifor Dudka i Aleksei Pobehailo." *Zemskii sbornik Chernigovskoi guberni*, 1903, no. 4, p. 61; Ignat Khotkevich, "Neskol'ko slov ob Ukrainskikh banduristakh i lirnikakh." *Etnograficheskoe obozrenie*, 1903, vol. 2, p. 102; Konstantin Bich-Lubenskii, "Banduristy i lirniki na Khar'kovskom XII arkheologicheskom s"ezde." *Russkaia muzykal'naia gazeta*, 1902, no. 37, p. 835.

8. Lesia Ukrainka, letter to Filaret Kolessa, March 18, 1913, *Zibrannia tvoriv u dvanadtsiaty tomakh*. Kiev: Naukova dumka, 1979, vol. 12, pp. 446–47.

9. Klyment Kvitka, "Profesional'ny narodni spivtsi i muzykanty na Ukraiini. Prohrama dlia doslidu iikh diial'nosti i pobutu." *Izbrannye trudy v dvukh tomakh*, Moscow: Sovetskii kompozitor, 1973, vol. 2, pp. 289–96.

10. Hrushevs'ka, *Ukraiins'ki narodni dumy*, vol. I, p. cx.

11. Lavrov, *Kobzari*. pp. 30–31. See also IMFE 1–4/248, M. Polotai's information on Petro Tkachenko, which notes the latter's political activity.

12. Interview, March 30, 1996.

13. IMFE 3–3/134, ark. 100. Another copy is IMFE 3–3/376, ark. 36.

14. Speranskii, *Iuzhno-russkaia pesnia*, p. 108.

15. *Trudy XII Arkheologicheskogo S"ezda v Khar'kove*, vol. II, pp. 386–87.

16. IMFE fond 11–4/940, ark. 13.

17. IMFE fond 11–4/810, ark. 2.

18. O. Slastion(ov), "Kobzar' Mikhailo Kravchenko i ego dumy." *Kievskaia starina*, 1902, vol. V, pp. 313–14.

19. Kyrdan and Omel'chenko, p. 96–97; V. Hnatiuk, "Lirnyky, lirnyts'ki pisni, molytvy, slova, zvistky." *Etnohrafynyi zbirnyk*, 1896, vol. II, p. 8.

20. IMFE fond 11–4/940, ark. 12. Minstrels were not supposed to reveal the details of apprenticeship. Nonetheless, Martynovych recorded detailed accounts from the *lirnyk* Petro Dryhavka and the *kobzar* Ivan Kuchuhura-Kucherenko. Both Dryhavka and Kuchuhura-Kucherenko listed much of the specific information which a master imparts to his pupil: highly structured, formulaic sayings which seem to have been developed over a long period of time. Prohibitions against drink are among these formulaic sayings.

21. IMFE fond 11–4/592, ark. 46. The informant seems to be Hrytsenko.

22. IMFE fond 6–2/23(1), ark. 71.

23. IMFE fond 11–4/940, ark. 3–4.

24. IMFE fond 11–4/940, ark. 12.

25. Panteleimon Kulish, *Zapiski o iuzhnoi Rusi*. St. Petersburg, vol. I, 1856, pp. 45–50.

26. Borzhkovskii, p. 666.

27. Borzhkovskii, p. 672. The statement in Borzhkovskii's article reads as follows:

"Christ chose twelve pupils and twelve apostles for the preaching of his word, and upon his ascension, he added the blind and the lame."

28. Martinovich, *Ukrain's'ki zapisi Porfiriia Martinovicha*, 1906, pp. 52–53.

29. Slastion(ov), "Kobzar' Mikhailo Kravchenko i ego dumy," pp. 304–5.

30. Grigorii Bazilevich, "Mestechko Aleksandrovka Chernigovskoi gubernii, Sosnitskogo uezda," *Etnograficheskii sbornik*, 1853, no. 1, pp. 329–33.

31. M. Hrinchenko and F. Lavrov, *Kobzar Fedir Kushneryk*. Kiev: Tsentral'na drukarnia naukovoho tovarystva URSR, 1940, p. 24; Malynka, "Kobzari Semen Vlasko, Dem'ian Symonenko, ta lirnyk Antin Ivanyts'kyi: ikhnii repertuar," *Pervisne hromo-dianstvo*, 1929, pp. 105–7.

32. Taras Shevchenko, "Perebendia," *Kobzar*, Kiev: Dnipro, 1976, pp. 44–47.

33. Cossacks shaved their entire heads except for one section at the very top. Here they left a circle of hair approximately three inches in diameter and let it grow out as long as it would go. This lock of long hair is called a *chupryna*. Legend has it that the *chupryna* is part of warrior bravado, a handle by which the enemy could carry a Cossack's head, should he succeed in severing it.

34. Slastion(ov), "Kobzar' Mikhailo Kravchenko i ego dumy," pp. 307–8.

35. Martynovych, "Pan Tvardovs'kyi, liakh: Spohady pro kobzariv," IMFE fond 11–4/594, ark. 3.

36. Quoted in Kyrdan and Omel'chenko, p. 119.

37. Slastion(ov), "Kobzar' Mikhailo Kravchenko i ego dumy," p. 308. "Bulo iak siade, iak zashkriaba, iak zatuzhyt', to i sam plache, i vsi za nym, a midiaki to iak toi horokh, til'ky tr . . . , tr . . . , tr . . ."

38. Kyrdan and Omel'chenko, p. 118; Slastion, p. 308.

39. Slastion, "Kobzar' Mikhailo Kravchenko i ego dumy," p. 308.

40. Martynovych, IMFE fond 11–4/594, ark. 2–3. A *karbovanets* is roughly equivalent to a Russian ruble.

41. Zhemchuzhnikov's collection efforts are noteworthy. He included some unprecedented and very valuable accounts of audience reaction and the circumstances of performance. He also provided the first description of the process by which a master *lirnyk* taught his apprentice. See Lev M. Zhemchuzhnikov, "Poltavshchina (Iz zapisnoi knizhki 1856 goda)." *Osnova*, 1861, no. X, pp. 77–90; and *Moi vospominaniia iz proshlogo*, Leningrad, 1927.

42. A.A. Rusov, "Ostap Veresai, odin iz poslednikh kobzarei malorusskikh," *Zapiski Iugo-zapadnogo otdela russkogo geograficheskogo obshchestva*, vol. I, Kiev, 1874, pp. 309–37 (contains the texts recorded by Chubyns'kyi as an appendix). Lysenko, "Kharakterystyka muzychnykh osoblyvostei," first appeared following Rusov's article in the same volume, pp. 338–60.

43. "Kief et le congres archeologique: souvenirs de vojage, par M. Alfred Rambaud," *Revue des deux Mondes*, vol. VI, pp. 801–35.

44. My field work in Kiev and L'viv, 1987. Hryhorii Tkachenko and Pavlo Suprun would proudly tell me that a song they were about to perform was the Veresai version. The only other reference to any sort of authorship was to recent *kobzari*, and usually made when the item about to be sung was a new composition by one of these men.

45. As quoted in Kyrdan and Omel'chenko, pp. 109–11.

46. See, for example, B.P. Kirdan's history of nineteenth-century scholarship, *Sobirateli narodnoi poezii: Iz istorii ukrainskoi fol'kloristiki XIX veka*, Moscow: Nauka, 1974.

47. Oleksa Horbach, *Argo ukraiins'kykh lirnykiv*, Munich: Naukovy zapysky Ukraiins'koho vil'noho universytetu, 1957, pp. 7–44 and separately; *Zbirnyk narodnykh pisen' i dum* (no author, collector, or date given), Winnipeg: Ukrainian Publishing;

George Tarnawsky and Patricia Kilina, translators, *Ukrainian Dumy; editio minor*, Toronto and Cambridge: Canadian Institute of Ukrainian Studies and Harvard Ukrainian Research Institute, 1979; Zenovii Shtokalko, *Kobzars'kyi pidruchnyk*, ed. Andrij Hornjatkevych, Edmonton/Kiev: Canadian Institute of Ukrainian Studies, 1992.

48. Malinka, "Zametki o dvukh lirnikakh Chernigovskoi gubernii, Alekseia Terent'evicha Masliukova i Egoria Esinovicha Okhremenko," *Etnograficheskoe obozrenie*, 1902, vol. 2, p. 149.

49. Efimenko, "Bratstva i soiuzy nishchikh," p. 314.

50. Borzhkovskii, p. 672.

51. Interview with Pavlo Suprun, March 31, 1996.

52. Speranskii, pp. 106–7; Studyns'kyi, p. 258.

53. Borzhkovskii, "Lirniki," pp. 665–68.

54. Borzhkovskii, p. 674.

55. Borzhkovskii, p. 670.

56. Kharkiv, IMFE, fond 6–2/23 (1), ark. 51.

57. Efimenko, "Shpitali v Malorossii," *Kievskaia starina*, 1883, vol. IV, pp. 723–25.

58. Horbach, p. 10.

59. Lavrov, *Kobzari*, p. 30–38; see also the description of Petro Tkachenko's revolutionary activities, IMFE fond 1–4/248.

Notes to Chapter 4

1. See, for example, Rose L. Glickman, "Peasant Women and Their Work," in Beatrice Farnsworth and Lynne Viola, eds., *Russian Peasant Women*, New York/Oxford: Oxford University Press, 1992, pp. 54–72.

2. Cathy A. Frierson, "*Razdel*: The Peasant Family Divided," in *Russian Peasant Women*, pp. 73–88.

3. Nancy M. Frieden, "Child Care: Medical Reform in a Traditionalist Culture," in David L. Ransel, ed., *The Family in Imperial Russia*, Urbana/Chicago/London: University of Illinois Press, 1978, pp. 236–59.

4. The belief that running water is pure became evident after the 1986 Chornobyl disaster, when peasants continued to drink such water even though it was contaminated with radiation.

5. "Territorial'noe raspredelenie ostro-zaraznykh boleznei," *Trudy Pirogovskoi Komissii po rasprostraneniiu gigienicheskikh znanii v narod*, addendum pp. 4–49.

6. V.V. Khizhniakov, *O bolezni glaz nazyvaemoi trakhomoiu: Kak uberech' ot trakhomy svoi glaza i ne peredat' ee drugim. Sovety zdorovym i bol'nym*, Pirogov Commission, pamphlet no. 11, Moscow, 1901.

7. Pirogov Commission, pamphlet no. 11.

8. Andrii Shut, Ivan Kravchenko-Kriukovs'kyi, Mykhailo Kravchenko, and others are reported as making harnesses and ropes. Kravchenko-Kriukovs'kyi complained that the hemp used in rope-making did terrible things to his finger-tips and interfered with his playing the *bandura*. V. Gorlenko, "Bandurist Ivan Kriukovskii (tekst deviati dum s biograficheskoi zametkoi)," *Kievskaia starina*, 1882, vol. 12, p. 484; F. Kolessa, *Melodii Ukrains'kikh narodnikh dum*, p. 101. According to material collected by Kharkiv in 1930, Nazar Denisovych Bokish made not only ropes, but *liry*, for himself and for sale; IMFE, fond 6–4, 161/4, ark. 27. See also Polotai, "Notatka pro kobzaria Tkachenka (Halushku)," IMFE fond 1–4, ark. 248.

9. Kharkiv, "Vidomosti pro lirnykiv, kobzariv ta sopilkariv," IMFE fond 6–4, ark. 185.

10. Malinka, "Kobzari i lirniki Terentii Parkhomenko, Nikifor Dudka i Aleksei Pobehailo," pp. 70–71.

11. IMFE fond 11–4/673, ark. 22; collected 1904, no performer given.

12. Volodymyr Kharkiv, "Sposterezhennia nad lirnykamy ta kobzariamy Val'kivs'koho raionu na Kharkivshchyni: Dopovid chytana na zasidanni Etnohrafichnoii Komisii VUAN, 1929," IMFE fond 6–2/23(2), ark. 48.

13. See, for example, Amfian Lebedev's discussion of the role and meaning of charity, "Izmeneniia v dukhe i napravlenii blagotvoritel'nosti v period torzhestva khristianstva; Blagotvoritel'nye uchrezhdeniia drevnikh khristian; Drevnie monastyri so storony ikh blagotvoritel'noi deiatel'nosti." *Sbornik Khar'kovskogo istoriko-filologicheskogo obshchestva*, vol. 15, 1908, pp. 251–68.

14. V. Danilov, "Sredi nishchei bratii," pp. 202–3.

15. Malinka, "Kobzari i lirniki." *Zemskii sbornik Chernigovskoi gubernii*, 1903, no. 4, pp. 66–70; Malinka, "Svedeniia poluchenye ot A. Malinki," *Trudy XII Arkheologicheskogo s"ezda v Khar'kove*, vol. 3, Moscow, 1905, p. 408.

16. Malinka, "Zametki o dvukh lirnikakh," pp. 148–60; the part about the cup is on p. 149.

17. Malinka, "Prokop Chub: Perekhodnyi tip kobzaria," *Etnograficheskoe obozrenie*, 1892, vol. 4, p.166 and Malinka, "Lirnik Andrii Kornienko," *Kievskaia starina*, 1895, p. 59; Malynka, "Kobzari Semen Vlasko, Dem'ian Symonenko, ta lirnyk Antin Ivanyts'kyi, pp. 105–7; Malinka, "Lirnik Evdokim Mykytovich Mokroviz," *Kievskaia starina*, 1894, vol. IX, p. 434; E. Chikalenko, "Lirnik Vasilii Moroz," *Kievskaia starina*, 1896, vol. III, p. 79.

18. P.E. Petrov, "K repertuaru lirnikov," vypusk I, Nezhin, 1913; D. Revuts'kyi, Iu. Vynohrads'kyi, T. Pashchenko, F. Senhalevych, "Kobzari i lirnyky," *Etnohrafichnyi visnyk*, bk. 3, Kiev 1926, pp. 64–69. The diagnosis that colds and hypothermia can cause blindness would not stand up to contemporary medical scrutiny, but chills were greatly feared by nineteenth-century peasants, who believed them to be the cause of a great variety of aches and illnesses.

19. Malinka, "Kobzar' Petro Haras'ko i Lirnik Maksym Pryshchenko," *Kievskaia starina*, 1893, vol. IX, p. 441.

20. Malinka, "Lirnik Ananii Savvovich Homyniuk," *Kievskaia starina*, 1898, vol. X, Dokumenty, p. 1. For a discussion of the meanings of *chorna bolist'* or *chorna khvoroba* (also black sickness), see Viktor Petrov, "Viruvannia u vykhor i chorna khvoroba,"*Etnohrafichnyi visnyk*, bk. 3, Kiev, 1926, pp. 102–16.

21. M.T. Ryl's'kyi and F.I. Lavrov, *Kobzar Ehor Movchan*, Kiev: Akademiia Nauk URSR, 1958, p. 18.

22. Martynovych, IMFE fond 11–4/ 594, ark. 55.

23. Malynka, "Kobzari Semen Vlasko, Dem'ian Simonenko, ta lirnyk Antin Ivanyts'kyi," pp. 105–7; Borzhkovskii, "Lirniki," pp. 668–69; Malinka, "Zametki o dvukh lirnikakh Chernigovskoi gubernii," p. 158; Hnatiuk, "Lirnyky," p. 8.

24. Hrinchenko and Lavrov, *Kobzar Fedir Kushneryk*, pp. 21–24.

25. A. Rusov, "Kobzar' Ostap Veresai; ego muzyka i ispolniaemye im narodnye pesni," *Zapiski Iugo-zapadnogo otdela Russkogo geograficheskogo obshchestva*, vol. I, Kiev, 1874, p. 316.

26. Malinka, "Kobzar' Petro Haras'ko i Lirnik Maksim Pryshchenko," pp. 441–42.

27. Borzhkovskii, "Lirniki," pp. 668–69.

28. Hrinchenko and Lavrov, *Kobzar Fedir Kushneryk*, pp. 23–24.

29. Malynka, "Kobzari Vlasko, Symonenko, ta lirnyk Ivanyts'kyi," pp. 105–7.

30. Martinovich, *Ukrain's'ki zapisi*, pp. 52–53. The biography published by Martynovych ends soon after the well incident. Martynovych's work, while one of the earliest collections of data on performers, was not published until the turn of the century. Furthermore, what did finally appear is labeled a fragment. In the Martynovych manu-

scripts available in the archives of IMFE, there is no material on Ivan Kravchenko-Kriukovs'kyi other than what has already appeared in print. The manuscript is labeled a fragment, just like the printed autobiography. Some information on the rest of Kravchenko-Kriukovs'kyi's life is available from Horlenko. Using Martynovych's data and possibly data from other sources, Horlenko published a long article on Kravchenko-Kriukovs'kyi in 1882. See below.

31. V. Gorlenko, "Bandurist Ivan Kriukovskii (tekst deviati dum, s biograficheskoi zametkoi)," *Kievskaia starina*, 1882, vol. XII, pp. 483. It is noteworthy that Horlenko's article makes no mention of the beatings. It simply states that Kravchenko-Kriukovs'kyi went blind at the age of fifteen. (Martynovych's biography, p. 52, gives the age of blindness as ten.) Kravchenko-Kriukovs'kyi's biography is unique. Virtually all of the others attribute blindness to illness, if they give the cause at all. Horlenko's failure to mention injuries, however, makes it seem possible that what happened to Kravchenko-Kriukovs'kyi happened to others and simply went unreported. After all, Horlenko was quite familiar with Ukrainian minstrelsy. He published extensively on performers and did much of his own collecting. If someone so knowledgeable chose not to mention the beatings, it is possible that injury was the reason for blindness in at least some of the cases where no cause is given.

32. Martynovych, IMFE fond 11–4/589 (1885–86), ark. 19.

33. "Kolektsiia Iavronyts'koho," IMFE fond 8–60, ark. 88.

34. Slastion(ov), "Kobzar' Mikhailo Kravchenko i ego dumy," p. 313.

35. Iavronyts'kyi, IMFE fond 8–60, ark. 88

36. Malinka, "Kobzar' Petro Haras'ko i Lirnik Maksim Pryshchenko," p. 441–42.

37. Hnatiuk, "Lirnyky," p. 8.

38. Chikalenko, "Lirnik Vasilii Moroz," p. 82.

39. Martynovych, IMFE fond 11–4/592, ark. 55.

40. Malinka, "Kobzari i lirniki Terentii Parkhomenko, Nikifor Dudka, i Aleksei Pobehailo," p. 9.

41. Malynka, "Kobzari Vlasko, Symonenko, ta lirnyk Ivanyts'kyi," pp. 105–7.

42. Malinka, "Lirnik Ananii Savvovich Homyniuk," p. 1.

43. Kharkiv, IMFE fond 6–2/23(2), ark. 50. See especially the interview with Kolisnyk.

44. Malinka, "Zametki o dvukh lirnikakh Chernigovskoi guberni," p. 149.

45. Before the introduction of metal strings, the *lira* had some advantages over the *bandura* because it could be heard better when people were dancing. Thus, it could be used both for accompanying the voice when a minstrel was begging and at various celebrations to provide dance music.

46. Khotkevich, "Neskol'ko slov ob ukrainskikh banduristakh i lirnikakh," pp. 87–106; see esp. pp. 99–100. Khotkevych, who states that Parkhomenko learned no epic songs from his master, says that he never met anyone so enamored with *dumy* and so anxious to learn them. Khotkevych (p. 97) also reports that Parkhomenko went so far as to hire a literate guide so that the guide could help him learn material, and especially epic songs, from books. Khotkevych's statement about what Parkhomenko learned from his master and what he learned from other sources, such as books, contradicts the reports of other scholars; but then, other scholars (Speranskii, Studyns'kyi) note that, in an effort to provide the collector with the data he was seeking, Parkhomenko and other minstrels would often contradict themselves.

47. Speranskii, pp. 107–11.

48. Hrinchenko and Lavrov, *Kobzar Fedir Kushneryk*, pp. 24–25.

49. Kolessa says that Veresai was particularly gifted as a musician. He was especially good at playing the *bandura*, and according to his own words, could arouse the

emotions of his audience with ease, should he choose to do so. Filaret Kolessa, *Ukraiins'ki narodni dumy*, L'viv: Prosvita, 1920, p. 58. See also Veresai's biography as reported by Rusov, p. 331.

50. Rusov, "Kobzar' Ostap Veresai," p. 318.

51. Rusov, p. 324–25. Veresai seems to have been a most difficult apprentice. He himself describes nagging a master for a smoke so much that the man finally hit him. He attributes a voracious appetite to himself and gives an account of overeating corn on the cob, again to the dismay of his master.

52. Hnat Khotkevych, "Vospominaniia o moikh vstrechakh so slepymi," *Tvory v dvukh tomakh*, Fedir Pohrebennyk, ed., vol. 1, Kiev: Dnipro, 1966, p. 460.

53. Studyns'kyi, "Lirnyky: Studiia," p. 260.

54. Malinka, "Zametki o dvukh lirnikakh," pp. 149, 158.

55. V. Gorlenko, "Kobzari i lirniki," pp. 49.

56. Ryl's'kyi and Lavrov, *Kobzar Ehor Movchan*, p. 18.

57. Hrinchenko and Lavrov, *Kobzar Fedir Kushneryk*, p. 15; about Nykonenko: see Kolessa, *Ukraiins'ki narodni dumy*, p. 57.

58. Polotai, "Notatka pro kobzaria Tkachenka (Halushku)," 1926, IMFE fond 1–4/248.

59. Rusov, "Ostap Veresai, odin iz poslednikh kobzarei malorusskikh," p. 319.

60. Chikalenko, "Lirnik Vasilii Moroz," p. 79.

61. Kvitka, "Profesional'ny narodni spivtsi i muzykanty na Ukraiini," p. 333.

62. Martynovych, interview with *kobzar* Petro Dryhavka, "Od pana ottsia nauka," IMFE 11–4/810, ark. 15 presents a section called "the training of girls" (*divchacha nauka*). Fond 11–4/590, ark. 7, among others, indicates that there was a special women's repertory. Fond 11–4/714, ark. 315 has a statement about Hanna Rudykha which praises her repertory and says that even though she was a woman, she was as smart as a man.

63. IMFE fond 6–2/23(2), ark. 50.

64. What was most often recorded from beggars was their begging song. It is possible that at least some beggars could go on from the begging song to other texts, just as minstrels did, but that they were never asked to do so by collectors.

65. The two songs that Borzhkovskii (pp. 664–65) says were being sung by groups of blind beggars are common in most minstrel repertories.

66. Danilov, "Sredi nishchei bratii," p. 203.

67. My experiences with the Supruns indicate that the blind do indeed develop better memories. To negotiate their way, the Supruns need to remember where things are. When placed in new surroundings, as when Suprun was staying at our home, he quickly learned and remembered where various objects such as tables, chairs, and staircases were located and was able to make his way without a walking stick and without bumping into furniture or falling down stairs. Kvitka (pp. 330, 338) says something similar about blind minstrels knowing the roads that they travelled.

68. Interview, October 21, 1987.

69. Speranskii, pp. 115–16.

70. Hnatiuk, p. 1.

71. Hnatiuk, p. 2.

72. IMFE fond 6–2/23(1), ark. 50–51

73. It is possible that the guild helped the minstrel with the bride-price. In the follow-up to his description of beggar guilds, Efimenko states that guilds give a sum of money to any member who marries, especially to a member who will then cease to be a beggar. "Bratstva i soiuzy nishchikh," p. 315.

74. IMFE fond 11–4/940, ark. 3.

75. Kvitka, "Profesional'ny narodni spivtsi i muzykanty na Ukraiini," p. 339.

76. A. Malinka, "Zametki o dvukh lirnikakh Chernigovskoi guberni," pp. 149 and 158.

77. IMFE fond 11–4/592. The references to women appear throughout; the statement about learning from the wife is ark. 27. The spelling of Hrytsenko's name as Khvedir instead of Fedir is an accepted variant. The only reason to doubt that it was Hrytsenko who said he learned psalms from his wife is folder 11–4/590. Here, on ark. 7, an almost identical statement is attributed to Iaremenko. It is possible that Iaremenko and Hrytsenko both learned from their wives, and it is also possible that the statement is misattributed in folder 592.

78. Bratytsia is in Gorlenko "Kobzari i lirniki," p. 42; Iaremenko is in Martynovych IMFE fond 11–4/590, ark. 17; Khrystenko is in Kharkiv, IMFE 6–2/23(1), ark. 69; Dimnych is in Borzhkovskii, p. 667.

79. Kvitka, p. 339.

80. Hnatiuk, p. 9.

81. Polotai, IMFE fond 14–3/1059, ark. 105

82. Malynka, "Kobzari Vlasko, Symonenko, ta lirnyk Ivanyts'kyi," p. l06; Kulyk is in Vynohrads'kyi, p. 66. For information of Dimnych, see the discussion below.

83. Kvitka, p. 339.

84. Rusov, p. 327. "Okh! Odruzhyla mene z tsim didom ioho bandura: iak priide mene svataty—do i vyzhenu, a iak zahrae na banduri—do i zavernu."

85. V. G(orlenko), "Kobzar' Kriukovskii (nekrolog)," *Kievskaia starina*, vol. 12, 1885, p. 741.

86. Gorlenko, "Kobzari i lirniki," p. 42.

87. Malynka, "Kobzari Vlasko, Simonenko, ta lirnyk Ivanyts'kyi," pp. 105–7.

88. Petrov, "K repertuaru lirnikov," p. 18.

89. Kharkiv, IMFE fond 6–2/23(1), ark. 69.

90. IMFE fond 11–4/590 and 592.

91. IMFE fond 14–3/1059, ark. 105.

92. Borzhkovskii, "Lirniki," pp. 665–67. The idea of a blind person taking care of small children is an interesting one. It is possible in the Ukrainian setting because infants are swaddled and children under a certain age are constantly held. With a very small child, then, a blind person would know where the child was and what the child was doing by touch.

93. Borzhkovskii; the material on Dimnych is on p. 667; Dovhaliuk/Zoria is on p. 668; Nikon is on p. 672. The material from Humeniuk is in Kvitka, p. 339.

94. Gorlenko, "Kobzari i lirniki," p. 30. Horlenko comments on the maturity and trustworthiness of the minstrel's son.

95. Vynohrads'kyi, pp. 64–66.

96. Gorlenko, "Kobzari i lirniki," p. 42; perhaps their poor financial circumstances were the reason for the lack of generosity that Bratytsia's wife displayed.

97. Malinka, "Lirnik Evdokim Mykytovich Mokroviz," p. 434.

98. Chikalenko, p. 80.

99. Malynka, "Kobzari Vlasko, Symonenko, ta lirnyk Ivanyts'kyi," pp. 105–7.

100. Malinka, "Kobzari i lirniki Terentii Parkhomenko, Nikifor Dudka, i Aleksei Pobehailo," p. 10; Malinka, "Prokop Chub: Perekhodnyi tip kobzaria," p. 166.

101. Gorlenko, "Bandurist Ivan Kriukovskii," p. 484.

102. Slastion(ov), "Kobzar' Mikhailo Kravchenko i ego dumy," pp. 309–10.

103. Malinka, "Kobzari i lirniki Terentii Parkhomenko, Nikifor Dudka, i Aleksei Pobehailo," p. 7.

104. IMFE fond 14–3/1059, ark. 106.

105. Hnatiuk, p. 7.

106. Kvitka, p. 339.

107. IMFE fond 6–2/23(1), ark. 50–51.

108. Kolessa, *Melodii*, p. 313.

109. IMFE fond 6–4/161/4, ark. 30.

110. IMFE fond 14–3/1059, ark. 106.

111. Gorlenko, "Bandurist Ivan Kriukovskii," p. 486.

112. Kyrdan and Omel'chenko, p. 82.

113. IMFE fond 11–4/810, ark. 15.

114. IMFE fond 11–4/591, ark. 3.

115. See the references to wives teaching their husbands "women's psalms," above. The quote about the cups is in IMFE fond 11–4/594, ark. 47. The preceding folio has some description of women's repertory.

116. IMFE fond 11–4/714, ark. 315 contains the quote about Hanna Rudykha. The huge collections from women are 11–4/601 from Motrena Bondarykha Hnatykha, 11–4/605 from Uliana Hantenko, and 11–4/606 from Oksana Kobylanka.

117. IMFE fond 6–4/161/4, ark. 52.

118. IMFE fond 6–4/161/4, ark. 52; date of collection 1930.

119. Kyrdan and Omel'chenko, pp. 82–83.

120. Kolessa, *Melodii*, pp. 53–56. It should be noted that the material on this woman is far less voluminous than the material on male performers. The biography is not as full as for male minstrels.

121. P.S. Ivashchenko, "Pavlo Bratytsia i Prokip Dub, kobzari Nezhinskogo uezda, Chernigovskoi gubernii," *Zapiski Iugo-zapadnogo otdela russkogo geograficheskogo obshchestva*, 1875, p. 110.

122. A number of scholars published lists of minstrels supplied to them by other minstrels, presumably in the hope that someone would go and collect from these. One example is Slastion(ov), "Kobzar' Mikhailo Kravchenko i ego dumy," p. 307. Another is "Svedeniia poluchennyia ot A. Malinki," pp. 406–8. Sumtsov published an actual call to collect data plus a twelve-step guide to use in data collection, "Kobzari i lirniki," *Russkaia muzykal'naia gazeta*, 1902, nos. 23–24, pp. 601–2.

Notes to Chapter 5

1. Borzhkovskii, p. 653, Speranskii, p. 111.

2. After complaining that Mykhailo Kravchenko was very reluctant to talk about guilds and always steered the conversation in another direction, Slastion expressed the hope that he could win the *kobzar*'s trust and gain more information, especially since the minstrel owed him for a trip to St. Petersburg. "Mikhailo Kravchenko i ego dumy," pp. 314–15.

3. Speranskii, pp. 120–21.

4. Speranskii, p. 117.

5. Speranskii, p. 113.

6. Kvitka, p. 336.

7. Speranskii, p. 117.

8. Mykhailo Kravchenko, for example, travelled to Myrhorod, Poltava, Kharkiv, Odessa, Ekaterinoslav and Ialta. Ivan Kravchenko-Kriukovs'kyi said that he travelled over all of Ukraine and mentioned specifically Poltava, Kharkiv, and Romny.

9. N. K. Moyle, "Izha ta kul'tura kharchuvannia," introduction to M. Nomys, *Ukraiins'ki prykazky, prysliv'ia i take inshe.* South Bound Brook, NJ: The Publishing Fund of the Ukrainian Orthodox Center, 1985, pp. 33-40.

10. The texts of most begging songs say exactly that. See, for example, Borzhkovskii, pp. 655–57 and 660–61 and Part 2, Songs, pp. 211–215.

11. Borzhkovskii, p. 661.

12. IMFE fond 11–4/940, ark. 12.

13. G(orlenko), "Kobzar' Kriukovskii (nekrolog)," p. 740.

14. Hnatiuk, pp. 8–9.

15. Efimenko, "Bratstva i soiuzy nishchikh," pp. 314–15. Evidence for a super-guild comes from a response to Efimenko's work on organizations of and for the poor. As Efimenko later reported in the journal *Kievskaia starina*, when he presented his original observations at the Kharkiv Historico-Philological Society, a man named M.D. Linde responded by supplying him with material he had collected on a related topic in the 1870s.

16. IMFE fond 6–2/23(1), ark. 70.

17. Borzhkovskii, p. 654.

18. Speranskii, p. 117.

19. Hnatiuk, p. 2

20. IMFE fond 11–4/940, ark. 13.

21. Borzhkovskii, p. 668.

22. Borzhkovskii, p. 658.

23. Horbach is essentially an analysis of the origins of the language and its derivational principles.

24. Horbach, pp. 12–42.

25. Studyns'kyi's "Lirnyky, Studiia" is primarily about the relationship of the *lebiiska mova* to other secret languages. He explains who the *shapovaly* (hatters), *ofeny* (peddlers), and *zlodii* (thieves) were (pp. 285–86) and gives the legend of the origin of the *lebiiska mova* at the time of the Polish domination of Ukraine (p. 285).

26. Horbach, pp. 9–11.

27. Studyns'kyi, p. 284; Borzhkovskii, p. 659.

28. Borzhkovskii, p. 659.

29. Borzhkovskii, p. 668.

30. Hnatiuk, p. 1.

31. Studyns'kyi, p. 284; K. Vyktoryn (pseudonym for Studyns'kyi) "Didivs'ka (zhebrats'ka) mova," *Zoria*, 1886, vol. VII, part 13–14, pp. 237–39.

32. Studyns'kyi, p. 258: "lirnyky nabyraiut' cherez tse bil'shoii s'milosty i uvazhaiut' toho, khto znaie iikh movu, za *svoho* cholovika."

33. IMFE fond 11–4/940, ark. 4.

34. IMFE fond 11–4/940, ark. 11. The line break replicates that found in the manuscript.

35. Studyns'kyi, p. 286.

36. Speranskii, p. 117.

37. IMFE fond 11–4/903, ark. 1.

38. Speranskii, pp. 113, 119; Efimenko, "Bratstva i soiuzy nishchikh," pp. 313–14.

39. Borzhkovskii, p. 658.

40. Speranskii, p. 113.

41. Speranskii, p. 115.

42. Speranskii, pp. 118–19.

43. IMFE fond 11–4/591, ark. 1; the accusations are on the back of ark. 2.

44. Speranskii, p. 113; Borzhkovskii, p. 658.

45. IMFE fond 11–4/590, ark. 7; fond 11–4/592, ark. 47; fond 11–4/714, ark. 36.

46. Powiesci Jozefa Dzierzkowskiego, as quoted in Studyns'kyi, "Lirnyky, Studiia," p. 258.

47. Studyns'kyi, p. 260. Studyns'kyi's informant, Zakhar Holovatyi, said that minstrels make a special effort to conceal this dance from the general public and post someone at the door when the dancing starts because they are afraid that awareness of such frivolity would cost them respect.

48. Bich-Lubenskii, "Banduristy i lirniki na Khar'kovskom XII arkheologicheskom s"ezde," p. 836. *Bich-Lubenskii uses the term pan-otets rather than tsekh-meister,* but he is clearly referring to the same office in the guild. The term *pan-otets* had much wider currency than *tsekh-meister;* the latter means guild head only, while *pan-otets* can be used for any master minstrel, as well as for the guild head. It was also the appropriate form of address for an apprentice to use when referring to his teacher, and the proper way for any person to address a priest.

49. IMFE fond 1–2/303, ark. 2; collected from Vasyl' Andriiev Hovtan, Nov. 26, 1930; collector not given.

50. IMFE fond 11–4/591. Collected by Martynovych in 1885.

51. Speranskii, p. 119.

52. Speranskii, p. 117.

53. Speranskii, p. 115.

54. Borzhkovskii, p. 658.

55. Speranskii, p. 113; Drahomanov, "Novyi variant kobzars'kikh spiviv," Central Academic Library, Kiev (henceforth TSNB), fond 172, ark. 10.

56. IMFE fond 11–4/591, ark. 1. The second rite is variously called *vyzvilka* and *vyzvilok.* The amount and type of variation between the terms is not unusual in folk speech. The first rite has similarly variant names: *odklynshchyny, odklianshchyna,* and so forth. It should be noted that, in many areas, the term *vyzvilka* or *vyzvilok* is used for the initiation rite. Usually, these areas have a rite for admission to the guild only; they do not have a second rite that confers permission to teach. In these areas, if a second rite is attested, it is also called a *vyzvilka* or *vyzvilok.*

57. Borzhkovskii, p. 658.

58. Kyrdan and Omel'chenko, p. 96.

59. Drahomanov, TSNB fond 172, ark. 10, cites V. Tomachyns'kyi as saying that masters did indeed sit home and exploit their apprentices.

60. Speranskii, pp. 127–28.

61. Chikalenko, "Lirnik Vasilii Moroz," pp. 79–80.

62. Borzhkovskii, p. 674.

63. Studyns'kyi, pp. 259–60.

64. Studyns'kyi, p. 259.

65. Speranskii, p. 116; Drahomanov, TSNB, fond 172–10 and Part 2, pp. 302–3.

66. Speranskii, pp. 117–20, Studyns'kyi, p. 260.

67. Speranskii, p. 121, and Part 2, pp. 206–8.

68. Hnatiuk, p. 2.

69. Slastion(ov), "Kobzar' Mikhailo Kravchenko i ego dumy," pp. 313–14.

70. IMFE fond 6–2/23(1), ark. 50.

71. Hnatiuk, pp. 8–9. The full text of Zlatarskyi's autobiography appears in chapter 6.

72. Rusov, p. 317.

73. IMFE fond 11–4/589, ark. 16; IMFE fond 11–4/591, ark. 1.

74. IMFE fond 11–4/810, ark. 6.

75. IMFE fond 1–2/303, ark. 1.

76. IMFE fond 11–4/592, ark. 46.

77. IMFE, fond 11–4/592, ark. 46.

78. IMFE fond 6–4/161/4, p. 28: the initiation fee is given as one-half pail of vodka and refreshments, usually fish. IMFE fond 1–2/303, ark. 1: the fee is vodka and fish, amount not stated. IMFE fond 11–4/591: the fee is a quarter pail for the initiation rite and half a pail for the rite that grants permission to be a teacher. IMFE fond 11–4/810, ark. 5 and IMFE fond 11–4/589, ark. 15: the old fee was half a pail for the initiation and a pail for the right to teach. Now it is a quarter pail and a half pail, respectively.

79. Hnatiuk, p. 5.
80. Kharkiv, IMFE fond 6–4/161–4, ark. 28; Martynovych, IMFE fond 11–4/591, ark. 1.
81. Kharkiv, IMFE, fond 6–2/23(1), ark. 72.
82. See, for example, Kharkiv, IMFE fond 6–2/23 (1), ark. 55.
83. IMFE fond 6–2/23(1), ark. 70–71.
84. IMFE fond 11–4/714, ark. 402.
85. Malynka, "Kobzari Vlasko, Symonenko, ta lirnyk Ivanyts'kyi," pp. 105–7.
86. IMFE fond 6–4/23 (1), ark. 51–52, 72.

Notes to Chapter 6

1. V. Hnatiuk, "Lirnyky," p. 7.
2. Borzhkovskii, "Lirniki," p. 668.
3. IMFE fond 11–4/810, ark. 15.
4. Speranskii, p. 117.
5. Rusov, p. 324.
6. Kyrdan and Omel'chenko, p. 96 is an example of the claim that Veresai was dismissed from his final apprenticeship because his talent was superior to that of his master.
7. Slastion(ov), "Kobzar' Mikhailo Kravchenko i ego dumy," p. 311.
8. Lavrov, p. 88.
9. IMFE fond 11–4/810: Martynovych collecting from Dryhavka, ark. 15; Speranskii, p 117.
10. Borzhkovskii, p. 659.
11. Hnatiuk, p. 5.
12. IMFE fond 11–4/591, ark. 4 and ark. 9–10. Both of these give two types of greetings, the one that a novice addresses to a full member of the guild and the one used between established minstrels. See also IMFE fond 11–4/592, ark. 47 for a list of the days of the week in minstrel secret language.
13. Natalie K. Moyle, "The Changing Concept of the Asik: Repertory and Learning Techniques." *II Milletlerarasi Turk Folklor Kongresi Bildirleri*, Ankara: Basbakanlik Basimevi, 1982, pp. 61–69.
14. Slastion(ov), "Kobzar' Mikhailo Kravchenko i ego dumy," pp. 307–8.
15. Borzhkovskii, p. 664.
16. Malinka, "Zametki o dvukh lirnikakh Chernigovskoi gubernii," p. 149.
17. Gorlenko, "Bandurist Ivan Kriukovskii," pp. 484, 486.
18. Rusov, p. 330.
19. Borzhkovskii, p. 663.
20. IMFE fond 6–4/161/4, 1930, ark. 47. It should be noted that a towel, a piece of linen which could be sold in the market, was considered a particularly good form of payment.
21. IMFE fond 6–2/23(1), ark. 23.
22. IMFE fond 6–2/23(1), ark. 53.
23. The word in the text is *khlopets*. This means both "boy" and "apprentice."
24. Hnatiuk, pp. 8–9.
25. Hnatiuk, p. 2; Kharkiv, IMFE, fond 6–2/23(1), ark. 50–51.
26. Borzhkovskii, p. 658, Kvitka, p. 334.
27. Kvitka, pp. 333, 336.
28. IMFE fond 6–2/23(1), ark. 51.
29. Kvitka, p. 334.

30. Kyrdan and Omel'chenko, p. 96.

31. Malynka, "Kobzari Vlasko, Symonenko, ta lirnyk Ivanyts'kyi," p 106; Malinka, "Kobzari i lirniki Terentii Parkhomenko, Nikifor Dudka, i Aleksei Pobehailo," pp. 6–7; Petrov, "K repertuaru lirnikov," p. 15.

32. Vetukhov, "Doklad A.V. Vetukhova," *Materialy komiteta o kobzariakh i lirnikakh*, 1902, p. 385.

33. Gorlenko, "Bandurist Ivan Kriukovskii," p. 504; Martinovich, "Slipets-kobzar' Ivan Kravchenko," *Kievskaia starina*, 1904, vol. II, p. 283.

34. Hnatiuk, p. 2.

35. Horbach, *Argo*, pp. 7–8.

36. Borzhkovskii, pp. 654–57.

37. Hnatiuk, p. 1.

38. Studyns'kyi,"Lirnyky, Studiia," p. 260.

39. Speranskii, p. 124.

40. Kharkiv, IMFE fond 6–2/23(1), ark. 50. It should be noted that minstrels did have to travel on their own. Dovhaliuk's father told Borzhkovskii (p. 670) that his son was once travelling with a group of fellow minstrels who forgot about him and left him all alone. Dovhaliuk successfully made his way home through what sounds like a whole string of villages.

41. Dryhavka is in IMFE fond 11–4/810 and Kuchuhura-Kucherenko is in IMFE fond 11–4/940. The manuscripts are hard to follow since they date late in Martynovych's career and the handwriting is difficult, full of the peculiar stress marks which Martynovych used after he suffered a stroke. Also, they are stream-of-consciousness or stream-of-narration texts, with virtually no commentary from Martynovych himself. The texts seem to be a straight transcription of the informant's speech, and it is often difficult to tell where the minstrel is talking about his training and where he is reciting a text learned during apprenticeship. Much of the wisdom learned from the master is formulaic and resembles minstrel poetry. Martynovych himself wrote some of it down as prose and some of it as verse, making it even more difficult to distinguish song texts from descriptions of training. In spite of their difficulties, these two accounts of apprenticeship are invaluable.

42. IMFE fond 11–4/763, ark. 10

43. IMFE fond 11–4/763, ark. 1, 2.

44. IMFE fond 11–4/763, ark. 1.

45. Dryhavka, IMFE fond 11–4/810, ark. 2; Kuchuhura-Kucherenko, IMFE fond 11–4/940, ark. 3.

46. Dryhavka, IMFE fond 11–4/810, ark. 2, 3; Kuchuhura-Kucherenko, IMFE fond 11–4/940, ark. 1, 12, 13.

47. IMFE fond 11–4/940, ark. 2. The translation reproduces the line divisions and the punctuation of the manuscript.

48. Kvitka, pp. 331–32, gives Humeniuk's description of the components of a full, multi-song minstrel performance and mentions the begging song as an integral part. See also the discussion of a typical performance in chapter 1.

49. Hnatiuk, p. 2

50. For a discussion of the relationship between music and text, see Kolessa, *Melodii ukraiins'kykh narodnykh dum*, pp. 50–59.

51. IMFE fond 11–4/810 and IMFE fond 11–4/940.

52. Hnatiuk, p. 2.

53. Ignat Khotkevich, "Bandura i ee mesto sredi sovremennykh muzykal'nykh instrumentov," *Ukrainskaia Zhizn'*, no. 5–6, 1914, pp. 39–58. M.V. Lysenko, "Narodni muzychni instrumenty na Ukraiini," *Ridnyi krai*, 1907, no. 11–13 and separately, Kiev:

Mystetstvo, 1955. H. Khotkevych, "Pidruchnyk hry na banduri," Archives of the Literature Institute, Ukrainian Academy of Science, Fond 62–20.

54. Kharkiv, IMFE, fond 6–2/23(2), ark. 51. The information about tying the apprentice's fingers to the master's appears in Kharkiv, IMFE fond 6–4/161/4, ark. 52, and Speranskii, p. 124.

55. Kharkiv, IMFE, fond 6–2/23 (2), ark. 62.

56. IMFE fond 11–4/810 and fond 11–4/940. Kuchuhura-Kucherenko provided a whole secret language dictionary for Martynovych. The words are grouped by meaning, such as items of clothing, food stuffs, and so forth.

57. Danilov, "Sredi nishchei bratii," pp. 200–6; Shchepot'ev, "Starechi prokhannia," pp. 30–40; V. Danyliv, "Dodatky do literatury starechykh prokhan'," *Etnohrafichnyi visnyk*, bk. 8, 1929, pp. 181–83.

58. Martynovych IMFE fond 11–4/715, ark. 7

59. IMFE fond 11–4/673, ark. 22.

60. Bich-Lubenskii, "Banduristy i lirniki na Khar'kovskom XII arkheologicheskom s"ezde,"p. 836.

61. Danilov, pp. 204–6.

62. IMFE fond 11–4/810, ark. 15.

63. IMFE fond 11–4/594, ark. 47.

64. Iaremenko is in IMFE 11–4/590, ark. 4. The titles of five women's songs are given the same fond, ark. 7, where the informant adds, "These are still called women's psalms, though now men as well as women sing them." Fond 11–4/977, ark. 29, labels an item as a women's song. Fond 11–4/592, ark. 25, labels an item as a woman's song, and the same fond, ark. 28, has the male performer noting that a certain song was taught to him by his wife.

65. IMFE fond 11–4/611, ark. 218–19. The performer, whose gender can be determined by the endings of the past tense verbs, says, "This is the sort of song that makes me cry right away. (She is speaking about 'The Escape of Three Brothers from Azov,' an epic song and something that women were not supposed to sing.) See, this is how I cry even for other people's sons. Oh, my God, oh my God! Even my head hurts."

66. Speranskii, pp. 120–21.

67. Kvitka, pp. 335–36.

68. IMFE fond 11–4/591, ark. 3.

69. IMFE fond 11–4/591, ark. 4.

70. Borzhkovskii, pp. 657–58.

71. Martinovich, *Ukrains'ki zapisi*, pp. 76–77.

72. This constitutes a difference between Western and Eastern Ukraine. Zlatars'kyi is describing the West. In other areas, taverns were used frequently for initiations. All occasions when large numbers of minstrels assembled, fairs included, were considered suitable times for the ritual.

73. It is not clear whether the elders are invited by the master and apprentice jointly or by one or the other of them alone.

74. Hnatiuk, pp. 4–5.

75. Speranskii, pp. 113–15.

76. Speranskii, pp. 117–18.

Notes to Chapter 7

1. Lord, *The Singer of Tales*.

2. Horbach, pp. 7–8.

3. Speranskii, p. 124.

4. IMFE fond 6–4/161/4, ark. 52.

5. IMFE fond 6–4/23(1), p. 50.

6. Lord, *The Singer of Tales*, pp. 124–28.

7. Kvitka, p. 332; Horbach, p. 7; Borzhkovskii, p. 657.

8. Drahomanov, "Novi varianty kobzars'kykh spiviv," *Zhyte i Slovo*, 1895, vol. IV, p. 33.

9. Kharkiv, IMFE fond 6–2/23(1), ark. 51 and 67–68.

10. Speranskii, pp. 124–26.

11. Speranskii, p. 124.

12. Kharkiv, IMFE fond 6–2/23(1), ark. 62 and 67.

13. Rusov, pp. 331–32.

14. Slastion(ov), "Kobzar' Mikhailo Kravchenko i ego dumy," p. 305.

15. Gorlenko, "Bandurist Ivan Kriukovskii," p. 486.

16. Borzhkovskii, p. 657.

17. Kvitka, p. 330; Ivan Humeniuk does say that he is repeating the words of his father, Sidor.

18. Malynka, "Kobzari Vlasko, Symonenko, ta lirnyk Ivanyts'kyi," p. 105.

19. Gorlenko, "Bandurist Ivan Kriukovskii," pp. 483–484.

20. "Materialy komiteta o kobzariakh i lirnikakh, sobrany i sgrupirovany E.K. Rednym," pp. 384–87.

21. IMFE fond 11–4/592, 1885. Although it is impossible to tell from the manuscript, Hrytsenko is probably the famous *kobzar* who is also called Kholodnyi. His master was Nazarenko.

22. Polotai, IMFE fond 14–3/1059, ark. 105–7.

23. Malinka, "Lirnik Ananii Homyniuk," p. 1.

24. IMFE fond 1–4/248.

25. Malinka, "Prokop Chub: Perekhodnyi tip kobzaria," pp. 164–67.

26. Malinka, "Kobzari Vlasko, Symonenko, ta lirnyk Ivanyts'kyi," p. 107.

27. IMFE fond 6–2/23 (1), ark. 62.

28. IMFE fond 6–2/23(2), ark. 50–51.

29. Malinka, "Kobzari i lirniki Terentii Parkhomenko, Nikifor Dudka, i Aleksei Pobehailo," pp. 6–9; Speranskii, pp. 136–44.

30. Kharkiv, IMFE fond 6–2/23(1), ark. 50.

31. Kharkiv, IMFE fond 6–2/23(1), ark. 71.

32. Kvitka, p. 332.

33. Kharkiv, IMFE, fond 6–2/23(1), ark. 71.

34. Gorlenko, "Kobzari i Lirniki," p. 42. See also the discussion about minstrel wives in chapter 4. In the obituary for Ivan Kravchenko-Kriukovs'kyi (*Kievskaia starina*, vol. XII, 1885, pp. 741), for example, Horlenko accused the deceased minstrel's wife of unseemly behavior.

35. Speranskii, p. 124. Kiashko's reluctance to share is ironic because his source must have been a printed one, one Parkhomenko could have gotten himself. Khmel'nyts'kyi *dumy* disappeared from the oral tradition around the middle of the nineteenth century. Thus Kiashko's source must have been a published collection.

36. Borzhkovskii, p. 673.

37. Chikalenko, "Lirnik Vasilii Moroz," p. 80.

38. *Trudy XII Arkheologicheskogo S"ezda v Khar'kove*, vol. II, Moscow 1905, pp. 386–87.

39. Malinka, "Lirnik Evdokim Mykytovich Mokroviz," p. 435.

40. Malinka, "Zametki o dvukh lirnikakh Chernigovskoi guberni," p. 150.

41. Malynka, "Kobzari Vlasko, Symonenko, i lirnik Ivanyts'kyi," p. 105.

42. Speranskii, p. 125.

43. Gorlenko, "Kobzari i lirniki," pp. 41–50.

44. Speranskii, p. 125.

45. IMFE fond 6–2/23(2), ark. 69.

46. Khotkevych, "Vospominaniia o moiikh vstrechakh so slepymi," pp. 457–78; the tuning is discussed on pp. 457–58; doctoring the voices of the mendicants is described on p. 460. The discussion of setting up an ensemble appears throughout, see esp. pp. 460–61. The rest is a description of planning the program, which shows some of Khotkevych's attitude toward his charges, and an account of the actual proceedings of the congress. Having learned to play the *bandura*, Khotkevych produced *Pidruchnyk hry na banduri*, a small handbook on how to play this instrument (L'viv: drukarnia Naukoho Tovarystva im. Shevchenka, 1909).

47. While in Ukraine in the 1980s, I sang in an amateur folk choir. The job of the choir director was to make sure that all of the folk songs we performed publicly were free of objectionable elements: all references to religion, anything that might be construed to have a Ukrainian nationalist flavor.

48. Interview, October 21, 1987.

49. June 15, 1994. On one occasion I did notice that one of Suprun's cupboards was full of Braille sheets, presumably his transcriptions of song texts.

50. October 21, 1987.

51. Kononenko, "Duma pro Chornobyl': Old Forms, New Topics," pp. 133–54.

52. "Epos Ukraiiny" (no author given). Photographer: I. Iaiits'kyi, *Sotsialistychna Kul'tura*, 1990, no. 8, pp. 32–33. Suprun sent me a copy through a friend.

53. Letter from Suprun, March 6, 1993.

54. Speranskii, p. 125.

55. Kharkiv, IMFE fond 6–2/23(2), ark. 65

56. Gorlenko, "Bandurist Ivan Kriukovskii: Tekst deviati dum s biograficheskoi zametkoi," p. 485.

57. Speranskii, p. 110.

58. IMFE fond 14–3/1059, ark. 105, material collected by Polotai.

59. Anna Astakhova, *Byliny Severa*, pp. 70–89. Astakhova was a Russian folklorist who collected and published the texts of Russian epics (*byliny*) and wrote about epic performers.

60. Lavrov, *Kobzari*, pp. 24–26.

61. Miller, *Folklore for Stalin*, pp. 2–24.

62. Natalie K. Moyle, *The Turkish Minstrel Tale Tradition*, New York and London: Garland Publishing, 1990, pp. 155–207.

63. IMFE fond 14–3/1059, ark. 106.

64. IMFE fond 6–2/23 (2), ark. 70.

65. Kolessa, *Ukraiins'ki narodni dumy*, pp. 1–62 and esp. 51–55. Jakobson, "Slavic Epic Verse: Studies in Comparative Metrics," pp. 414–63; p. 445.

66. Kononenko, "Women as Performers of Oral Literature: A Re-examination of Epic and Lament," *Women Writers in Russian Literature*, eds. Toby W. Clyman and Diana Greene, Westport, Conn., and London: Greenwood Press, 1994, pp. 17–33.

67. Gender awareness is not characteristic of Slavic folklore scholarship, and Jakobson, cited above, claims that only women lamented in Ukraine, which is not true. See I. Sventsiits'kyi and V. Hnatiuk, "Pokhoronni holosinnia, Pokhoronni zvychaii i obriady," *Etnografichnyi zbirnyk*, 1912, vols. XXXI and XXXII, for a collection of lament texts and descriptions of the funeral rite, which includes laments by men.

68. Kolessa, *Ukraiins'ki narodni dumy*, pp. 51–55. Kolessa cites the passage where a relative asks the deceased when he will return and then responds for the dead person,

saying: "take yellow sand, sow it upon a white rock, water it with your tears. When the yellow sand sprouts green periwinkle, when the green periwinkle blooms with purple blossoms, then I will return." As Kolessa shows, this striking image appears in both laments recorded by Sventsiits'kyi and in epic songs such as the "Duma about a Sister and a Brother."

69. Hnatiuk, "Lirnyky," p. 2.

70. Demuts'kyi, p. 37.

71. IMFE fond 6–2/23(2), ark. 54.

72. IMFE fond 11–4/592, ark. 37.

73. Malinka, "Lirnik Ananii Savvovich Homyniuk," pp. 1–8.

74. *Ukrain's'ki zapisi Porfiriia Martinovicha*, pp. 16–23. See also Slastion(ov), "Kobzar' Mikhailo Kravchenko i ego dumy," p. 305.

75. Martinovich, *Ukrain's'ki zapisi*, p. 23.

76. Gorlenko, "Bandurist Ivan Kriukovskii: Tekst deviati dum s biograficheskoi zametkoi," pp. 508–10.

77. Kirdan, "Var'irovanie Kobzarem M. Kravchenko dumy 'Bednaia Vdova i Tri Syna,' " *Tekstologicheskoe izuchenie eposa*, eds. V.M. Gatsak and A.A. Petrosian, Moscow: Nauka, 1971, pp. 47–63.

78. IMFE fond 6–2/23 (2), ark. 70.

79. Slastion(ov), "Kobzar' Mikhailo Kravchenko i ego dumy," p. 313.

80. Speranskii, p. 137.

81. Slastion(ov), "Kobzar' Mikhailo Kravchenko i ego dumy," p. 313.

82. IMFE fond 11–4/592, ark. 6.

83. IMFE fond 11–4/714, ark. 168.

84. IMFE fond 11–4/714, ark. 205.

85. IMFE fond 11–4/597, ark. 2. Here the informant is the *lirnyk* Mykolai Doroshenko, judging from the texts collected—a good, though not outstanding—minstrel. When dictating the epic about the "Escape of Three Brothers from Azov," he first used the line *U nediliu rano po-ranenko* (On Sunday, early in the morning). He then replaced this with *Barze rano po-ranenko* (Very early in the morning) and insisted that the line he first produced belonged in the song about "The Widow and Her Three Sons" while the line he substituted was the one and only line appropriate to the song at hand.

86. IMFE fond 11–4/597, ark. 13.

87. IMFE fond 11–4/611, ark. 219. The song being discussed is the epic "The Escape of Three Brothers from Azov." The informant acknowledges two possible endings. There are actually three endings attested in the tradition.

88. It is probably not incidental that among the beggars who were not minstrels but merely chanted their requests for alms, women had a reputation for greater skill (Danilov, "Sredi nishchei bratii," p. 203). If they learned poetic and improvisational skills outside of apprenticeship, performing wedding and funeral laments as part of their family ritual duty, then even with minimal training, they would have the knowledge and skill to produce better begging chants than men, because men had less experience in lamentation.

Notes to Chapter 8

1. Borzhkovskii, p. 672. The statement in Borzhkovskii's article reads as follows: "Christ chose twelve pupils and twelve apostles for the preaching of his word, and, upon his ascension, he added the blind and the lame."

2. Studyns'kyi, p. 258.

3. Kharkiv, "Sposterezhennia nad lirnykamy ta kobzariamy Valkivs'koho raionu na Kharkivshchyni," IMFE fond 6–2/23(1), ark. 55. This document give a series of quotes about the David legend. Borzhkovskii (p. 672) got a similar statement from the *lirnyk* Nikon.

4. IMFE fond 1–2/303, ark. 2, collected from Vasyl' Andriivych Hovtyn', Nov. 26, 1930. The words *volol* and *zakharbet* are in quotes in the text itself. They are translated by the speaker as horse and begging bag (*torba*). Ukrainian minstrels did not have horses, and traveled by walking, hence the confusion.

5. Speranskii, p. 112.

6. Kvitka, "Profesional'ny narodni spivtsi i muzykanty na Ukraiini," pp. 330–31.

7. Kharkiv, IMFE fond 6–2/23 (2), ark. 54.

8. Speranskii, pp. 110–11.

9. Frank E. Sysyn, *Between Poland and Ukraine: The Dilemma of Adam Kysil, 1600–1653*, Cambridge: Harvard Ukrainian Research Inst./Harvard Univ. Press, 1985, pp. 14–17; Zenon E. Kohut, *Russian Centralism and Ukrainian Autonomy: Imperial Absorption of the Hetmanate, 1760s–1830s*, Cambridge: Harvard Ukrainian Inst./Harvard Univ. Press, 1988, pp. 24–26. A discussion of Ukrainian history from the point of view of Ukrainian epic appears in Kolessa, *Ukraiins'ki narodni dumy*, pp. 10–27.

10. Sysyn, pp. 29–31; Kohut, pp. 26–27; Metropolitan Ilarion, *The Ukrainian Church: Outlines of the History of the Ukrainian Orthodox Church*. Trans. O. Ferbey, Winnipeg: Millennium Committee of the Ukrainian Church of Canada, 1986, pp. 138–40.

11. Metropolitan Ilarion, pp. 133–34.

12. Kohut, p. 24.

13. Kohut, p. 27.

14. M. Hrushevs'kyi, "Khmel'nyts'kyi i Khmel'nyshchyna." *Zapysky naukovoho tovarystva im. Shevchenka*, vol. XXIII–XXIV, p. 8.

15. Ia.D. Isaievych, *Bratstva ta iikh rol' v rozvytku ukraiins'koii kul'tury XVI-XVIII st*, Kiev: Naukova Dumka, 1966, pp. 45–70. It would be interesting to know if the church brotherhoods admitted women, as minstrel brotherhoods seem to have done. Unfortunately, Isaievych does not address this question.

16. Metropolitan Ilarion, p. 134; Isaievych, pp. 65–67.

17. Metropolitan Ilarion, pp. 135–36; Isaievych, pp. 71–126.

18. Isaievych, pp. 127–95.

19. To give just one example of the continuing importance of institutions founded by church brotherhoods: the Kievan Mohyla Academy has remained a symbol of enlightenment and independence to this day. It was the first degree-granting institution, free of government control, to be established in post-Soviet, independent Ukraine. Attempts in 1987 to raze the building which had once housed the Academy, or as rumor had it, turn it into a grocery store (*gastronom*), got people so upset that they helped make a historical preservation group, UKK (the Ukrainian Cultural Committee), a leader among Ukrainian nationalist forces.

20. Russell Zguta, *Russian Minstrels: A History of the Skomorokhi*. Philadelphia: University of Pennsylvania Press, 1978. Zguta argues that *skomorokhi* are a native phenomenon rather than an import and that they originated in an East Slavic pagan priesthood, adopting the role of entertainers when pagan remnants became unacceptable. If Zguta is correct, the *skomorokhi* may be the ancestors of the *kobzari* and *lirnyky*.

21. Efimenko, "Shpitali v Malorossii," p. 720.

22. Efimenko, p. 715; pp. 719–20.

23. Efimenko, p. 709–14, 725–27.

24. Efimenko, pp. 714, 716.

25. Efimenko, pp. 715–17; 723–24.

26. Efimenko, pp. 722.

27. Metropolitan Ilarion, p. 136.

28. Iastrebov, "Gaidamatskii bandurist," pp. 379–88.

29. K.F.U.O., "Kodenskaia Kniga i tri Bandurista," *Kievskaia starina*, 1882, vol. II, pp. 161–66.

30. V.G., "Pridvornyi bandurist v begakh," pp. 21–23; Lavrov, pp. 63–64.

31. Borzhkovskii, "Lirniki," p. 665.

32. P. Zhitetskii, *Mysli o narodnykh malorusskikh dumakk*, Kiev: Kievskaia starina, 1893, pp. 39–41. See also Gregory L. Freeze, "Caste and Emancipation: The Changing Status of Clerical Families in the Great Reforms," in *The Family in Imperial Russia*, pp. 124–52, for a discussion of hereditary clerical positions in Russia and the problems this system caused.

33. Zhitetskii, pp. 41–45.

34. Zhitetskii, pp. 41–46; pp. 167–73.

35. (no author given), "Avtobiografiia Iuzhno-russkogo sviashchennika 1–oi poloviny VXIII st," *Kievskaia starina*, 1885, vol. II, pp. 318–32; Zhitetskii, pp. 46–47.

36. "Avtobiografiia Iuzhno-russkogo sviashchennika," pp. 318–32, and Zhitetskii, pp. 47–48.

37. It is surprising that Zhytets'kyi, in his efforts to establish school influence on *dumy*, did not pick up on the fact that songs based on Skovoroda's poetry were routinely sung by minstrels. Perhaps he was not familiar enough with living minstrels and their repertories to know that "To Every City Its Rights and Mores" was, in fact, quite popular. See also the secret song *Zhachka*, translated, in the appendix, and its corresponding notes. The song may well be a composition by a church school student which found its way into minstrel repertory.

38. Efimenko, pp. 715–17.

39. Borzhkovskii, p. 666.

40. IMFE fond 6–2/23(2), ark. 50–51.

41. Demuts'kyi, *Lira i iii motivy*. The influence of scripture is not discussed by Demuts'kyi, but he does note the written source of each song based on scripture, and the number of these is significant.

42. Zhitetskii, p. 85.

43. Khotkevich, "Neskol'ko slov ob ukrainskikh banduristakh i lirnikakh," p. 87.

44. Zhitetskii, p. 167.

45. Danilov, "Sredi nishchei bratii," pp. 202–3, reports that at the Lavra, the beggars with the more gruesome wounds, sores, or deformities did better financially because they got more attention. Kharkiv, IMFE fond 6–2, talks explicitly about the parallel between using music to get sympathy and displaying a physical impairment. He quotes V. Honchar on the topic of pity (*zhalist'* or *zhalib*) and using singing and playing to affect the emotions of the public. Bakhmut apparently told Kharkiv that the *lira* was a good instrument because it was particularly suited for evoking pity.

46. Rusov, "Ostap Veresai, odin iz poslednikh kobzarei malorusskikh," p. 330.

47. IMFE fond 11–3/562, ark. 8; no collector given, but it is probably Martynovych, taking notes during Veresai's appearance in St. Petersburg.

48. Danilov, pp. 202–3.

Notes to Chapter 9

1. Speranskii, *Iuzhno-russkaia pesnia i sovremennye ee nositeli*, p. 123; Kharkiv, IMFE fond 6–2/23(2), ark. 49.

2. Malinka, "Kobzar' Petro Haras'ko i lirnik Maksym Pryshchenko," pp. 441–50; Malinka, "Kobzari i lirniki Terentii Parkhomenko, Nikifor Dudka, i Aleksei Pobehailo," pp. 60–92; and especially, Malinka, "Prokop Chub, perekhodnyi tip kobzaria," pp. 164–78.

3. Khotkevich, "Neskol'ko slov ob Ukrainskikh banduristakh i lirnikakh," p. 101, and Gorlenko, "Bandurist Ivan Kriukovskii," pp. 485, 495.

4. Malinka, "Prokop Chub, perekhodnyi tip kobzaria," p. 165; Kolessa, *Melodii Ukraiins'kykh narodnykh dum,* pp. 59–64.

5. S. Famintsyn, *Domra i srodnye ei muzykal'nye instrumenty russkogo naroda,* St. Petersburg, 1891; *kobza,* pp. 87–109, and *bandura,* pp 110–70. Khotkevich, "Bandura i ee mesto sredi sovremennykh muzykal'nykh instrumentov," pp. 39–58; Lysenko, "Narodni muzychni instrumenty na Ukraiini"; Khotkevych, "Pidruchnyk hry na banduri."

6. Kolessa, *Ukraiins'ki narodni dumy,* p. 49; Kohut, *Russian Centralism and Ukrainian Autonomy.*

7. Malinka, "Kobzar' Petro Haras'ko i lirnik Maksym Pryshchenko," p. 445.

8. Khotkevich, "Neskol'ko slov ob Ukrainskikh banduristakh i lirnikakh," p. 100.

9. P. Bezsonov, *Kaleki perekhozhie: Sbornik stikhov i issledovaniia.* Moscow: Tipografiia A. Semena, 1861–64. Reprinted in two vol. with a new introduction by the Very Reverend Sergei Hackel, London: Gregg International Publishers, Ltd. 1970. Bezsonov publishes all sorts of material, including texts from the South Slavs, Ukraine, Belarus, and the adjacent areas of Russia proper. Songs included are begging songs and religious verses, plus songs and beliefs about mendicants. See also Speranskii, "Kurskii lirnik T.I. Semenov," *Etnograficheskoe obozrenie,* vol. LXVIII-LXIX, 1906, pp. 3–28.

10. Speranskii, *Iuzhno-russkaia pesnia i sovremennye ee nositeli,* pp. 110–11.

11. See chapter 5.

12. Hrushevs'ka, *Ukraiins'ki narodni dumy,* vol. I, pp. XIII-XVII, has a detailed account of the use of the term *duma.*

13. Kolessa, *Ukraiins'ki narodni dumy,* p. 8.

14. Hrushevs'kyi offers a quote from Sahaidachnyi which is meant to show that the Cossacks were not indifferent to religion. In it, Sahaidachnyi claims that the Cossacks are by nature pious. He also gives various instances of their support of the church. Mykola Hrushevs'kyi, *Istoriia Ukraiiny-Rusi,* vol. VII, part 2, pp. 391–92.

15. See, for example, the *duma* about Samiilo Kishka in Kirdan, *Ukrainskie narodnye dumy,* pp. 148–49. According to Kyrdan's notes (p. 447), all three religious establishments do in fact exist, only the one in Mezhihorsk is a monastery rather than a church. All were founded and supported with the moneys of the Cossack regiments affiliated with them. At least Mezhihorsk, but possibly also the other places, had a hospice where impoverished or disabled Cossacks could receive care.

16. Efimenko, "Shpitali v Malorossii," pp. 715–16.

17. Efimenko, p. 715.

18. Demuts'kyi, *Lira i iii motivy,* pp. 52–54.

19. Demuts'kyi, pp. 27–29.

20. Demuts'kyi, pp. 34–35.

21. Demuts'kyi, pp. 33–34.

22. "The Passion of Christ" (*Strasti Khrystovi*); "Christ Crucified" (*Rospynanie Khrysta, Khrystu na Kresti*), Demuts'kyi, pp. 1–7. The briar belt and the slivers of willow are p. 1. The birth pangs of the Virgin are p. 4.

23. Demuts'kyi, pp. 39–47.

24. In his description of a religious fair (p. 664), Borzhkovskii tells about a *lirnyk* with a large crowd of crying women gathered about him. The song that he sings to attract so large an audience is "The Orphan Girl" (*Syritka*).

25. The Slavic understanding of an orphan is different from ours: the loss of one parent makes a child an orphan. See Andrejs Plakans, "Parentless Children and the Soul Revisions: A Study of Methodology and Social Fact," *The Family in Imperial Russia*, pp. 77–102.

26. Demuts'kyi, pp. 54–56.

27. "The Three Brothers of Samara" *(Try braty Samars'ki)* is printed in seven variants in Hrushevs'ka, vol. I, p. 138–44; Kirdan, *Ukrainskie narodnye dumy*, pp. 99–100.

29. The variants of Fedir Bezridnyi are printed in Hrushevs'ka, vol. II, pp. 113–23, and Kirdan, pp. 81–88. The variants of Ivas' (or Ivan) Konovchenko are in Hrushevs'ka, vol. II, pp. 12–106; total of 42. Kirdan published 6 variants, pp. 224–57. Number 6 is a new printing from archival sources.

30. Antonovich and Dragomanov, *Istoricheskie pesni malorusskogo naroda*; "Baida" is in vol. I, 1874, pp.145–59; P. Lukashevich, *Malorossiiskie i Chervonorusskie narodnye dumy i pesni*, Sankt-Peterburg: Tipografiia Eduarda Pratsa, 1856; "Baida" is on pp. 9–12; "Morozenko" is on pp. 28–29. "Morozenko" was a particular specialty of the minstrel Parkhomenko. See N. D-vin, "Pesnia pro Morozenka," *Etnograficheskoe obozrenie*, 1903, vol. LVI, no. 1, pp. 115–16. Suprun performs both "Baida" and "Morozenko," and for the latter, he uses Parkhomenko's version.

31. The horror of watching animals awaiting his hero's death emphasizes, the extreme nature of the torment in a number of *dumy*. In "The Death of a Cossack in the Kodyma Valley" (Kirdan, pp. 99–100), for example, after enduring the misery of watching the scavengers and recalling the pain of his losses, the hero prays to his mother for one extra bit of strength and uses it to fire his rifle at the vultures circling above his head. Then he collapses, surveys the scene one last time, and dies.

32. "The Flight of Three Brothers from Azov" *(Utecha tr'okh brativ z Azova)* is on pp. 88–137 in Hrushevs'ka, vol. I; total of 24 variants. It is on pp. 150–223 in Kirdan; 18 variants. Variants 4, 5, 6, 7, 11, 12, 14, 15, 16, 17, 18 of Kirdan are published for the first time and previously available only in the archives of IMFE.

33. "The Captives" *(Nevil'nyky)* is in 6 variants in Hrushevs'ka, vol. I, pp. 1–9, and "The Captive's Lament" *(Plach nevil'nyka)* is in 4 variants, vol. 1, pp. 10–13. Kirdan gives 5 variants of the former, number 5 of which is a new printing of archival materials, and 3 variants of the latter, number 2 of which is new; pp. 101–13. "Marusia Bohuslavka," the story of a woman who sacrifices her life so that Cossack prisoners might escape, is in Hrushevs'ka, vol. I, pp. 21–27, and Kirdan, pp. 122–34.

34. See the preceding chapter and Danilov, "Sredi nishchei brat'i," pp. 202–3.

35. As discussed in Plakans's article, most children who lost a parent were hired out—sometimes to relatives, but hired out nonetheless. The position of hirelings was very difficult, even when they were living with relatives. Thus, the mother in this *duma* does her sons a great service by protecting them from the normal fate of children with only one parent.

36. The variants of "The Widow and Her Three Sons" *(Udova)* are in Hrushevs'ka, vol. II, pp. 233–76; total of 42 variants. In Kirdan, this *duma* is on pp. 346–84; 14 variants. Variants 8, 9, 10, 13, and 14 of Kirdan are from archival sources and do not appear in Hrushevs'ka.

37. Kirdan, p. 360.

38. The variants of "Sister and Brother" *(Sestra ta brat)* are in Hrushevs'ka, vol. II, pp. 276–90, with an additional text on p. 298; total of 20 variants. Kirdan has 12 variants; numbers 5, 7, 8, 10, 11, and 12 are publications of archival material; pp. 326–44.

39. The variants of "Cossack Life" *(Kozats'ke zhyttia)* are in Hrushevs'ka, vol. II, pp. 210–16; total of 4 variants. Three of these are in Kirdan, pp. 307–11.

40. The variants of the *duma* about the stepfather, here called "The Farewell of a

Cossack to His Kin" (*Proshchannia kozaka z rodynoiu*) are in Hrushevs'ka, vol. II, pp. 216–26; 11 variants. There are no additional variants in Kirdan, though there is some discussion of the correct readings of lines, based on his archival research, on pp. 312–24.

41. Zhitetskii, *Mysli o narodnykh malorusskikh dumakh*, pp. 157–59.

42. Kirdan, pp. 119–21; Hrushevs'ka, vol. I, pp. 20–21.

43. Borzhkovskii, "Dve lirnitskie pesni," pp. 637–40. The song contains a unique scene. Usually, the recognition of sin leads to salvation. Typically, heroes who repent are mourned by a cuckoo or a sister, and their souls are saved, even though their bodies cannot escape death. In the song here, a bird does arrive and does promise to care for the dying brothers. The bird is an eagle rather than a cuckoo, and instead of bringing the brothers water to drink as he promises, or informing the parents of the demise of their children so that they can perform the proper rites, the bird attacks, ripping out the brothers' eyes and eating their flesh. This scene is followed by another statement to the effect that the brothers are being punished for their sins by their parents' curses.

44. Kirdan, pp. 122–34; Hrushevs'ka, vol. I, pp. 21–28.

45. Kirdan, pp. 135–49; Hrushevs'ka, vol. I, pp. 35–54.

46. Kirdan, p. 125 is just one example.

47. Demuts'kyi, p. 22.

48. Demuts'kyi, pp. 39–42.

49. Demuts'kyi, pp. 38–39.

50. Demuts'kyi, p. 43.

51. Demuts'kyi, pp. 48–51.

52. Kirdan, p. 93. The song is "The Three Brothers by the River Samarka." Similar lines appear in another version of the same epic, p. 97.

53. The Ukrainian Oleksii Popovych is probably related to the Russian epic hero Aleksei Popovich in name only, the narratives about them being radically different. Both heroes are brash, and this may be the basis for the shared name.

54. Kirdan, pp. 384–405; Hrushevs'ka, vol. I, pp. 63–78.

55. Kirdan, pp. 406–11; Hrushevs'ka, vol. I, pp. 82–86.

56. Kirdan, pp. 166–67.

57. Kirdan, pp. 224–57; Hrushevs'ka, vol. II, pp. 12–109.

58. Demuts'kyi, pp. 52–54.

59. See chapter 4.

60. Kononenko, "The Influence of the Orthodox Church on Ukrainian *Dumy*," *Slavic Review*, 1991, vol. 50, No. 3, pp. 566–75. See also Orest Subtelny, *Ukraine: A History*, Toronto/ Buffalo/London: Univ. of Toronto Press, 1988, 666 pp. In the introduction, Subtelny states that one of the major themes of his book is Ukrainian statelessness.

Notes to Chapter 10

1. D.K. Zelenin, *Ocherki po russkoi mifologii: umershie neestestvennoiu smertiu i rusalki*, Moscow: Indrik, 1995 (reprint of the 1916 original with a new introduction by N.I. Tolstoi).

2. Sventsiits'kyi, pp. 44–50, 59–62; Chubinskii, *Obriady: Rodiny, krestiny, svad'ba, pokhorony, Trudy etnografichesko-statisticheskoi ekspeditsii v zapadno-russkii krai*, 1877, vol. 4, pp. 697–712, especially pp. 700–2 and 703–4. See also, Gail Kligman, *The Wedding of the Dead: Ritual, Poetics, and Popular Culture in Transylvania*, Berkeley/Los Angeles/London: Univ. of California Press, 1988. Kligman describes Romania, but much of what she says is applicable to the Slavs in general and the Ukrainians in particular.

3. Hrushevs'ka, vol. I, p. xxxvi.

4. Sumtsov probably articulates this theory most clearly. See, for example, his "Kobzari i Lirniki Khar'kovskoi guberni." *Trudy XII Arkheologicheskogo s"ezda v Khar'kove*, vol. II, 1905, p. 308. It is also voiced by many others: Malinka, "Kobzari i lirniki Terentii Parkhomenko, Nikifor Dudka i Aleksei Pobehailo," p. 62; Khotkevich, "Neskol'ko slov ob Ukrainskikh banduristakh i lirnikakh," p. 88; Kulish, *Zapiski o iuzhnoi Rusi*, p. 193; Drahomanov, "Tvortsi kozats'kikh dum," TSNB fond 172, ark. 26; Suprun presented a version of this theory in our interview of Nov. 27, 1987.

5. Zhitetskii, *Mysli o narodnykh malorusskikh dumakh*; the entire first section, up to the texts, is devoted to presenting this argument (249 pp.). The crux of the argument appears in chapter 5, "Tvortsy i pevtsy dum," pp. 157–76.

6. Kolessa, *Ukraiins'ki narodni dumy*, pp. 1–62 and esp. 51–55; "Ukraiins'ki narodni dumy u vidnosheniu do pisen', virshiv i pohoronnykh holosin'," *Zapysky naukoho tovarystva imeni Shevchenka*, 1920, vol. CXXXII, pp. 1–37.

7. Kirdan, *Ukrainskie narodnye dumy*, p. 330. Compare Sventsiits'kyi, pp. 108–11. St. Peter's day, actually Saints Peter and Paul, is June 29. Untimely blossoming of trees is actually a bad omen, usually indicating that someone will soon die. Hnatiuk, "Pokhoronni zvychaii i obriady," p. 407.

8. Jakobson, "Slavic Epic Verse: Studies in Comparative Metrics," pp. 414–63; p. 445.

9. Kolessa, *Ukraiins'ki narodni dumy*, pp. 12–13 and 54–55.

10. Hrushevs'ka, vol. II, pp. 113–23, and Kirdan, pp. 81–88.

11. Hrushevs'ka, vol. II, pp. 12–106; Kirdan, pp. 224–57.

12. Kirdan, pp. 295–97.

13. Hrushevs'ka, vol. I, pp. 78–85; Kirdan pp. 408–11.

14. "Marusia Bohuslavka" is in Hrushevs'ka, vol. I, pp. 21–27; Kirdan gives 7 variants, pp. 122–34. Numbers 5, 6, and 7 are new publications of archival material. He also lists a number of published sources for additional variants. It should be noted that this interpretation of Marusia's fate is shared by performers, if not by scholars. Hryhorii Tkachenko said in an interview on Oct. 18, 1987 that this *duma* is particularly sad because the heroine dies.

15. Sventsiits'kyi, pp. 44–50, 59–62; Chubinskii, pp. 697–712, especially pp. 700–2 and 703–4. See also, Kligman, *The Wedding of the Dead*, and Elsa Mahler, *Die Russische Totenklage: Ihre Rituelle und Dichterische Deutung*, Leipzig: Veroffentlichungen des Slavischen Instituts, 1935, pp. 391–408; see especially pp. 392–96.

16. Antonovich and Dragomanov, vol. I, pp. 270–72.

17. See Sventsiits'kyi and Hnatiuk for detailed accounts of funeral practices by region. Many are transcripts of the actual words spoken by the informants and contain invaluable data on omens of impending death; proper methods of washing, dressing and internment; lament texts; and ideas about the soul and what happens to it after death, including when the death is premature.

18. Hnatiuk, pp. 260, 408.

19. Hnatiuk, p. 287, is but one example.

20. Kirdan, pp. 89–90.

21. Kirdan, pp. 87–88.

22. Kirdan, "Ivas' Konovchenko" is on pp. 228–29, 234, 240–41, 245, 252–53, and 257. "Death of a Cossack in the Kodyma Valley" is on pp. 99–100 and "Death of Bohdan Khmel'nyts'kyi" is on pp. 291 and 294.

23. Kirdan, pp. 150, 156, 158, 163, 173, 178, 183, 191, 197, 202, 203 (Turks rather than animals), 220.

24. Kirdan, "Fedir, the Man Without Kin," p. 87; "The Three Brothers of Samara," p. 91.

25. Kirdan, pp. 160, 171, 175, 186, 205, 210.

26. Kirdan, p. 218.

27. Kirdan, pp. 161, 206.

28. Kirdan, finding the head: pp. 228, 240–41, 252, 257; winning the body back from the Turks: p. 234.

29. Kirdan, p. 317. See also pp. 315, 320.

30. Kirdan, p. 157.

31. Kirdan, p. 153. The lamenting cuckoo also appears on pp. 179, 186, 190, and 194.

32. Hnatiuk, *Pokhoronni zvychaii i obriady*, and Chubinskii's funeral section are good examples.

33. Antonovich and Dragomanov, vol. I, pp. 270–72.

34. Kirdan, pp. 140–49; the passage quoted is on p. 149.

35. Kirdan, pp. 298–306; the quote is from version 1, p. 302.

36. Kirdan, pp. 271, 274, 282, 289.

37. Kirdan, pp. 307 and 311.

38. Jakobson, p. 444.

39. Sventsiits'kyi, pp. 79–80; 129. According to an informant, "Normally women sing laments and men do not, but there are exceptions."

40. Kononenko, "Women as Performers of Oral Literature," pp. 17–33.

41. See Kligman's book. She recorded the laments sung by all of the relatives at the funeral of a young girl. It was just assumed that all of the women could lament, and when the time came, this is exactly what they did.

42. See, for example, D.M. Balashov, Iu.I. Marchenko, and N.I. Kalmykova, *Russkaia svad'ba: Svadebnyi obriad na Verkhnei i Srednei Kokshen'ge i na Uftiuge (Tarnogskii raion Vologodskoi oblasti)*, Moscow: Sovremennik, 1985.

43. Sventsiits'kyi and Hnatiuk, p. 357. This section contains various statements about laments, including the comment that "men do not usually lament, but there are exceptions."

44. Kolessa, *Ukraiins'ki narodni dumy*, pp. 51–52.

45. A good discussion in English is Miller, *Folklore for Stalin*.

46. Sventsiits'kyi and Hnatiuk, pp. 18–20, discuss humorous laments. Post-funeral games are described on pp. 227–31, 238–43, 266–77, and 292–97.

47. Zguta, *Russian Minstrels*.

48. Kirdan, p. 149. See also Kirdan, p. 302, among others.

49. N.N. Veletskaia, *Iazycheskaia simvolika slavianskikh arkhaicheskikh ritualov*, Moscow: Nauka, 1978.

50. pp. 67–68.

51. Veletskaia, pp. 63–65.

52. See Chapter 8.

53. See Chapter 2.

54. See Chapter 2.

55. IMFE fond 6–4/161/4, ark. 22. Dated 1930.

56. IMFE fond 11–4/580, ark. 18. The informant is Mykola Doroshenko, a *lirnyk*; date of collection 1885–86.

57. Sventsiits'kyi and Hnatiuk, p. 302.

58. The desert experience and living underground are equated in religious songs. In "Oleksii, Man of God," the hero wanders in the desert for thirty years, and in "Varvara," the female equivalent of Oleksii, the heroine is forced to endure entombment for an equal length of time. Both Oleksii and Varvara achieve salvation as a result of their suffering.

59. Lavrov, *Kobzari*, pp. 57–59.

60. Kolessa, *Ukraiins'ki narodni dumy*, p. 35, argues that there is an absence of plot in the Khmel'nyts'kyi *dumy*.

61. A nice example is Horlenko's search for Khmel'nyts'kyi *dumy*. Horlenko became quite excited when he found Bratytsia and discovered that he, in contrast to most *kobzari*, could perform *dumy* from this cycle. His excitement turned to disappointment when he figured out that Bratytsia had learned his material from books and that this material was not part of the living tradition. See "Kobzari i lirniki," pp. 41–50.

62. Kolessa, *Ukraiins'ki narodni dumy*, pp. 39–45, gives numerous comparisons between the Khmel'nyts'kyi *dumy* and written literature. The literary influence Zhytets'kyi finds in all *dumy* Kolessa attributes to this cycle and this cycle only.

Conclusion

1. My family accompanied me to Ukraine in 1993. We visited the Supruns on August 18.

Notes to Texts

A Religious Festival

1. *Otpust*, Ukrainian *vidpust*, is a religious holiday for the forgiveness of sins.

2. *Panshchyna* refers to the time when Ukraine was under the domination of the Polish-Lithuanian Commonwealth, and the song is one which protests oppression by the Polish nobility (*pany*). The song is widely known, but being secular, is inappropriate to a religious setting.

3. *Akathistos hymnos*, literally a hymn chanted without sitting, is a long prayer service to the Holy Tirnity, the Savior, the Virgin, a feast, or a saint, chanted ritually by a priest and the congregation on certain Saturdays of Lent. It can also be recited by a solitary worshipper at any time, as is the case here.

The Minstrel Initiation Rite

1. The use of a bowl rather than a bottle appears frequently. Apparently, dipping vodka out of a bowl with spoons was a good way for blind people to avoid spilling it and wasting a precious commodity.

2. This is a formula found in many accounts of the initiation rite. It means that money tempts one to drink, but the purpose here, though drink will be served, is solemn; it is the initiation of a new member.

3. See chapter 5 for an explanation of the key-keeper and his role.

4. The confusion between wine and vodka appears in a number of initiation rite descriptions. Apparently, the drink used was vodka, but the verbal formulas that went with the drink, perhaps under the influence of the words accompanying the Eucharist, refer to wine. See, for example, IMFE fond 1–2/303, ark. 1, where the minstrel informant himself acknowledges and explains the confusion.

5. See note number 1, above.

Notes to Songs

Special thanks to Andrij Hornjatkevych for help deciphering some of the manuscript material and especially for help with religious references. Although the minstrels were associated with the church through their guilds, they had little theological training. In their songs, apocryphal material is mixed with Biblical references. Religious terminology is often confused or misused. Hornjatkevych was very helpful in reconstructing the theological material from which terms and passages found in minstrel songs derive.

The Begging Song and The Song of Gratitude

1. The person addressed is the woman of the house; it is not the singer's mother. Because kin was so important and mothers especially were revered, addressing a stranger as "mother" was a standard way to show respect.

2. This, again, is a term of respect; the singer is not addressing his father.

3. Ilion is not a Biblical personage, but a figure regularly used in Ukrainian folk song as a representation of an archetypical, miserly rich man.

4. The division of a cloth, cloak, or mantle into three pieces is sometimes ascribed to Mary and sometimes to Paraskovia Piatnytsia. It is apocryphal and appears in folksong, especially the begging song, and in folk painting.

5. "Registered" may refer to the book of the family dead kept at the local church. The names in the book would be read during Lent and also at commemorations of the dead, such as Radunytsia. The unregistered would be those whose names were not entered in this book. Since it is unlikely that a deceased family member would not be registered, the distinction may also derive from one between categories of Cossacks. Registered Cossacks had legal status. They were entitled to pay, when pay from the tsar or the king of the Polish-Lithuanian Commonwealth was forthcoming. When land allotments were made, they were entitled to land allotments. Unregistered Cossacks were men who joined the ranks of the Cossacks of their own initiative and had no legal standing. They received a share of the booty when Cossacks were engaged in a military campaign. At times of peace, they were usually allowed land and fishing rights, though these were not recognized beyond the local administration.

6. See previous notes 1, 2, and 3, above.

7. Akathistos here is not used in its normal meaning (see note 3, Religious Festival), and is probably confused with Scripture.

8. A towel, meaning a piece of cloth, rather than literally a towel, was considered a particularly good gift. The towel did not spoil like gifts of food and could be sold in the marketplace. The towel also had symbolic meaning, probably derived from the apocryphal story of Mary/Paraskovia dividing her mantle and from the association between cloth, especially the ritual towel (*rushnyk*), and power.

9. God will know what you have given to the poor and will take this into account when deciding the fate of your soul after death. This is apparently a quotation from the minstrel himself. It appears as a footnote in the manuscript.

10. In Ukrainian belief, all people who died young and violently had the potential to become unquiet dead. The prayers of minstrels were especially necessary in the case of such deaths, and helped the troubled souls find peace in the afterlife.

Religious Songs

1. There is obviously some confusion between this song and a Last Judgement song, where the distinction between the righteous and sinners would be more logical. Here, the righteous should not want to be released from Heaven, and sinners would likely be guilty of the sins listed. See also note 17, ch. 2.

Epics (Dumy)

1. In the mind of the performer, all Muslim countries are grouped into one category.
2. "Speaking with words" and "crying with tears" are typical stylistic features of *dumy*. This ornamental repetition heightened the emotional impact of the song.
3. The word is *tyshlyk*. The performer says that he does not know what this is. It could be a *tashlyk*, a stone hammer or cudgel.
4. The implication is that he should have no rest in the Heavenly Kingdom.

Satirical Songs

1. A device which enabled a person to carry large, bulky loads.

Secret Songs

1. The song is difficult to decipher because there are no other texts to use for comparison and because the performer did not know Scripture and misused and confused terms. I thank Andrij Hornjatkevych, Norman Ingham, and Valentina Izmirlieva for help with this text.
2. Presumably referring to the Apostles Peter and Paul.
3. The literal translation is tablets of brass. Please note that this and the preceding line are rendered differently in subsequent verses.
4. Presumably Saints Basil the Great, John Chrysostom, and Gregory the Theologian, though usually the number three refers to the Holy Trinity.
5. This is an aside that appears in the manuscript. It is spoken by someone present, presumably Hanna Iaremenkiva.
6. There should be nine choirs of angels, but such confusion is not unexpected in an oral source.
7. Explanatory comments made by Hanna Iaremenkiva which appear in the manuscript after the song text.
8. Explanatory comments made by Roman Iaremenko which appear at the bottom of the manuscript folio.

Notes to Bibliographic Essay

1. *Drevnie Rossiiskie Stikhotvoreniia Sobrannye Kirsheiu Danilovym*, Vtoroe dopolnennoe izdanie podgotovili A.P. Evgen'eva i B.N. Putilov, Moscow: Izdatel'stvo Nauka, 1977.
2. Hrushevska's speculation on Tsertelev and Lomykovs'kyi, Introduction, vol. I, pp. XVIII-XXI.
3. Nikolai Tsertelev, *Opyt sobraniia malorossiiskikh pesnei*, St. Petersburg, 1819.
4. Hrushevs'ka suggests that Tsertelev did begin collecting spontaneously. She adds that the idea of publishing what he had collected came to Tsertelev after the appearance of Danilov's book.
5. Mikhail Maksimovich, *Malorossiiskiie pesni*, Moscow, 1827; *Ukrainskie narodnye pesni*, Moscow, 1834; *Sbornik ukrainskikh pesen'*, Kiev, 1849.
6. Izmaiil Sreznevskii, *Zaporozhskaia starina*, I-III, Kharkiv, 1833–38.
7. Panteleimon Kulish, *Ukraina: od pochatku Vkrainy do bat'ka Khmel'nytskoho*, Kiev, 1843.

8. Lomykovs'kyi's collection states that the songs were written down from a *kobzar* Ivan. Thus this early and out-of-the-mainstream collection, which was not published until late in the nineteenth century by Zhytets'kyi and was thus known to only a few people, gives at least the first name of the performer who was the source of its texts. Tsertelev also had at least an oblique reference to the oral performers who were his sources. First of all, his work was called *An Experiment in Collecting Little Russian Songs*. Second, in an article he wrote about his work in *Vestnik Evropy*, 1827, June, no. 12, p. 275, called "O narodnykh stikhotvoreniiakh (pis'mo k g-nu Maksimovichu)," he mentions collecting from two blind men and being especially impressed by one of them.

9. Kirdan, *Sobirateli narodnoi poezii*, pp. 52–137.

10. Kirdan, *Sobirateli narodnoi poezii*, pp. 28–51. Kyrdan not only gives a history of early collecting and publication, he does text comparisons for virtually every scholar he discusses. Thus he compares the first and subsequent editions of Tsertelev, showing that at least some editing took place. Kyrdan also gives the contemporary critical reaction to each of the collections he discusses. Tsertelev's collection, though well received, was criticized for its "incorrect" (meaning non-standard) orthography. It is likely that Tsertelev strove to respond to and please his critics.

11. For Sreznevskii, the three volumes of *Zaporozhskaia starina* cited above; for Kulish, *Ukraina*, already cited, and *Istorie vozsoedineniia Rusi*, St. Petersburg, 1856–57.

12. Antonovich and Dragomanov, *Istoricheskie pesni malorusskogo naroda*.

13. Lukashevich, *Malorossiiskie i Chervonorusskie narodnyia dumy i pesni*.

14. The quote is: "podchinennye muzyke, buduchi vytverzhyvaemy slovo v slovo, ili pochti tak, oni podlezhali men'shemu vliianiiu vremeni, pravil'nee sokhranili svoe soderzhanie."

15. Tsertelev, "O starinnykh malorossiiskikh pesniakh." *Syn otechestva*, 1818, no. 45, book XVI, p. 124. The quote reads: "razvaliny, svidetel'stvuiushchie o krasote razrushennogo zdaniia."

16. The first quote is, "postepenno otkhodiat ot pervobytnogo vida" (p. XX). The quote describing Maksymovych's editorial work goes as follows: "Ia staralsia slichat' i soglashat' raznoglasiia; sluchalos' svodit' inogda dve v odnu, libo odnu razdeliat' na dve; ia izbiral, kak nakhodil skhodstvennee s pravil'nym smyslom i—skol'ko ponimal—s dukhom i iazykom nadornym."

17. Kirdan, pp. 66–68.

18. The quote reads: "Ia imel vozmozhnost' chasto usmatrivat' iasno te izmeneniia, kakie proiskhodili s nimi chastiiu ot dolgovremennogo i nepravil'nogo peniia onykh, chastiiu i ot izobretatel'nosti samikh pevtsov i pevits: takim obrazom ia mog predstavit' ochen' mnogie pesni v ispravneishem vide" (p. iv).

19. The Central Government Archive of Literature and History (TSGALI), fond 314, Maksimovich, M.A., opis I, unit 12, folios 101–3. Cited in Kirdan, *Sobirateli narodnoi poezii*, pp. 218–19.

20. Bazilevich, "Mestechko Aleksandrovka Chernigovskoi gubernii Sosnitskogo uezda."

21. Bazylevych's article appeared in the premier issue of *Etnograficheskii sbornik*, the new publication of the Russian Imperial Geographical Society (*Imperatorskoe russkoe geograficheskoe obshchestvo*).

22. *Ukrainskie melodii: Sochinenie Nik. Markevycha*, Moscow, 1832, pp. 116–17.

23. *Kievskaia starina*, 1897, vol. XI, p. 278.

24. Kirdan, *Sobirateli narodnoi poezii*, pp. 214–16.

25. The composite texts made up from the songs of Shut and Beshko were turned over to Metlyns'kyi and published by him in *Narodnye iuzhnorusskie pesni*. They were also given to Bodians'kyi, but he never got his materials out in print.

26. Olena Pchilka, introduction to "Letters to Ostap Veresai from P.A. Kulish and L.M. Zhemchuzhnikov." *Kievskaia starina*, 1904, Feb., pp. 213–14.

27. P. Kulish, *Zapiski o Iuzhnoi Rusi*, vol. I, p. 64.

28. Antonovich and Dragomanov, *Istoricheskie pesni malorusskogo naroda*.

29. *Narodnye iuzhnorusskie pesni*, izdanie Amvrosiia Metlinskogo, Kiev: Universitetskaia tipografiia, 1854. This is the collection which printed a number of the texts collected by Kulish on his expedition to Aleksandrivka in 1853, including the composite texts he made out of his recordings from Shut and his former apprentice, Beshko.

30. On July 12, 1854, Bilozers'kyi wrote to O. Lazarevs'kyi in Petersburg about his hopes of publishing his guide for collectors and a complete version of his register of performers. The letter is in the archives of the Central Library of the Ukrainian Academy of Sciences, Kiev, fond 1/3394.

31. Markevych, *Iuzhnorusskie pesni s golosami*.

32. Kolessa, *Melodii ukraiins'kykh narodnykh dum*; Lysenko, *Kharakterystyka muzychnykh osoblyvostei ukraiins'kykh dum is pisen' u vykonanni kobzaria Veresaia*; Lysenko, *Narodni muzychni instrumenty na Ukraiini*, ed. by M. Shchhol', Kiev: Mystetstvo, 1955 (reprint).

33. Rambaud, "Kief et le congres archeologique, souvenirs de voyage, par M. Alfred Rambaud."

34. Rusov, "Ostap Veresai: odin iz poslednikh kobzarei malorusskikh." *Zapiski Iugo-zapadnogo otdela Imperatorskogo russkogo geograficheskogo obshchestva*, 1873.

35. Rusov, "Kobzar' Ostap Veresai: ego muzyka i ispolniaemye im narodnye pesni," *Zapiski Iugo-zapadnogo otdela Russkogo geograficheskogo obshchestva*, vol. I, Kiev, 1874. Lysenko, *Kharakterystyka muzychnykh osoblyvostei ukraiins'kykh dum i pisen' u vykonanni kobzaria Veresaia*.

36. *Ukrain's'ki zapisi Porfiriia Martinovicha*.

37. What makes the Martynovych materials so special is that he recorded not just one initiation rite or other text normally concealed from people who were not members of minstrel guilds, but many. Also, his sources were the minstrels themselves. He did not have to turn to people peripheral to the profession, such as guides, to get his information.

38. Borzhkovskii, "Lirniki"; Gorlenko, "Bandurist Ivan Kriukovskii (tekst deviati dum s biograficheskoi zametkoi)"; Gorlenko, "Kobzari i lirniki"; Sumtsov, "T.M. Parkhomenko," *Vestnik Khar'kovskogo istoriko-filologicheskogo obshchestva*, 1911, vol. X; Sumtsov, *Ukrains'ki spivtsi i baikari*, Kharkiv: Pechatne dilo, 1910 (pamphlet); P. Tikhonovskii, "Kobzari Khar'kovskoi guberni," *Sbornik Khar'kovskogo istoriko-filologicheskogo obshchestva: Trudy Khar'kovskogo predvaritel'nogo komiteta po ustroistvu XII Arkheologicheskogo s"ezda*, Kharkhiv, 1902; K.F. Ukhach-Okhorvych, "Kobzar' Ostap Veresai, ego dumy i pesni," *Kievskaia starina*, 1882, vol. VIII; Malinka, "Kobzari i lirniki Terentii Parkhomenko, Nikifor Dudka i Aleksei Pobehailo"; "Kobzari Semen Vlasko, Dem'ian Symonenko, ta lirnyk Antin Ivanyts'kyi: ikhnii repertuar"; "Prokop Chub, perekhodnyi tip kobzaria"; "Kobzar' Petro Haras'ko i lirnik Maksym Pryshchenko"; "Lirnik Evdokim Mykytovich Mokroviz"; "Lirnik Andrei Kornienko"; "Lirnik Ananii Savvovich Homyniuk"; "Zametki o dvukh lirnikakh Chernigovskoi gubernii: Alekseia Terent'evicha Masliukova i Egoria Esinovicha Okhremenko"; "Svedeniia o kobzariakh i lirnikakh."

39. Slastion(ov), "Kobzar' Mikhailo Kravchenko i ego dumy."

40. V. Ivanov, "Arteli slepykh, ikh organizatsiia i sovremennoe polozhenie," *Trudy XII Arkheologicheskogo s"ezda v Khar'kove*, vol. III, 1905, pp. 303–11; Khotkevich, "Neskol'ko slov o banduristakh i lirnikakh."

41. Khotkevich, "Vospominaniia o moikh vstrechakh so slepymi." Khotkevych notes his attempts to improve the voices of his charges by feeding them a mixture of

honey and lemon juice. He even acknowledges his attempts to retune their musical instruments for them, until he realized that the traditional tuning was indeed suitable to traditional recitative style.

42. M. Speranskii, *Iuzhno-russkaia pesnia i sovremennye ee nositeli (po povodu bandurista T. M. Parkhomenka)*.

43. Lavrov, *Kobzari: Narys z istorii kobzarstva Ukraiiny*; Kyrdan and Omel'chenko, *Narodni spivtsi-muzykanty na Ukraiini*.

44. Slastion, "Melodii Ukraiins'kikh dum i iikh zapysuvannia," *Ridnyi krai*, Ch. 35: 4-6, Ch. 36: 6-8, Ch. 37: 5-7, Ch. 38: 5-7, Ch. 41: 5-7, Ch. 42: 4-5, Ch. 43: 4-7, Ch. 44: 8-9, Ch. 45:8-13, Ch. 46: 3-8, 1908.

45. Hrushevs'ka, vol. I, pp. clxxvii-cxcix.

46. Kolessa, *Melodii ukraiins'kykh narodnykh dum*.

47. Studyns'kyi, "Lirnyky, Studiia," *Zoria*. Under the pseudonym of Kost' Vyktoryn, "Didivs'ka /zhebrats'ka mova," *Zoria*.

48. Hnatiuk, "Lirnyky, lirnyts'ki pisni, molitvy, slova, zvistky."

49. Sventsiits'kyi, *Pokhoronni holosinnia*; Hnatiuk, *Pokhoronni zvychaii i obriady*.

50. Hrushevs'ka, *Ukraiins'ki narodni dumy*; Kvitka, "Profesional'ny narodni spivtsi i muzykanty na Ukraiini: Prohrama dlia doslidu iikh diial'nosti i pobutu."

51. Kharkiv, "Sposterezhennia nad lirnykamy ta kobzariamy Valkivs'koho raionu na Kharkivshchyni," IMFE fond 6–2; "Vidomosti pro lirnykiv, kobzariv ta sopilkariv," IMFE fond 6–4/185; texts of various songs are in IMFE fond 6–4/161, ark. 1–4; Kirdan, *Ukrainskie narodnye dumy*.

52. O. Pravdiuk, *Romens'kyi kobzari Evhen Adamtsevych*, Kiev: Muzychna Ukraiina, 1971; Ryl's'kyi and Lavrov, *Kobzar Ehor Movchan*; Hrinchenko and Lavrov, *Kobzar Fedir Kushneryk*.

53. Lavrov, *Kobzari*; Kyrdan and Omel'chenko, *Narodni spivtsi-muzykanty na Ukraiini*.

54. Kirdan, "Var'irovanie kobzarem M. Kravchenko dumy 'Bednaia Vdova i Tri Syna.'"

Bibliography

Abramov, I. "Perezhytki tsekhovoi organizatsii v mestechke Berestechke." *Zhivaia starina*, 1908, vol. III, p. 261.

Afanas'ev, Aleksandr. "Dve starinnye malorusskie dumy (dostavleny A.S. Afanas'evym)." *Izvestiia akademii nauk* (Pamiatniki i obraztsy narodnogo iazychestva i slovesnosti), 1853, vol. II, pp. 206–24.

Afanas'ev-Chubinskii, A. "Byt malorusskogo krest'ianina (preimushchestvenno v Poltavskoi gubernii)." *Vestnik geograficheskogo obshchestva*. 1855, vol. XIII, bk. 1, part 2, pp. 129–56.

Antonovych, Volodymyr, and Mykhailo Drahomanov (Antonovich, Vladimir, and Mikhail Dragomanov). *Istoricheskie pesni malorusskogo naroda*. 2 vols. Kiev: Izdatel'stvo russkogo imperatorskogo geograficheskogo obshchestva, 1874–75.

Astakhova, Anna. *Byliny Severa; Tom pervyi, Mezen' i Pechora*. Moscow/Leningrad: Akademii nauk, 1938.

"Avtobiografiia iuzhno-russkogo sviashchennika 1-oi poloviny VXIII st." *Kievskaia starina*, 1885, vol. II, pp. 318–32.

Balashov, D.M., Iu.I. Marchenko, and N.I. Kalmykova. *Russkaia svad'ba: Svadebnyi obriad na verkhnei i srednei Kokshen'ge i na Uftiuge (Tarnogskii raion Vologodskoi oblasti)*. Moscow: Sovremennik, 1985.

Bazylevych, Hryhorii (Bazilevich, Grigorii), sviashchennik. "Mestechko Aleksandrovka, Chernigovskoi gubernii, Sosnitskogo uezda." *Etnograficheskii sbornik*. 1853, vol. I, pp. 313–36 (reprinted in *Chernigovskie gubernskie vedomosti*, 1854, nos. 12–14).

Bezsonov, P.V. *Kaleki perekhozhie: Sbornik stikhov i issledovanie*. 6 vols. Moscow: Tipografiia A. Semena, 1861–64 (reprinted in 2 vols. with a new intro. by Very Rev. Sergei Hackel; London: Gregg International Publishers, 1970).

Bogdanovskii, A.V. *Sbornik svedenii o Poltavskoi gubernii*. Poltava, 1877.

Boian. "Narodni muzychni strumenty na Vkraiini." *Zoria*, 1894, pp. 17–19, 87–89, 112–14, 135–37, 161–62, 185–87, 211–12, 231–33.

Borzhkovskii, Valerian. "Dve lirnitskie pesni." *Kievskaia starina*, 1889, vol. XII, pp. 637–42.

———. "Lirniki." *Kievskaia starina*, 1889, vol. IX, pp. 653–708.

———. "Parubotsvo kak osobaia gruppa v malorusskom sel'skom obshchestve." *Kievskaia starina*, 1887, vol. VII, pp. 765–76.

———. "Predanie i pesnia ob ekzamene diaka v starinnoi Malorossii." *Kievskaia starina*, 1892, vol. VI, pp. 456–58.

Bych-Lubens'kyi, K. (K. Bich-Lubenskii). "Banduristy i lirniki na Khar'kovskom XII arkheologicheskom s''ezde." *Russkaia Muzykal'naia Gazeta*, 1902, no. 37, pp. 834–42; no. 38, pp. 866–73.

———. "Muzykal'nyi vecher XII arkheologicheskogo s''ezda." *Kharkovskie gubernskie vedomosti*, 1902, no. 217.

Chubyns'kyi, Pavlo P. (P.P. Chubinskii). *Obriady: Rodiny, krestiny, svad'ba, pokhor-ony: Trudy etnograficheskostatisticheskoi ekspeditsii v zapadno-russkii krai.* St. Petersburg, 1877, vol. 4.

Chykalenko, E. (E. Chikalenko). "Lirnyk Vasilii Moroz." *Kievskaia starina,* 1896, vol. III, pp. 79–87.

D-vin, N. "Pesnia pro Morozenka." *Etnograficheskoe obozrenie,* 1903, vol. LVI, no. 1, pp. 115–16.

Danilov, Kirsha. *Drevnie rossiiskie stikhotvoreniia sobrannye Kirsheiu Danilovym.* Vtoroe dopolnennoe izdanie podgotovili A.P. Evgen'eva i B.N. Putilov. Moscow: Izdatel'stvo Nauka, 1977.

Danyliv, V.V. (V.V. Danilov). "Dodatky do literatury starechykh prokhan'." *Etnohraf-ichnyi visnyk,* 1929, bk. 8, pp.181–83.

———. "Malorusskaia narodnaia pesnia v starinnykh i novykh lubochnykh izdaniiakh." *Russkii filologicheskii vestnik,* 1910, vol. LXIV, bk. 3–4, pp. 232–42 and separately. Warsaw, 1910.

———. "Nositeli pokhoronykh prichitanii v Malorossii." *Kievskaia starina,* vol. IV, pp. 30–33.

———. "Sredi nishchei brat'i." *Zhivaia starina,* 1907, vol. IV, pp. 200–6.

———. "Sredi kobzarei i lirnikov." *Istoricheskii vestnik,* 1911, vol. CXXVI, October, pp. 301–12.

Dashkevych, N. (N. Dashkevich). "Rezultaty issledovannia ob Oleksii Popovyche i dumy pro buriu na chornom more." *Chteniia v obshchestve Nestora Letopistsa,* 1904, bk. XVIII, pp. 28–30.

———. "Duma ob Ivane Konovchenko." *Chteniia v obshchestve Nestora Letopistsa,* 1908, bk. XX, pp. 64–65.

Dei, O.I. *Dumy.* Kiev: Dnipro, 1982.

Demuts'kyi, P. *Lira i iii motivy; zibrav v Kyiivshchyni P. Demuts'kyi.* Kiev: Notopechatnaia i drukarnia I.I. Cholokova, 1903.

Dmytryiv, M. "Kobzari mynuloho i budushchyny." *Ridnyi krai,* 1907, no. 16, pp. 8–9.

Domanyts'kyi, V.I. (V.I. Domanitskii). "Kobzari i lirniki Kievskoi gubernii v 1903 godu." *Pamiatnaia kniga Kievskoi gubernii,* 1904, vol. IV, pp. 1–65 and separately. Kiev: Izdatel'stvo Kievskogo gubernskogo statisticheskogo komiteta.

Drahomanov, Mykhailo P. (M.P. Dragomanov). "Malo-rossiia v ee slovesnosti." *Vestnik evropy,* 1870, vol. VI, pp. 754–80.

———. "Nepevnii variant dumy." *Zhitte i Slovo,* 1895, vol. III, pp. 350–51.

———. "Novyi variant kobzars'kykh spiviv." Central Academic Library, Kiev, fond 172, ark. 10, and *Zapysy naukovoho tovarystva imeni Shevchenka u L'vovi,* vol. III, pp. 265–73, and vol. IV, pp. 14–34.

———. "Rozbir dumy pro buriu na Chornim mori." *Zhitte i Slovo,* 1894, vol. I, pp. 300–3.

———. "Tvortsi kozats'kykh dum." *Zhitte i Slovo,* 1894, vol. I, p. 289.

"Dukhovnye pesni XVI veka: Psalmy lirnikov i banduristov." Kiev: Universitetskii kontsert, 1916.

"Duma pro Handzhu Andybera." Izdanie knizhnogo magazina B. Khavkina i D. Poluekhtova, Kharkiv, 1886 (reprint).

Efimenko, A.Ia. "K voprosu o bratstvakh." *Izvestiia khar'kovskogo XII arkheo-logicheskogo s''ezda,* 1902, no. 14, pp. 225–26.

Efimenko, P. "Bratstva i soiuzy nishchikh." *Kievskaia starina,* 1883, vol. VII, pp. 312–17.

———. "Shpitali v Malorossii." *Kievskaia starina,* 1883, vol. IV, pp. 709–27.

"Epos Ukraiiny" (no author given). Photographer: I. Iaiits'kyi. *Sotsialistychna Kul'tura,* 1990, no. 8, pp. 32–33.

Erofeiv, Ivan. "Ukrains'ki dumy i iikh redaktsii." *Zapysky ukraiins'koho naukoho tovarystva u Kyevi*, 1909, bk. VI, pp. 69–83, and bk. VII, pp. 17–64.

Famintsyn, A.S. *Domra i srodnye ei muzykal'nye instrumenty russkogo naroda.* St. Petersburg, 1891.

———. *Skomorokhi na Rusi.* St. Petersburg: Tipografiia Arngol'da, 1891.

Farfarovskii, S. "Kobzari na Kubani." *Sbornik Khar'kovskogo istoricheskogo obshchestva*, 1913, vol. XIX, pp. 181–87.

Franko, Ivan. "Khmel'nychchyna (dumy, pisni, virshi)." *Zibrannia tvoriv*, Kiev: Naukova dumka, vol. 43, 1986, pp. 7–193.

———. "Pisnia pro Baidu." *Zibrannia tvoriv*, vol. 42, 1984, pp. 161–89.

———. "Pisnia pro pravdu i nepravdu." *Zibrannia tvoriv*, vol. 43, 1986, pp. 280–351.

———. "Pisnia pro smert' brativ Strusiv." *Zibrannia tvoriv*, vol. 42, 1984, pp. 456–66.

Freeze, Gregory L. "Caste and Emancipation: The Changing Status of Clerical Families in the Great Reforms." *The Family in Imperial Russia: New Lines of Historical Research*, ed. David L. Ransel, Urbana/Chicago/London: University of Illinois Press, 1978, pp. 124–50.

Frieden, Nancy M. "Child Care: Medical Reform in a Traditionalist Culture." *The Family in Imperial Russia*, pp. 236–59.

Frierson, Cathy A. "*Razdel*: The Peasant Family Divided." *Russian Peasant Women*, eds. Beatrice Farnsworth and Lynne Viola, New York/Oxford: Oxford University Press, 1992, pp. 73–88.

G. "Bandurist Ostap Veresai." *Nedelia*, 1874, no. 17, pp. 630–43.

Gendych, P.A. "Materialy po narodnoi slovesnosti Poltavskoi guberni." Poltava: Izdanie Poltavskoi uchenoi knizhnoi komissi, 1915.

Glickman, Rose L. "Peasant Women and Their Work." *Russian Peasant Women*, eds. Beatrice Farnsworth and Lynne Viola, New York/Oxford: Oxford University Press, 1992, pp. 54–72.

Kh.H. "Z nahody kobzars'koii mandrivky." *Ridnyi krai*, 1903, no. 21, p. 8.

Haidai, Mykhailo. "Narodni holosinnia." *Etnohrafichnyi zbirnyk*, 1928, bk. 7, pp. 67–71.

———. "Zhebrats'ki retsytatsii." *Etnohrafichnyi zbirnyk*, 1928, bk. 6, pp. 85–97.

Haliun, Ivan. "Novi kobzars'ki pisni." *Etnohrafichnyi visnyk*, 1928, bk. 7, pp. 54–59.

Hnatiuk, Volodymyr. "Lirnyky: Lirnyts'ki pisni, molytvy, slova, zvistky i t.i. pro lirnykiv povitu Buchats'koho." *Etnohrafichnyi zbirnyk*, 1896, vol. II, pp. 1–76 and separately, L'viv, 1896.

———. "Zhebrats'ki blahal'nytsi." *Zapysky naukoho tovarystva imeni Shevchenka*, 1912, vol. CX, pp. 158–63.

Horbach, Oleksa. *Argo ukraiins'kykh lirnykiv* (offprint from "Naukovy zapyski Ukraiins'koho Vil'noho Universitetu"). Munich, 1957.

Horlenko, Vasyl' P. (Vasilii Gorlenko). "Bandurist Ivan Kriukovskii (tekst deviati dum s biograficheskoi zametkoi)." *Kievskaia starina*, 1882, vol. 12, pp. 481–518.

———. "Dve malorusskie dumy c predisloviem V. Kallasha." *Etnograficheskoe obozrenie* 1892, vol. XV, pp. 138–46.

———. "Dve poezdki s N.I. Kostomarovym." *Kievskaia starina*, 1886, vol. I, pp. 111–23.

———. "Kobzar' Kriukovskii (nekrolog)." *Kievskaia starina*, vol. 12, 1885, p. 741.

———. "Kobzari i lirniki." *Kievskaia starina*, 1884, vol. I, pp. 21–50, and vol. XII, pp. 639–56 and separately. Kiev, 1884.

———. *Ukrainskie byli: Opisaniia i zametki.* Kiev, 1899.

Hrinchenko, Borys D. (B. Grinchenko). *Dumy kobzars'ki.* Chernihiv, 1897.

———. "Dumy pro Turets'ku nevoliu i pro Samiila Kishku." Kiev: Vydae knyharnia P.F. Panchshykova, 1886.

————. "Pisnia pro Doroshenka i Sahaidachnoho." *Zapysky ukaiins'koho naukovoho tovarystva u Kyevi*, 1908, bk. 1, pp. 44–71 and separately. Kiev, 1908.

Hrinchenko, M.O. "Ukraiins'ki narodni dumy." *Vybrane: Z pytan' muzychnoho fol'kloru*, ed. M. Hordiichuk. Kiev: Derzhavne vydavnytstvo muzychnoii literatury URSR, 1959, pp. 15–121.

————, and F. Lavrov, *Kobzar Fedir Kushneryk*. Kiev: Tsentral'na drukarnia naukovoho tovarystva URSR, 1940.

Hrushevs'ka, Kateryna. *Ukraiins'ki narodni dumy*. 2 vols. Kharkiv-Kiev: Derzhavne vydavnytstvo Ukraiiny, 1927–31.

————. "Ukraiins'ki narodni dumy u frantsuzs'kykh perekladakh." *Zapysky naukoho tovarystva imeni Shevchenka*,1930, vol. XCIX, pp. 1–10.

Hrushevs'kyi, Mykhailo. (Grushevskii, Mikhail). "Baida Vyshnevetskii, v poezii i istorii." *Zapysky ukraiins'koho naukovoho tovarystva u Kyevi*, 1909, bk. II, pp. 108–39 and follow-up: 1912, bk. X, pp. 14–18.

————. *Istoriia Ukraiiny-Rusi*. Available in abridged form in English translation as *A History of Ukraine*. Archon Books, 1970.

————. "Khmel'nyts'kyi i Khmel'nyshchyna." *Zapysky naukovoho tovarystva im. Shevchenka*, vol. XXIII-XXIV, p. 8.

Hrytsa, Sofia I. *Melos ukraiins'koi narodnoi epiky*. Kiev: Naukova dumka, 1979.

Huslystyi, K.H. "Do pytannia pro istorichni umovy vynyknennia ukraiins'kykh dum." *Istorichnyi epos skhidnykh slov'ian*, ed. M.T. Ryl's'kyi. Kiev: Akademiia nauk, 1959, pp. 119–35.

M.L.I. "Malorossiskoe nishchenskoe prichetanie." *Kievskaia starina*, 1903, vol. I, pp. 6–7; vol. IX, pp. 106–10; vol. XII, pp. 128–31.

P.I. "Sila roditelskago proklitia po narodnym razskazam Kurianskogo uezda Khar'kovskoi gubernii." *Etnografichesko obozrenie*, 1889, vol. III, pp. 41–50.

Ianchuk, N. "Kratkii otchet o muzykal'no-etnograficheskoi ekspeditsii v malorossiiu." *Otchet o deiatel'nosti otdelenia russkogo iazyka i slovesnosti imperatorskoi Akademii Nauk*. St. Petersburg, 1912, pp. 76–81.

Iastrebov, V. "Gaidamatskii bandurist." *Kievskaia starina*, 1886, vol. X, pp. 378–88.

————. "Novye dannye o soiuzakh nezhenatoi molodezhy." *Kievskaia starina*, 1896, vol. X, 110–28.

Ilarion, Metropolitan. *The Ukrainian Church: Outlines of the History of the Ukrainian Orthodox Church*, trans. O. Ferbey. Winnipeg: Millennium Committee of the Ukrainian Church of Canada, 1986.

Isaievych, Ia.D. *Bratstva ta iikh rol' v rozvytku ukraiins'koi kul'tury XVI-XVIII st.* Kiev: Naukova Dumka, 1966.

Ivanov, P.V. "Komu i v kakikh sluchaiakh narod molitsia." *Etnograficheskoe obozrenie*, 1898, vol. XXXIX, no. 4, pp.141–42.

Ivanov, V. "Arteli slepykh, ikh organizatsiia i sovremennoe polozhenie." *Trudy XII arkheologicheskogo s''ezda v Khar'kove*, vol. III, 1905, pp. 303–11.

Ivashchenko, P.S. "Pavlo Bratytsia i Prokip Dub, kobzari Nizhinskogo uezda Chernigovskoi gubernii." *Zapiski iugo-zapadnogo otdela russkogo geograficheskogo obshchestva*, 1875, vol. II, pp. 109–29.

Jakobson, Roman. "Slavic Epic Verse: Studies in Comparative Metrics." *Selected Writings*. The Hague and Paris: Mouton and Co., 1966, vol. IV, pp. 414–63.

A.K. "Do kobzars'koi spravy." *Ridnyi krai*, 1902, no. 12, p. 4.

"K istorii starykh obychaev bratstv i koliad na Volyni." *Kievskaia starina*, 1901, vol. X, pp. 15–18.

"K izucheniiu kobzarskogo iskusstva." *Kubanskie oblastnye vedomosti*, 1903, no. 55, and *Kievskaia starina*, 1903, vol. IV, p. 33.

Kadlubovskii, A.P. "K istorii russkogo dukhovnogo stikha o Varlaame i Iosafate." *Izvestiia XIV arkheologicheskogo s''ezda*, 1908, pp. 123–24, and *Trudy XIV arkheologicheskogo s''ezda*, vol. 3, pp. 114–15.

Kalachov, N. "Arteli v drevnei i nyneshnei Rossii." *Etnograficheskii sbornik*, 1864, vol. VI, pp. 1–64.

"Kaleka-predskazatel'nitsa v sele Patsetselakh, Anan'skogo uezda." *Kievlianin*, 1872, no. 61.

Kargonol'tsov, I.P. "Malorossiiskie banduristy." *Putevoditel' po Dnepru i ego porogam*. Ekaterinoslav: Tipografiia I.Ia. Pavlovskogo, 1888, pp. 303–11.

Khalanskii, M. "Malorusskaia duma pro Baidu." *Sbornik Khar'kovskogo istoriko-filologicheskogo obshchestva*, 1908, vol. XV, pp. 205–19 and separately. Kharkiv, 1908.

Khat., A.G. "Zasedanie muzykal'no-etnograficheskoi komissii v Moskve." *Kievskaia starina*, 1900, vol. VII-VIII, pp. 12–16.

Khotkevych, Hnat (I. Khotkevich). "Bandura i ee mesto sredi sovremennykh muzykal'nykh instrumentov." *Ukrainskaia zhizn'*, 1914, no. 5–6, pp. 39–58.

———. "Deshcho pro bandurystiv ta lirnykiv." *Literaturno-naukovyi vistnyk*, 1903, bk. I, pp. 30–46.

———. "Lektsiia o banduristakh i kobzariakh i issledovanie narodnoi muzyki." *Iuzhnyi krai*, 1903, no. 7775, and *Kievskaia starina*, 1903, vol. IX, pp. 118–19.

———. "Neskol'ko slov o banduristakh i lirnikakh." *Izvestiia XII Arkheologicheskogo s''ezda*, 1902, no. 6, pp. 81–83, and *Trudy XII arkheologicheskogo s''ezda*, pp. 310–11.

———. "Neskol'ko slov ob Ukrainskikh banduristakh i lirnikakh." *Etnograficheskoe obozrenie*, 1903, vol. LVII, no. 2, pp. 87–106.

———. "Pidruchnyk hry na banduri." Archives of the Literature Institute, Ukrainian Academy of Sciences, Fond 62–20, and L'viv: Drukarnia Naukoho tovarystva im. Shevchenka, 1909.

———. "Vospominaniia o moikh vstrechakh so slepymi." *Tvory v dvokh tomakh*, ed. Fedir Pohrebennyk, vol. 1. Kiev: Dnipro, 1966, pp. 455–518.

Kligman, Gail. *The Wedding of the Dead: Ritual, Poetics, and Popular Culture in Transylvania*. Berkeley/Los Angeles/London: University of California Press, 1988.

"Kobzar Ostap Veresai." *Dzvonok*, 1892, no. 13.

"Kobzari i lirniki." *Russkaia muzykal'naia gazeta*, 1902, no. 38, pp. 601–2.

"Kobzarskii kontsert." *Ridnyi krai*, 1908, part 34, pp. 7–8.

Kohut, Zenon E. *Russian Centralism and Ukrainian Autonomy: Imperial Absorption of the Hetmanate, 1760s–1830s*. Cambridge: Harvard Ukrainian Inst./Harvard University Press, 1988.

Kolessa, F. "Etnograficheskaia ekskursiia." *Etnograficheskoe obozrenie*, 1908, vol. LXXVIII, no. 3, pp. 198–99.

———. "Formuly zakinchennia v ukraiins'kykh dumakh u zv'iazku z pytanniam pro naverstvuvannia dum." *Zapysky naukoho tovarystva im. Shevchenka*, 1937, vol. CLV, pp. 29–67.

———. *Melodii ukraiins'kykh narodnykh dum*; first printed as volumes XIII and XIV of *Materialy do ukraiinskoi etnolohii*. L'viv: Etnohrafichna komisiia naukovoho tovarystva im. Shevchenka, 1910–13; reprinted separately in one volume, ed. by S.I. Hrytsa, Kiev, 1969.

———. "Uber den melodischen und rythmischen Aufbau den ukrainischen rezitierende Gesange der sogenannten Kozakenlieder." *III Kongress der international Musikgesellschaft*, Vienna, 1909, pp. 276–99.

———. *Ukraiins'ki narodni dumy*, L'viv: Prosvita, 1920.

————. "Ukraiins'ki narodni dumy u vidnosheniu do pisen', virshiv i pohoronnykh holosin'." *Zapysky naukoho tovarystva im. Shevchenka*, 1920, vol. CXXX, pp. 1–18, vol. CXXXI, pp. 1–63, vol. CXXXII, pp. 1–64.

————. "Varianty melodii ukraiins'kykh narodnikh dum; iikh kharakterystyka i hrupovann'e: Studiia." *Zapysky naukoho tovarystva imeni Shevchenka*, 1913, vol. CXVI, pp.126–65.

Kononenko, Natalie (Moyle). "*Duma* pro Chornobyl': Old Genres, New Topics." *Journal of Folklore Research*, 1992, vol. 29, no. 2, pp. 133–54.

————. "The Influence of the Orthodox Church on Ukrainian *Dumy.*" *Slavic Review*, 1991, vol. 50, no. 3, pp. 566–75.

————. *The Turkish Minstrel Tale Tradition*, New York and London: Garland Publishing, 1990, pp. 155–207.

————. "Women as Performers of Oral Literature: A Re-examination of Epic and Lament." *Women Writers in Russian Literature*, eds. Toby W. Clyman and Diana Greene. Westport, Conn. and London: Greenwood Press, 1994, pp. 17–33.

Kornilovich, M.I. "Iz oblasti mestnogo narodnogo tvorchestva." *Kievskaia starina*, 1898, vol. X, pp. 8–13.

Kostomarov, Nikolai. "Istoricheskoe znachenie iuzhno-russkogo narodnogo pesennogo tvorchestva." *Beseda*, 1872, vol. IV, pp. 1–68, vol. V, pp. 75–123, vol. VI, pp. 1–55, vol. VII, pp. 1–76, vol. X, pp. 1–55, vol. XI, pp. 1–54, vol. XII, pp. 28–49; and *Sobranie sochinenii: Istoricheskie monografii i issledovaniia*, St. Petersburg, bk. 8, vol. XXI.

Krist, E. "Kobzari i lirnyky Khar'kovskoi guberni." *Sbornik Khar'kovskogo istoricheskogo obshchestva*, 1902, vol. XIII, part 2, pp. 121–33 and separately. Kharkiv: Pechatnoe delo K. Gagarina, 1902.

————. "Svedeniia o kobzariakh i lirnikakh, sobrannye po programme Sumtsova." *Khar'kovskie gubernskie vedomosti*, 1902, no. 140.

Kudrinskii, F. "Tsekhovye bratstva v mestechke Stepani (Volynskoi gubernii, Rovenskogo uezda)." *Kievskaia starina*, 1890, vol. VII, pp. 88–104.

Kulish, Panteleimon. *Istoria vossoedineniia Rusi*, St. Petersburg, 1856–57.

————. *Ukraina: od pochatku Vkrainy do bat'ka Khmel'nytskoho*, Kiev 1843.

————. *Zapiski o iuzhnoi Rusi*, 2 vols. St. Petersburg, 1856–57.

Kvitka, Klement. "Profesional'ny narodni spivtsi i muzykanty na Vkraiini: Prohrama dlia doslidu iikh diial'nosti i pobutu." *Zbirnyk istoricho-filolohichnoho viddilu Ukraiins'koi Akademii Nauk*, no. 13, Pratsi etnohrafichoi komisii, vol. 2, Kiev, 1924; reprinted in *Izbrannye trudy*, vol. II, Moscow, 1973, pp. 279–345.

Kyrdan, Borys P. (B.P. Kirdan). *Sobirateli narodnoi poezii: Iz istorii ukrainskoi fol'kloristiki XIX veka.* Moscow: Nauka, 1974.

————. *Ukrainskie narodnye dumy.* Moscow: Nauka, 1972.

————. *Ukrainskie narodnye dumy (XV-nachalo XVII vv.).* Moscow: Akademiia nauk, 1962.

————. *Ukrainskii narodnyi epos.* Moscow: Nauka, 1965.

————. "Var'irovanie kobzarem M. Kravchenko dumy 'Bednaia Vdova i Tri Syna.' " *Tekstologicheskoe izuchenie eposa*, ed. V.M. Gatsak and A.A. Petrosian. Moscow: Nauka, 1971, pp. 47–63.

————, and Andrii Omel'chenko. *Narodni spivtsi-muzykanty na Ukraiini.* Kiev: Muzychna Ukraina, 1980.

O.L. "Vladimir-Volynskoe bratstvo." *Kievskaia starina*, 1889, vol. VII, p. 289.

P.L. "Sovremennyi banduristy i lirniki v Poltavskoi guberni." *Poltavskie gubernskie vedomosti*, 1902, no. 219.

Lavrov, Fedir. *Kobzari: Narys z istorii kobzarstva Ukraiiny.* Kiev: Mystetsvo, 1980.

————. "Tvortsi ta vykonavtsi ukraiins'koho heroiichnoho eposu." *Istorichnyi epos skhidnykh slov'ian*, ed. M.T. Ryl's'kyi. Kiev: Akademiia nauk, 1959, pp. 59–85.

————. "Tvortsy i ispolniteli ukraiinskogo geroicheskogo eposa." *Issledovaniia po slavianskomu literaturovedeniiu i fol'kloristike*, ed. V.I. Chicherov. Moscow: Akademiia nauk, 1960, pp. 217–39.

Lebedev, Amfian. "Izmeneniia v dukhe i napravlenii blagotvoritel'nosti v period tor-zhestva khristianstva; Blagotvoritel'nye uchrezhdeniia drevnikh khristian; Drevnie monastyri so storony ikh blagotvoritel'noi deial'nosti." *Sbornik Khar'kovskogo istoriko-filologicheskogo obshchestva*, vol. 15, 1908, pp. 251–68.

Legasov, A., *Bandurist: Zbirnyk malorossiiskykh pisen'*. Moscow: Knigorpodavets E.A. Gubanov, 1887.

"Lirnyts'ka shkola." *Ridnyi krai*, 1907, no. 11, p. 13.

Lisovskii, A.N. "Opyt izucheniia malorusskikh dum." *Poltavskie gubernskie vedomosti*, 1890 and separately. Poltava: Izdatel'stvo Poltavskogo gubernskogo statisticheskogo komiteta, 1890.

Lord, Albert B. *Singer of Tales*. Cambridge, Massachusetts and London: Harvard University Press, 1960.

Luhovs'kyi, Borys. "U desiatukhu: Startsi v Chernihovi na iarmarku v chervni 1924 roku." *Ukraiina*, 1924, bk. 4, pp. 62–74.

————. "Sotsiial'na satyra z iarmarkovoho starechoho repertuaru." *Ukraiina*, 1926, bk. 18, pp. 51–54.

Lukashevych, Platon. (P. Lukashevich). *Malorossiiskie i Chervonorusskie narodnye dumy i pesni*. St. Petersburg: Tipografia Eduarda Pratsa, 1856.

Lysenko, Mykola. (N.V. Lysenko). "Duma o Bohdane Khmel'nytskom i Barabashe, s motivom (zapisannaia ot Kobzaria Pavla Bratytsi v Nezhyne)." *Kievskaia starina*, 1888, vol. VII, pp. 15–23.

————. *Kharakterystyka muzychnykh osoblyvostei ukraiins'kykh dum i pisen' u vykonanni kobzaria Veresaia*, originally published in vol. I of *Zapiski iugo-zapadnogo otdela russkogo geograficheskogo obshchestva*, 1874, pp. 338–60; reprinted 1978, new edition prepared by M. Hordiichuk, Kiev: Muzychna Ukraina.

————. "Narodni muzychni instrumenty na Ukraiini." *Ridnyi krai*, 1907, nos. 11–13, and separately, ed. M. Shchhol'. Kiev: Mystetstvo, 1955.

L.M. "Malorusskoe nishchenskoe prichetan'e." *Kievskaia starina*, 1903 (izvestiia i zametki), pp. 6–7.

————. "Pis'ma k Ostapu Veresaiu P.A. Kulisha i L.M. Zhemchuzhnikova." *Kievskaia starina*, 1904, vol. II, pp. 211–28.

Mahler, Elsa. *Die Russische Totenklage: Ihre Rituelle und Dichterische Deutung*. Leipzig: Veroffentlichungen des Slavischen Instituts, 1935.

Maksymovych, Mykhailo (Mikhail Maksimovich). *Malorossiiskie pesni, izdannye M. Maksimovichem*. Moscow: Tipografiia Avgusta Semena, 1827.

————. *Sbornik ukrainskikh pesen'*. Kiev: Tipografiia Feofila Gliksberga, 1849.

————. *Ukrainskie narodnye pesni*. Moscow, 1834.

Malynka, Oleksandr (A. Malinka). "Kobzar Petro Haras'ko i Lirnyk Maksym Pryshchenko." *Kievskaia starina*, vol. IX, pp. 441–50.

————. "Kobzari i lirniki Terentii Parkhomenko, Nikifor Dudka i Aleksei Pobehailo." *Zemskii sbornik Chernigovskoi gubernii*, 1903, no. 4, pp. 60–93 and separately, Chernihiv, 1903.

————. "Kobzari Semen Vlasko, Dem'ian Symonenko, ta lirnyk Antin Ivanyts'kii: Ikhnii repertuar." *Pervisne hromodianstvo*, 1929, pp. 105–21.

————. "Lirnik Ananii Homyniuk." *Kievskaia starina*, 1898, vol. X, pp. 1–8.

————. "Lirnik Andrei Kornienko." *Kievskaia starina*, 1895, vol. IX, pp. 59–64.

————. "Lirnik Evdokim Mykitovych Mokroviz." *Kievskaia starina*, 1894, vol. IX, pp. 434–44.

————. "Nemota i kosnoiazychie (Narodnyi sposoby lechenia na Ukraine)." *Etnograficheskoe obozrenie*, 1895, vol. XXIV, no. 1, pp. 179–80.

————. "Prokop Chub, perekhodnyi tip kobzaria." *Etnograficheskoe obozrenie*, 1892, vol. XII, no. 1, pp. 164–78.

————. "Svedeniia poluchenye ot A. Malinki." *Trudy XII Arkheologicheskogo s''ezda v Khar'kove*, vol. 3, Moscow, 1905, p. 408.

————. "Zametki o dvukh lirnikakh Chernigovskoi gubernii: Aleksei Terent'evich Masliukov i Iagor Esypovych Okhremenko." *Etnograficheskoe obozrenie*, 1902, no. 2, pp. 148–60.

"Malorossiiskie banduristy." *Russkii khudozhestvennyi listok*, 1859, no. 12.

Malorossiiskie pesni, Malorossiiskie dumy. Ukrainskii Al'manakh. Kharkiv: Universitetskaia tipografiia, 1831.

Markevych, M. (N. Markevich). *Iuzhnorusskiia pesni s golosami.* Moscow, 1853.

————. *Ukrainskie melodii: Sochinenie Nik. Markevicha.* Moscow, 1832.

Martynovych, Porfirii (P. Martinovich). *Ukrain's'ki zapisi Porfiriia Martinovicha. Kievskaia starina*, 1904 and separately, 1906.

————. "Slipets-kobzar Ivan Kravchenko." *Kievskaia starina*, 1904, vol. II, pp. 261–313.

Maslov, A.L. "Lirniki Orlovskoi guberni v sviazi s istoricheskim ocherkom instrumenta." *Etnograficheskoe obozrenie*, 1900, vol. XLIV, pp. 1–13.

————. "Ukrainskaia narodnaia muzyka, s notami." *Ukrainskaia zhizn'*, 1912, no. 12, pp. 62–72.

Maslov, S. "Lirniki Poltavskoi i Chernigovskoi gubernii." *Sbornik Khar'kovskogo istoricheskogo obshchestva*, 1902, vol. XIII, part 2, pp. 217–26.

Metlyns'kyi, Amvrosii (A. Metlinskii). *Narodnye iuzhnorusskie pesni.* Kiev: Universitetskaia tipografiia, 1854.

Miller, Frank J. *Folklore for Stalin: Russian Folklore and Pseudofolklore of the Stalin Era.* Armonk, New York and London, England: M.E. Sharpe, 1990.

Miller, O.F. "Malorusskie narodnye dumy i kobzar Ostap Veresai." *Drevniaia i novaia rossiia*, 1875, nos. 3–5.

Murashov, M. "Pesni liudei bozhiikh." *Etnograficheskoe obozrenie*, 1915, vol. CVII-CVIII, no. 3–4, pp. 15–61.

"Narodnyi predanie o Save Chalom." *Kievskaia starina*, 1887, vol. IX, p. 194.

Naumenko, V. P. "O proiskhozhdenii malorusskoi dumy o Samuile Koshke." *Chteniia v obshchestve Nestora Letopistsa*, 1888, bk. II, p. 188.

————. "Lysty Holovats'koho do M. Maksymovycha ta Pl. Lukashevycha." *Ukraiins'kii naukovyi zbirnyk*, Moscow, 1915, pp. 34–44.

Noll, William (Vil'am Noll). "Parallel'na kul'tura v Ukraiini u period Stalinizmu." *Rodovid*, 1993, no. 6, pp. 16–26.

Novyts'kyi, Ia.O. (Ia.P. Novitskii). "Malorusskie pesni, preimushchestvenno istoricheskie, sobrannye v Ekaterinslavskoi guberni v 1874–1894 godakh." *Sbornik Khar'kovskogo istoricheskogo obshchestva* 1894, vol. VI, pp. 49–160 and separately. Kharkiv, 1894.

K.F.U.O. "Kodenskaia kniga i tri bandurista." *Kievskaia starina*, 1882, vol. II, pp. 161–66.

"O tom kak vospevaiut startsy na Ukraine." *Dukhovnye chteniia*, 1871, bk. 12, p. 120.

L.P. "Sovremennye banduristy i lirnyki v Poltavskoi guberni (Po soobshcheniu korrespondentov poltavskogo gubernskogo statisticheskogo komiteta)." *Poltavskie gubernskie vedomosti*, 1901, no. 219.

Pashchenko, T., and F. Senhalevych. "Kobzari i lirnyky." *Etnohrafichnyi visnyk*, 1926, bk. 3, pp. 63–75.

Pavlii, P.D., ed. *Ukraiins'ki narodni dumy ta istorychni pisni.* Kiev: Vydavnytstvo akademii nauk Ukraiins'koii RSR, 1955.

Pavliuk, Mykola. "De-shcho pro nashykh kobzariv." *Ridnyi krai*, 1902, no. 11, pp. 11–12.

Pchilka, Olena. "Starosvits'ki 'dumy' v novomu vykonanniu i poiasnenniu." *Ridnyi krai*, 1908, part 1, pp. 11–14.

————. "Nove kobzarstvo: Kobzar Hryts'ko Kozyshko." *Ridnyi krai*, 1912, no. 12, pp. 21–23.

Perets, Volodymyr. "Ukraiins'ki dumy v novomu vydanni K.M. Hrushevs'koi." *Etnohrafichnyi visnyk*, 1928, bk. 7, pp. 73–132.

Petliura, S.V. "Kobzari, ikh polozhenie i znachenie." *Izvestiia obshchestva izucheniia kubanskoi oblasti*, 1903, vol.VI.

Petrov, P. "K repertuaram lirnikov." Vypusk 1. Nezhin, 1913.

Pirogov Commission, pamphlet no. 11: V.V. Khizhniakov, *O bolezni glaz nazyvaemoi trakhomoiu, kak uberech'ot trakhomy svoi glaza i ne peredat' ee drugim: Sovety zdorovym i bol'nym.* Moscow, 1901.

————. "Territorial'noe raspredelenie ostro-zaraznykh boleznei." *Trudy Pirogovskoi Komissii po rasprostraneniiu gigienicheskikh znanii v narod*, addendum, pp. 4–49.

Plakans, Andrejs. "Parentless Children and the Soul Revisions: A Study of Methodology and Social Fact." *The Family in Imperial Russia*, pp. 77–102.

"Poslednii kobzar, Ostap Veresai." *Kievlianin*, 1873, no. 121–122.

Pravdiuk, O. *Romens'kyi kobzar Evhen Adamtsevych.* Kiev: Muzychna Ukraiina, 1971.

"Programma dlia etnograficheskogo opisaniia iugo-zapadnogo kraia." *Kievskie gubernskie vedomosti*, 1869, no. 79, pp. 211–12.

"Programma dlia sobiraniia svedenii o kobzariakh i lirnikakh (k XII arkheologicheskomu s''ezdu v Khar'kove)." Kharkiv, 1900.

Pryvalov, N. "Lira (ryle, rele): Russkii narodnyi muzykal'nyi instrument." *Zapiski otdeleniia russkoi i slavianskoi arkheologii Imperatorskogo russkogo arkheologicheskogo obshchestva.* 1907, vol. V, part II, pp. 23–46.

Rambaud, Alfred M. "Kief et le congres archeologique, souvenirs de voyage, par M. Alfred Rambaud." *Revue des deux Mondes*, vol. VI, pp. 801–35.

————. "L'Epopee Petite-Russienne: Les Derniers Kobzars." *Russie Epique.* Paris, 1875, pp. 435–55.

Rawita, Franciszek. "Ostap Weresaj, ostatni kobzarz ukrainski." *Nowa Reforma.* Krakow, 1886, II, no. 203.

Rednyi, E.K. "Materialy komiteta o kobzariakh i lirnikakh, sobrany i sgrupirovany E.K. Rednym." *Izvestiia Khar'kovskogo XII arkheologicheskogo s''ezda*, 1902, pp. 384–87.

Revuts'kyi, Dmytro. "Suchasna parodiia na ukraiins'ku narodniu dumu." *Etnohrafichnyi visnyk*, 1925, bk. 1, pp. 69–71.

————. *Ukraiins'ki dumy ta pisni istorychni.* 2nd ed. Kharkiv/Kiev: Derzhavne vydavnytsvo Ukraiiny, 1930.

————, and Iu. Vynohrads'kyi, T. Pashchenko, F. Senhalevych. "Kobzari i lirnyky." *Etnohrafichnyi visnyk*, bk. 3, Kiev, 1926, pp. 64–69.

Rudchenko, I.Ia. *Chumatskie narodnye pesni.* Kiev: Tipografiia M.P. Fritsa, 1874.

Rusalka Dnistrova (Ruthenische Volkslieder). Budim, 1837.

Rusov, A.A. "Ostap Veresai, odin iz poslednikh kobzarei malorusskikh." *Zapiski iugozapadnogo otdela imperatorskogo russkogo geograficheskogo obshchestva.* Kiev, vol. I, 1874, p. 309–38.

Ryl's'kyi, M.T. (M.T. Ryl'skii). "Heroichnyi epos ukraiins'koho narodu." *Istorichnyi epos skhidnykh slov'ian.* Kiev: Akademiia Nauk, 1958, pp. 39–58.

————. "Itogi i zadachi izucheniia ukrainskikh dum i istoricheskikh pesen." *Issledovaniia po slavianskomu literaturovedeniiu i fol'kloristike*, ed. V.I. Chicherov. Moscow: Akademiia nauk, 1960, pp. 193–216.

————, ed. *Narodni spivtsi radians'koi Ukraiiny*. Kiev: Akademiia nauk, 1955.

————, and F.I. Lavrov. *Kobzar Ehor Movchan*. Kiev: Akademiia nauk URSR, 1958.

Shchepot'ev, Volodymyr. "Glavnye temy religioznogo pesennogo tvorchestva ukrainskogo naroda v khristianskii period." *Trudy II arkheologicheskogo kongressa*, 1910, no. VII, pp. 1–4.

————. "Starechi prokhannia." *Etnohrafichnyi zbirnyk*, 1928, bk. 6, pp. 30–40.

Shtokalko, Zinovii. *Kobzars'kyi pidruchnyk* (ed. Andrij Hornjatkevych), Edmonton/Kiev: Canadian Institute of Ukrainian Studies, 1992.

Sichyns'kyi, Myroslav. *Istorychni pisni*. L'viv: Naukove tovarystvo im. Shevchenka, 1908.

M.Sh-KO. "Pisnia lirnyka pro Sotskoho." *Zoria*, 1895, no. 13, p. 258.

Slastion, Opanas (Slastionov, A.G.). "Kobzar' Mikhailo Kravchenko i ego dumy." *Kievskaia starina*, 1902, vol. V, pp. 303–31 and separately. Kiev, 1902.

————. "Kobzari." *Ridnyi krai*, 1910, part 43, pp. 11–12.

————. "Melodii ukraiins'kikh dum i iikh zapysuvannia." *Ridnyi krai*, 1908, part 35, pp. 4–6; part 36, pp. 6–8; part 37, pp. 5–7; part 38 pp. 5–7; part 41, pp. 5–7; part 42, pp. 4–5; part 43, pp. 4–7; part 44 pp. 8–9; part 45, pp. 8–13; part 46, pp. 3–8.

Sokalskii, P.P. *Russkaia narodnaia muzyka-velikorusskaia i malorusskaia v ee stroenii, melodicheskom i ritmicheskom, i notatsii ob osnove sovremennoi garmonicheskoi muzyki*. Kharkiv, 1888.

Speranskii, M.N. *Iuzhno-russkaia pesnia i sovremennye ee nositeli (po povodu T.M. Parkhomenka)*. Kiev, 1904.

————. "Kurskii lirnik T.I. Semenov." *Etnograficheskoe obozrenie*, 1906, vol. LXVIII-LXIX, pp. 3–28.

————. "Malorusskaia pesnia v starinnykh russkikh pesennikakh." *Etnograficheskoe obozrenie*, 1909, vol. LXXXI-LXXXII, no. 2–3, pp. 120–44 and separately. Moscow, 1909.

Srebnitskii, I.A. "Sledy tserkovnykh bratstv v vostochnoi malorossii." *Trudy IV arkheologicheskogo s''ezda v Rossii*, 1891, vol. II, pp. 10–26.

S(reznevskii), I(zmail). *Zaporozhskaia starina*. Parts I-III. Kharkiv: Universitetskaia tipografiia, 1833–8.

Stanyslavs'kyi, V.I. "Duma pro Sorochiyns'ki podii." *Ukraiina*, 1924, bk. 1–2, pp. 171–74.

Studyns'kyi, Kyryl. "Lirnyky, Studiia." *Zoria*, 1894; no. 11, pp. 257–61; no. 12, pp. 284–6; no. 14, pp. 324–6; no. 15, pp. 345; no. 16, pp. 365–6; no. 17, pp. 385–7; no. 18, pp. 425–6 and separately. L'viv: Vyd. V. Lukicha, 1894.

————. Vyktoryn, Kost' (pseudonym). "Didivs'ka (zhebrats'ka) mova." *Zoria*, 1886, vol. VII, no. 13–14, pp. 237–39.

Subtelny, Orest. *Ukraine: A History*. Toronto/Buffalo/London: University of Toronto Press, 1988.

Sumtsov, Mykola (N.F. Sumtsov). "Bandurist Kucherenko." *Iuzhnyi krai*, 1907, no. 9258.

————. "Bohdan Khmel'nytskii v pesniakh." *Iuzhnyi krai*, 1907, no. 9165.

————. "Duma ob Oleksee Popovyche." *Kievskaia starina*, 1894, I, pp. 1–20, and II, pp. 324–26.

————. "Kobzari i lirniki." *Russkaia muzykal'naia gazeta*, 1902, nos. 23–24, pp. 601–2.

————. "O kobzariakh i lirnikakh." *Russkaia muzykal'naia gazeta*, 1900, p. 601.

————. "O kobzariakh i lirnikakh Khar'kovskoi gubernii." *Izvestiia II arkheologicheskogo s''ezda*, 1902, no. 6, pp. 77–80.

———. "Ocherki istorii iuzhno-russkikh apokraficheskikh skazanii i pesen." *Kievskaia starina*,1887, vols. VI-VII, pp. 215–68; vol. IX, pp. 1–54; vol. XI, pp. 401–55; and separately. Kiev, 1888.

———. "Parkhomenko, nekrolog." *Vesti Khar'kovskogo istoriko-filologicheskogo obshchestva*, 1911, vol. X, pp. 43–45.

———. "Sovremennoe izuchenie kobzarstva." *Trudy XIII arkheologicheskogo s''ezda*, Kharkiv, 1905, pp. 270–75.

———. "Ukrains'ki dumy." *Zapysky naukoho tovarystva im. Shevchenka*, 1913, vols. CXVII and CXVIII, pp. 227–34 and separately. L'viv, 1914.

———. *Ukrains'ki spivtsi i baikari. Sbornik Khar'kovskogo istoricheskogo obshchestva*, 1910, vol. XIX, and separately. Kharkiv: Pechatne dilo, 1910.

———. "Zapiska o kobzariakh i lirnikah na XII arkheologicheskom s''edze." *Volyn'*, 1903, no. 2, and *Kievskaia starina*, 1903, vol. II, p. 85.

Sventsiits'kyi, Ilarion. "Pokhoronne holosin'e i tserkovno-religiina poeziia." *Zapyski naukovoho tovarystva im. Shevchenka*, 1910, vol. XCIII, pp. 5–39.

———, and V. Hnatiuk. *Pokhoronni holosinnia; Pokhoronni zvychaii i obriady: Etnografichnyi zbirnyk*. L'viv: Etnografichna komisiia naukoho tovarystva im. Shevchenka, vol. XXXI-XXXII, 1912.

Sysyn, Frank E. *Between Poland and Ukraine: The Dilemma of Adam Kysil, 1600–1653*. Cambridge: Harvard Ukrainian Research Institute/Harvard University Press, 1985.

Tarnawsky, George, and Patricia Kilina, translators. *Ukrainian Dumy; editio minor*. Toronto and Cambridge: Canadian Institute of Ukrainian Studies and Harvard Ukrainian Research Institute, 1979.

Tersakovec, Michajlo. "Beziehungen der Ukrainischen historischen Lieder resp. Dumen zum sudslavischen volksepos." *Archiv fur slavische Philologie*, 1907, Bd. 29, pp. 221–46.

Tikhanov, P.I. "Chernigovskie startsy (Psalmy s kriptoglossom)." *Izvestiia chernigovskoi arkheologicheskoi komissii*, 1899, vol. II, pp. 65–158 and separately. Chernihiv, 1899.

Tikhonovskii, P. "Kobzari Khar'kovskoi gubernii." *Sbornik Khar'kovskogo istoriko-filologicheskogo obshchestva: Trudy Khar'kovskogo predvaritel'nogo komiteta po ustroistvu XII arkheologicheskogo s''ezda*. Kharkiv, 1902, vol. XIII, pp. 135–38.

Timchenko, E. "Do pytannia pro stosunok ukraiins'kikh dum do pivdenno-slavianskoho eposu." *Zapysky ukraiins'koho naukoho tovarystva u Kyevi*, 1908, bk. II, pp. 239–47.

Tkachenko-Petrenko, E. "Dumy v izdaniiakh i izsledovaniiakh." *Ukraiina*, 1907, vol. III, bk. VII-VIII, pp. 144–85 and separately. Kiev, 1907.

Tomachinskii, V.V. "Zapis dumy pro Ivana Konovchenka, s primechaniem." *Kievskii telegraf*, 1872, no. 58.

Tsertelev, Nikolai. "O starinnykh Malorossiiskikh pesniakh." *Syn Otechestva*, 1818, part 45, no. XVI, pp.124–36.

———. *Opyt sobraniia starinnykh malorossiiskikh pesnei*. St. Petersburg, 1819.

"Tvortsy i pevtsy narodnykh malorusskikh dum." *Pravoslavnyi vestnik*, 1892, no. 261.

Tykhovskii, I. "O kobzariakh." *Izvestiia XIV arkheologicheskogo s''ezda*, 1908, p. 100.

Ukrainka, Lesia. Letter to Filaret Kolessa, March 18, 1913, *Zibrannia tvoriv u dvanadtsiaty tomakh*, Kiev: Naukova dumka, 1979, vol. 12, pp. 446–47.

———. "Z repertuaru kobzaria Hnata Honcharenka." *Zibrannia tvoriv*, vol. 9, pp. 146–63.

Ukhach-Okhorvych, K.F. "Kobzar' Ostap Veresai, ego dumy i pesni." *Kievskaia starina*, 1882, no. 8, pp. 259–60.

Umanets, M. "Antin Holovatyi, Zaporozhskii deputat i kobzar." *Pravda*, 1891 and separately. L'vov, 1891.

G.V. "Pridvornyi bandurist v begakh." *Kievskaia starina*, 1888, vol. X, pp. 21–23.

Varnitskii, D.I. *Zaporozh'e v ostatkakh stariny i predaniiakh naroda.* St. Petersburg: Izdatel'stvo L. Panteleeva, 1888.

Vasylenko, M. (N. Vasilenko). "K voprosu o shkole dlia banduristov i lirnikov v Poltavshchine." *Kievskaia starina*, 1903, vol. I, pp. 12–17.

———. "Kobzari i lirniki Kievskoi gubernii v 1903 godu." *Pamiatnaia kniga Kievskoi gubernii na 1904 god*, 1904, part V, pp. 1–65.

Vasylenko, V. (V. Vasilenko). "Banduristy i lirnyky." *Khar'kovskie gubernskie vedomosti*, 1902, no. 329.

———. "Derevnia i ee razvlechenie (ocherki i nabliudeniia)." *Kievskaia starina*, 1904, vol. IV, pp. 135–43.

———. "Po voprosu o prizrenii slepykh i vsiakikh nishchikh." *Kievskaia starina*, 1904, vol. VII-VIII, pp. 131–51.

Veletskaia, N.N. *Iazycheskaia simvolika slavianskikh arkhaicheskikh ritualov.* Moscow: Nauka, 1978.

Veresai, Ostap, obituary for, *Kievskaia starina*, 1890, vol. VII, pp. 132–34.

Volovid, Mykola. "Lysty Ostapa Veresaia do pryiatelia." *Pravda*, 1868, nos. 19, 21, 23, 36, 39.

———. "Ostap Veresai, Sokirenskii kobzar." *Pravda*, 1868, nos. 15, 17, 18.

Zaleskii, A. "Variant pesni o Nechae." *Kievskaia starina*, 1887, vol. VIII, pp. 787–88.

Zbirnyk narodnykh pisen' i dum (no author, collector, or date given). Winnipeg: Ukrainian Publishing.

Zelenin, D.K. *Ocherki po russkoi mifologii: Umershie neestestvennoiu smertiu i rusalki.* Moscow: Indrik, 1995 (reprint of the 1916 original, with a new introduction by N.I. Tolstoi).

Zguta, Russell. *Russian Minstrels: A History of the Skomorokhi.* Philadelphia: University of Pennsylvania Press, 1978.

Zhemchuzhnikov, Lev Mikhailovich. *Moi vospominaniia iz proshlogo.* Ed. M. Dmitrenko. Leningrad: Isskustvo, 1970.

———. "Poltavshchina (Iz zapisnoi knizhki 1856 goda). *Osnova*, 1861, no. X, pp. 77–90.

Zhuk, "Neskol'ko slov o sleptsakh i banduristakh." *Vestnik iuga*, 1903, no. 463.

Zhytets'kyi, P. (P. Zhitetskii). *Mysli o narodnykh malorusskikh dumakh.* Kiev: Kievskaia starina, 1893.

———. "Starinnaia zapis' narodnykh malorusskikh dum s obzorom variantov dum." *Kievskaia starina*, 1893, vol. XL, pp. 95–125.

———. "Zametki o raznykh metodakh izucheniia narodnykh malorusskikh dum." *Etnograficheskoe obozrenie*, 1895, vol. XXVII, no. 4, pp. 108–21.

Index

Natalie Kononenko's interest in folklore goes back to her childhood and the many Ukrainian and other tales she heard from her mother and her grandfather. Her interest in the handicapped can also be traced to her early family life and growing up with a deaf brother. Ms. Kononenko received her doctorate in both Slavic and Near Eastern Languages and Literatures from Harvard University, where she studied with Albert Lord. She is the author of *The Turkish Minstrel Tale Tradition*, coeditor of *Ukrainian Dumy*, and editor of *The Magic Egg and Other Ukrainian Stories*, to which she contributed a number of tales. She currently teaches folklore and East Slavic languages at the University of Virginia.